Also by Thomas Byrne Edsall

**THE NEW POLITICS OF INEQUALITY**

# POWER
# AND MONEY

# POWER AND MONEY

Writing about Politics,
1971–1987

## Thomas Byrne Edsall

W · W · NORTON & COMPANY

NEW YORK · LONDON

First Edition

The text of this book is composed in Avanta, with display type set in Univers and Avanta. Composition and manufacturing by the Haddon Craftsmen, Inc. Book design by Marjorie J. Flock.

Library of Congress Cataloging-in-Publication Data
Edsall, Thomas Byrne.
    Power and money: writing about politics, 1971–1987 / Thomas Byrne
Edsall.
    p.    cm.
    Includes index.
    1. Campaign funds—United States. 2. Political parties—United States. 3. Income distribution—United States. 4. United States—Politics and government—1945–    5. Maryland—Politics and government—1951–    I. Title.
JX1991.E27 1988
324.7'8'0973—dc 19                                                                                      87–31484

ISBN 0-393-02571-3

W. W. Norton & Company, Inc., 500 Fifth Avenue, New York, N. Y. 10110
W. W. Norton & Company Ltd., 37 Great Russell Street, London WC1B 3NU
1 2 3 4 5 6 7 8 9 0

For my wife Mary

And for my daughter Lexa,
who points out my ignorance, broadens my horizons,
and teaches me about the future

# CONTENTS

Introduction     13

Acknowledgments     25

**1** **BALTIMORE AND MARYLAND:** *Power, Money,*
*Race, and Class—American Politics Writ Small*     29

The Power of Willie Adams Is Clear, but It's Tenuous
and at Critical Point     32
*The Evening Sun,* March 11, 1971

Maryland: The Governor Raiseth     38
*The Washington Monthly,* February 1972

Analysis: Black Political Conflict     46
*The Evening Sun,* May 13, 1972

Mandel Contributors Benefit from State     50
*The Evening Sun,* October 24, 1972

Vetoes, Appointments Favorable     57
*The Evening Sun,* October 25, 1972

Big Givers to Mandel Kitty Do Well     62
*The Evening Sun,* October 26, 1972

Mandel Contributors Have Big Business Relationships     66
*The Evening Sun,* October 27, 1972

Money and Morality in Maryland     70
*Society,* May/June 1974

Decline and Fall of Baltimore's Machine     82
*The Sun,* July 8, 1977

Maryland: A Government Serving Private Gain     90
*The Sun,* October 16, 1977

## 2 THE CONSERVATIVE REARMAMENT                               94

Congress Turns Rightward                                        95
*Dissent,* Winter 1978

Business Lobbying Helps Aid Effort                             103
*The Sun,* July 23, 1979

Constituents' Economic Interests Lead to Conservative's
Switch on Foreign Aid                                         108
*The Sun,* July 24, 1979

Business Learns to Play New Politics                          112
*The Sun,* February 25, 1980

Business's Winning Way with Democrats Shows in Battle
over Authority of FTC                                         118
*The Sun,* February 26, 1980

Business Coalitions Form to Win Congressional Clout           122
*The Sun,* February 27, 1980

The Battle of the Budget                                      128
*The Nation,* May 10, 1980

House Majority Leader Wright in for Tough Election Fight      134
*The Sun,* September 24, 1980

Money, Technology Revive GOP Force                            139
*The Washington Post,* June 17, 1984

Donors, Voters Pinpointed                                     144
*The Washington Post,* June 18, 1984

## 3 THE EARLY YEARS OF THE REAGAN
ADMINISTRATION                                                149

Reagan Wins May Be Far-Reaching                               150
*The Washington Post,* August 13, 1981

Three Who Sowed Tax Provision Reap Its Business Bonanza       154
*The Washington Post,* October 5, 1981

Why the Republicans Can't Lose                                157
*The Washington Post,* January 17, 1982

How a Lobbyist Group Won Business Tax Cut                     164
*The Washington Post,* January 17, 1982

GE Gets Tax Refund on Billions Profit 168
*The Washington Post*, March 16, 1982

Democrats Find Budget Fight Waged on Republican Terms 170
*The Washington Post*, May 2, 1982

How Democrats Sold Out—for Nothing 173
*The Washington Post*, August 1, 1982

Business Tries Hand at Feeding GOP Early in Marginal
Races 176
*The Washington Post*, September 12, 1982

PACs Bankrolling GOP Challengers 180
*The Washington Post*, September 14, 1982

New Power Network 183
*The Washington Post*, October 8, 1982

Up from Watergate 186
*The Washington Post*, August 16, 1984

**4 MONEY AND CONNECTIONS IN WASHINGTON** 190

Fund-Raisers Are New Elite of Campaigns 192
*The Washington Post*, December 12, 1983

Partners in Political PR Firm Typify Republican New Breed 194
*The Washington Post*, April 7, 1985

Good Connections 198
*The Washington Post*, October 27, 1985

Rollins's New Quest: Making a Fortune 203
*The Washington Post*, October 27, 1985

Democrats for Profit 205
*The Washington Post*, October 28, 1985

Corporate Chiefs Put Heart into Contributions to GOP 209
*The Washington Post*, August 29, 1986

Firms, Lobbies Provide Much of Democrats' Funds 213
*The Washington Post*, August 12, 1986

Money (and Politics) in Both Parties 217
*Dissent*, Fall 1986

GOP Committees a Bonanza for Ex-Aides and Relatives 222
*The Washington Post*, January 13, 1987

Breakfast with the Senate Finance Chairman for $10,000        225
*The Washington Post,* February 3, 1987

Congress' Free Rides                                           227
*The Washington Post,* June 14, 1987

**5 PARTIES IN CRISIS: THE ELUSIVE MAJORITY**                 233

Boom and Bust: Economic Ills Strain Alliance of Oilmen
and the GOP                                                   234
*The Washington Post,* April 25, 1983

Boom and Bust: The Hard Times of the Independent Gas
Industry                                                      239
*The Washington Post,* April 26, 1983

'84 Politics: "New Patriotism" vs. New Class Allegiances      244
*The Washington Post,* February 5, 1984

Exploiting the New Affluence: The GOP's Road to
Dominance                                                     248
*The Washington Post,* August 19, 1984

More Bad News for Mondale                                     253
*The Washington Post,* October 21, 1984

An Extremely Fluid Electorate, without Partisan Roots         258
*The Washington Post,* November 4, 1984

Politics and the Power of Money                               262
*Dissent,* Spring 1985

Onward, GOP Christians, Marching to '88                       265
*The Washington Post,* June 30, 1985

New Politics of Rich Man, Poor Man                            271
*The Washington Post,* December 22, 1985

An Enduring Republican Majority?                              275
*Dissent,* Winter 1986

Jockeying for Position: Only 1,000 Days to Go                 280
*The Washington Post,* February 9, 1986

Shifts in the Political Alignments                            283
*Dissent,* Spring 1986

Slicing the Pie                                               288
*The New Republic,* March 3, 1986

Republican America                                                      296
  *The New York Review of Books,* April 24, 1986

Money Paves Way for GOP                                                 304
  *The Washington Post,* May 22, 1986

Stockman as the Judge and the Judged                                    309
  *Boston Sunday Globe,* May 25, 1986

New Right Finally Gains Control of Huge Southern Baptist
Convention                                                              314
  *The Washington Post,* June 14, 1986

Why the GOP Is Still Waiting on Realignment                             316
  *The Washington Post,* September 14, 1986

Massachusetts: A Model for Democrats?                                   321
  *The Washington Post,* October 5, 1986

A Grass-Roots Battle to Control Redistricting                           324
  *The Washington Post,* November 2, 1986

Why the Democrats Are Still Losers                                      327
  *The Washington Post,* January 11, 1987

Political Changes in the South                                          332
  *Dissent,* Winter 1987

Dole's Transformations                                                  335
  *The Washington Post,* March 9, 1987

The Political Impasse                                                   342
  *The New York Review of Books,* March 26, 1987

Right Turn?                                                             352
  *Tikkun,* Vol. 2, No. 2

How the GOP Got into the Tall Cotton                                    357
  *The Washington Post,* May 3, 1987

The Southern GOP's New Button-Down Personality                         360
  *The Washington Post,* June 14, 1987

The GOP's Right-Wing Center                                             364
  *The Washington Post,* November 22, 1987


Epilogue                                                                367
Suggested Reading                                                       373

# INTRODUCTION

**T**HERE ARE serious criticisms to be made of a journalism that focuses the heart of its attention on money. Nonetheless, writing about politics without writing about money is like talking about human anatomy without discussing the circulatory system. This book in no way provides a complete examination of the vital relationship between cash and public policy, but throughout these pages I attempt to explore the importance of integrating the issue of money—not only campaign money, but changing patterns in the distribution and growth of income and wealth across the country—into the larger fabric of political news. Following the trail of money is one way to cut through the camouflage of the political process, to determine both the underlying goals of the exercise of power and the social and economic consequences of changes in the balance of power.

When I first began covering Baltimore politics in the late 1960s, among my initial assignments was an upcoming election in two of the city's six councilmanic districts. As I was putting together a story describing the Fifth District contest in the northwest corner of the city, I was told by a source that one of the candidates for the city council, a local lawyer named Allan Spector, was "working both sides of the street." Although Spector had lined up publicly with the district's anti-machine reform clubs, he had privately arranged to be carried on the ticket of James H. (Jack) Pollack, the last of Baltimore's great bosses. Having never been exposed to the protocol governing machine endorsements, I had very little understanding of the driving role of ward organizations and clubs, either in city elections or in the operation of municipal government. I mistakenly assumed that when Pollack carried Spector on his ticket, Pollack had agreed to run and finance Spector's campaign, and that in return, Spector would march to Pollack's tune. I sought out Spector and asked him how much Pollack was paying of the cost of his campaign. "Not a dime," said Spector. It was my impression that he was telling the truth. I went back to my source who told me that I had asked the wrong question: "If you run for the council, Pollack doesn't pay you, you pay Pollack." I returned to Spector and asked him how much he had paid Pollack for a slot on his ticket. The answer, as it turned out, was $10,000.

What is most clearly revealed in this story is my own ignorance, and this book is in many ways an expansion upon that theme. One of the virtues of daily reporting is that it is possible to at least partially correct today's mistakes in tomorrow's paper; assembling a collection of articles amounts to rectifying past mistakes by putting them on exhibition a second time.

At another level, however, the brief anecdote of the relationship between political boss and candidate reveals something else: that one definition of power is the ability to make others pay. If there is a central element in political journalism that makes the work interesting day after day, it is the continuous discovery of the scope, consequences, and complexity of power. Although the incident involving the payment of $10,000 to Pollack occurred in the context of a decaying system of machine politics, there has been no diminution in the role of money in political campaigns, and, over the last twenty years, new mechanisms to handle monetary transactions have emerged—political action committees, telemarketing, direct mail, earmarked donations, politicized tax-exempt foundations and so on—as both special and ideological interests have proliferated.

I would not have thought of bringing together a collection of news stories and essays. Once committed, however, I struggled to find central themes, occasionally touched upon in these pieces. All too often such themes emerged through the discovery of what I had omitted. Each of these themes involves the relationship of the press to power, a relationship that has grown in importance in direct proportion to the increasing centrality of the media in the political and legislative processes.

At this juncture in American politics, when traditional partisan loyalties are in the process of dealignment—that is, as reliable voter loyalty to either the Democratic or the Republican party decomposes—the public portrayal of issues, campaigns, and the course of legislation becomes critically important. The press is, in effect, a forum in which much of the competition between interests seeking to gain the loyalty of a majority of the electorate will be fought out. The aggressiveness, thoroughness, competitiveness, and doggedness of the press—or, conversely, its passivity, maleability, superficiality, and inaccuracy—will be critical factors, not just in the outcome of the struggle between Democrats and Republicans, but in the outcome for rich and poor, black and white, the powerful and the less powerful, the established and the newly arrived, as the battle for majority party status determines basic policy on such fundamental issues as social equity, productivity, economic growth, foreign intervention, arms control, and the national defense.

The American press has achieved high levels of distinction not only at such turning points in national history as the civil rights movement, Watergate and the Vietnam War, but also in providing sustained, detailed coverage of the operations of government and of the political process. The long tradition of a readiness to challenge authority and to force public officials at every level of government to give a public accounting of their actions and decisions has nourished the growth of a press corps increasingly well equipped by training and background to absorb a flow of information that has grown exponentially. The high standards of much of the press have not always been accompanied, however, by a commitment to explore how, for example, the burdens and dislocations resulting from the drive for equality in the civil rights movement, as well as from the social upheavals of the women's movement, are shared by all sectors of society. In addition, the press, either explicitly or implicitly, has often become an advocate of reform without anticipating its unintended consequences. The press, for example, failed to forsee the accelerated deterioration of political organizations and clubs in working and lower-middle class communities resulting from the reforms of the Democratic presidential selection process in the wake of the 1968 election. Similarly, the media endorsed strict campaign finance reform in the mid-1970s, following upon Watergate disclosures of secret contributions to Richard M. Nixon's reelection fund, without any recognition that such reforms would provide legally sanctioned mechanisms—in the form of political action committees (PACs)—to institutionalize special interest contributions, and that the new method of raising money from individuals would encourage the political mobilization of the upper-middle class, at the same time that organized representation of those in the lower strata of the income distribution deteriorated.

As the educational requirements, status, and pay of journalists have risen, the political and world-view of reporters has became increasingly divergent from the views of large segments of the general electorate, particularly from those of the working and lower-middle classes. Survey after survey* conducted by those on the right and on the left, and by the media itself, show that on social issues—school prayer, abortion, homosexuality, pornography—as well as on questions of defense spending, crime, and capital punishment, the views of reporters and editors are consistently more liberal than those of the general public. This generally liberal vision extends to support for programs aimed at assisting the poor, but it comes to an abrupt halt on issues related to altering the distribution of income: on questions involving government action to lessen the gap between the incomes of rich and poor, there is a higher level of opposition to government intervention

---

* "Los Angeles Times Poll on the Media," Los Angeles Times, August 11, 12, 13, 14, 1985.

Schneider, William and Lewis, I.A., "Views on the News," Public Opinion, August/September 1985.

Verba, Sidney and Orren, Gary R., Equality in America (Harvard University Press, 1985).

Weaver, David H., and Wilhoit, G. Cleveland, The American Journalist (Indiana University Press, 1986).

Lichter, S. Robert, Rothman, Stanley, and Lichter, Linda S., The Media Elite (Bethesda, MD: Adler & Adler, 1986).

"Research and Forecasts, Inc.," The Connecticut Mutual Life Report on American Values in the '80s (Hartford, CT, 1981).

Gannett Center for Media Studies, The Media and the People (Columbia University, 1985).

American Society of Newspaper Editors, Newspaper Credibility: Building Reader Trust (New York: ASNE, 1985).

MORI Research Inc., Journalists and Readers: Bridging the Credibility Gap (San Francisco, CA: The Associated Press Managing Editors Association, October 1985).

Burgoon, Judee K., Burgoon, Michael, and Atkin, Charles K., The World of the Working Journalist (The Newspaper Readership Project, NY, September 1982).

The Gallup Press Agenda Study, "Gallup Surveys the Press," Editor and Publisher, December 31, 1983.

among journalists than among the general public.

The consequences of the ideological gap between a large body of the national media* and the public have been distorted by the arguments of conservatives who contend that journalists are biased in favor of liberalism. In fact, the political consequences are more complex and subtle, involving a growing linkage between the views of the media and of what might loosely be called the liberal establishment; media identification on economic issues with the most well-to-do sector of the population; and, finally, a kind of blindness on the part of the national media to the sense of status displacement, as well as to the deep sense of moral dislocation or moral disorder, often felt by middle- and lower-income workers. One of the basic functions of the press is to give voice to the competing interests in society. Over the past two decades, the national media has not performed this function adequately for those groups whose views are most distant from their own, the largely working and lower-middle class voters who are far more conservative than journalists on social issues and on civil liberties. Reportorial neglect of significant segments of the population has meant that the press has abdicated its claim to fully represent the concerns of the public at large. At the same time, this neglect has fed trends towards increasingly low voter turnout among those in the bottom half of the income distribution, and contributed to the creation, in the 1970s, of an opening for conservative interests, both ideological and economic, to successfully manipulate the political process without facing the kind of powerful scrutiny that a press with a legitimate and broad base of public support can offer. The result, by the beginning of the 1980s, was the enactment of government policies producing regressive changes in the distribution of income to the advantage of conservative elites.

The intermittent, but growing, ideological conflict between the two parties has forced to the surface basic issues involving the tensions between some of the inherent inequities of free enterprise capitalism and the goal of political equality under democracy—basic issues that the press is not prepared to explore in full detail. On the one hand, on major newspapers there is a bureaucratic separation of political and economic assignments creating a false distinction between the two beats. Even more important, however, is the strong reform tradition in political reporting that encourages reporters to look upon the political exercise of economic power as inherently corrupt, as inextricably entwined with favoritism and patronage; or to look upon it solely as a tactic to win reelection, through the carefully timed expenditures of federal funds and the creation of election-based economic cycles. In fact, political power is an integral—and driving—part of economic life, often used to either force open a closed private sector, or to further restrict it in ways which have broad consequences for, among other things, the scope of individual economic opportunity, for the long-range distribution of

---

*By national media I mean to refer to the three networks, PBS, the four newspapers with national circulation—the *New York Times,* the *Washington Post,* the *Wall Street Journal,* the *Los Angeles Times*—and the three newsmagazines: *Time, Newsweek,* and *U.S. News and World Report.*

income, for the availability of housing, health services, and other basic necessities, and for the rate of growth in jobs and in overall productivity. The media has been strongly inclined to either distort this function of politics, or to disregard it altogether.

The press, in many ways, carries obligations similar to those of a political party: both, in order to have credibility, must be able to make the case that they are representative of broad public interests. In the case of American political parties, the basic goal is to represent at least a majority of the voting electorate. In the case of the press, the fundamental obligation is to give balanced voice to the competing interests in the nation and the community.

Over the past twenty years, the forces that have given rise to the conservative movement in American politics have been a testament to the alienation of the media from large segments of the electorate, and a testament to its failure to perform the basic role of fairly exploring all segments of society. The tax revolt of the 1970s; the sustained erosion of Democratic party loyalties among northern, white working and lower-middle class voters; the rise of the Christian right; the surge of support for Ronald Reagan that allowed passage of his 1981 budget and tax proposals, are all developments the media neither anticipated, nor stayed abreast of, until they had become dominant forces on the political landscape.

These developments were driven by groups largely outside the scope of the political press corps: workers and small businessmen whose moderate incomes were, in the 1960s, progressively whittled away by a system of marginal tax rates that in effect penalized modest increases in earnings; homeowners who saw their property taxes rise precipitously without any improvement in the quality of government services; an industrial workforce caught between weakened union representation and employers intent on cutting costs; a corporate community that, in the 1970s, achieved a degree of political mobilization unseen for nearly fifty years; a well-financed and aggressive national drive to shift to the right the intellectual content of the legislative and political debate; the pressures of international competition on domestic relations between business and labor.

While the business community has gained increasing sophistication in making its views known to the press and to the public, the gulf between the press and the working and lower-middle classes has become wider. The dissonance between the press and large segments of the public has become even more acute for members of the Washington press corps, who live and work in an economy unlike that of any other section of the country. Successful national print reporters make from $60,000 to $120,000 a year, and considerably more for some of those in television—wage levels placing them well within the top five percent of the country, and at rough parity with many of the lobbyists, politicians and elected officials they cover. A number of the most prominent, recognizable reporters have, furthermore, become highly paid speakers in their own right, addressing gatherings of just those associations and lobbying organizations directly dependent on the decisions of the federal government covered by the press. The economic distance of Washington reporters from much of the nation is compounded by the fact that they work in a city with one of the highest levels of the cost of living, costs exerting a constant and corrosive pressure on both reporters and on the men and women they cover. It is a city that has no traditional manufacturing-based, blue-collar working class, white or black, and a poor population that is by national standards disproportionately black.

Outside of Washington, many of the political responses of the white working and lower-middle classes over the past twenty years have been covered without full exploration of the economic pressures and consequences of social change. In its news coverage of the white reaction to court-ordered busing, of the trade union response to apprenticeship integration requirements, and in its coverage of referenda mandating lowered state and local taxes, the press, particularly the liberal press, has, through its own cultural and economic assumptions, placed itself in the position of dictating, at least implicitly, to a far less affluent and less privileged segment of society the taxes they should be willing to pay, the schools their children should go to, and the rules governing their unions' hiring and apprenticeship programs. It was from those voters who felt most adversely affected by the civil rights movement and the liberalization of cultural norms in the 1960s and 1970s, that George Wallace drew much of his support in 1968. Even larger numbers turned out for Ronald Reagan.

The cultural and economic distance between the press and large blocs of the electorate—blocs constituting what was loosely described in the 1970s as the "silent majority"—effectively prevented accurate coverage of the forces at work within the neighborhoods and communities that have become key battlegrounds in the struggle between the Democrats and Republicans for majority party status—areas such as southeast Chicago, the river wards of Philadelphia, northwest Birmingham, Dearborn, Michigan, and south Boston. Once bastions of Democratic strength—Dearborn cast one of the highest percentages of votes for John F. Kennedy of any city in the nation—these communities have over the past twenty years become fertile terrain for movements of social conservatism and for the Republican party, particularly in presidential elections. The cultural distance between the press and key voting blocs is not restricted to white working and lower-middle class communities, but is visible also between the press and many Asian and Hispanic immigrant groups, and also between the press and many blacks—those middle-class blacks who are socially conservative, as well as, progressively over the course of two Reagan administrations, black elites, the black working poor, and the black underclass.

What makes the contemporary alignment of the media with the well-educated, generally liberal elite particularly damaging to its credibility is that it compounds a much more long-standing parallel alliance. The press is, in many ways, strongly tied to the progressive reform movement which has periodically surfaced as a powerful force in American politics, a movement which goes back into the nineteenth century and which resurfaced again earlier this century during the administrations of Theodore Roosevelt and Woodrow Wilson. While the news media are technically both objective and non-aligned, their inner workings allow, and sometimes encourage, the enforcing of progressive reform standards, a progressive reformism which has been overwhelmingly dominated by one wing of the educated and articulate middle class. While the history of reform and reform journalism in this century has made a lasting imprint on government and has much to its credit—successfully pressing among other things for a strong civil service, competitive bidding on public contracts, the elimination of discriminatory voter registration requirements, fair housing, equal employment opportunities, and enactment of legislation to regulate the financing of political campaigns—the willingness of the press to accept, without further criticism or analysis, reform standards has also seriously constricted the ability of the media to develop a fully coherent and representative vision of American politics. While focusing on the ethical-reform issues of government, the press has often failed to recognize a basic, underlying economic function of government at all levels—city, state and federal. That is, that political power is an integral component of the economic marketplace at large, and that the holding of political power translates into the power to influence the distribution of economic rewards and penalties in the private sector.

Contrary to the views of reformers who have historically sought new ways to regulate the use of political power in order to keep it from permeating or even intersecting with the private sector, the exercise of political power is vital to the forcing of democratic access to the private marketplace. Patronage and favoritism in the awarding of contracts—as well as a host of other discretionary powers available to public officials—have, in many cases, served as hammers to break down the walls of closed establishments. While not infrequently misused—often to reward the already powerful—political authority to grant construction and defense contracts, to select consultants, to determine the location of roads and highways, to define land use, to regulate the private workplace, and to license private businesses, from nursing homes to racetracks to television stations to liquor stores, has been used by public officials to open private markets previously closed to competition.

As Irish, Italian, Polish, Asian, Hispanic, and black Americans gain both influence and status, the shifting flow of public money has altered the balance of private power. While these newer arrivals to, and participants in, American public life begin to buy into insurance companies, banks, asphalt paving firms, paper cup distributors, real estate concerns, architectural partnerships, cement suppliers, and so on—protected establishments have been forced to expand to include a broader segment of the nation's racial and ethnic mix.

The strict enforcement of middle-class standards of government to prevent favoritism and patronage functions, then, in some ways, to protect the powerful and to inhibit the democratic expansion of economic power. At the same time, reform standards have been critically important in preventing traditional abuses of power. While the media has often exercised its watchdog functions well, it has also demonstrated a consistent inability to recognize and to chronicle ambiguous outcomes, and particularly to both record and share responsibility for the unintended consequences of new rules established to regulate the political process.

In this context, the reform tradition underlying much political reporting has functioned to seriously distort and to divert resources from coverage of the basic issue underlying government: who gets what and how much? This weakness is most apparent in the treatment by the press of campaign finance. A fundamental premise of the reform movement—and of the press—is that political money is by its nature suspect, and that strict limits should be placed on the amount of money any individual or organization can give to a candidate or political party. The series of campaign finance bills enacted in the 1970s, in the aftermath of Watergate, effectively institutionalized these reform goals, turning them into law. The maximum that any individual can, at this writing, give to candidates and to political parties for federal elections is $25,000 annually, with a ceiling of $2,000 to any specific candidate, $5,000 to a political action committee (PAC) and $20,000 to a national political party. Any individual contributor is legally precluded from dominating the finances of any candidate for federal office.

At the same time, however, campaign finance law has functioned, paradoxically, to convert what was excessive influence exercised by individual donors into a system that has given one class of society, the well-to-do, a much stronger influence in the political process. Campaign finance reforms of the mid-1970s set the stage for the establishment of a financially powerful Republican party, outfitted with innovative computerized technology, able to raise nearly $300 million over each two-year election cycle through the solicitation of small contributions by mail. Targets of political direct-mail appeals are the affluent, with an average income in excess of $75,000, placing them within the top three percent of the national income distribution, and far more inclined to support the Republican than the Democratic party. The Republican mobilization of a large segment of the affluent into a politically active community of campaign donors became a major force in the shift to the right of American politics in the late 1970s, and it was this group of donors that, as a class, benefited most from the Reagan administration's tax and budget initiatives of the early 1980s.

By isolating campaign finance from the larger *cui bono* or "who benefits" issue of American politics, reformers and the press contribute to a general misapprehension as to the forces at work in the nation's political arena. Campaign finance is one indicator—and a strong one—of where power is located and who holds it. At the same time, the inverse is true: the near absence of campaign contributions by the middle class, and the virtually total absence of such donations from the poor, in combination with the steady decline in voter turnout as income falls, are strong indicators of a lack of political power, and of a lack of ability to influence the outcome of government decisions. Political money is more than a probable source of corruption. Money used to finance political campaigns is one of a number of forces contributing to the formation of policies that determine the national distribution of income and wealth; the relationship of the federal government to the workplace—including policies toward worker safety and labor unions; trade, monetary, and foreign policy; as well as strategies for economic growth.

The continuing struggle over these issues takes place within a basic national consensus supporting a political and economic system in which income and wealth effectively trickle from the top down, with a disproportionate share going to those on top, and the rest going in unequal amounts to managers, white and blue-collar workers, the unemployed, welfare recipients, and so on. In this context, the most important goal of any political party is economic growth, which provides the opportunity to better the living conditions of large numbers of people, no matter what the specific distributional policies of the party in power.

Beyond that, however, the core issues of politics involve distributional issues at the margin, disputes over policies that will result in the bottom fifth of the income distribution receiving four percent or six percent of personal income; or the shift of a fraction of the roughly thirty percent of national wealth now held by the top one percent of the population down to those in the top five percent. While the scope of change is modest, the consequences for those getting more or less can be enormous, particularly for those in the bottom quintile of the income distribution: increasing the share of personal income from four percent to six percent means that the income of individuals and families within this group rises by fifty percent, enough to make a significant difference in the quality of housing and food.

These kinds of distributional issues come to the fore when the political system is in the midst of a dealignment, or a realignment—that is, a transferring of reliable partisan loyalty from one party to the other—as may now be the case. The end of majority status for the Democratic New Deal coalition has placed the two parties in a head-on competition to build new majority bases. In the elections of 1980 and 1984, Ronald Reagan twice established majority coalitions, which, in economic terms, were the mirror opposites, or pyramidal inversions, of the New Deal coalition. While Roosevelt and Truman received their largest margins among the poor and working class, Reagan received his strongest majorities among the affluent, declining in strength steadily as the income of voters dropped, although he succeeded in ending Democratic voting traditions in a large number of white, blue-collar communities. The attempt to develop new coalitions dominated by those in the top half of the income distribution is not an isolated phenomenon; a "plurality of the affluent," has been central to the successful strategy of the conservative party under Margaret Thatcher in England.

The shifting partisan balance of power and the development of new political alliances in a period of realignment place an additional burden on political journalism. The news coverage of a realignment struggle requires an attempt to address the question of "who gets what, and how much" in the broadest possible terms; in other words, an attempt to determine how the benefits of economic growth, or the penalties of the kind of stagnation that emerged during the Carter administration, are distributed among the rich and poor, black and white, North and South, the manufacturing industries and the service industries, urban centers and rural outposts. At the same time, an essential ingredient of political journalism needs to be the attempt to determine the degree to which the policies of the parties and their candidates increase the opportunities for democratic competition in the private sector, or insulate established wealth and corporations from new challenges. This kind of concerted attempt to identify the economic consequences of partisan conflict becomes critically important as the split between Democrats and Republicans has been determined increasingly by income, particularly in 1980 and 1984. On two counts, those in the bottom half of the income distribution lack leverage to influence the distributional policies adopted by government: they lack the financial resources to influence the political process, and they turn out at the polls in far lower percentages than those in the top half. For the press, which functions to provide a marketplace for ideas and strategies in the political and distributional competition, one of several basic obligations is to insure representation of those groups that are the least well equipped to make their case to elected officials and to the larger public.

Such tasks are particularly difficult for a national press with very little institutionalized capacity for thorough research, and a press facing political strategists from both parties expert in the manipulation of public opinion and in shaping the content of political conflict. The press is neither equipped to resolve the partisan conflicts created by a realignment battle, nor to act as judge. The press is, however, an active participant in the political process, and its independent strength will be determined in large part by the respect, grudging or otherwise, it earns from the general public, and by the resourcefulness, aggressiveness, and commitment to exaustive examination that it brings to the fray. The prospect of partisan realignment, and all that shifts in the balance of power bring, means that the press, no matter what its intention, will play a central role in determining the scope of public understanding of political and economic issues at stake. The opportunity offered the press to explore the potential consequences of new majority coalitions to the electorate at large should not be lost because of a failure to commit the resources the job requires, a reluctance to address the broader issues raised by intensified political conflict, or because of an allegiance to one political elite.

The work in this volume can be legitimately criticized from a number of larger vantage points. My own work embodies the shortcomings I have laid at the feet of the press. In addition, for some, reporting like mine, which concentrates on the imperfections of politicians and of the political system, often seems too critical, harping on the negative while overlooking larger public achievements. For others, this kind of reporting, which implicitly endorses the resilience and efficacy of the two-party system and of the division of power between local, state, and federal governments, fails to raise broad, ideological challenges, tending rather to reinforce the existing distribution of power and to obstruct efforts to fundamentally change either the political or the economic structure. Third, much reporting, including my own, treats political elites—from the city council to the majority leadership of the Senate—as representative of larger constituencies, while those on both the left and right argue that these elites often profoundly misrepresent constituent interests. All these criticisms are valid, but the function of the mainstream political press is not, in my opinion, to direct the operations of government and elections, but rather to explore them. In this context, if I and some of my colleagues have been negligent, it has been in failing to diligently and aggressively pursue the consequences of decisions made by elites for those who must pay the price, to examine the conflicting social and economic pressures on voters, which are then selectively capitalized upon by politicians and their backers for specific advantage, and to insure that the portrayal of the political and economic pressures on all groups is, within the boundaries of the possible, fair and accurate.

Journalism is, by definition, a craft producing work not designed to stand up to future scrutiny. Readers of these stories will find a fair degree of repetition from one piece to the next. Clearly, the original articles were not meant to be consumed at one sitting, or even by one reader. I suggest that the reader skip over familiar arguments and formulations. Furthermore, a selection of 70 articles out of the upwards of 4,000 I have written over the past 20 years necessarily will convey a disconnected and often spotty narrative. There is no way in such a relatively small selection of writing by one reporter to fill in all the missing connective tissue. Since a certain amount of discontinuity is inevitable, I have decided that there is little to be gained by substantially rearranging the sequence in which these articles first appeared. As a result, section by section, the pieces are generally laid out in chronological order. In real life, after all, that is the way the news happens.

The first chapter details at a state and municipal level some of the interlocking aspects of money and power: *Baltimore and Maryland: Power, Money, Race, and Class—American Politics Writ Small*. The last five sections—Chapter Two, *The Conservative Rearmament;* Chapter Three, *The Early Years of the Reagan Administration;* Chapter Four, *Money and Connections in Washington;* Chapter Five, *Parties in Crisis: The Elusive Majority;* and the Epilogue, which attempts to look at some future trends both in politics and in political journalism—may be of greater general interest. Most readers will find more that has been left out, overlooked, or misunderstood than they will find to praise. In any case, I hope my colleagues, present and future, will draw inspiration from all the work that remains to be done.

*Greensboro, Vermont*
*August 1987*

# ACKNOWLEDGMENTS

**M**ANY JOURNALISTS far worthier than I have contributed to my education—those I have known and those I have only read—particularly David Broder, Haynes Johnson, Robert Sherrill, and I.F. Stone.

My gratitude to *The Providence Journal* for a spartan and exacting introduction, twenty-three years ago, to the principles of newspapering—to the police blotter, the town meeting, the accident ward, and the night shift.

I am indebted for basic training to my betters at *The Baltimore Sun:* Phil Evans, Ernie Imhoff, Bob Keller, Jim Keat, Gil Watson, Jerry Kelly, and William F. Schmick III.

My thanks to *The Washington Post:* Don Graham, Ben Bradlee and Len Downie at the top who set the standards—rigorous, competitive, scrupulous and tough; Bob Kaiser, who has provided me with intellectual stimulation and the encouragement to think things through; Dan Balz and Ann Devroy, who not only run the political coverage with insight and imagination, but who are called on regularly to fill in the considerable gaps in my expertise; Steve Luxenberg, a thoughtful editor as well as a listener and a friend; Dave Ignatius on Outlook, and Meg Greenfield and Ken Ikenberry of the editorial pages, who provide a much appreciated outlet for pieces with a point of view; Peter Silberman, who first gave me a berth at *The Post* and who more than once gave me a hand; Frank Swoboda and Peter Behr of the financial section, who gave me friendship and a couple of lucky breaks when I needed them.

Additional gratitude for all I have learned from my colleagues in the profession, whose achievements routinely and inescapably eclipse mine: Mary McGrory, Jules Witcover, Jack Germond, Bob Healy, Bob Kuttner, William Greider, Fred Barnes, Adam Clymer, Marty Tolchin, E. J. Dionne, Al Hunt, Dave Rogers, Mark Shields, Steve Nordlinger, Carl Leubsdorf, Fred Hill, Bob Dowling, Jon Margolis, Lou Cannon, Helen Dewar, Bill Peterson, Jim Dickenson, Ward Sinclair, Paul Taylor, Mike Barone, Sidney Blumenthal, Chuck Babcock, Maralee Schwartz, Milt Coleman, Dan Morgan, George Wilson, George Lardner, Spencer Rich, Ed Walsh, Jim Rowe, Peter Milius, David Maraniss, David Hoffman, Juan Williams, Howie Kurtz, Mike Issikof, Tom Reid, Peter Perl, and Morton Mintz. I am indebted to editors Don Phillips, Noel Epstein, Bob Webb, Steve Barr, Bill Elsen, Henry Allen, and Jerry Knight; to James P. Jordan for insight and advice; and for invaluable research assistance to Ken John and Colette Rhoney. Special appreciation to James P. Jordan for insight and advice; to Karl W. Deutsch, John T. Edsall, and Burt Hoffman, wise counsel of many years.

My special thanks to the magazine editors whose support has allowed me, at welcome intervals, to write at leisure and at length: Bob Silvers at *The New York Review of Books;* Charlie Peters at *The Washington Monthly;* and Irving Howe at *Dissent.*

In an age of media monopoly, I have been particularly lucky to work for two family-run newspapers, *The Washington Post* and *The Baltimore Sun,* whose commitment over several generations to the unambiguous separation of editorial decisions from business judgments, and to the vigilant protection of an independent newsroom, has given dignity and credibility to American journalism.

Special thanks to Donald S. Lamm, the president of W. W. Norton & Company and the editor every writer dreams of, without whom this book would not have come into being; and to his assistant, Amy Cherry, who worked her way through a mountain of stale newsprint, who edited and selected, and who in the end created order out of turmoil.

# POWER
# AND MONEY

# CHAPTER ONE

# BALTIMORE AND MARYLAND
## Power, Money, Race, and Class— American Politics Writ Small

THE ARTICLES AND ESSAYS reprinted in this section describe a period of transition in the political order of both Baltimore and Maryland—the final days of a city politics dominated by ward and district organizations, and of a state politics still subject to manipulation through patronage and through contract awards handed out by the Board of Public Works. In one basic respect, there has been no change between the 1969–75 period, when this material was written, and the present: the Democratic party continues to dominate both the state and the city. Within that party structure, however, there have, been a series of internal realignments.

At the time I was writing about Baltimore politics, blacks had started to win citywide offices, most often in contests in which one black candidate faced two or more white candidates who split the white vote. In the intervening years, blacks have gained a slim voting majority in the city and have flexed their political muscle, winning the presidency of the Baltimore city council and the state's attorney office in head-on contests against whites. In 1987, Kurt Schmoke, a Yale-educated Rhodes scholar and city prosecutor, became Baltimore's first elected black mayor. Unlike other majority black communities such as Detroit, Atlanta, and New Orleans, the shift in control of city hall from white to black took place without a racially divisive contest for the mayoralty. William Donald Schaefer, a white, served as mayor for fifteen years, from 1971 to 1986 when he won the governorship. Schmoke won the office in 1987 by beating another black, Clarence "Du" Burns, an organization politician who had worked his way up from high school janitor to president of the city council, in a contest without a white candidate.

During the fifteen years of Schaefer's mayoralty, the underlying politics of the city changed dramatically. There continues to be a network of traditional Democratic political organizations and clubs, but their ability to produce a decisive vote in all but the closest of elections has disappeared. Television has now become a factor not only in contests for major offices, but also in city council and state legislative races, while the steady replacement of patronage with civil service jobs has continued.

Dominic (Mimi) DiPietro (see page 821), who in 1975 represented the last of the strong, old-guard leaders, is, as of this writing, still a member of the city council, but at 82 he no longer qualifies as one of the pillars of power when politicians map legislative or campaign strategies.

William L. (Little Willie) Adams (page 32), the powerful and deliberately reclusive millionaire who controlled Metro Democrats, a west Baltimore political club, was, at the time I was covering the city, a figure of vast influence in the black community. Adams, a former numbers operator looked upon with some suspicion by Baltimore's black civil rights leadership, had, by the late sixties, built a real estate and corporate empire as powerful as any in the state. For more than a decade no black in Baltimore politics moved without looking to see where Adams stood. In September 1979, Adams was charged with three counts of violating state lottery (gambling) laws. The case dragged through the courts for nearly five years and did not come to trial until June 1984, when he was acquitted. During these legal proceedings, Adams, who who was 70 in 1984, dropped off of center stage in city politics. Adams played no significant role in the 1987 election that produced the city's first elected black mayor, as an entire new generation of blacks—and some whites—emerged to form the nucleus of the city's political operatives and strategists.

At the state level, the gubernatorial election of 1978 marked a major turning point in Maryland politics. For generations, the state house had been controlled by governors in the tradition of Marvin Mandel, Millard Tawes, and Spiro T. Agnew. With each new administration, the universe of favored road contractors, builders, insurance firms, architects, engineers, developers, and racetrack operators changed, with state government serving as an engine of economic advancement. The power of the governor over the legislature depended in large part on the chief executive's ability to guarantee allegiance through the adept use of patronage.

The indictment and conviction of Governor Marvin Mandel and five associates in 1978 on charges of mail fraud and racketeering brought this style of government to an abrupt halt. Although the convictions were overturned in 1987, a system of state government amounting to a pyramidal accumulation of deals, each based on economic self-interest, is unlikely to return to Maryland.* Instead,

---

*Governor Mandel and five associates were convicted in 1978 on 15 counts of mail fraud and on one count of racketeering. The conviction was based on charges of legislative maneuvers—including a gubernatorial veto—designed to raise the value of the Marlboro Race Track in Prince George's County, a track owned by five Mandel associates: Irvin Kovens, Harry W. Rodgers, William Rodgers, Ernest Cory and W. Dale Hess. Mandel spent 19 months in jail and was paroled on December 20, 1981; he was disbarred in October 1982. In 1987, in an unrelated case, *McNally* vs. *U.S.*, the Supreme Court held that the federal mail fraud statute was not meant to be used in situations, such as that of the Mandel case, in which the government argued that citizens were deprived of their "intangible rights" to the loyal and faithful service of public officials. On August 14, 1987, following the decision in *McNally*, Mandel and his associates filed motions in federal court to have their convictions overturned. On November 12, 1987, U.S. District Court Judge Frederick N. Smalkin ruled in Mandel's favor. Smalkin said in his ruling that "The evidence of concealment of ownership of Marlboro shares and of Mandel's secret financial arrangements certainly showed that something fishy, and perhaps dishonest, involving Maryland's governor and some of those personally and politically closest to him was going on . . . Mandel may well have been bribed. His codefendant might well have bribed him. But however strong the evidence of dishonesty or bribery, the jury was told

Mandel's conviction forced an abrupt and permanent shift in the conduct of government in Maryland, as he was replaced by former state senator Harry Hughes, a reform Democrat who won two terms in large part because of his aura of exemplary honesty. In 1986, Schaefer, the former four-term Mayor of Baltimore and a politician with a genius for the exercise of executive power, won the governorship. Schaefer, however, faces a legislature substantially different from the one which first elected Mandel in 1969, when Spiro T. Agnew left the governorship to assume the vice-presidency. The steady rise in the population of such suburban jurisdictions as Montgomery, Prince Georges, Anne Arundel, and Baltimore counties—while Baltimore city's population has fallen from 41 percent of the total population of Maryland (1950), to 18 percent in 1984—insures that there will never be a return to the free-wheeling style of patronage and favoritism exercised under Mandel and his predecessors, a kind of politics that depended on a firm base of urban power unrestricted by inhibitions concerning official propriety and public ethics.

Maryland has remained one of the most Democratic states in the nation. In fact, the strength of the Republican party in the state legislature has fallen from 33 of 185 seats in 1967 to 23 of 188 seats in 1987, despite the endemic corruption during the 1970s within the state's Democratic party, and despite the rising national strength of the GOP under Ronald Reagan. The Maryland Democratic party has maintained its resiliency in large part because it has retained the capacity to provide representation to both whites and blacks, city and suburb, old-guard and reformer. In the long run, however, the demographic changes taking place in the state point toward the prospect of increasing internal dissension within the Democratic party, and suggest that over time the Republican party will become more and more competitive. Not only do the suburban communities that now dominate the state provide fertile territory for the GOP—as evidenced by their strong support for Ronald Reagan and their rejection of Walter F. Mondale in 1984—but growing suburban strength in the legislature is likely to produce the kind of political conflict pitting affluent, and largely white, suburban jurisdictions against less affluent, and largely black, Baltimore city, and, to a lesser extent, against Prince Georges County, just under 40 percent black. It is this kind of conflict that often results in the destruction of Democratic hegemony, and in the emergence of political divisions along Republican–Democratic lines.

The articles in this section touch upon one stage in the evolution of Maryland politics, a stage of intense internal conflict within the dominant Democratic party that has not yet, as it has in many other states, resulted in a major erosion of the party's strength.

In this chapter I have also included a series of stories on the campaign finances of Mandel's 1970 gubernatorial election, the details of which, 18 years

---

it could not convict for something that did not amount to a federal crime." Prosecutors said they would appeal Smalkin's decision.

later, may seem numbing. As a way of looking at a campaign, however, the stories have, I hope, some continuing interest. Today, reporting about campaign finance—even of the *quid pro quo* documented here—has become more common, but at the time that these stories appeared, this kind of journalism was, as far as I know, nonexistent.

A number of the facts I reported in the Mandel series were later used by federal prosecutors to obtain the conviction of the former governor and his associates. My goal in unearthing the connections between campaign donations, executive action, and the awarding of city and state contracts was not, however, to provoke federal prosecution, but to illuminate the systematic and structural interaction—quite apart from questions of legality—at the city and state levels between government and the private sector. It was the pervasiveness of this kind of interactivity, not allegations of its criminality, which I felt deserved attention. The District Court ruling in 1987 overturning the Mandel conviction suggests that prosecutors had overstepped the boundaries of the law to force an alteration of state government that might best have been left to the general public to determine on election day.

# The Power of Willie Adams
# Is Clear, but It's Tenuous
# and at Critical Point

*The Evening Sun,* March 11, 1971

As success builds upon itself with the election of a state's attorney, congressman, supreme bench judge, and expanded representation in the legislature, black politicians are tracking the scent of a mayoral victory in Baltimore this year.

They are moving toward an increasingly visible goal without, however, the roots of established political organization in five of the city's six districts, organizations with access to that lubricant of success, money.

Black voters are turning out in numbers for the first time to vote for local candidates. But the finances necessary to run major campaigns are not available within the black community, making one of the differences between winning and losing the ability to draw white contributors with interests in the spending of city taxes and in the actions of regulatory agencies—a difference that has given William L. (Little Willie) Adams particular significance.

Capitalizing on the natural affinity between the white Democratic financial establishment and a black politician with economic, rather than ideological, interests, Mr. Adams, a 57-year-old black millionaire, has the respect of contractors, banks, racetrack owners, liquor interests, insurance companies and, in fact, most of the people and corporations who bankroll elections.

Benefiting from the mystique of 21 years in the numbers racket (from 1930 to 1950) without, he has said, spending a night in jail, and from his more recent business investments and connections with urban renewal projects, tavern operators, and the financial machinery of the Democratic party, Mr. Adams's influence is reflected in the prestigious patronage falling to close associates.

Delegate Lloyd Randolph, (D-4th), was chief clerk of the city's elections board until his resignation last year; George L. Russell, Jr., is city solicitor and before that an appointed judge on the Supreme Bench; Solomon Baylor is a Municipal Court judge and before that a member of the zoning board; Kenneth O. Wilson replaced Mr. Baylor on the zoning board; and Henry Parks, Jr., the former councilman, is now treasurer of the state Democratic party and a member of the Metropolitan Transit Authority.

Mr. Adams's friendship and close association with Marvin Mandel became one of his strongest assets when Mr. Mandel became governor.

In the world of white politics, where the increasingly affluent voter has forced a shift in the distribution of backroom power from the ethnic boss whose constituency is becoming more unreliable, to those with the cash to finance the growing cost of campaigns, Mr. Adams is assured of continued strength.

But in the black political community, where power based on the holding of elected office will increase geometrically during the next ten years, Mr. Adams's status is at a critical turning point: As intense competition begins, he has the initial advantages of influence and financial resources, advantages which are threatened as black bases of electoral strength extend beyond the Fourth District into the Second and Fifth, and, to a lesser extent, the Third and Sixth Districts.

Representative Parren Mitchell (D-7th, Md.), won election with the endorsement, but without the active support of, Metro Democrats, Inc., Mr. Adams's political organization. Clarence W. Blount, the Fifth District's first black state senator, has a loose alliance with Metro, but is also building up an independent organization in northwest Baltimore.

In the Second District, Mr. Adams has provided financial support to some of the members of the East Side Democratic Organization, which in 1967 and 1970 elected a black councilman, a state senator and two delegates. But the group's success at the polls serves only to increase the danger to Mr. Adams of independent action.

Metro, itself, was able to elect only four out of seven delegates from the Fourth District in November. The group has the allegiance also of two city councilmen, Mr. Adams's wife, Victorine, and Robert Marshall. But it has been unable to maintain control over either of the district's state senators, and Mr. Marshall is said to owe some political debts to James (Jack) Pollack, the declining boss of northwest Baltimore.

The tenuousness of Mr. Adams's current advantages, then, has turned this year's mayorality race, in part, into a test of his ability to limit the major black candidacies to only Mr. Russell, the city solicitor, formerly Mr. Adams's personal attorney and one-time joint investor.

Mr. Russell's candidacy has attracted whites from the old guard, some of

whom have worked against the interests of blacks but who see a black candidacy
as inevitable and are looking for a man they can work with or, in a phrase heard
repeatedly, 'you need a black in there to say no to the "militants." ' The presence
of Lou Grasmick, who ran the Mahoney "Your Home is Your Castle" campaign,
and of John A. Pica, the city contractor and former center of councilmatic
opposition to civil rights, in the Russell testimonial committee, sticks like a bone
in the throat of black activists.

It has never been Mr. Adams's strategy to attack the status quo within the
white community. He has worked, instead, within the black community to
develop his economic base—first in the numbers and later in real estate, vending
machines, the Parks Sausage Company and urban renewal development.

One of the rewards for this strategy, a reward of recognition, was a small
testimonial last year in Little Italy for Mr. Adams. It was arranged by a group
of 42 men, composed largely of First District conservatives, Mahoney supporters
and Block bar owners who less than five years ago put up a bitter battle against
integration.

With a new found prestige based on his old friendship with Governor
Mandel, and with the recent recognition of county machine politicians who
identify him with the black vote in Baltimore, Mr. Adams is moving out into the
open more.

He attended not only Mr. Russell's testimonial in December but also a
pre-primary fund-raiser in January for William Donald Schaefer, the City Council president and one of Mr. Russell's white competitors, as well as the opening
of the General Assembly.

He is, in the eyes of some observers, calculatingly making people aware of
his presence, making the delegates think about the fact that he can call up
Governor Mandel or Irvin Kovens, the former racetrack owner and a monied
decision maker behind the Governor, and get what he wants.

Always watching, letting others seek him out, he is seen as trying to turn a
reputation into a presence. At the opening of this year's General Assembly he
stood in front of the entrance to the House of Delegates' chamber, as those who
have worked with him moved quickly to shake his hand, while some who did not
know him asked quietly, "Is that Willie Adams?"

Light skinned, with an accountant's paunch and horn-rimmed glasses, he
looks altogether too mild and inconsequential to be Little Willie Adams. He lives
in the center of the black bourgeoisie, plants tomatoes in his back yard, got a high
school degree at night and attended business classes at Loyola College and the
Johns Hopkins University.

He was asked several times for an interview but refused unless certain conditions guaranteed what he considered a favorable article.

A millionaire on the basis of his stock in Parks Sausage Company alone, Mr.
Adams, in the words of an associate, "is too smart to go in for too much show
and pomp. He lives a good life but he doesn't show it off in a way that's going
to make a white person say 'they always buy Cadillacs.' "

His taste in cars runs to sedate Buicks and Chryslers and at public gatherings he often wears baggy brown suits. His home is a separate brick house at 3103 Carlisle Avenue, a social step above a row house but not as impressive as the homes up the hill from it in the Ashburton section along North Hilton street.

Mr. Adams is an early riser, on his way to work before 8 A.M. He conducts much of his activity from his real estate office in the 1500 block Pennsylvania Avenue, which is considered the most likely place to reach him on any given afternoon.

Mr. Adams has become a gentleman farmer on weekends at an estate he owns with Mr. Russell and Charles Burns, a pharmacist, in the Whitehall section of Baltimore county.

Along with growing squash, greens, and tomatoes at the farm, Mr. Adams invites friends there in the fall to hunt.

The Little Willie reputation began when Mr. Adams went before the Kefauver Committee to Investigate Interstate Crime in 1951, at which he described his rise from running numbers in East Baltimore at 16 to numbers banker at 36, with 10 lieutenants and a daily handle of $1,000 or more. He said he left the racket in May 1950.

Numbers operators have come and gone, however, and the real basis for the widespread but inflated belief that Little Willie Adams is behind every enterprise in the ghetto is the more limited reality of his connections with real estate, bars and urban renewal. Mr. Adams and his wife's commercial acquisitions are centered in the 1500 block of Pennsylvania Avenue where they have owned 11 of the properties, and now own 7.

Once a center of numbers activity and more recently considered a focal point of narcotics traffic, the 1500 block was the hub of black nightlife before its reputation for street crime, decay and the opening of other areas through desegregation brought about its demise.

"For a young Negro who thought he had some moves, the 1500 block was the place he proved it," a former habitué commented. "It didn't hurt Willie's reputation that while most of us had to go there to show what we had, Willie owned it."

The glamour of having a piece of the sporting life was enhanced by Mr. Adams's part ownership of Carrs Beach, an amusement park and swimming area packed on summer days when other beaches were segregated.

The glamour, however, did not include Mr. Adams's buying and selling of residential properties, attacked last year in a report by Activists, Inc., a civil rights group. Mr. Adams's company, A and L Realty, was one of many cited for profiting from the purchase of homes from whites who felt threatened by Negro migrations and who then sold to blacks at inflated prices.

Over the years, Mr. Adams built up connections, both direct and indirect, with a group of highly reliable contributors to local elections: bar owners and operators who are regulated by politically appointed liquor inspectors and commissioners.

His links to bars are ownership of buildings in which others operate bars, family ties and contractual arrangements. In no case is Mr. Adams the licencee of any liquor outlet.

He and his wife own the Club Casino property in the 1500 block Pennsylvania Avenue as well as a neighborhood tavern he once operated himself and lived above, Little Willie's Bar, in the 2400 block Druid Hill Avenue.

Across the street from the Casino, Mr. Adams sold and mortgaged the York Tavern to Delegate Randolph; his father-in-law runs a bar on Pressman street; two of the men arrested with Mr. Adams in a 1949 raid (Mr. Adams was acquitted, the 16 others were convicted) operate taverns; a close friend who retired as a lieutenant of the police force three years ago, James Hiran Butler, owns a portion of Cherry Hill Liquors; his business partner at Carrs Beach, Askew Gatewood, runs the Red Rooster on McKean Street.

These links expanded through the Biddison Music Company, which Mr. Adams helped found in 1947, a firm leasing juke boxes, pinball machines and other vending devices to restaurants and bars.

The political utility of these connections is reflected in the large number of advertisements taken out by the liquor outlets in the literature printed for events held by the Metro Democrats and by Woman Power, an organization run by Mrs. Adams, and in the ticket sales to the periodic affairs held by the political club.

Real estate and connections to bars are the kind of interests which force the respect of machine politicians; in fact, they are the kind of interests the politicians are quick to understand and trust. They are not, however, enough to guarantee the respect of the banks, insurance companies and prestigious law firms that also bankroll the Democratic party.

Mr. Adams has established financial credibility through Parks Sausage, a company he founded with Mr. Parks in 1951. Mr. Adams is now a director, and owns 26 percent of the stock in the company. And Mr. Adams has easy access to the highest levels of the Equitable Trust Company in his financial dealings.

Mr. Parks, also a millionaire and a Negro, has blended in with the financial establishment and the Democratic party organization, lunching regularly at the Center Club and taking over as treasurer of the State Democratic party shortly after his resignation from the City Council.

Since Mr. Adams and Mr. Parks became actively involved in politics in the early 1960s, Parks Sausage has been sold two tracts of city-owned land in the Camden Industrial Park, and last year became the first company in the city to receive a special $1.37-million loan guaranteed by the city and state at a 6.5 percent interest rate, at that time less than the prime lending rate. The low rate was allowable under a new state industrial financing program.

In the 20 years of its existence, the firm has steadily grown, and is now listed on the New York Stock Exchange with company officials predicting gross sales of $10 million a year.

The sale of land to the company raised a conflict-of-interest question for Mr.

Parks while he was serving on the council; the council quickly resolved the problem by passing an amendment to the conflict provisions of the city charter permitting special exemptions covering the Parks sales.

Mr. Parks resigned from the council in part because the exemption did not permit him to invest in a combination office-building-parking garage in the Inner Harbor renewal area. The building is to be developed by Allen Quille, president of Quille Parking Lots, Inc., and Mr. Adams's wife's uncle. Mr. Adams is a director of the parking lot company.

Although Mr. Adams's corporate interests provide the financial base for political muscle, they require the maintenance of good relationships with those in power, a delicate balance that can be disturbed by a dispute over ideological issues.

"With these kinds of interests, Adams isn't going to use up the political debts he is owed to change things like school policies or hiring practices. There's nothing in it for him," a member of the General Assembly commented.

There are a number of black politicians who say in private that Mr. Adams's opportunities to expand his influence through the election of top city officials will be limited to the present period while there is a continued dependence on money from white sources to elect a black in a citywide election.

Their thinking is based on two major weaknesses they see in Mr. Adams's organization, Metro Democrats, weaknesses shared by Metro's major competitor, the Fourth District Democratic Organization.

The first is that while both organizations have fought over prominent and well-paying jobs, they have not set up machinery to obtain minor city posts for constituents, the kind of machinery which helped establish more permanent bases of power for white organizations in working-class sections.

A second weakness often referred to is the dominance in these organizations of men and women well over 40 who are considered out of touch with younger more aggressive people and groups.

Black city councilmen, including those associated with Mr. Adams, have not made serious efforts to bring the problems of the black community into the forum of city government for airing and debate. Mr. Parks, for example, when he was a councilman would never let a racial issue get in the way of his friendships and alliances with white councilmen.

These weaknesses, combined with an inability to control the black vote with any sureness, and Mr. Adams's economic involvement with the actions of government, reduce his ability to bargain independently without raising the danger of economic sanctions imposed against his own interests.

# Maryland: The Governor
# Raiseth

*The Washington Monthly,* February 1972

With the decline of organization control of large blocs of votes and a waning reform movement in the Democratic party, a quiet transfer of power is taking place in Maryland politics, a transfer based on the use of money as an exclusive force in winning office.

The importance of money in 1972 is not particularly noteworthy in itself, since politicians, with rare exceptions, have always depended on cash to win elections. But the significance of recent developments lies in the techniques that those with money, or with access to it, have developed. Contrary to the expectations of those who were optimistic following the decline of the political machine, these techniques have given a small number of people even greater influence, without the restrictions that applied to the power held by bosses in the first half of the century.

An examination of this transfer requires some history of power centers in elections and an explanation of the failure of efforts in the 1960s to reform state politics, a failure based in part on the internal contradictions between the claimed aims of the reformers and their sources of financial support.

The sources of cash for the candidates have been, and continue to be, the various interests affected by the actions of state government. These interests can be broken down into three general categories: 1) the state-regulated industries, including liquor outlets and manufacturers, nursing homes, racetracks, and finance companies; 2) the contractors, developers, consultants, and real estate dealers who gear their activities to state projects; and 3) the large banks, law firms, and insurance companies that want to maintain their control over the methods used to sell bonds and to store monies.

Aside from lining up contributors, candidates had always been required to seek out the support of the local political machines, which also had to be paid off. In local elections the machines often tried to win seats, and in isolated cases a particular machine's candidate might run for statewide office. In most cases, however, the local machine merely bargained with various candidates over the price of votes, and the votes were paid for with money and jobs. The money, in turn, financed the printing of ballots and the "walking around" expenses of precinct and ward workers; the jobs kept these workers employed between elections. As the machine leaders developed their own interests, such as construction firms or real estate, the bargaining often expanded to include the promise of contracts for beneficial land deals.

The political boss was, then, the third point in the triangular relationship between the financial interests and the candidates. He was the vehicle to the vote, particularly in a predominantly Democratic state where a guarantee of a large turnout for a specific candidate in a primary election often assured final victory. The boss also became the intermediary between the money and the men who ended up winning the elections—the city councilmen, state delegates, and state senators whose votes were essential on zoning, bond, and budget questions.

There are obvious criticisms to be made of this system, all justified. The boss was rarely interested in broad policy questions and could often only control his constituency with the promise of jobs; special interests were provided the advantage of dealing with a private power, rather than needing to submit to public questions; government bureaucracies were overloaded with incompetents appointed for their loyalty rather than their ability; the boss, through his business activities, often became a special interest himself.

The system, however, provided one major limitation to the ability of the boss to influence public decisions with impunity: he had to maintain the allegiance of those who would go to the polls every election and vote the way they had been told. In the cities, these voters were most often working class, and their concerns—the right to organize, minimum wages, and even the right to a fair deal at the racetracks—often conflicted with the monied interests. This forced the boss, who was caught between the two, to at least compromise. Another more subtle limitation was the background of the boss himself. Although rural political brokers often grew out of local elites, in urban areas the boss often rose directly from his own constituency. Men like Thomas J. D'Alesandro, Jr., Frank Kelly, and Jack Pollack of Baltimore began as city workers, prizefighters, or laborers.

Although the successful boss had always been inclined to join ranks with the bankers and contractors, he also enjoyed forcing the privileged classes to seek out the favors of the urban minorities. But whatever his inclinations, it was necessary for the boss to force compromises or he would be treated as easy game.

The reasons for the decline of the machine are well known: civil service replaced patronage, television appealed directly to the voter, the ethnic vote began to dissolve as education improved and as people moved to the suburbs. The magnitude of this decline can be seen in the fact that in 1950 a powerful Democratic boss in Maryland, Jack Pollack, threw the gubernatorial election to the Republican candidate in retaliation for the ousting of one of his associates from the state central committee. Yet in 1971, the same boss was only able to deliver enough votes for his candidate for the presidency of the Baltimore city council to run a weak fourth in the Democratic primary.

This decline coincided with the focus in the 1960s on such issues as civil rights and poverty; it was a period when a vacuum of entrenched power permitted the development of a political climate appropriate for the election of what were considered reformers. In Maryland, this was typified by the election in 1964 of Joseph Tydings to the U.S. Senate. Tydings based his campaign on opposition to the special interests that dominated state government. Although his opponent in the Democratic primary was Louis Goldstein, he campaigned against the incumbent governor, J. Millard Tawes, and against a beer lobbyist influential in the Tawes administration, George Hocker, treating Goldstein as a tool of the "Hocker-Tawes machine."

Tydings's failure to win reelection in 1970 can be attributed to a number of factors: his support of civil rights, the opposition of the gun lobby, his failure to build up a reform element within the rank and file of the Democratic party. But equally important was the fact that Tydings permitted himself to be outflanked by the same interests he opposed in 1964. The maneuver forced him to run with the descendants of those he had defeated; it also exemplified the resurgence of money as the controlling factor in elections.

While the defeat of Tydings shows the negative effects of political money, the use of the same force to win is reflected in the 1970 election of Governor Mandel. The elevation of Mandel to the governor's office in 1969 had been the result of a political accident: the selection of Spiro T. Agnew as the Republican vice-presidential candidate. Mandel did not have to win a general election to become governor; instead, he needed only a majority of the 185 senators and delegates who depended on him, as House speaker, for passage of their legislation. Although his selection by the legislators was almost assured, Mandel had another debt to collect: as chairman of the Democratic party during the 1968 election, he had been responsible for the distribution of money for the Humphrey campaign, most of which went to the organizations with which the legislators were affiliated.

Mandel's elevation to the governorship was unremarkable except in its long-term significance: the special interests that once had depended on Agnew, whose political future within the state was tenuous, now had a member of the majority party in office. The problem was to assure his actual election in 1970.

Without the advantage of incumbency, Mandel would have been an unlikely candidate. He avoided taking stands on public issues, specializing instead on the manipulation of votes and legislation; he was associated in the public mind with the secretiveness characteristic of the legislative process in the state capital. Mandel had never been a major vote-getter in his own legislative district, the Fifth, a predominantly Jewish section of Baltimore. There he had been able to depend on his religious identification and the support of the two major political factions.

To prevent the development of significant opposition well before the 1970 Democratic primary, Mandel's associates began immediately to line up the support of the approximately 1,000 corporations and officials of corporations who can be depended upon to kick in $500 or more to state campaigns. Although Mandel might well have been the choice of the machines of earlier days, the power of giving initial approval to his candidacy would have rested with the bosses instead of the money brokers. In the past the contributors usually played an essentially passive role, permitting local bosses and organizations to select candidates, and then giving to whichever candidate appeared most likely to win, hedging their bets in close contests by backing two or more candidates for the same office. Until 1970, this process had still not been altered in recognition of the reduction of the organization-controlled vote.

Mandel and his associates recognized that the bloc vote had been eliminated, and concentrated on the one variable they could control—money. They knew that the increased cost of campaigns made that variable even more important. In addition, they proved that stricter elections laws made it easier, rather than more difficult, to corner the market on contributions.

The three men who systemized the use of money in the Maryland campaign represent the areas that are most essential to the process. Harry Rodgers, III, is the president of Tidewater Insurance Company, a firm providing coverage to government employees and corporations that do business with the state or are concerned with state regulatory activities. W. Dale Hess is the former majority whip of the House of Delegates. As a legislator, he developed wide contacts with the state's lobbyists. He is a real estate speculator who profited from advance knowledge of pending decisions of the state roads commission. Since his retirement from the House, Hess has taken over public relations for Tidewater. Irvin Kovens is the former owner of the Charlestown, West Virginia, racetrack, which draws heavily on Maryland racing enthusiasts, and the operator of M. Kovens Company, a large installment sales company.

The three men approached every known "giver" and succeeded in raising adequate funds to conduct a primary before the election began. They developed what seems to be turning into a standard tactic, the pre-primary testimonial dinner held well before the election. Although important as a means of raising money, the testimonial dinner serves other essential functions. If successful, it creates a steamroller effect: potential backers who are reluctant to support anyone early in a campaign are forced to consider the possibility that further delay could turn them into latecomers. The dinner is held while the incumbent has at least six months, and preferably more, to go in his term so that all those firms with interest in the day-to-day decisions of current government—contractors with pending "extras," for example—will be more inclined to line up behind him.

Perhaps most important of all is the necessity of giving the incumbent, particularly an untested one such as Mandel, credibility within the financial community—to make it appear that his stock is rising and that now is the time to buy in before the price becomes prohibitive.

Rodgers, Hess, and Kovens have developed the ability to identify and cultivate the "constituency" from which money can be raised. The make-up of the constituency is always changing, depending upon a number of factors, the most important of which is the time period of the campaign. In the pre-primary period, there is a specific group which can be drawn on for support. It is composed of the corporations and men who are financially dependent on the discretionary powers of state officials: consulting engineers and architects who do not bid competitively for contracts, real estate dealers whose investments depend on road routes and interchanges, liquor people concerned with the diligence of inspectors, insurance companies seeking higher rate scales. The vulnerability of this group is one of the major advantages held by an incumbent running for reelection; he has a ready source available to try to create the steamroller effect at the appropriate moment.

If the initial phase is successful, as it was in the case of Mandel's testimonial, when he raised over $600,000 nine months before the primary, the pressure is applied to swing the more secure potential contributors into line. This group is composed of the contractors who have dealt so long with state officials that they know the middle-level bureaucracy cannot turn against them; the banks and bonding companies so prestigious that no governor would attempt to offend them; the law firms with former partners secure on the civil and criminal benches. Assured of maintaining their income sources from the state, these groups are primarily interested in preventing any tampering with the overall system of state budgeting. They also like to avoid any major misuse of money which might become public knowledge, thus jeopardizing the state's bond rating, and consequently its ability to finance new construction. Much of the financial establishment tends to be very close-mouthed about any questionable activities in government, largely because it is in their interest to see that whatever problems arise are settled "in house" without any public controversy.

Clearly, in the two-stage process of winning first the vulnerable money and then the secure money, the first step is the more important. The natural guideline used by the secure group to determine a candidate's chances is the amount of money already collected.

The vulnerable money sources in Maryland have developed a unity of interest with a major element of the Democratic party, a unity which is based on land speculation and the ancillary means of profit: insurance, marginally regulated lending companies, legal fees, and contracting. One of the characteristics of this speculative atmosphere is that those who operate within it encourage cooperation as much as, if not more than competition. The land buyer is concerned less with potential competitors for the land than with winning the cooperation of both public and private officials: zoning commissioners, road designers, money lenders, and potential developers. The degree to which this atmosphere has absorbed public officials is reflected in the governor's former ownership of a real estate company and savings and loan firm, both of which were used for speculative investment; the participation of the attorney general and chief judge of the state district court system in a Florida land investment scheme; the inclusion of former Governor Agnew in a limited partnership investing in the Virgin Islands; and the present lieutenant governor's extensive landholdings in the suburban Washington area.

The talent that Rodgers, Hess, and Kovens bring to this scene is an extension of past success in their own business ventures. Rodgers's cultivation of contacts through his political activities has turned Tidewater into one of the leading insurance companies in the state; Hess's real estate ventures have been so lucrative that they have been submerged in a myriad of corporations; Kovens recently sold his racetrack for a profit of $5.7 million.

If these men had been bosses, their activities would have damaged their credibility within their constituencies, particularly if the outward signs of their success were as visible as, for example, Kovens's chauffeur-driven Cadillac. But within their present political world—those who feel the need to protect their interests through contributions—business success and the techniques used to achieve it are respected. The encouragement of cooperation within the ethic of speculation has served to increase its attractiveness to contributors and politicians alike; Kovens, for example, has a reputation as a man willing to cut others in on a deal.

The combined effort of Kovens, Hess, and Rodgers to raise money for Governor Mandel effectively put Mandel over the most critical phase of his 1970 campaign. Sargent Shriver, the former ambassador to France, who was considering making a challenge, discovered that the available sources of money had been dried up before he was able to announce his candidacy.

The success of Governor Mandel's associates in lining up liberal donors in the old-line camp created a major overlap between Mandel money and Tydings money. There is in Maryland what might be described as a residue of liberal givers, centered in Baltimore and suburban Washington areas. They include men like Jerold Hoffberger, whose decision to back a candidate is significant not only in itself but also because it will prompt lesser liberal money to flow in the same direction. Hoffberger, as president of the company producing National Beer and Colt 45 and as the owner of the Baltimore Orioles baseball team, is not in a position to completely alienate influential state politicians, and once the Mandel campaign began moving, he joined the supporters.

This was a major blow to Shriver, but it also was a big factor in the decision of Senator Tydings to make an about-face from the style of his campaign of 1964. Faced with a primary fight, the opposition of the gun lobby, the suspicion of liberals over his sponsorship of preventive detention legislation and a possible split within his party, Tydings chose to line up on the side where he shared financial support—with Governor Mandel, the heir of the machine he ran against in 1964.

Tydings became the advocate of unity and cooperation within the Democratic party, counseling Shriver behind closed doors not to run, telling his supporters not to help Shriver even indirectly, opposing a reform challenge which would force him into the conflict not only as a candidate seeking votes but also as a candidate seeking cash.

Mandel's supporters also used the state election law to advantage. The major regulation in Maryland is a blanket prohibition on contributions totaling more than $2,500 in any election by any corporation, individual, or union. This has proved to be to the advantage of Governor Mandel for several reasons. It does not apply to contributions made at fund-raising events held before the politician officially files his candidacy for election. This gives the incumbent running for reelection leverage to collect twice from those who think it is economically wise to contribute: once (or more) during the pre-announcement phase, and secondly after the formal campaign begins. If the law were tightened up to cover the period before the formal announcement, the incumbent would continue to have a major advantage in that he could bring more pressure to bear on donors to give the maximum well before the campaign begins, thereby eliminating them as potential sources of support for his opponent.

Governor Mandel's handling of the Humphrey money in the state in 1968 had been the subject of a federal grand jury investigation, and to avoid any possible complications in 1970, he went beyond the letter of the law and reported all purchasers of tickets to his pre-primary testimonial. At the same time, however, his aides encouraged reporters to believe that there was some doubt about the interpretation of the law. The doubt, in turn, was reflected in newspaper stories.

Despite whatever assurances they may have received, those who had already given to the Mandel testimonial were reluctant to contribute to anyone else, since there was some apprehension that the second donation might be illegal.

In the one-sided competition for financial support between Mandel and Shriver, another factor working in Mandel's favor was the fact that the ceiling on contributions has a built-in loophole: anyone who wants to exceed the ceiling can give additional money to his wife, child, or secretary, who in turn gives it to the candidate. It is an accepted practice, but Shriver was dependent to a much larger degree than Mandel on the type of contributor who is concerned with maintaining the appearance of propriety and who is, therefore, the most difficult to persuade to use these techniques.

The result of these maneuverings was Mandel's election to a four-year term in office. The election represented the resurgence within the Democratic party of most of the financial interests which had been influential through the 1950s and early 1960s. The difference, however, is that these interests, through the guiding hands of Kovens, Hess, and Rodgers, are no longer dependent on the bosses and organizations as they were ten years ago. Mandel's election is the first in the state in which the vacuum of power created by the decline of the boss has been recognized and filled by those who understand the consequent increase in the importance of money.

The absorption of the powers of the boss has had an extremely significant effect on the processes and style of state government. On the surface, the legislative and executive branches have been made more efficient. The committees have been better structured to process legislation; the governor has centralized control over the chaotic complex of agencies through the creation of cabinet-level posts to oversee the various functions of state government.

These changes are portrayed by the elected leaders and by the press as if they represent major alterations in the function and direction of state government. In fact, they represent only the imposition of corporate efficiency on institutions which are now more directly attuned to the needs of business. The vast majority of legislation continues to be unrelated to the needs and interests of the general population; instead, the measures are most often directed to the profit relationships of two related business endeavors: Should the savings and loans be given a rate advantage over the commercial banks, should changes in the insurance legislation benefit the agents, the underwriters, or, best of all, both?

The elimination of the old-style boss control of politicians has given an air of propriety to what remains the same legislative process. The legislators now look less like ward heelers and more like department store managers. This shift in the superficial appearance of state leadership has insulated the politician from some criticism in the press. The business community, including the newspapers, has always viewed with distaste the necessity of dealing with the political hacks who filled city councils, legislatures, and the governor's office. These institutions have now been made more acceptable, and the lines of authority and responsibility have been defined in patterns following systems developed in private enterprise. The press is neither equipped nor inclined to raise the general question of the obligation of officials to their constituents. Incidental complaints are made, but the overall view of the press is favorable towards the changing face of state government.

Governor Mandel has portrayed himself as an integral part of this change: a northwest Baltimore political functionary who learned the ropes and developed the skills to outgrow the machine. Two of the bills Governor Mandel fought hardest for in the state legislature last winter combined his interest in maintaining control of political money with his concern for increasing the appearance of efficiency.

The first bill provided for the state takeover of the cost of local school construction. There was no real opposition to the concept of the proposal; the fight developed over the governor's insistence that he gain ultimate control over the entire process of letting contracts. On the surface, the governor's position was that centralized control would permit better coordination of the program and the creation of uniform standards; at another level, the governor was operating on a political fact of life, that corporations donate to the campaigns of the politician who has the final say over their business activities. Passage of the bill meant, in effect, that Mandel had shifted a major source of contributions—school architects and contractors—from the level of mayors and county executives to the gubernatorial level. He not only developed a new area from which to raise money for a 1974 campaign; he also reduced the resources of potential opponents now holding office in local governments.

The second measure had the identical intent: it gave the governor veto power over the leases to be arranged with the airlines using Friendship International Airport. The leases, in turn, are to finance approximately $500 million worth of capital improvements at the airport, another major source of contributions.

As Governor Mandel continues to expand his resources for reelection, the men behind him are in the process of acquiring an interest in an increasing number of politicians. In the recent elections in Baltimore city—the largest political entity next to the state—Kovens raised the funds for the successful campaign of the man who will probably be the city's last white mayor. Aware, however, of the growing political strength of the blacks, who now comprise just under 48 percent of the city, Kovens has offered his money-raising talents to the black candidate defeated in the 1971 mayoral election, George L. Russell, Jr., who is considering a 1972 challenge of Parren J. Mitchell, the state's first black congressman. By refusing to work within the confines of the Democratic party, Mitchell has become a threat to the ability of Mandel and Kovens to insure that their political dominance will continue to extend into the black community. The threat has been increased by the growing evidence of Mitchell's willingness in local elections to support candidates running against those put up by the established black clubs.

Unlike the Irish and Italians, blacks are at the point of winning majority political power at a time when they must depend on money to finance television campaigns; the same forces behind the decline of the machine are acting to prevent the formation of black organizations with any degree of independence from predominantly white sources of financial support. Kovens's backing of Russell is an attempt to capitalize on this weakness within the black community while internal competition still makes it most vulnerable.

Kovens was unsuccessful in his effort to control the election of the Baltimore city council president, but he has recouped the loss by volunteering to help raise the money to pay off the $33,000 debt incurred by the winner, Walter S. Orlinsky. Hess had already been active in Mr. Orlinsky's campaign.

This steady acquisition of politicians has created a forced unity among elected officials which supersedes conflicting ideologies and differing constituencies. The knowledge is shared, particularly among the ambitious, of the strength of controlled political money; delegates vote for or against abortion bills but join forces on insurance matters; city councilmen differ over free school lunches but back each other's zoning bills.

The continued control of elective politics by the small group of men who can manipulate existing sources of money is unlikely to be altered as long as state government remains in large part an appendage of the business community. More than any other level of government, the state has remained insulated from pressures to go beyond the role of arbiter of demands for wider markets and increased profits by various industries. State officials have encouraged the process of permitting local and federal governments to become focal points for social questions while issues at the state level remain isolated from the public.

# Analysis: Black Political Conflict

The Evening Sun, May 13, 1972

The Seventh Congressional District primary election May 16 is the first major test of a basic conflict among black politicians between those active in the elective process for the traditional benefits—jobs and contracts—and those whose roots are in civil rights, the peace movement and black activism.

Although the candidates represent a mixture of interests, the conflict places Democratic Representative Parren J. Mitchell in a camp motivated primarily by ideological reasoning, while George L. Russell, Jr., represents those concerned primarily in the bread and butter of politics.

The contest between Mr. Mitchell, the incumbent, and Mr. Russell, the city solicitor, has become the focal point of what is perceived by the candidates, their backers and workers as a competition to determine which groups and individuals will dominate as the city becomes increasingly black.

At stake in the long run are not only the winning of major offices and the consequent influence over jobs, construction and policy, but also a determination of which white factions will continue to have influential voices in the city's political machinery.

The split here—seen also in other cities—began soon after black organizations, particularly the Fourth District Democratic Organization, established firm bases in west Baltimore in the early part of the last decade.

Reluctant to endanger their new-found ability to bargain with the predominantly white Democratic establishment over jobs and the beginnings of economic bases, most black elected officials largely rejected the privately voiced pressure from civil rights groups for aggressive leadership.

The result was two divergent trends: the organizations improved their ability to dominate district elections and, with the exception of state Sen. Clarence M. Mitchell, III, (D-4th) civil rights activists continued the protest movement, leaving the establishment of permanent clubs to the politicians.

This tacit agreement for a separate peace was abruptly altered in 1967 when Joseph C. Howard, an outsider often critical of the established clubs, demonstrated the strength and significance of the black vote in a citywide election by winning a seat on the Supreme Bench.

Judge Howard's successful campaign, run in large part by Larry Gibson, now a member of the school board, forced a sudden recognition of the widened scope of elective offices available to blacks. This was a major alteration that the established black and white factions were among the slowest to act upon.

Instead, in campaigns that stressed the candidates' "blackness" to appeal to black votes, two more major victories were achieved in 1970 by Representative Mitchell and Milton B. Allen, the present state's attorney.

Not until 1971, in the mayoral election, did a majority of the black clubs and a significant number of white groups and backers take the initiative and actively support the candidacy of a black for a position above the legislative or council district level.

Mr. Russell's unsuccessful bid for the mayoralty had the support of the Metro Democrats, the Eastside Democratic Club in the Second Council District and the Five-In-Five Democratic club in the Fifth Council District.

Many of the leaders and workers in the Howard, Allen and Mitchell campaigns sat out the Russell effort, in part because his candidacy represented a threat to their own dominance of the more prestigious black victories and also because of the presence of whites associated with activities considered against the interests of blacks.

Among those prominent in the Russell campaign were Louis J. Grasmick, coordinator of George P. Mahoney's "Your Home Is Your Castle" gubernatorial campaign in 1966; and William L. Siskind, director of a lending institution that provided large sums to finance the sale of homes to blacks in racially changing neighborhoods for prices viewed as excessive by civil rights groups.

Mr. Russell, unlike previous black candidates for major office, was able to draw upon the intensive resources of William L. (Little Willie) Adams, the black businessman and former head of a numbers operation: corporations in which Mr. Adams has an interest and business partners contributed and loaned over $10,000 to the Russell campaign.

The mayoral contest, however, left entirely unresolved the conflict between Mr. Russell's backers and what might be termed loosely the Mitchell faction.

The entry of Clarence Mitchell, Parren Mitchell's nephew, into the mayoral race, proved embarrassingly futile. It resulted only in an intensification of the belief that his role was to ruin Mr. Russell's chances in part of larger strategy to permit Representative Mitchell and his allies to dominate city politics in the future.

The belief received further support when Representative Mitchell took an active part in the council election in the Fifth District. He supported Norman Reeves, suggesting in radio advertisements that Mr. Reeves was the only legitimate black candidate running, with the implicit indication that the candidate fielded by the Five-in-Five club, Pinkney Howell, was not.

This belief, along with the widely held view of Representative Mitchell as a militant bent on excluding whites from the political process, was a major factor in uniting white politicians and financial backers behind Mr. Russell's current congressional campaign.

In an effort to avoid a repetition of the charges that Mr. Russell is controlled by white bosses, the white backers have been carefully kept in the background, surfacing only recently.

Among the traditionally conservative white groups and individuals who are supporting Mr. Russell's campaign are James (Jack) Pollack, once the boss of northwest Baltimore; state Senator Harry J. McGuirk (D-6th) and the Bohemian clubs in East Baltimore.

More important, however, has been the participation of backers closely associated with Governor Mandel who have been both raising money and determining how it is to be spent.

They include Irvin Kovens and W. Dale Hess, two of the most important parts of Governor Mandel's successful effort to corner most of the political money in 1970, in a move that prevented Democratic competitors for getting campaigns off the ground.

Mr. Kovens has been one of the few white backers to develop strong contacts within the black political organizations, maintaining a close relationship with both Mr. Adams, who is an influential member of Metro Democrats, and Sen. Verda F. Welcome (D-4th), a leading force in the FDDO.

Mrs. Welcome has been accused by the Baltimore Afro-American of supporting Mr. Russell because of $5,000 given to her club. In addition, however, the Russell campaign offered support for her campaign to be a Democratic convention delegate. A defeat of Representative Mitchell in the May 16 primary would improve her chances of running for reelection in 1974 if she faces Clarence Mitchell in a single-member district.

The view of Representative Mitchell as a leader of a militant faction of blacks bent on taking over city politics, encouraged in political circles by his own claim that he is fighting a battle against the Mandel-dominated Democratic machine, fails to take into account one of the inherent weaknesses Mr. Mitchell has demonstrated.

Mr. Mitchell and supporters sympathetic to him have not lived up to the claim of presenting an alternative to the established Democratic organizations, failing entirely to build up any permanent organization and neglecting the lower level of politics, except in the single, and unsuccessful, case of Mr. Reeves candidacy for the council.

Although he has some supporters among members of the House of Delegates, they do not represent strong organizations capable of either pulling out a large vote or providing the day-to-day services to the poorest constituent group in the state.

He has won the support of one of the established clubs, the Five-in-Five, but that decision was made after extensive consideration by state Senator Clarence W. Blount, (D-5th), whose support is by no means assured in future elections.

In addition, even some reform politicians are critical of Representative Mitchell's public opposition to the use of "walkaround money" to pay precinct workers. "It's a little arrogant to assume you are so great that masses of people are willing to spend a day passing out ballots for you. Most people who do that need the twenty bucks," one Fifth District reformer commented.

The failure of Representative Mitchell to establish any permanent organization has forced him to adopt a crisis strategy, trying to piece together support in the newly drawn district as the threat of a Russell challenge becomes more realistic. Mr. Mitchell has run into a number of rejections, prompted by his unwillingness to maintain contacts and to pay due respect to the sensitive egos of political workers.

A defeat for Representative Mitchell would be a major setback to the faction he is now representing; it would eliminate him from his position of political spokesman for the black caucus and lend major encouragement to his opposition in future elections.

Because of the failure to build up permanent organizations, a defeat would be more serious for the Mitchell faction than for those backing Mr. Russell because it would eliminate an essential base of power, the possession of elective office.

For Mr. Russell, a defeat following his failure in the mayoral primary would result in a major lessening of his credibility as a candidate.

For some of those supporting him, however, the election is being viewed as an opportunity to expand contacts, win or lose, with backers who have the ability to raise funds to finance major campaigns.

Members of the Eastside Democratic Club, for example, are starting fledgling electronics, funeral, and contracting businesses that can only benefit from increased exposure to members of the Democratic party who are influential in providing assistance to these kinds of economic endeavors.

The white backers and black clubs behind the Russell campaign have already demonstrated their staying power in recent years and a Russell defeat would be a blow, but not a permanent setback.

# Mandel Contributors Benefit from State

*This is the first in a series of articles examining large contributors to Governor Mandel's 1970 campaign and some of their business dealings with the state.*

*The Evening Sun,* October 24, 1972

Contributors of $1,000 or more to the 1970 campaign of Governor Mandel have since benefited from governmental action ranging from more than $31 million in discretionary awards to executive advocacy of favorable legislation.

In addition these contributors have been involved in secondary mechanisms for profiting from governmental and political activity. These dealings extend from the selection of bonding agents by contractors to the choice of advertising firms by state regulated businesses.

The overwhelming proportion of large contributors—both individuals and corporations—not only profess a general interest in good government, as do all contributors, but also have immediate economic interests in the operation of state government.

Many noncontributors also have financial dealings with the state.

The financial involvement of the large contributors centers primarily on Governor Mandel's control of the Board of Public Works, although it also includes his influence in the legislature, his appointive power, his authority over regulatory agencies and the growing political and financial muscle of close associates.

The Board of Public Works, made up of Governor Mandel, John A. Luetkemeyer, state treasurer, and Louis L. Goldstein, state comptroller, is the strongest agency in state government, having the power to approve or disapprove most expenditures.

The legislature in effect ceded control of the board to Governor Mandel when it confirmed his choice of Mr. Luetkemeyer as treasurer instead of exercising its independent authority to make the appointment.

Under the Mandel administration, the power of the board over state spending has been widened to cover both previously independent state agencies and entirely new areas of state financial responsibility.

The most significant expansion of the board's power came with the creation of the state Department of Transportation. Among other things, this eliminated the state Roads Commission and transferred final approval for the selection of road consultants to the Board of Public Works.

Consultants form the single largest group contributing to the governor's campaign in 1970.

The purchase of Friendship International Airport by the state earlier this year placed under board control the selection of contractors and consultants for major capital improvements at the facility.

Finally, the assumption by the state of most of the cost of school construction formerly paid by the subdivisions gave the Board of Public Works power to set requirements for:

"The approval of sites, plans and specifications for the construction of new school buildings or the improvement of existing buildings, site improvements, competitive bidding, the hiring of personnel . . . the actual construction of school buildings . . . and any other requirements involving school construction."

Mandel campaign records show, according to an *Evening Sun* survey, a total of 293 contributions of $1,000 or more from individuals and corporations, producing a total of $422,262, or 37 percent of the $1.14 million the governor reported spending. Another $27,700, or 2.4 percent, was given in amounts of $1,000 or more by unions.

Of the money from these large contributors, $165,900, or 40 percent, was from interests that profit from the decisions of the Board of Public Works. These contributors fall into three categories: architects and engineers, contractors, and owners of property rented by the state.

Another $212,467, or just over 50 percent of the large contributions, was raised from sources financially interested in a wide scope of other state government activities to be examined later in this series.

Ten percent of the large contributions were from sources who could not be shown to have direct financial interests in government decisions.

Completely excluding contracts awarded on the basis of competitive bidding, the ratio of discretionary awards in money given architects, engineers, contractors and owners of rental property under the Mandel administration to their contributions of $1,000 or more has exceeded 100 to 1 and grows with each new meeting of the Board of Public Works.

These ratios did not apply to individual cases where awards and contributions varied widely.

In addition, many discretionary awards were given to firms and individuals, who did not contribute to the governor's campaign.

Architects and engineers in the $1,000-or-more category contributed $99,300 and received noncompetitive awards of $14.8 million, or $100 in awards for every 67 cents contributed.

The ratio is larger for contractors who gave a total of $51,600 in amounts of $1,000 or more and were granted extras, change orders and subcontracts of $13.69 million, or $100 in unbid payments for each 39 cents contributed.

Owners of property for which the state approved new leases contributed $17,300 in amounts of $1,000 or more and are to be paid a total of $2.69 million for the duration of the leases, or $100 in rent for each 64 cents contributed.

Many of the awards given to architects and engineers by the board list a specific price. Those that did not, however, were calculated using one of two methods.

When the architect or engineer was listed in conjunction with the award of a project to a contractor, the fee was calculated at the conservative rate of 5 percent of the construction cost. Actual fees are based in almost all cases on two sliding scales which run from either 4½ percent to 7 percent or 6 percent to 10 percent.

In calculating fees for preliminary design work, the figure used was the amount set aside for that purpose in the capital budget.

Because of the record-keeping system maintained by various state departments, the proportion of extras, subcontracts and consultant fees awarded to contributors and to noncontributors could not be determined; discretionary awards are also made to corporations that do not appear as contributors.

Of the 28 contractors contributing $1,000 or more, however, 26, or 93 percent, received extras or subcontracts.

In addition, the contributing contractors received extras totalling more than 6 percent of the bid price on at least 10 contracts of $1 million or more. Six percent is generally considered the cutoff limit on reasonable contract cost increases.

All but one of the architects and engineers contributing to the Mandel campaign received awards given on a noncompetitive basis.

A spokesman for the one firm which did not receive any awards, Rackoff Associates, of Columbus, Ohio, said the company was considering the establishment of a Maryland office at the time the contribution was made but later dropped the idea.

In terms of the authority of the Board of Public Works over awards at the beginning of the Mandel administration, the contributing individuals and corporations and the awards they have received include the following:

The interlocking firms of Gaudreau, Inc., and Bacharach Associates. Officials of these firms contributed a total of $10,000 and received design awards of $1.05 million.

The design contracts awarded to Gaudreau, Inc., include a $3.12 million student union building at Morgan State College and a $2.04 million central utility plant in Baltimore.

Bacharach Associates has been awarded under the Mandel administration design contracts for a $2.57-million physical education building at Bowie State College and a $1.58-million addition to the chemical engineering building at the University of Maryland in College Park.

In addition, Paul L. Gaudreau, the president of Gaudreau, Inc., and a director of Bacharach Associates, is chairman of the state Board of Architectural Review, which oversees the quality of design work.

A Hagerstown engineer, Harold E. Wibberley, Jr., a partner in the firm of Baker-Wibberley-Coble-Berger and Associates, contributed $2,500 to Governor Mandel; his firm received awards of $321,780, including the development of a program for a 400-bed maximum security institution at Jessup and a 100-bed community correction center.

Other architectural and engineering firms and officials of firms, the amount they contributed and the value of awards they received are as follows:

• Wilson T. Ballard, Jr., president of the Wilson T. Ballard Company, Owings Mills, contributed $4,500 and the firm received $160,535 in awards.

• Whitney A. Sanders, president of Sanders and Thomas, of Pottstown, Pa., contributed $1,000. He said his firm has received awards of "about $25,000" although it did not appear on state records examined for this series.

• Fenton and Lichtig, 2219 Maryland Avenue, has been awarded two contracts for which no price was given on Board of Public Works Records and a third for an estimated $20,000. The firm contributed $1,000.

• Arthur G. VanReuth, president of VanReuth and Widner, 5509 York Road, contributed $1,000 and the firm received $67,299 in contracts.

• Purdum and Jeschke, 1023 North Calvert Street, contributed $1,000 and received "more than $20,000 a year" from the state, according to a company spokesman. No record of the firm was found on board records.

• Watkins and Magee, 2526 St. Paul Street, contributed $1,000 and received $50,000 in contracts.

• Lester L. Buchart, president of Buchart Associates and Buchart-Horn, both of York, Pa., contributed $1,000. His firms received awards totaling $79,376.

• Buddy Harris, of Gruen Associates, 1401 K Street, Washington, contributed $1,000. The firm received approximately $140,000 in design contracts.

• James C. Angeleras of Bethesda, Md., president of A. B. Engineering, contributed $2,000 and the firm received $66,319 in awards.

• Miller, Schuerholz and Associates, of 315 St. Paul Street, contributed $1,100 and received $87,440 in awards.

• Benjamin Brotman, an architect with offices at 2118 Maryland Avenue, contributed $1,300 and received awards of $159,200.

• William Bouton Kelly, a partner in Tatar and Kelly, 800 North Charles Street, contributed $1,400. The firm received $70,425 in contracts.

• Irving Bowman and Associates, of Charleston, W. Va., contributed $1,000 and has received contracts of at least $27,250.

• Greenhorne and O'Mara, of Riverdale, Md., contributed $2,000 and has received awards of $199,130.

• John B. Funk Associates, Towson, contributed $1,000 and received awards of $9,400.

• Lyon Associates, of 6707 Whitestone Road, contributed $2,500. A firm with identical directors, Maryland Surveying and Engineering, received awards of $60,000.

The contractors receiving extras and change orders—changes in the cost of a project approved after it has been bid and awarded—and subcontracts—portions of bid awards given by prime contractors to smaller ones with the approval of the state—are:

• Willard Hackerman, the president of Whiting-Turner, Company. He contributed $1,000 and, primarily from road work, the company received subcontracts of $495,000 and extras totaling $728,265.

These extras and subcontracts result largely from work on the second Chesapeake Bay Bridge. Although competitively bid-work is not the subject of this series, the extent of the involvement of Whiting-Turner with state work is reflected in the award of $11.23 million in bid-work to the firm.

• Lawrence Construction Company, 5710 Bellona Avenue, contributed $1,000, received extras and change orders totaling $827,225 all from projects under supervision of the Board of Public Works, including a $2.85 million education building and a $3.45 million library building, both at Morgan State College.

• The Carney Equipment Company, which has identical directors with the John Matricciani Company, 408 South Caroline Street, contributed $1,000. The Matricciani firm is the subcontractor on $495,003 in road work.

• Ames-Ennis, Inc., 2224 North Charles Street, which contributed $1,000, has received extras totaling $447,278 on work, including a $6.74 million vocational rehabilitation center at Montebello State Hospital.

• Baltimore Contractors, Inc., 711 South Central, contributed $1,000 and has received change orders totaling $175,724.

• Two interlocking firms, the Corle Corporation and P. Flanigan and Sons, contributed a total of $3,500. P. Flanigan and Sons is subcontractor on $1.69 million in road work and has received extras totaling $32,836.

• A $1,500 contributor, Leimbach Construction Company, 3906 Hickory Avenue, has received $61,841 on projects which include $1.88 million in renovations to the dental-pharmacy building at the University of Maryland.

• The Williams Construction Company, 8960 DeSoto Road, gave $1,000 to the Mandel campaign and has received $69,839.

• The Regal Construction Company, Upper Marlboro, Md., a $2,500 contributor, has received $26,491 in road-work extras.

• Drummond and Company, of Race Road, a $1,500 contributor, is the subcontractor on $127,505 in road work.

• In a more complex case, The Raymond-Dravo-Langenfelder partnership of corporations gave $3,500 and the Raymond Metal Products Company, a subsidiary of Raymond International, a Houston-based firm and a part of the partnership, gave another $3,500.

Raymond International has been the subcontractor on $425,769 in road work. The Raymond-Dravo-Langenfelder combine, which won a $39.68 million contract on the second bay bridge, has received extras on the job totaling $6.42 million.

In addition, two other subsidiaries of Raymond International, Raymond International Engineering and Raymond Concrete Pile Division, have received unbid consultant awards totaling $13,774.

• Ralph Marcantoni and Sons, of Broening Highway, a $1,500 contributor, has received $2,634 in extras.

• James A. Openshaw, Jr., vice president of Cherry Hill Sand and Gravel Company, contributed $1,000, and the company an additional $2,500. A total of $63,626 in extras have gone to the company.

• Michael Callas, president of Callas Construction Company, Hagerstown, contributed $1,000. His firm received extras of $56,803 on state work including a $1.28 million alteration-of-housing contract at the Maryland Correctional Institution in Hagerstown.

• Another $1,000 contributor, the A. H. Smith Sand and Gravel Company, of Branchville, Md., received extras on road work of $16,693 and was awarded $75,120 in informal contracts, the requirements for which are less stringent than competitively bid contracts.

• Harry W. Rodgers, III, a $2,000 contributor, is a partner in buildings which have been rented by the school construction program and the Department of Education. Over a three-year period, these leases will produce a total of $968,250 in rent.

• Two corporations which contributed a total of $1,000 to the Mandel campaign, Spruel Development Company and Prince George's Center Inc., share the same officers, Hershel, Goldine and Marvin Blumberg.

The state leased space under the Mandel administration from the Spruel Development Company at 3700 East–West Highway in Hyattsville, Md., for a total cost of $119,610.

• Bernard Gewirz, who appears on campaign finance records as the agent giving money to the campaign from Julian Farms, which gave a total of $1,300, is also one of the persons with whom the state negotiated a lease for space for $17,244 over three years at 1730 K Street, N.W., Washington.

Mr. Gewirz said he is "connected" both with Julian Farms and the Washington building but declined to comment further.

• A total of $5,000 was contributed by two corporations controlled by the S. L. Hammerman Organization. The public defender system has taken a five-year lease for a total rent of $39,985 in the Jefferson building in Towson which is owned by Valley Green, Inc., a part of the Hammerman organization.

• After Fair Lanes, Inc., a bowling lane chain, gave up most of the space in 610 North Howard Street, the Department of Motor Vehicles and the Department of Health and Mental Hygiene have taken out three-year leases producing a total rent of $676,367.

Fair Lanes, Inc., contributed $2,500 to Governor Mandel's campaign. A second company on which many of Fair Lane's directors also sit, Rolling Road Plaza, Inc., rented space to the University of Maryland in Baltimore county on a four-year lease producing a total rent of $22,650.

• A $1,000 contributor, Nottingham properties, is the owner of 111 Allegheny Avenue in Towson in which the District Court System has rented space on a ten-year lease for a total of $557,550.

• Another $1,000 contributor, John W. Steffey, is an officer of Charles H. Steffey, Inc., which rented space for a year to the public defender system at 407 Crain Highway for $2,400.

• A major political supporter in the black community, William L. Adams, an influential force in Metro Democrats, Inc., rented vacant land to the state for use as a parking lot at 407–417 West Biddle Street for $17,625 over three years.

The extent of the financial interests of consultants in the expanded powers of the Board of Public Works under the Mandel administration is reflected in the following contributors who derive a significant portion of their government work from school construction and road design.

• Two joint engineering firms, Ematech and Ewell, Bomhart and associates, both of 1800 North Charles Street, contributed $8,000. The firms were awarded $291,002, much of which was from the Department of Transportation.

• Green Associates and Management Consultants, both interlocking companies with offices at 1130 North Charles Street, contributed a total of $10,000. The two firms have been awarded $1,785,311 in fees under the Mandel administration.

• A San Francisco architectural firm, Skidmore, Owings and Merrill, a $2,000 contributor, was awarded the contract to be chief of the design concept team for the East–West Expressway in 1967.

Payments to the consultant however, were regularly approved by the state through the duration of the contract which was terminated in December 1971, when total payments exceeded $7 million.

• Jersey Testing Laboratories, of Newark, N.J., a $1,000 contributor, performed an estimated $12,000 in consulting work.

• An Annapolis Engineering firm which contributed $1,000, C. D. Messick, Jr., and Associates, was recently awarded $30,837 in consulting road work on Route 197.

• A $2,000 contributor, Stack, Cohen and Purdy, of 5008 York Road, a firm specializing in road work, has received contracts totaling $128,767.

In terms of school contracts, local authorities continue to select consultants but the Board of Public Works has the power to set rules over specifications and other procedures.

In June 1971, for example, local authorities submitted $21.26 million school construction for approval by the Board of Public Works.

An architect designing two of the projects, Ronald S. Senseman, a $2,000 contributor, was listed as the recipient of $138,579 in fees for the designs. He has also been awarded $118,000 for work that has traditionally gone through the Board of Public Works.

A member of the firm of Walton, Madden, Cooper and Auerbach, John M. Walton, of Riverdale, Md., contributed $1,000.

Among the school projects approved by the board was a $1.3 million elementary school in Prince George's county for which the firm was to be paid $51,880.

The Walton, Maden, Cooper and Auerbach firm has also been awarded design fees of $177,135 which were approved by the Board of Public Works under the Mandel administration.

# Vetoes, Appointments Favorable

*This is the second in a series of articles examining large contributors to Governor Mandel's 1970 campaign and some of their business dealings with the state.*

*The Evening Sun,* October 25, 1972

Governor Mandel has advocated and killed legislation and has made executive appointments in ways favorable to the interests of several contributors of $1,000 or more to his 1970 campaign.

Specific incidents range from legislation of major importance for the racing industry to minor local bills of direct financial interest only to individual businesses.

The gubernatorial actions involved include the approval and vetoing of legislation, the appointment of contributors to regulatory boards, and the appointment of commissions which have issued decisions favorable to contributors.

No predetermined connections between gubernatorial decisions and contributions were found; Governor Mandel made many decisions favorable to corporations and individuals who did not contribute to his campaign.

The decisions involving contributors do not affect the profits of contributors in the form of direct payments of state monies; instead, the issues involve such questions as the expansion of a market, the avoidance of a tax or the provision of state services where none existed before.

In May 1969 when Governor Mandel and his supporters were making initial plans for the campaign, the governor vetoed a local bill which would have permitted the Cecil County commissioners to impose a tax of 1 to 5 cents on every ton of sand and gravel quarried in the county.

In his veto message to the House of Delegates, the governor said the measure would create an unfair competitive disadvantage for the operators of quarries in the county.

Two and a half months later, on July 14, 1969, York Building Products, Inc., a Pennsylvania-based firm with a quarry in Cecil County and a major supplier to state road contractors, contributed $2,000 to Governor Mandel's campaign.

A more complex case started with a sudden withdrawal of gubernatorial opposition to a racing bill passed in the 1971 session of the General Assembly, and continued through the 1972 session. In the end, over the governor's objection, the track legislation failed.

Governor Mandel vetoed the racing bill passed in the 1971 session, a measure which authorized the transfer of 18 days from the track at Hagerstown to the Marlboro racetrack.

When the 1972 session began, however, influential legislators commented privately that they had received word from gubernatorial lobbyists that "the governor would not object" if the veto were overridden. The veto was overridden.

Between the veto and the beginning of the session, the track had changed hands. The new owners include two close associates of Irvin Kovens, Governor Mandel's chief campaign fund-raiser, and three other persons who gave a total of $6,500 to the Mandel campaign.

The addition of days to Marlboro's season—known as consolidation—gave the track's officials more justification for participation in consolidation legislation introduced with gubernatorial backing later in the 1972 session.

This bill gave additional days and revenue to the following tracks:

• Pimlico was to receive new racing dates and an increase in the percentage of the daily amount bet—the handle—worth $828,000 annually, on the basis of 1971 revenue figures.

Officials of the track and the track itself gave $10,500 to the Mandel campaign.

• Laurel Race Course was to receive new racing dates and increased revenues worth, again on the basis of 1971 figures, $761,000 a year.

The Laurel track contributed $4,000 to the Mandel campaign and a related corporation, Boston Metals, gave $2,000.

• The Bowie Race Track was to be purchased by the state for $8 million. This price included the purchase of the racing dates held by the track which had originally been granted to the track without cost.

C.D.R.H., the corporation owning Bowie, gave the Mandel campaign $2,500 and the chief officer of the track, F. G. Tucker, gave another $2,500.

• Marlboro was to get 58 new racing days and be permitted to race them at Laurel and Pimlico, far more profitable locations.

The full ownership of Marlboro remained hidden to the public and the legislature throughout the legislative session.

An ownership declaration filed three months ago at the State Racing Commission shows, however, the following owners:

Irving (Tubby) Schwartz holds 57,000 shares of the 200,000 shares of outstanding stock; he is the largest stockholder. Harry Klaff is listed as owning 30,000 shares. Both men are close associates of Mr. Kovens.

Another 20,000 shares is held by Harold E. Wibberley, Jr., a Hagerstown engineer who gave the Mandel campaign $2,500. Ernest N. Cory, Jr., the holder of 30,000 shares, is the senior partner in the Laurel law firm of Cory, Boss and

Rice, which gave $2,000 to the Mandel campaign. Eugene Casey, the president of Marlboro, who owns 2,500 shares, heads nine corporations which gave a total of $2,000.

Although the tracks and their owners stood to gain the most from the consolidation legislation, three other special interests involved in Maryland racing would have gained from the measure:

The Horsemen's Benevolent and Protective Association, which gave $2,500; the Independent Association of Racetrack Employees, which gave $2,000; and American Totalisator, the firm providing computer services to the tracks, gave $1,000.

The consolidation bill was opposed by a strong coalition of state legislators and community groups who contended that more racing crowds would disrupt adjacent neighborhoods.

The measure received strong gubernatorial backing and was on the verge of final passage on the last day of the session only to be killed by Sen. Julian L. Lapides (D-2nd), Baltimore city, who threatened to stop all legislative action with a filibuster.

In addition to the contributions from the racing industry, Governor Mandel derived extensive campaign support from individuals who were later to be appointed to the Racing Commission, and from members who were to come up for reappointment during his administration.

The most generous was Milton Polinger, appointed to the commission in May 1971. He personally gave $2,500. Three corporations he controls, the Polinger Company, Majestic Builders Corporation and Seventy-S Associates, gave $1,400.

In addition, Mildred Colodny, the comptroller of the Polinger corporations, gave $2,500.

Robert Furtick, a lobbyist for the trucking industry appointed to the Racing Commission in 1971, gave $1,500.

J. Newton Brewer, of Rockville, who was appointed chairman of the Racing Commission in August 1969, and re-appointed to the post May 20, 1972, gave the Mandel campaign $1,000. His wife gave an additional $1,000.

Samuel Stoffberg, an associate of Mr. Kovens whose term on the commission was due to expire in 1973, gave $1,000 in his own name and $2,000 through two corporations, Allied Bedding and Stanley's Realty. Mr. Stoffberg died August 17, 1972.

In terms of appointments, Governor Mandel several times has appointed large contributors to positions which give them power to oversee or regulate areas in which they have a financial interest. In some cases state law requires that members of the regulated industry serve on the regulating commission.

Roger C. Lipitz, the president of the House in the Pines nursing home chain, was appointed in June 1970, to a three-year term on the state Board of Nursing Home Examiners, a board created in 1970 to regulate nursing homes, with the power to revoke licenses.

Mr. Lipitz had contributed $3,000 to the Mandel campaign.

William L. Wilson, a former director of the First National Bank and Trust Company of Western Maryland, was appointed banking commissioner empowered to regulate all state banks in 1971.

Mr. Wilson, a former Democratic party treasurer, contributed $700 to the Mandel campaign and is listed on reports as the supplier of $700 more from other donors in the Cumberland area.

Mr. Wilson, however, was apparently Governor Mandel's second choice, selected only when a controversy over his first choice, Joel Kline, a suburban Washington developer, forced the Governor to back down.

The controversy centered on charges, leveled by Sen. Meyer Emanuel (D-Prince Georges) and others, that Mr. Kline had used widespread campaign contributions as a lever to get the appointment.

Mr. Kline gave the Mandel campaign $2,500 himself and $2,500 through a corporation he controls. He and his corporations gave $10,000 to the campaign of Lt. Gov. Blair Lee, Governor Mandel's running mate, and lent that campaign $25,000.

I. D. Shapiro, a $2,000 contributor, was appointed in 1970 to the Governor's Commission on Abandoned Automobiles. Mr. Shapiro is president of United Iron and Metal Company, a major processor of junked and abandoned automobiles.

T. Hammond Welsh, president of the Maryland State Savings and Loan Association, a private company, was appointed chairman of the state Board of Building, Savings and Loan Association Commissioners in 1970. He contributed $1,400 to the Mandel campaign.

A contributor of $2,000, Samuel W. Barrick, was appointed judge in the Sixth Judicial Circuit in 1970.

The 1970 reorganization of state government resulted in the creation of administrative positions, called departmental secretariats, paying $36,100 a year.

Two government employees elevated to these positions contributed $1,000 each, John R. Jewell, secretary of licensing and regulation, and James P. Slicher, secretary of budget and fiscal planning.

In addition, two former members of the House of Delegates, who made large contributions, were appointed to state jobs.

Thomas J. Hatem, defeated Hartford county delegate, gave $1,000; he was appointed state insurance commissioner in 1971, at $23,500 a year. Harvey Epstein, who retired from his city Fourth District seat, gave $1,000, and his law partner, Ronald L. Lapides, gave another $1,000; Mr. Epstein was appointed commissioner of labor and industry at $20,600 a year June 17, 1972.

A case in which the legislative and appointive powers overlap involves a contribution of $2,700, $1,700 in cash and $1,000 in goods and services, from R and W, Inc., the parent company of the Easy Method Driving School, a chain active in the Baltimore–Washington corridor.

In 1971, Governor Mandel appointed, at the request of the General Assembly, a commission to study driver education programs.

The commission has subsequently recommended, against the advice of the Department of Education, that legislation be passed to permit commercial driving schools, including the Easy Method Driving School, to teach driving in the public schools, which they are not allowed to do under existing law.

Legislation has been of particular interest to two industries which contributed to the Mandel campaign: beer manufacturers and developers.

The beer industry, and individuals connected with it, gave a total of $13,750 to the Mandel campaign.

For three legislative sessions, Governor Mandel successfully fought efforts to raise Maryland's tax on beer, which, at three cents on the gallon, was the second lowest in the country.

Faced, in the latter part of the 1972 session, with an unexpected lack of revenues, at a time when he had committed himself to no increase of general taxes, Governor Mandel reluctantly acceded to an increase in the beer tax.

More than half of the $13,750 contributed by beer interests, $7,250, was from members of the Hoffberger family or corporations connected with National Beer, which, in turn, is owned by the Hoffbergers. The Hoffbergers also control the Orioles baseball team.

In the 1971 session of the legislature, Governor Mandel pushed through a $7 million bond for improvements at Memorial Stadium, where the Orioles play. This marked the first involvement of the state in stadium finances.

This was done, in part, to accommodate the demands for improvements issued by Carroll Rosenbloom, a $1,000 contributor, who was the owner of the Colts football team until this summer.

The issue resurfaced in the 1972 session, when Governor Mandel successfully sponsored legislation creating a stadium authority empowered to issue revenue bonds to finance a new sports facility in downtown Baltimore for the baseball and football teams.

The developers, who are centered primarily in the suburban Washington area, provided a total of $49,500 to the Mandel campaign.

Governor Mandel vetoed in 1970 the mechanics' lien law, legislation designed to increase the liability of developers for debts to subcontractors.

This law was meant to remedy a recurrent problem in the suburban Washington area, where unsuspecting homebuyers discovered that they were liable for the debts incurred by developers to the subcontractors.

The governor then appointed a commission to study the problem, too late in the year, however to make any recommendations to the 1971 session.

The commission finally proposed legislation, well after the 1972 session began, which died in the committee of introduction in the house after no gubernatorial effort was made to get it to the floor.

The governor vetoed a second consumer protection bill after the 1971 session which would have given purchasers of defective goods the right to refuse to make payments to small loan or industrial finance companies if such a company was an active participant in the sale.

The Household Finance Corporation, a Chicago-based firm with over 30 small loan companies in Maryland, contributed $1,000 to the Mandel campaign.

The governor vetoed in 1970 another bill of direct financial interest to small loan companies. The measure would have permitted banks to go into direct competition with them by allowing banks to charge equally high interest rates on small loans.

After the 1969 session, Governor Mandel signed two local bills of direct financial interest to a contributor of $1,000, George's Radio and Television, a suburban Washington chain.

The chain, which had hired two lobbyists to press for the legislation, succeeded in winning a change in the blue laws to permit stores with a maximum to six, instead of three, employees to stay open Sundays.

One reason for this legislation was to allow the chain to compete on Sundays, with nearby drugstores which are allowed to stay open and which also sell radios and televisions.

# Big Givers to Mandel Kitty Do Well

*This is the third in a series of articles examining large contributors to Governor Mandel's 1970 campaign and some of their business dealings with the state.*

The Evening Sun, October 26, 1972

At its meeting, September 15, the Board of Public Works approved 27 discretionary awards totaling $1,479,370 to 16 companies which had made contributions of $1,000 or more to Governor Mandel's campaign, either through the corporations themselves or corporate executives.

The value of the awards at this one meeting was about $350,000 above the average going to contributors at the monthly meetings of the board. Since the beginning of 1970, more than $31 million in noncompetitive awards and subcontracts has been granted to contributors.

With the exception of the hiring of consultants for design of capital improvements at Friendship International Airport, the awards were neither discussed nor individually voted upon; instead, they were approved in blanket fashion as small parts of entire sections of the multipage agenda. These included many awards given to noncontributors.

The state Department of Transportation, for example, received approval to hire the consulting firm of Matz, Childs & Associates for engineering work on Maryland Routes 189 and 75 for a minimum cost of $185,835. The state Department of Forests and Parks extended the firm's contract for design for roads and other facilities in Rocky Gap Park.

In addition, the Department of Transportation hired Matz, Childs & Associates to perform construction supervision and inspection services and other work on Interstate Route 95, jointly with Knorle, Bender, Stone & Associates, for an amount not to exceed $782,980.

Matz, Childs & Associates gave the Mandel campaign $2,000. Knorle, Bender, Stone & Associates gave $2,500, and Maurice E. Bender, of the firm, gave $2,500.

The September 15 awards brought the total given Matz, Childs & Associates since early 1970 to $384,185. The two firms working jointly have been awarded $1.73 million.

These awards, and others discussed in this article, are granted on a noncompetitive basis.

The elimination of the State Roads Commission under the Mandel administration and the creation of the Department of Transportation placed under the control of the gubernatorially controlled board all road consulting contracts.

Among the others approved that day were:

Two consultant awards were given to Maps, Inc., for topographical studies on an interchange in Anne Arundel County, and for the proposed National Freeway in Western Maryland, totaling $21,876. This brought the total to Maps, Inc., to $107,979.

The president of Maps, Inc., Thomas L. Collins, contributed $1,000 to the Mandel campaign.

DOT won approval from the board to give a $29,960 contract for engineering services on a rest area along Interstate Route 70 to Greiner Environmental Systems, Inc., a part of the J. E. Greiner Company.

The Greiner company, in turn, is part of a conglomerate which contributed a total of $6,000 to Governor Mandel's campaign. The Greiner company has received noncompetitive awards of at least $1,091,091 under the Mandel administration.

For initial work on what is to become $30 million in capital improvements at Friendship International Airport, DOT was authorized to hire a joint venture which includes Ewell, Bomhardt & Associates, a local firm, and the New York firm of Howard, Needles, Tammen & Bergendoff. They are to be paid at the rate of 6.5 percent of construction cost.

Ewell, Bomhardt & Associates, which contributed a total of $8,000, has received awards of $291,082 during the Mandel administration. On September 15, the firm was also paid $1,263 for supervision of borings at Frostburg College.

The airport contract was the first state award for the New York firm; H. C. Lamberton, Jr., of Whippany, N.J., a partner, contributed $1,000.

A seventh company receiving a consultant award from DOT was George William Stephens, Jr., & Associates, which is to be paid $82,500 for engineering services on Maryland Route 462.

This, and additional awards of $10,000 from the Department of Forests and

Parks and about $7,000 from Towson State College, granted the same day, brought the total given to the Stephens firm under the Mandel administration to $157,577. George William Stephens, Jr. contributed $1,000.

These awards from the Department of Transportation were not under the control of the Board of Public Works when Governor Mandel first took office. Prior to his reorganization of state government, road consultants had been approved by the now defunct State Roads Commission.

In addition to the road consultants, the board approved on September 15 the selection of a series of architectural and engineering consultants for other state agencies which included the following campaign contributors:

The firm of John F. Harms, Jr., & Associates, of Pasadena, was hired to design modifications to the Jessup sewage treatment plant for a cost not to exceed $24,250.

Prior to September 15, the Harms firm had received $108,771 from the state during the Mandel administration. The president, John F. Harms, Jr., contributed $2,000 to the Mandel campaign.

The architectural firm of Rogers & Vaeth, 6 South Calvert Street, a $2,000 contributor, was granted by the board two extensions of existing contracts, both for the Department of Forests and Parks for work in state parks.

Rogers & Vaeth had already been awarded under the Mandel administration architectural contracts totaling $160,270.

Another extension on a contract was given to Bacharach Associates, an engineering firm mentioned in the first part of this series. Officers of the firm gave the Mandel campaign $10,000.

An engineering firm, which had already received at least 13 awards totaling $232,779, Albert B. Gipe & Associates, was awarded on September 15 a contract to prepare detailed plans for water lines at Rosewood State Hospital for a fee estimated in the capital budget at $7,000.

In addition to the water line contract, the Gipe firm, which had contributed $4,500 to the Mandel campaign, was awarded September 15 a contract to study the communications system at Towson State College at a cost not to exceed $10,000.

The payment schedule on the third contract which had been awarded the Gipe firm October 12, 1971 for design of a new boiler plant was changed from a "B" schedule to a "C" schedule September 15. The effect of this is to increase the payment to the engineering company from approximately 5 percent of the construction cost to 6.5 percent.

A $1,000 contributor, Elgi & Gomph, engineers, was awarded a design contract for a 2,000-ton chiller at the Baltimore County campus of the University of Maryland for an unspecified price.

Prior awards to Elgi & Gomph under the Mandel administration total $91,-207.

The Department of Forests and Parks was given approval September 15 to hire the engineering firm of Dalton-Dalton-Little, formerly called Loewer &

Associates, to prepare a master plan and design for the development of Gunpowder State Park. Some $200,000 has been allocated in the capital budget for this design work.

Loewer & Associates, 1800 North Charles Street, a $2,000 contributor, had already received awards of $115,000.

A Salisbury-based engineering firm, George, Miles & Buhr, a $1,000 contributor, was appointed by the board September 15 to design a storm drain to the Tonytank Creek at Salisbury State College at a cost estimated in the capital budget at $8,000.

In addition, the firm was paid $150 for consultation on water main leaks at Assateague State Park.

The Salisbury firm had been awarded prior to September 15 contracts totaling $350,569, including work on a $1.48 million auditorium at the Eastern Shore campus of the University of Maryland and a $5.09 million center for retarded children in the same area.

Although most of the awards to contributors September 15 were to architectural and engineering consultants, three leases were taken or extended on property owned by another contributor, and an extra on a major construction contract was granted to a firm owned by a fund-raiser in the Mandel campaign:

The governor's Commission on Law Enforcement and the Administration of Justice took out a new lease, approved September 15, with Maryland Properties, Inc., a subsidiary of McCormick & Co. for space in the Executive Plaza One Building in the Greater Baltimore Industrial Park.

On the same day, the Board of Public Works approved two extensions of leases in the same building for the commission, which altogether will produce payments to the subsidiary of McCormick & Co. of $44,966 for the duration of the leases.

These leases raise to $312,533 the amount to be paid in rent to the subsidiary under agreements approved since Governor Mandel took office.

Maryland Properties is also a prime contractor which has received extras of $167,358 on work for the state.

At the September 15 board meeting, an extra of $45,305 was approved for the Consolidated Engineering Company, prime contractor on the $19.9 million North Hospital Building at the University of Maryland. This brought the total number of extras on the project to over $1.59 million, more than 8 percent over the contract bid price.

Consolidated Engineering was purchased in October 1971, by William L. Siskind, a fund-raiser for Governor Mandel.

Many of the extras on the hospital contract were approved before Mr. Siskind took over the company.

# Mandel Contributors Have
# Big Business Relationships

*This is the last in a series of articles examining
large contributors to Governor Mandel's 1970
campaign and some of their business dealings
with the state.*

*The Evening Sun,* October 27, 1972

Contributors of $1,000 or more to the 1970 campaign of Governor Mandel in some cases form pyramids through which state money passes from level to level.

Control of the finances in these transactions often is only nominally held by the state, delegated in fact to the contributors themselves, either through accepted practice or necessity. There is nothing illegal in this.

In the case of the second Bay Bridge, for example a massive, $117 million public works project, the state granted the engineering contract to the J. E. Greiner Company, one subsidiary of a conglomerate which gave the Mandel campaign $7,000.

The initial award was made to the Greiner company before Governor Mandel took office, but the decision to continue the project, despite predicted cost overruns, was made under the Mandel administration.

Sitting on top of the pyramid, the Greiner Company was first allowed to renegotiate bids on two sections of work which were $7.1 million over the firm's estimates.

The Greiner firm worked out an arrangement with the Raymond-Dravo-Langenfelder joint venture—a partnership which gave $3,500 to the Mandel campaign, and one member of which gave another $3,500—an arrangement reducing a bid from $42.5 million to $39.7 million. The renegotiation was approved by the Mandel administration April 28, 1969.

The consulting engineers then renegotiated a $2.8 million bid from P. Flanigan & Sons, so that the cost would be lowered to $1.8 million. The Flanigan firm contributed $2,500 to the Mandel campaign and a related corporation, Corle, Inc., gave $1,000. The new contract was approved May 23, 1969.

The supposed savings negotiated by the Greiner company with the Raymond-Dravo-Langenfelder partnership have since been largely eaten up by $2.4 million in extras, approved by the state on the recommendation of the Greiner company, resulting from a wage escalation clause inserted during the renegotiations.

In addition, the R D L joint venture was granted, without competitive bidding, additional work to provide supporting piers at both ends of the span for a net cost of $4.6 million.

Since the renegotiation of the Flanigan contract, the firm has been given extras totaling $81,222, and $79,272 has been eliminated from the contract.

Describing the role of the J. E. Greiner Company as consulting engineer for the project, Walter E. Woodford, Jr., chief engineer for the State Highway Administration, said "the consulting engineer acts as a representative of the state" in evaluating changes in contracts.

Moving to the third level of the pyramid the R D L joint venture subcontracted, with approval of the state, $100,000 worth of work to the Whiting-Turner Contracting Company on August 29, 1969. Willard Hackerman, president of Whiting-Turner, gave the Mandel campaign $1,000.

Just over a year later, October 26, 1970, Whiting-Turner won another portion of the contract: $6.3 million for decking of the bridge and other work. Its only competitor was the R-D-L joint venture.

Acting on the recommendation of the J. E. Greiner Company, the state has approved extras of at least $250,000 for the Whiting-Turner Contracting Company.

The Raymond-Dravo-Langenfelder partnership has also purchased state-required property damage liability and bodily injury liability insurance through Tidewater Insurance Agency.

The owner of one sixth of the stock in Tidewater is Harry W. Rodgers, III, one of Governor Mandel's chief fund-raisers, who gave $2,000 of his own to the campaign.

Tidewater was also the agent for the $35 million bond to cover another part of the bridge contract won by a division of United States Steel (which does not appear as a contributor of $1,000 or more to the Mandel campaign).

The most consistent participants generally in these pyramid relationships are contractors, engineers and architects.

Others, however, include insurance companies and their officers:

Poor, Bowen, Bartlett & Kennedy is an agent on state contract bonds and has been paid premiums of $387,419 over three years for coverage of state facilities. The agency contributed $1,000 to the campaign.

Fidelity and Deposit Company of Maryland has underwritten bonds on state projects totaling at least $51 million over the last three years.

Roy E. Julie, Jr., the F. & D. vice president who contributed $1,000 to the campaign, has recently joined the Tidewater Insurance Agency.

Tidewater is one of a number of corporations in which Mr. Rodgers has an investment. These corporations appear repeatedly as recipients of state moneys.

In addition to Mr. Rodgers's own contribution of $2,000 and a corporate gift of $1,000, other officials of Tidewater gave a total of $4,200. Edward Dickenson, a land development partner of Mr. Rodgers, gave $1,000 and Charles Zollman, president of an engineering firm owned by Tidewater, gave $1,000.

A close personal friend of Governor Mandel, Mr. Rodgers deals with the state through the writing of at least three different kinds of insurance, through rentals of property to the state, and through awards without competitive bidding to Zollman associates, an engineering firm.

In another major bridge project, the Outer Harbor Crossing, for example,

Zollman Associates, a wholly owned subsidiary of Tidewater Insurance, shares the $3.7 million design and supervision contract with the New York firm of Singstad, Kehart, November & Hurka for the approaches to the span. This is one of the largest noncompetitive engineering awards to be given during the Mandel administration.

Mr. Rodgers estimates that Tidewater does about $200,000 a year in bond business, about half of which comes from state and local government contracts.

Of the insurance company's $6 million gross, about 10 percent, or $600,000 comes from property damage and bodily injury coverage on state projects, he said.

In addition, the state payroll department deducts about $70,000 a year from paychecks of workers in the AFL-CIO American Federation of State County and Municipal Employees, and sends the money to Tidewater to cover a health and life insurance program.

Another $23,270 is paid by the state annually to Tidewater for premiums on state property coverage.

Rentals from corporations of which Mr. Rodgers is a stockholder include a three-year lease to the Department of Education of $295,000 a year and another three-year lease to the Executive Department's School Construction Program for $27,750 a year.

Mr. Rodgers was part of the triumvirate which controlled fund-raising for Governor Mandel. The other two are W. Dale Hess, the former majority whip of the House of Delegates who retired in 1970 to join Mr. Rodgers in many of his business activities, and Irvin Kovens, the former owner of the Charlestown Race Track in West Virginia.

The three men are expected to be called on again for the 1974 reelection campaign of Governor Mandel, who has already started tentative plans for a fund-raising testimonial in May 1973.

One of the major strengths Mr. Rodgers and his two associates are able to draw on in their role as fund-raisers is their access to Governor Mandel.

"I could expedite an extra," Mr. Rodgers said. "If a contractor had an extra, I could go talk to the governor about it," he said, contending that his efforts would be successful only if the extra (an added charge to a contract) were "legitimate."

Mr. Rodgers said he regularly takes requests from contributors to Governor Mandel refusing, however, to estimate what proportion involved questions of payment of state moneys.

The fund-raisers active in the Mandel campaign have power based not only on the ability to raise money, but also on their access to the governor and their ability to convey the impression that they are speaking for the governor.

Two state senators said, for example, that during the last session of the General Assembly Mr. Kovens encouraged them to vote for a proposed racetrack consolidation bill.

Speaking only on the condition that they not be identified, the senators said they both assumed that Mr. Kovens was speaking for the governor, but could not be sure.

This kind of power based on the assumption that the fund-raiser speaks for the governor gives Mr. Kovens even more leverage as a fund-raiser.

Various sources said that in the mayoral campaign last year, racetrack interests contributed over $10,000 to William Donald Schaefer, primarily to retain access to the legislature and the governor's office through Mr. Kovens, who was the Schaefer campaign's chief fund-raiser. The owners of the track refused to discuss their contributions.

Control of the campaign spending itself is another position of leverage from which money can be raised.

Edwin B. Early, president of Twentieth Century Printing, contributed $1,000. In addition to state work which includes the biannual printing of the Maryland Manual, Twentieth Century Printing was paid $28,213 by the Mandel campaign.

Bluefeld Caterers, another $1,000 contributor, was paid $87,383 for services to the Mandel campaign. The Schaefer campaign in which Mr. Kovens was also active, paid the caterers $27,738.

One of the contracts most vulnerable to changes of administrations has been the advertising account for the tourism division of the Department of Economic and Community Development.

Although the two agencies involved in the competition for the contract, the Robert Goodman Agency, Inc., and the Lou Rosenbush Advertising Agency, both contributed $1,000 to the campaign, the Rosenbush firm provided advertising services to the Mandel campaign.

The Goodman firm, in contrast, has associated itself with Republican campaigns here, including the gubernatorial campaign of Spiro T. Agnew in 1966.

When Mr. Agnew took office in 1967, the Rosenbush firm was taken off the tourism account, currently worth $170,000 a year, and was replaced with the Goodman firm.

The Agnew tenure as governor was brief, however, and shortly after Governor Mandel took office in 1969, a major portion of the contract—fees for the placement of ads—was transferred to the Rosenbush firm.

Robert Goodman, president of the Goodman agency, said an attempt was made at that time to take the entire contract away from his firm.

He said he contacted some associates, whom he refused to identify but indicated were politically influential, and was able to temporarily retain the portion of the contract for the production of advertisements.

He lost this portion, however, to the Rosenbush firm in January 1972.

This transfer of advertising accounts from administration to administration is not limited to the state; Mr. Goodman said that during the Agnew administration he picked up part of the account for the Pimlico Race Track, a state-regulated enterprise, only to lose it the the Rosenbush firm after Governor Mandel took office.

This interrelationship between political activity and financial dealings has also resulted in benefits for Mr. Rodgers and Mr. Hess, the part owners of Tidewater Insurance Agency.

Mr. Rodgers said the owners of companies doing business with the state have approached him to offer Tidewater their insurance without even being solicited.

In addition to gaining increased business, the major fund-raisers in the Mandel campaign have developed a power to raise money for campaigns that is independent of the candidates they are supporting.

Mr. Rodgers acknowledged this power in a boast when he said that an executive who claimed to have given money to the Schaefer campaign because of Mayor Schaefer's policies was lying: "He did it because I told him to."

The comment, however, reflects strength independent of the governor which has been most recently demonstrated in the defection of Mr. Rodgers, Mr. Hess and Mr. Kovens from the Democratic party for the current presidential election, a defection to Democrats for Nixon against the wishes of the governor.

The inability of the governor to control his own fund-raisers results, in part, from the fact that his debt to the fund-raisers far exceeds any favors he can do for them.

A critical factor in the election of Governor Mandel was the fund-raising effort conducted by his supporters well before the 1970 primary.

The success of a testimonial which raised more than $600,000 nearly a year before the campaign even began was one of the major reasons R. Sargent Shriver and other potential opponents in the Democratic primary decided against challenging Governor Mandel.

Not only did the money—the credit for which goes largely to Mr. Rodgers, Mr. Kovens and Mr. Hess—scare off the opposition, but it also guaranteed support from the traditional political clubs for Governor Mandel, who had no major base of voting strength.

This dependence of the governor on his fund-raisers is surfacing now in the current plan to repeat the 1970 tactic and to hold a testimonial for the governor in May 1973, to again raise adequate funds to scare off potential opposition, in this case a year and four months before the primary election.

To accomplish the same feat, however, Governor Mandel will again turn to his fund-raisers, according to his staff, demonstrating his willingness to forget the embarrassment they have caused him while he has been chairman of the George McGovern campaign this year.

# Money and Morality
# in Maryland

*Society,* May/June 1974

Over the past two years, symptoms of corruption have been surfacing in both major parties in Maryland. Some have received nationwide publicity because of testimony before the Senate Watergate Committee. The Hearings disclosed an illicit $50,000 loan by the Committee to Re-Elect the President to the organizers of a local testimonial dinner for Spiro T. Agnew. The loan was designed to create an inflated impression of public support for the vice-president. Another disclosure involved the secret transfer of $180,000 from a White House controlled fund to the 1970 campaign of Maryland Senator J. Glenn Beall, Jr. On November 19, 1973, the seven-member Agnew dinner committee pleaded guilty to four counts of violation of state election law and a $2,000 fine was imposed on the group. The treasurer of the committee, Blagden H. Wharton, still awaits trial on perjury charges. Because of a one-year statute of limitations in Maryland election law, a grand jury failed to hand down an indictment in connection with the $180,000 transfer to the Beall campaign.

Other cases, although not so widely publicized, illustrate the same symptoms of corruption in both parties. In suburban Baltimore County, a center of Democratic strength, federal prosecutors have accepted a guilty plea from William E. Fornoff, former chief administrative officer, on a minor tax charge in return for testimony. That testimony was used in the trial of N. Dale Anderson, the Baltimore County executive convicted of 32 counts of bribery, extortion and tax evasion.

The Fornoff testimony was also the key to widening federal inquiry on matters of local corruption to include the county and gubernatorial administrations of Spiro T. Agnew. After extensive plea bargaining, Agnew avoided facing charges of bribery and extortion, and on October 10 pleaded *nolo contendere* to tax evasion in a Baltimore federal court.

The United States Attorney's office for Maryland has obtained grand jury testimony from local architects and engineers implicating Joseph W. Alton, the Republican executive of Anne Arundel County. The federal prosecutors have also subpoenaed records of consultant awards made during the administration of incumbent Gov. Marvin Mandel, a Democrat.

A separate investigation by the state attorney general has resulted in the conviction on 16 counts of bribery and related charges of Samuel A. Green, Baltimore County state's attorney, the local equivalent of a district attorney. Mr. Green's chief investigator, Louis W. Irvin, was found guilty on December 28, 1973, of conspiracy to cover up a $750 bribe and of false pretenses.

Finally, the state legislature considered this year legislation mandating an investigation into the sale of stock in a state chartered bank to chief fund-raisers for Governor Mandel. A board member of the bank has charged that its founders were pressured into selling stock to the fund-raisers through suggestions that the sale would gain prompt approval for the opening of the financial institution from state officials.

Most of these manifestations of alleged illegal activity by elected officials are related directly or indirectly to the elective process. This process, particularly campaign financing, is under close scrutiny, and a number of reforms ranging from stricter legislated regulation to a public takeover of campaign costs are under consideration.

The case of Maryland, a state generally considered to contain a demographic mix providing the best statistical reflection in federal elections of the nation's total voting patterns, and a state for which there is no evidence of exceptional corruption, indicates, however, that the financing of elections is only one part of a larger system. No reform will be adequate unless it deals with the broader questions of governmental power and access to it.

Concern with the excessive influence of special interests over public officials in Maryland led as long ago as 1954 to a state attorney general's ruling that a 1902 law required both registration of lobbyists and full disclosure of fees and expenses incurred during the legislative session for the purpose of affecting legislation. The decision to enforce the law was prompted by public reaction to the refusal of lobbyists who had successfully represented banks and nursing homes in the passage of questionable bills to reveal payments and expenditures. It was hailed by those who argued that special interests would be unable to sway the votes of state senators and delegates if required to operate without the cloak of secrecy.

Similarly, in 1957 the Maryland election code was amended to limit the maximum amount any individual could contribute during an election to $2,500, a step comparable to the legislation limiting contributions in federal elections to $3,000, which has been passed by the Senate and is under consideration by the House. Proponents of the limitation in Maryland argued successfully that such legislation would prevent any single person or corporation from "buying" a candidate by bankrolling his entire campaign.

At the more routine level of reform, in 1971 Gov. Marvin Mandel assumed the responsibility on the part of the state to pay a larger share of the cost of public education. The governor successfully sponsored legislation turning over to the state the cost of school construction. Operating on the reform principle that responsible administration requires centralized fiscal authority in the executive branch, Mandel's legislation transferred the expenditure of construction money from local boards controlled by county executives and city mayors to the gubernatorially controlled state Board of Public Works.

These bills are part of the fabric of reform built up over the past 80 years on a number of principles: that mandatory disclosure is a powerful weapon in the control of abuses of power; that the achievement of responsible government requires the elimination of diffuse fiscal and executive authority; that a knowledgeable electorate confronted with a comprehensible and businesslike structure of government will have adequate information to make correct decisions.

The efficacy of these principles has been made clear by the resulting legislation. No one would now argue that required lobbyist registration has demonstrably limited the influence of special interests in Maryland; on the contrary, the most significant use of the list of lobbyists is for mailings by legislators seeking contributions for their reelection.

The $2,500 campaign contribution limitation, intended to encourage elective competition, has reduced the ability of challengers to raise money while incumbents have been able and, in fact, encouraged by the law, to concentrate fund-raising efforts on a broad range of contractors, consultants and regulated businesses vulnerable to the discretionary powers of those already in office.

The transfer of fiscal responsibility for school construction from the subdivisions to the state has resulted in a parallel transfer of fund-raising leverage from the Baltimore mayor and the 23 county executives to the governor; the complex of corporations specializing in the building of schools—architects, engineers, contractors, lumber suppliers, hardware suppliers, electrical subcontractors and mechanical subcontractors—a complex that had formed the nexus of resource from which local campaigns were financed, has been added to the resources of an incumbent governor empowered to approve or reject school construction contracts. School construction, as a consequence, became part of the gubernatorial campaign fabric. The governor through the Board of Public Works would now control construction of schools as well as roads, bridges and state buildings. The Board of Public Works in Maryland, like boards in other states, has power over not only all forms of state construction but also over land acquisitions and state leases. It affects the entire economy of the state and provides a lever to either encourage or force contributions from a broad range of businesses.

The inability to perceive the economic function of government has been a major characteristic of reformers from the 1890s to the leaders of Democratic party reform efforts preceding the 1972 election; it also appears to be an element in the thinking of those who would attempt to remedy the Republican abuses of the 1972 campaign by the passage of restrictive campaign contribution legislation.

The procedural approach to reform fails to recognize that underpinning the outward structure of city and state government—the balance of authority between the executive and legislative branches, the varying degrees of responsibility granted competing bureaucracies, the extent to which elected officials are empowered to appropriate and spend—is a system based on the function of government as a market in which the statutory and constitutional power relationships serve as important elements in the rules and regulations of the marketplace.

Complementing the hierarchy of elected officials and civil servants who comprise the structure of government is another hierarchy from the private sector whose strength is largely based on financial resources. The latter comprises the substructure of government. The two interact in a marketplace where money and power are the currencies of exchange. Before turning to the effects of this market mentality on public policy, it is necessary to identify the motives and methods of the private substructure of government.

In Maryland, as in other states, a limited segment of the general constituency sees the state and local governments as more than providers of essential services; they are economic resources to be cultivated and directed to the advantage of those participants in the political process who have achieved adequate status through either their elective strength or their financial position, or both. To those who recognize this role of government and who are in a position to act upon it, the needs of society at large—for education, police protection, water, roads and for all the other functions that fill out expanding budgets—are potential sources of profit to be encouraged under controlled circumstances.

The processes of government, from this limited perspective, may be seen as a series of competitions over the distribution of budget appropriations, over efforts to determine the direction of new spending, over the power to regulate as a vehicle for profit, and over decisions that affect both land values and area development plans for industrial and commercial growth. Mediating these processes, a hierarchy emerges in which the competitive parties from the private sector find their places within a stratified system. On top are those commercial and industrial interests which ultimately have more usable and focused power in their immediate grasp than the state. The most prominent of these is the banking industry and the ancillary financial and legal communities which, through control of the flow of money, not only determine the ability of the state or city to borrow money and at what interest rate, but also determine through the granting or withholding of credit the success or failure of urban renewal projects, toll road facilities and a broad range of capital projects. This power is secondary, however, to the influence exercised by the banking community over the entire economy, ranging from the ability to facilitate the cashing of a welfare check to the authority to grant or withhold financial backing for major projects in the private sector, power that very few elected officials have either the capacity, interest or knowledge to challenge.

Forming a second level in this hierarchy are the commercial and industrial concerns that have some permanence in the economic system independent of state and local government decisions, but that also maintain major interest in the outcome of a variety of governmental questions. These include large developers, insurance companies, savings and loan firms, road and building consultants, trucking companies, wholesale liquor dealers, large construction companies and secondary law firms. One characteristic of new gubernatorial administrations is that each raises a new or varied group from a subordinate to a primary position of power.

The recent allegations of bribery and tax evasion involving Spiro T. Agnew centered around the persons and corporations raised to this position of influence under his administration: the road consulting firm of Matz, Childs and Associates; I. H. Hammerman, II, an investment banker and real estate developer; and Jerome D. Wolff, a former member of Agnew's staff, and later an executive with the J. E. Greiner consulting firm. They formed part of a favored constellation during Agnew's administration which also included the Robert Goodman Advertising Agency and the law firm of Buckmaster, White, Mindel and Clarke. When Agnew was replaced in 1969 by Marvin Mandel, the firms prominent in his administration were superseded by those to which Mandel had political ties. Zollman Engineering, a company headed by Harry W. Rodgers, III, has replaced Matz, Childs and Associates and the J. E. Greiner Company as the recipient of state contracts; the Rosenbush Agency has been given state advertising work, including the $1,000,000 lottery contract, and has acquired clients among state-regulated industries, including racetracks; and Weinberg and Green has the legal work for a broad range of industries doing business with the state or regulated by it.

At the base of the power hierarchy are those largely commercial interests which are almost entirely dependent upon government action for their existence, such as insurance premium lending companies that exist because state law mandates their use, and minor paving contractors who receive their entire income from government contracts; the owners of small parcels of land seeking zoning changes; silk-screen printers who would be unable to meet payrolls regularly without orders from the city or state; nursing homes subject to state-determined standards and specializing in the provision of service to medicaid patients, and so on.

The competition forming the substance of many governmental decisions takes place both vertically between these divisions and horizontally within a given stratum. The dispute over no-fault insurance exemplifies horizontal competition; it involves an effort by companies specializing in group insurance to increase the scope of their clientele, to the economic detriment of the larger automobile carriers currently providing policies to individuals through third-party liability coverage; the higher no-fault limits are set, the better the competitive position of the group insurers. Similarly, a decision over whether to build a bridge or a tunnel to provide transportation across a body of water will determine what set of contractors, subcontractors and consultants are eligible to profit from the public works project. Conversely, a proposal to allow finance companies to require collateral on small loans is vertically competitive because the increased leverage allowed the firms to collect debts would permit a strengthened ability to make loans at rates approaching those of banks and other lending institutions. More subtly, protective land-use legislation works to the advantage of prestigious developers specializing in the construction of expensive residential complexes, which provide adequate open space and sewage facilities, and works to the detriment of the marginal developer of garden apartments for blue-collar or lower-middle-class residents. In this context, differences in ideology or political belief within a city hall or state house are insignificant compared to the conflict of special interests. The exclusion of public financing of electoral campaigns has resulted in a system in which candidates are dependent on and largely defined by their financial resources, which in turn do not provide a cohesive point of view but instead a fragmented, and often internally conflicting, position from which the officeholder's votes must be cast.

Instead of a liberal–conservative split, analysis of the composition of the members of a city council or state legislature indicates that the significant division is between two different groups: one, the normally dominant faction often described in the press as "practical politicians," or the "old guard," which operates on a set of rules superseding ideology; and the other, whom we shall call "the critics," a diverse group of legislators who are unified only in their opposition to those holding power. Between these two is a third, less significant group composed of legislators who are generally unaware of the processes taking place around them but can be depended upon to provide the dominant faction with a majority because the rewards they seek involve the parochial satisfaction of local needs that can only be met through cooperation with the dominant faction. These legislators will be concerned with a bill raising the salary of a local sheriff, or a bill extending the Eastern Shore oyster season, or a bill exempting a court-house associate from civil service provisions; and their votes on larger matters will be bartered for support on these issues.

Working to the advantage of the dominant faction and serving to prevent the expression of conflict in ideological terms is the fact that on any given issue a sizeable block of the critics will join those behind a given proposal: legislation to expand state spending for water control and anti-pollution projects will draw in liberals and the conservationists, while a vote on the spending of state monies for a maximum-security penitentiary will pull in conservative support. Without a common purpose or program beyond procedural reform, the critics are consis-tently divided by their own internal ideological differences, a factor working to insure that they remain a minority even if they achieve a numerical majority.

The continued existence of a majority faction more attuned to the concerns of special interests than to the needs of their constituents is partially dependent on the seriousness with which its members attend to the details of the political and legislative process (bestowing awards for cooperative votes, marshalling votes from the critics on relevant issues, etc.). A more important base of support, however, is the structure of rules applying to both politics and the bureaucracy at city and state levels. The function of this structure is to guarantee that the basic process of government—the raising of taxes and the spending of these revenues—provides extensive opportunity for profit, both political and economic, to persons holding leverage within the political system. Although enlightened legislation may be passed, the content of programs is diluted from conception to implementation, invariably in ways weakening the basic intent. This can be described as a filtering process: when a certain amount of money is set aside for a given social purpose, the operating rules of the system require that the money, and plans for its expenditure, be filtered through a series of steps diverting the intent of the program and steadily reducing the amount of funds arriving at their formally intended destination.

What began, for example, as a proposal for a state takeover of the entire automobile insurance industry in 1970, became as it passed through the gover-nor's office, the legislature and the bureaucracy, legislation reaffirming the status of every financial interest from the private sector involved in the provision of car insurance. Legally required policies covering economic and health losses allowed insurance companies to reduce liability coverage and at the same time opened up a new type of mandatory coverage. The state limited its takeover to those drivers who had been rejected by insurance companies, thus relieving the compa-nies of the responsibility for maintaining a privately run assigned risk plan and permitting the governor to expand the bureaucracy and his own patronage in the state program. To prevent the possibility that the state might perform the function of agent and that it might develop a system of delayed payments for the poor, the legislation was further amended to set minimum fees for agents and mandated the use of premium loan companies by the state's high-risk clientele who needed time payments. Final passage of the legislation has served to eliminate pressure for no-fault insurance, a system opposed by trial lawyers seeking to protect the liability system under which they collect one-third of any judgment for their clients. Passage of this and similar legislation required the approval of a series of appointed and elected officials who determined that their function was to protect special interests rather than to represent a broader, general interest.

The typical politician learns quickly that his allegiance to a complex of special interests must supersede ideological considerations. Identifiable forces act on the lower-level politician—the candidate for the Maryland House of Delegates or for the Baltimore City Council—from the time he begins to seek nomination, through the period when he casts his vote, to the beginning of his active seeking of renomination. Although the individual legislator may draw psychological sustenance from the belief that his election embodied the will of the voters, the reality of his selection, in the majority of cases, involved a series of decisions which allowed him to be on a favored ticket, to obtain essential endorsements or to receive adequate funds, decisions which in the main he did not control and in which his role was to indicate acquiescence to the wishes and demands of others, not to affirm his own beliefs. In Baltimore, for example, the election of local politicians, both reform and old-line, is determined largely by the endorsement of clubs in the city's six districts. These clubs, in turn, offer political and financial backing from members of various groups who are not interested in legislation affecting large classes of people but in the preservation and expansion of narrow economic interests. A typical reform club is likely to receive support from that group within the AFL-CIO which controls the Committee on Political Action (COPA); from a segment of the Greater Baltimore Committee, an organization of the more prestigious downtown businesses; from the Hoffberger family, owner of National Beer, the Baltimore Orioles and active backers of liberal Democratic campaigns; from innovative developers, including James P. Rouse, the builder of the new town of Columbia; and from architects with civil libertarian politics who are, or want to be, involved in urban renewal. Conversely, old-guard organizations are likely to receive backing from the Building and Construction Trades Council, the faction of the AFL-CIO most opposed to integration; from the downtown merchants involved in sales to largely black customers or from those connected with the "Block," a row of nightclubs and strip shows; from the owners of the Pimlico Race Track who are involved in continuing conflicts with the neighboring northwest Baltimore community; from developers who have profited from haphazard zoning along commercial and residential streets; and from the established architects and engineers whose livelihoods have depended upon the receipt of discretionary public contracts.

The result of this diversity of support is evident in the later actions of the politician. He has become a part of a system in which, most often, his varied supporters have worked out a method of mutual nonconflict, and he must limit his actions in accordance with their tacit agreement: he can support legislation requiring union pay scales on government construction but must avoid involvement in efforts to raise or expand minimum-wage provisions. His advocacy of a program to provide low-income housing loans is acceptable as long as revenues to finance it do not come from an increase in the beer tax or from racing revenues.

The ideological blurring of a candidate increases as the candidate seeks higher office, where there is an increasing overlap between the various interests involved in the elective process. In the predominately Democratic politics of a state like Maryland, once a candidate has won a primary, all major interests tend to coalesce behind him unless the contest has been so divisive that the Republican appears to have a chance of winning. In that case, both candidates receive financial support from the same sources.

Once elected, the politician finds that he must operate on two terrains, each with its own set of rules. The first is the public arena where he must constantly try to convince a body of people, primarily his constituents, that he speaks and acts in their interest, either in so far as he perceives what their interests are or in direct response to their demands. The second is the smaller, but equally important, arena of the legislative process, in which his constituency is but one of a number of factors in the making of decisions. Within the latter, a system of cooperation prevails, entailing compliance with a set of rules that requires the politician to maintain public respect toward fellow legislators and their motives; to presume in public their integrity; to accept the principle that when ignorant of the content of legislation, vote with the leadership; to abide with the procedures within the legislative process and with the techniques used by the bureaucracy to implement legislative acts—in other words, to remain passive toward major elements of the lawmaking process and to assume that most events are out of one's control. This passivity is more than the willingness to play by the rules necessary for the operation of government; it involves a collective submersion of integrity for the protection of an undemocratic system.

To insure this result in a body of legislators, most of whom have a developed competitive drive, rewards and punishments are applied that function not only to control the politician's actions but also to control his perception of his goals. The most commonly enforced form of punishment is exclusion from the inner mechanics of the legislative process. Rewards are preferred in part because of the danger that punishment will result in open conflict, which in turn is likely to produce public debate on issues and activities, to the detriment of those holding power. An effective method of control is the encouragement of elected officials in the use of the rewards that go with office. These include such major rewards as the diversion of business to a selected lawyer or insurance agent; the power to have constituents' complaints to the bureaucracy quickly resolved; such minor rewards as the availability of free tickets to sports and entertainment events; cut-rate prices on consumer goods, ranging from cars to television sets; trips to conventions held by industries affected by state legislation. At one level these amenities provide not only economic rewards but also psychological sustenance in a job which entails exhausting efforts—speaking to groups at night, responding, often unsatisfactorily, to the requests of constituents and maintaining a constant alertness to the minor activities of fellow legislators that can indicate a weakness, a strength or a bargaining point. More important, however, is the implicit assumption that the legislator will learn to judge his own success on the basis of his ability to acquire what are essentially personal rewards. The rewards are used to reduce the vision of the legislator to the most immediate and self-centered level, and consequently serve to minimize whatever larger conceptions he initially held about the role and function of government and his purpose within it.

Liberals and reformers—politicians who claim to reject this system of rewards and who base their appeal on advocacy of open governmental procedures and on opposition to corruption and favoritism—have failed to produce significant alteration of the substance of government in part because of the unacknowledged economic self-interest motivating the efforts of some reformers. An essential difficulty within reform efforts is that a base of support lies among economically established persons and corporations, currently out of favor, who perceive the bias of an incumbent administration as a stepping stone for potential competitors. Their advocacy of competitive procedures and opposition to favoritism is in fact a method of protecting their own interests. This attitude is reflected in the complaint that Governor Mandel has awarded a disproportionate number of appointments, bank charters, racing date transfers and state related legal business to Jewish associates.

In apparent deference to the more influential members of their electorate, the liberals and reformers in Maryland have focused their activities on a superficial alteration of government. They have yet to center efforts on economic legislation; instead, the great bulk of their political energy is spent on such bills as mandatory financial disclosure, elimination of loopholes in the election law and environmental legislation, all subjects resulting in extensive newspaper coverage but which provide no significant alternative for the body of voters whose interests lie in what government does and how much government takes away in taxes. This focus on peripheral reform legislation allows the old-guard factions dominating the labor-union and lower-middle-class districts in the state to portray liberal opponents as politicians who have little or no concern for the working man, and to continue to use incidental patronage and the awarding of contracts as a means of proving their own allegiance to their constituencies.

The more critical failure of reformers in Maryland, however, has been their inability to perceive that the procedural changes they have imposed on government—civil service reform, the off-year municipal election, the elimination of party designation in some localities—do nothing to alter the economic balance outside of government and serve only to force the creation of new avenues of influence.

The reduction of the strength of the boss and of the machine through the passage of such measures as nonpartisan city elections, the replacement of party nominating conventions with open primaries and prohibitions against straight ticket lever voting, has not resulted in "open politics" but has, instead, created a vacuum which has been filled in recent years by political entrepreneurs, intermediaries who have capitalized on the simultaneous rise in the cost of elections and on the decline of the availability of a guaranteed block vote for statewide or local candidates. These men perform the same function—that of intermediary between corporate interests and elected officials—that the boss performed. They function, however, without either the limitations or restrictions of the boss. In Maryland the three persons who seem to have filled the vacuum are Harry W. Rodgers, III, W. Dale Hess and Irvin Kovens, each of whom has recognized that the one remaining elective variable subject to control is money. Harry Rodgers, an owner of Tidewater Insurance Company, a firm providing coverage to contractors and state employees and also a major stockholder in Zollman Engineering, a firm doing road consulting for the state, is a fund-raiser with wide contacts among businesses receiving government contracts. Dale Hess, former majority leader in the Maryland House of Delegates and currently a partner of Mr. Rodgers knows the lobbyists for every business concerned with the passage or defeat of state legislation. Irv Kovens, former owner of the Charlestown Race Track, has developed a broad range of contributors among the speculators active in real-estate development surrounding both Baltimore and Washington and along the Baltimore–Washington corridor.

No longer tied to the responsibility of producing a guaranteed vote, a responsibility that forced the bosses of the past fifty years to give at least token recognition to the interests of their working-class constituencies at a time of more intense industrial strife, the intermediaries have been able to specialize in a single function, the raising and distribution of campaign contributions.

For the special interests which have over the years financed elections, the intermediary has replaced the boss as a means of influencing the elected official. For the candidate for major office, the intermediary provides the ability to raise the increasing amounts needed to finance a campaign. For candidates for lower office and their organizations, the intermediary has become an essential source of money distributed during statewide campaigns—money that replaces inadequate revenues from bull roasts, crab feasts, socials, testimonials, kickbacks from patronage appointees and payments from merchants seeking regularity in the delivery of public services.

The 1970 gubernatorial election in Maryland represented the resolution of problems created by the elimination of the boss and by the consequent elimination of channels of influence for special interests over government decisions; it was a reassertion of money as the most important factor in a contest in which Kovens, Hess and Rodgers eliminated competition against their candidate, Marvin Mandel, before the campaign began. Recognizing Mandel as an unprepossessing figure associated in the public mind with boss-ridden Baltimore politics and secretive legislative deliberations, the intermediaries began fund-raising immediately upon Mandel's selection by the state legislature to replace Spiro Agnew as governor in January 1969. By holding a testimonial dinner nine months before the primary and a year before the election when state contractors, consultants and regulated businesses faced 12 more months of the governor's assured incumbency and his consequent control over the spending of the state budget and over policy decisions, the intermediaries proceeded to lock in the traditional contributors by persuading them to contribute the maximum allowed under state law, $2,500. This effectively eliminated these donors from funding opponents, the most prominent of whom was R. Sargent Shriver. When Shriver began campaigning, he discovered an almost complete absence of available financial backing and a consequent lack of political support from local organizations needing money of their own. The result was Shriver's decision to withdraw his candidacy, turning the primary election into a virtually uncontested victory for Mandel. It remains to be determined whether Governor Mandel's involvement in what promises to be a messy divorce will significantly weaken his ability and that of his intermediaries to make good use of money for victory in the 1974 gubernatorial election. Prior to the announcement in July of his separation from his wife, Mandel and his associates had already raised nearly a $1 million from a testimonial dinner held last May, 16 months before the primary.

A vital source of money and power, largely ignored in the pseudo-electoral contest in 1970 was control of the Board of Public Works, the single most powerful agency in state government through its authority to reject or give final approval to the spending of state monies in almost all areas except in the regular payment of salaries. At monthly meetings, the Board of Public Works approves the spending of 35 percent of the $2.8 billion annual state budget for capital construction, the hiring of consultants, rentals of buildings for agencies, contract extras, land acquisitions—the majority of the decisions in which most campaign contributors have financial interests. The Board of Public Works is composed of the governor; the state comptroller, an elected official; and the state treasurer, who is appointed by the legislature but in reality is selected by the governor. Paralleling the board at the city level is the Baltimore Board of Estimates, a five-man board on which the mayor and his two appointees hold a majority.

The boards are part of a larger process in the government's operation treated by the public and the press as part of a custodial routine, while the focus of attention rests on such questions as busing, handgun controls, election reform and financial disclosure legislation. Buried in the routine deliberations of the legislature and of the city council, and for that matter in the decisions of bureaucracies concerning water distribution, road plans and sewer lines, are issues which individually have little direct or immediate effect on large numbers of people but that alter the value of land, expand the opportunity for profit through the granting of incidental tax exemptions, determine the geographic direction of development, alter the permissible techniques used by utilities to justify rate increases and determine the accounting systems to be used by insurance companies in describing their assets.

This routine becomes part of a substructure in government in which public issues, the most consistent of which is race, become diversionary questions. Politicians debate these questions, fight over the passage of related bills and give surface expression to a democracy of differing opinions while beneath this surface, decisions are being made on the distribution of consultant contracts, the route of new roads, the location of bridges, the extent to which lawyers and insurance companies can continue to profit from an altered system of automobile coverage, decisions on which property can be converted to industrial or commercial use and to what extent the expansion of the state's regulatory role will protect existing industries from new competition.

In this light, the charges against former Vice-President Agnew, the illegal transfers of campaign contributions, and the use of criminal activities to influence the outcome of elections are only new incidents to add to the lengthy history of the direct or indirect purchase of power held by elected officials.

An attempt, however, to prevent a recurrence of the cases that are now in the public light by a repetition of the reform tactics used in the first half of this century, without a recognition of the essentially interactive relationship of the state and its politicians with the surrounding economy, will result only in a re-enactment of the process in which the boss was replaced by the intermediary, with the concomitant minimum amelioration that this effected.

The current focus of attention on the criminal investigations in Maryland will prompt the reform faction to capitalize on events to promote their candidacies and legislation. Anticipating this, Governor Mandel has already announced that he will return campaign contributions from engineering and architectural consultants awarded contracts on a noncompetitive basis. But these are simply superficial changes. If there is no recognition of the duality of state and local government—that for a limited segment of the population it is an economic resource, while for the majority it is the provider of routine services—the involvement of this wave of reformers will soon wane and there will be a reversion to the system in which there is a persistent diversion of state monies to those who have acquired economic and political leverage.

# Decline and Fall of Baltimore's Machine

*The Sun,* July 8, 1977

The heavy-set, 73-year-old man raised his right hand and flexed his forefinger to summon a waitress at Bud Paulino's Crab House on East Lombard street.

"Honey," Dominic Mimi DiPietro said, "get me a meat sandwich." The waitress, new to the job, looked bewildered, and Bud Paulino quickly stepped over.

Mr. Paulino took the waitress by the arm: "Tell the chef to make a meat sandwich for Councilman DiPietro." Within five minutes, she returned with an inch and a half of salami, pepperoni and bologna, fried and wedged between two slices of Italian bread.

It was the councilman's third meal that Saturday night. After a meeting of the 26th Ward Democratic Club, over which he presided, he joined the ranks for roast beef and beer. After a brief walk through an East Baltimore precinct, he had his ration of three crabs at about 10 P.M., when he first arrived at Bud's. He had a beer with the crabs, but much of it was used to wash his hands.

Throughout the night at Bud's, men stopped by the table to talk politics: Lou Cavaliere, head of the special projects section of Baltimore's Public Works Department; Tony DeAngelo, a public works foreman who had briefly filled a vacancy in the House of Delegates, and Bud Paulino's son-in-law, who came to check out the possibility of getting a zoning change.

All these men accorded Mr. DiPietro a deference and respect exceptional for the bars and clubs of East Baltimore. As he began his eighth decade, the councilman had achieved the status of a leader.

To maintain that status, he spends eight hours a day in his city council offices. At night he attends two or more meetings, gatherings that require observation of every subtle development.

Mr. DiPietro is a surviving remnant of what once was a broad collection of leaders controlling political fiefdoms across the lower two-thirds of the city.

Though they often feuded and were rarely under the control of a single, citywide boss, these leaders dominated the election of city council members, state senators and members of the House of Delegates. The candidate who won the backing of a majority of such leaders could, at one time, expect to be elected mayor. The role of these leaders in statewide contests was often critical.

This level of power is no longer present; what remain are parts of the old machinery, scattered in some sections of the city.

As the white constituents of the old clubs grow affluent and move out to the surrounding counties, there is a parallel shift to the suburbs in the potential for corruption. This is reflected in the recent prosecution of city elected officials for minor—in financial terms—crimes, while prosecutions of two former Baltimore County executives have involved major extortion schemes based on profiting from the massive development of the county.

At the core of Mr. DiPietro's power is his domination of one East Baltimore precinct, the Fifteenth Precinct of the Twenty-sixth Ward. It is a 16-block area that produces from 400 to 600 votes in an election.

The 15th has been Mr. DiPietro's precinct for 48 years, since 1929, and it has been his bargaining lever in the club known 30 years ago as the Hoffer-bert-D'Alesandro organization. Time and death have now made the club the Staszak-DiPietro organization, still the dominant faction in Baltimore's First Councilmanic District, which in turn is dominated by the Twenty-sixth Ward. Mr. DiPietro's home precinct is one of the few left where an organization endorsement virtually assures a significant margin of victory.

In a demonstration of that control in 1970, Mr. DiPietro refused to back the organization's candidate for state's attorney, George Helinski, who had participated in the unsuccessful indictment of Mr. DiPietro on charges of taking a bribe from pool hall operators. In a five-man race, Mr. Helinski overwhelmingly carried the Twenty-sixth Ward with more than 2,500 more votes than his nearest competitor. In Mr. DiPietro's Fifteenth Precinct, Mr. Helinski got 60 votes out of 432 cast.

Twenty-five years ago, Mr. DiPietro was a small but important part of what was a machine. To borrow a metaphor from Samuel Lubell, in 1950 the organization in Baltimore was the political 'sun' and all opposition the 'moon.' When the organization lost, it was because internal conflicts deflected elective energy to outsiders who, in turn, if they won, were often drawn into the ongoing and consistent power of a structure devoted to winning year after year and disdainful of any transitory notion of reform.

Today Mr. DiPietro is a part of a much more complex political landscape in which there is no organization or machine according to traditional definitions. The old machines grew and flourished in poor, waterfront sections of downtown Baltimore, in crowded, row house neighborhoods of Italians, Irish, Bohemians, Poles and Jews. Their political and economic adversaries were the North Baltimore wards of well-connected Protestants and Catholics who controlled the city's insurance companies, law firms and five major banks. The premise of the machine was that it would provide some of the benefits—jobs, food, coal, housing—not supplied by the men in control of private enterprise.

Although a variety of factors—an expanded civil service, government social welfare programs, the strengthened office of the mayor—are cited as contributing to the decline of the machine, in Baltimore perhaps the critical factor was the failure, two decades ago, of machine leaders to recognize the makings of a continued majority constituency: blacks.

In the early 1950s, the late James H. (Jack) Pollack demonstrated the ability to periodically meld many of the competing, old-line political clubs into a semblance of a unified machine. Beginning almost at exactly the same time as Mr. DiPietro, just before the Great Depression shift of voters to the Democratic party, Mr. Pollack organized the city's lower-class Jewish precincts, which would prove to have higher turnout than their Irish, Polish and Italian counterparts, and which served as ideal bases of strength in making alliances with the leaders of declining ethnic constituencies.

Unlike, for example, Chicago's late Mayor Richard J. Daley, Pollack never was capable of controlling the politics of the entire city, but he was the last politician capable of negotiating broad coalitions of white political clubs strong enough to make him the single most important leader in the city.

The Jewish precincts—his base of strength—were the most highly concentrated neighborhoods, adjacent to the city's rapidly growing black population.

Unlike the Chicago organization, which absorbed blacks into the system early—which may help to explain its continued vitality—Mr. Pollack perceived the rise of the black vote as a threat to his control over the Fourth Councilmanic district.

He devoted himself to splintering infant black organizations, making secret alliances with black Republicans to split general election results, and reluctantly ran token blacks on his own tickets.

The Pollack-black split in the 1950s has shaped much of what now takes place in Baltimore politics.

By turning himself into a symbol of white forces resisting black growth— he boasted until his death that his Trenton Democratic Club remained "98.5 percent white"—Mr. Pollack inadvertently encouraged the growth of black leaders whose campaign rhetoric and style were anti-machine. This, in turn, produced a generation of black leaders from the middle and upper class of black society—doctors, school principals, lawyers, real estate dealers and insurance agents.

With rare exceptions, there have been no black DiPietros—or Currans, Mahons, D'Alesandros or Hofferberts—in the Baltimore political spectrum, and the 30-year process shifting blacks from a relatively minor, "owned" segment of the Baltimore electorate to majority status appears likely to reach completion with scant distribution among the black lower classes of the kind of political benefits that went to white ethnic groups.

In large part because of the black-white split in Baltimore politics, the old-line whites have themselves become a major force in a current move to insulate the last bastion of patronage, the courthouse, from political whim. In an effort to protect loyal workers from the threat of firing in the event that a black court clerk is elected, the white political clubs are toying with the possibility of "grandfathering" all present workers into their jobs, and then imposing civil service restrictions on new workers.

In terms of citywide organization, the black-white split prevented any district-based politician from using an elective base to form coalitions strong enough to aim toward a majority alliance. Instead, the city has become a collection of minor fiefdoms, defined largely by the borders of councilmanic and state Senate districts—which in turn have largely been drawn along racial lines.

The reduction of the city political clubs to separate entities without a single guiding force has made city politics vulnerable to external pressures, particularly to suburban money. Without a single base to bargain for contributions in return for votes, each club faces a financial crunch as the constituencies get older and poorer, and the costs of paying election workers and maintaining a clubhouse either remain stable or increase.

In addition, the traditional illicit means of raising money are disappearing. A business considering a plant in the city no longer considers making a pay-off for a zoning change; instead, it wants a tax break for making the sacrifice.

Taking the place of the boss in recent years have been financial middlemen— persons who see candidates, vote-producing clubs and businesses with a financial stake in government decisions as clients. The interests these men have advanced, including their own, have been almost all suburban—shopping centers, highway construction, consultants, developers.

From a position of dominance over state politics thirty years ago, the city clubs have degenerated into seekers of the financial largesse of fund-raisers who, in turn, are promoting statewide candidates tied to corporations.

Just as the money is moving out of the city, so are the votes. "All I got is old people," Mr. DiPietro complains. "It used to be four or five votes in a family, now it's one." Maryland's Third Congressional District, the core of which is the white working-class neighborhoods the organization once dominated, now has the highest median age in the state.

As the death rate surpassed the birth rate among Mr. DiPietro's constituents and as downtown blacks moved farther into his Twenty-sixth Ward, an even more chilling development took place in the last election—for the first time in the history of the state, the total vote in Baltimore City was smaller than the total vote in neighboring Baltimore County, a 97 percent white suburb that forms a horseshoe around the city.

In terms of the politics of this state, the 1976 election results were a benchmark in a transition evolving since 1950, when the city stopped growing: The largest block of votes no longer lies in a Democratic stronghold where Republicans have been run over roughshod.

Instead, politicians seeking statewide office will now focus their attention on a jurisdiction whose growth has been founded in part on whites escaping from an increasingly black city. Although Democrats outnumber Republicans three-to-one in the county, their party loyalty is nominal at best. Baltimore County voted for Gerald R. Ford over Jimmy Carter by a 9 percent margin, and it was overwhelmingly carried by Richard M. Nixon in 1972.

With the flow of whites to the county has gone the flow of money, including the political money.

Baltimore County is the political birthplace of Spiro T. Agnew, whose successor as county executive was Dale Anderson, later convicted of 38 counts of bribery, tax evasion and extortion. In the county, there is the potential for profit in every zoning decision, sewer line and road extension.

In the city—long considered the root of all political evil in the state—corruption has been, by comparison, reduced to nickel-and-dime transactions. In an implicit courtroom commentary on urban democracy, the most recent convictions of city officials were on conflict of interest charges for holding an interest in a two-truck wrecking firm and on an extortion scheme in which schools would be vandalized to force the issuance of emergency, non-bid repair contracts.

In financial terms, the political stagnation of the organization clubs in Baltimore city is reflected in the payments of what is known as walk-around or Election Day money—payments to the organizations to place workers and to print sample ballots to be passed out at polling places across the city. Writing in 1911, Frank R. Kent estimated that a statewide candidate needed to pass out about $50,000 on Election Day if he expected the city machine to carry him.

Fifty years later, despite inflation, the amount remains the same.

"It used to be that a precinct captain went to your christening, your high school graduation and helped you move in after you got married. Now he doesn't know anybody," commented former Mayor Thomas J. D'Alesandro, III. To Mr. D'Alesandro, the organizations "are nothing. They can't produce any more. This state is wide open. You don't need the clubs when you've got television."

At one level, television has provided free home entertainment to those who might otherwise have dropped in at the local clubhouse for a few beers and some hands of nickel-ante poker. At another, it has provided the candidates with direct access to voters, circumventing their necessity of introduction by local political leaders and their organizations.

Before the advent of television, the clubs provided bull roasts, meetings, crab feasts, dances—the core political functions providing an avenue to the voter for the candidate. While television has served as an impersonal route, the clubs are losing their almost exclusive control of direct access to the increasingly assertive and independent neighborhood associations that have sprung up over the past decade in white neighborhoods.

In Baltimore, these groups developed in large part in response to a proposed East–West Expressway—planned to cut across every section of the city except the well-to-do north. This organizational root has resulted in an essential distrust of public officials and, in many cases, an adversary relationship with the clubs whose councilmen, state senators and delegates either supported the road or disappeared when the moment to express opposition arose.

"The neighborhood organizations don't have leaders like they used to have, they don't like to be led," Mr. DiPietro said, ruefully. Sitting in Bud's Restaurant surrounded by supporters, he added, "When you go to their meetings it ain't nothing like this. They treat you like dirt," he said, pointing to the floor.

The two Democrats in Maryland with seemingly the brightest national futures—Sen. Paul S. Sarbanes and Rep. Barbara A. Mikulski—both achieved elective success in large part because of neighborhood associations in the once machine-controlled Third Congressional District.

Mr. Sarbanes and Ms. Mikulski began their political careers as outsiders to the old-line clubs. But once they proved their ability to win, both reached accommodations with the clubs, and in recent elections have actively paid walk-around money for endorsements and poll workers.

The rapprochement of the two reformers—Mr. Sarbanes and Ms. Mikulski—with the clubs is, in fact, testimony to the continuing, if modest, strength the clubs can exert despite all the counterpressure and all the social forces working against them.

On their own turf, the clubs are dominant, although no longer exclusive, factors, in "bottom of the ticket" races—state central committee, House of Delegates, judgeships, state senators and councilmen.

But they have been unable since 1970 to elect one of their own to either the House of Representatives or the Senate—a strong contrast to the 1960s, when the city's three representatives were all products of clubs in various sections of the city.

The power of the clubs in a statewide election—for governor, senator, or in a presidential primary—is no longer definable by a percentage or precise margin.

One of the original functions of "walk-around money" was literally cash payments to local political leaders to walk around their precincts and promote one candidate while denouncing the opponent as a tool of monied interests. The leaders bought drinks in bars, talked to housewives on their marble stoops and served as escorts for their candidates at meetings and tours.

This once-secondary function of the clubs has been transformed into a major function. Although candidates are not bankrolling local leaders' bar tours to any significant level, the leaders still act to set a tone in voter perceptions of candidates. Their precinct captains continue to have respected voices within a multitude of small communities where candidates' strengths can be promoted and where the opposition candidates' weaknesses capitalized upon.

Former Democratic Senator Joseph D. Tydings was, for example, widely believed in early 1970 to be assured of reelection. As the contest progressed, however, a major weakness emerged. In working-class white neighborhoods, he was seen as a millionaire liberal with more interest in poverty programs than in urban whites trying to hold on to fading neighborhoods and tenuous weekly paychecks.

This is the kind of weakness that can be partially offset if local Democratic leaders line up behind the party's nominee.

In Mr. Tydings's case, many did not, and went instead to his Republican opponent, J. Glenn Beall, Jr., who had a secret $165,000 cash fund supplied by the Nixon White House to attract dissident Democrats. Mr. Tydings lost by a margin of 24,000 out of 956,000 votes cast.

In order to retain what little vitality remains, the city clubs are faced with a declining cash surplus. While the East Baltimore groups Mr. DiPietro tours at night show balance sheets moving closer and closer to the red, outside the city limits to the south, the Lake Shore Democratic Club is a thriving organization made up of men and women who have just made it over the city line into modest ranch houses on 10,000-square-foot lots.

Union foremen, craftsmen from the AFL-CIO unions and small contractors, the members own boats and have left the row houses behind them, but the social habit of meeting weekly at a political club remains.

Bi-weekly dances produce a steady flow of cash, fleshed out by summer crab feasts and bull roasts. The regular business meetings at mid-week are attended by fifty or more people, but even in the midst of election season, more time is spent on the treasurer's report than on endorsements.

The club backed the entire Democratic ticket in the last election, but privately over the free beer at the bar, members acknowledged that they would vote to reelect the area's conservative Republican congresswoman, Marjorie S. Holt.

Twenty-five years ago, Mr. DiPietro boasts, a member of his United 26th

Ward Democratic Club wept at the door after he was barred for life for secretly backing a Republican. No such strictures apply at suburban clubs, and in fact they do not apply any longer at Mr. DiPietro's club. Even though Mr. DiPietro's candidates still win in his precinct, the margin of victory will never again reach the 10-to-1 level assured from the depression through the Korean war, and the precinct's turnout has fallen from 750 to 500 votes over the past 24 years.

Mr. DiPietro is 73. His former boss, George Hofferbert, died in December at 74. His co-leader, Joseph J. Staszak, is 61. No one in the organization shows any real talent, or interest, in the drudgery of maintaining a political faction when there are fewer and fewer plums to hand out.

For Mr. DiPietro, politics has been the core of his existence, carrying him from precinct captain to councilman to leader—through two indictments, one conviction and one pardon. He did not marry until he was 62.

Today a politician needs more than Mr. DiPietro's fifth-grade education to present himself to the voters.

And in the city, the Democratic stronghold of the state, the ambitious candidate must look forward not only to the prospect of declining benefits to distribute but also to a political horizon constricted with every census. After 1970, the number of Baltimore congressmen fell from three to one within city boundaries, with another shared by the county; the number of state senators fell from 12 to 11. The census has become a 10-year hammer blow to the city's leverage in the state.

As the city steadily loses population, the one growing source of potentially unified voting strength, the black community, remains sharply divided by factional disputes dating back to the first black elective victories 20 years ago.

State Senator Verda F. Welcome engages in repeated duels with William L. (Little Willie) Adams; a persistent rivalry characterizes relations between East and West Baltimore; and the Mitchell family remains largely at odds with all other established factions.

The shift in the style and content of Maryland politics resulting from the decline of the city as a political force is most apparent in the gubernatorial candidacies of Theodore G. Venetoulis and Steny H. Hoyer, both of whom are operating from suburban bases.

Mr. Hoyer, the president of the state Senate, has his roots in a Prince Georges county organization that represents a significant step beyond the city club.

While the almost exclusive function of Mr. DiPietro's Twenty-sixth Ward United Democratic Club is the winning of elections—ideological disputes are nonexistent—the major function of the Prince Georges Democratic organization is to neutralize differences among opponents of busing, middle-class blacks, Common Cause activists, remnants of the defunct rural organization, developers and preservationists.

The concern of these groups with a specific interest, as opposed to simple elective victory, has forced the Prince Georges organization to maintain at least a semblance of democratic procedure unthinkable in a traditional city club.

Mr. Venetoulis, the Baltimore county executive, won election in 1974 without deep roots in his constituency.

If Mr. Hoyer represents a transition of political power from the city to the suburbs, Mr. Venetoulis represents a step farther—to a form of politics without permanent, solidified ties to the electorate.

In this style of politics, the media become a dominant factor and a candidate's newness ("freshness," in campaign rhetoric) becomes a positive attribute. Mr. Venetoulis managed the Maryland campaign of California Governor Edmund G. (Jerry) Brown, Jr., in which the prevailing method was the creation of events designed to have immediate television appeal—appearances before college audiences where large crowds were guaranteed, free beer at union hall rallies to assure a turnout, and the constant, but unspecified, claim by the candidate that he represents something other than traditional politics.

The success of this campaign style has been more damaging to machine politics than the reform legislation passed by the state and federal governments.

At the same time, however, lingering elements of machine politics remain a major interest of reformers. In the last Maryland U.S. Senate election, the issue of paying walk-around money was repeatedly raised, when in fact it has become a smaller and smaller percentage of campaign budgets. More attention was paid to the old-line backing of the Brown campaign than to the methods he used to win votes outside the city.

The consequence of this attention is that the city remains in the public eye a focal point of corruption, when the major convictions in recent years have all stemmed from activities in surrounding counties—Spiro T. Agnew and Dale Anderson, former Baltimore County executives, and Joseph W. Alton, Jr., a former Anne Arundel County executive.

# Maryland: A Government
# Serving Private Gain

*The Sun,* October 16, 1977

The conviction of Marvin Mandel and five associates has led to quiet rejoicing among reformers who feel that a faction of the Democratic party controlling the state for its own financial gain has been seriously wounded. Three of the co-defendants—W. Dale Hess, Harry W. Rodgers, III, and William Rodgers—built a minor empire of corporations profiting from government decisions: insurance, consulting engineers, leasing, janitorial services, even the sale of portable toilets for roadworkers. They have demonstrated exceptional success in a state where there is an evident connection between government decisions and private profits.

But there have been repeated reform drives before in Maryland, and all have died quiet deaths. One reason, perhaps, is that most liberal reformers in Maryland have lacked any continuing concern with the internal workings of state government.

There is very little in state government to hold the interest of the liberal reformer, in contrast to the city or federal levels of government. While mayors are caught in the vortex of fiscal crises, demands of the poor and busing fights, and while members of Congress debate tax reform, energy, ethics and other elevated topics, governors for the most part remain promoters of the industry within their states and seekers after new industry.

They build roads to encourage tourists and discuss their programs with the Chamber of Commerce. The industry they regulate is in large part only that left over from the federal regulatory system. Not much media mileage can be gained from calling for a crackdown on hearing-aid dealers or barbering schools. This is not the terrain for the ambitious reformer.

What a number of Mandel critics have not acknowledged or have failed to perceive is that state government, more than any other level, functions primarily as an arena of competition between different industries and businesses. In this context, the poor and the black are largely peripheral—they surface as significant factors briefly during legislative debates on welfare benefits and medicaid benefits—and without the poor and the black, there is very little ideological content at this time to political disputes.

Instead, at the state level the conflicts center on competition for the award of benefits—contracts, regulatory decisions, leases, etc.—between interests which already have a large share of these benefits and those which are seeking to break into the market. The theme of private benefit is pervasive in the history of Maryland politics. In the latter part of the nineteenth century, the apparent conflict between reformers and city bosses was in large part the B. & O. Railroad (reformers) against a collection of lesser railroads (the bosses) seeking a share of the state franchise.

In the 1920s, the state entered the field of racetrack legislation, and a fight between the major tracks for leverage in the executive and legislative branches has continued to the present.

In more recent years, legislative sessions have become the focal point for conflicts between insurance companies and trial lawyers; between the various levels of the lending industry: banks, savings and loans and finance companies; between doctors and chiropractors; barbers and beauticians. This was the universe that Governor Mandel and three of his co-defendants—Hess, Harry Rodgers and Irvin Kovens—had dominated over the past decade.

Hess, a farmer elected to the Legislature in 1955, initially established himself financially by buying up property where three interchanges were later constructed along the John F. Kennedy Highway.

Rodgers began his Tidewater insurance business by forming a partnership in 1959 with the son of then Gov. J. Millard Tawes, and Mr. Tawes's patronage dispenser, George Hocker. After Governor Mandel won, Rodgers bought out Mr.

Hocker and brought in Hess, a close Mandel associate.

Kovens bought the Charlestown (W. Va.) racetrack in 1965, sold 50 shares of the stock to the daughter and son-in-law of the Teamsters Union president, James R. Hoffa, got a $4 million Teamsters pension fund loan and received a vastly expanded racing season from West Virginia racing officials. By 1971, he was able to sell the track for a profit of $6 million.

In carrying out what federal prosecutors successfully charged was mail fraud and racketeering, Mandel and his colleagues did not alter the shape and style of state government. Instead, they used those elements of state government which have historically functioned to provide corporate and political profit.

• With little or no ideological content to state government, the financing of state political campaigns has been left almost entirely to persons and companies who benefit from state actions. Hess, Rodgers and Kovens took this political fact of life at face value and specialized in the cornering of all available campaign money to prevent the surfacing of any significant rival to Mandel, a politician of questionable public appeal who nevertheless won two terms without real opposition.

• Most of the benefits available from state government result from the discretionary and secondary decisions of public officials and contractors which are not subject to rules of competitive bidding. The Hess–Rodgers corporate structure was designed to fit into this unrestricted context: an insurance business, an engineering firm, racetrack stock, an interest in a state-chartered bank, buildings to be leased to the state.

Well before any criminal investigation began, most of this information found its way into the press, particularly into this newspaper, including details of an Eastern Shore land deal in which Mandel was given an interest at nominal cost. But instead of producing voter outrage, the major result of these news stories was to further encourage the cycle of profits: any state contractor wondering where to get the most for his insurance dollar had only to read the paper to find out. In fact, the fund raising, the notoriety and the receipt of state-related business all worked together, building to a crescendo of power. By the time of the 1974 election, no significant Democrat gave serious thought to running against Mandel.

A large sector of the state bureaucracy, particularly the regulatory agencies, and much of the deliberation of the General Assembly, particularly the bills before the Economic Affairs and Economic Matters committees, are devoted to a single question: Who will make money? In many cases, these are not moral decisions. The choice between an overpass or an underpass may make no difference to the taxpayer, but it will determine which set of contractors, engineers and architects will benefit.

More importantly, however, the potential for favoritism imbedded in the core of state government, contrary to the claims of some reformers, has served to perform a traditional American goal: increased opportunity for social and economic mobility.

Under the Mandel administration, the beneficiaries of the favoritism were a highly restricted group, and clearly there was no large-scale expansion of the distribution of contracts and other rewards. However, until the emergence of Tidewater Insurance, most of the state-related insurance work, including the broad range of services required on construction projects, was funneled to old-line agencies that had established their political ascendancy during earlier administrations. Similarly, the apparent lock on most of the road and bridge consulting work held by the J. E. Greiner Company was not significantly challenged until Hess and Rodgers acquired the Zollman engineering firm.

In a manner paralleling the provision of jobs to the immigrant by the turn-of-the-century machine, state government in Maryland has served as a vehicle for new competitors to break into terrain controlled by established corporations. The state can, and has, acted to create new wealth, a source, in a sense, of venture capital in the form of assured contracts, lax regulation and the passage of a favorable bill.

The reform ideal of a fair, impartial government, free of favoritism, often serves instead to reinforce the economic status quo: insurance contracts go to the entrenched firms with long records of service; bond counsel work goes to the law firms with the best contacts in the financial world; the largest banks are entrusted with state deposits; engineering contracts go to the firms which have demonstrated their abilities in past state work.

The successful prosecution of the governor and his associates was premised, in large part, on the demonstration that the relationship between Mandel and the five co-defendants extended beyond favoritism, that there was a return of benefits back to the governor in the form of loans, gifts, and interests in corporate ventures.

The charges against Mandel and his associates were more subtle than those filed against the politicians who preceded him up the steps of the federal courthouse in downtown Baltimore. Spiro Agnew, Joseph W. Alton and Dale Anderson were accused of taking cash pay-offs in return for contracts. Mandel and his friends were accused of participating in a pattern of corrupt give and take which spread throughout his administration.

In this context, the indictment of Mandel and the co-defendants was based in part on a legalistic and ideally-construed model of government, which has little relationship to the reality of governing, at least not in Maryland.

The expectation of a government free of bribery may be legitimate, but the legal presumption that a state governor be impartial, disinterested and unbiased in the routine carrying out of daily business, in the context of a system imbued with favoritism, may possibly stretch a democratic form of government beyond its credible limits.

# CHAPTER TWO

# THE CONSERVATIVE REARMAMENT

**T**HESE ARTICLES describe what might be called pre-Reagan Washington, the period during the mid and late 1970s when the conservative movement, first nourished by the 1964 presidential bid of Barry Goldwater and then stunted by Watergate, began to flower. It was an ideal moment for the coalescence of the right. Jimmy Carter, the weakened Democratic president who had promoted such issues as the Panama Canal Treaties and labor law reform, was the perfect target for both right-wing organizations and the Republican National Committee. A progressive system of taxation, originally designed to soak the rich, had, through a vastly accelerated rate of inflation, become a growing burden on the working and lower-middle classes—just those groups most in need of insulation from steadily rising marginal tax rates. Watergate provided false comfort to a Democratic party disastrously defeated in 1972, while forcing the GOP to regroup and to develop the most effective fund-raising apparatus in the nation's history.

While Democrats neglected to address their party's internal conflicts over race, economics, social issues, and the problems of the cities, national business organizations began to convert management and stockholders into highly effective lobbying arms, forming political action committees (PACs) and "grass-roots" pressure groups equipped to target key members of congressional committees to promote an agenda ranging from deregulation to lower tax rates to a foreign aid program largely benefiting American manufacturers. Well before the Reagan victory and the GOP takeover of the Senate, business organizations during the administration of Jimmy Carter strengthened their beachhead in the Democratic party, giving large sums to incumbent Democratic members of the House and Senate in a drive to protect business interests in the legislative process as long as Democrats were in power. As a legislative minority, without the fund-raising leverage provided by committee chairmanships, Republicans successfully turned to their party organizations, the Republican national, congressional and senatorial committees, to raise huge sums not only for incumbents but also for challengers and competitors for open seats. These committees, in turn, capitalized on an extraordinarily productive direct mail fund-raising base to move a quantum jump ahead of the Democrats in the high technology of campaigning. In 1980, when the possibility of Republican victories sharply increased, business abandoned many incumbent Democrats to support GOP challengers. The political momentum of the drive to the right was given substantial support by the creation and expansion of conservative think tanks and foundations which provided intellectual legitimation to the tax and regulatory changes sought by business interests.

These and other conservative forces coalesced in the election of 1980 and in the legislative session of 1981 with the kind of power and political muscle that had not been seen in Washington since 1965, when the height of the civil rights movement coincided with Lyndon B. Johnson's landslide victory to produce a brief national consensus in favor of a liberal agenda. The growing strength of conservative forces at that time is well illustrated by the 1980 reelection struggle of Texas Representative Jim Wright. Although the race was expected to be tight, Wright won decisively with 60 percent of the vote. Rising to succeed Thomas P. (Tip) O'Neill, Jr., as Speaker of the House in 1987, Wright, on economic issues, has remained firmly in the liberal camp, defying colleagues and advisers by calling for a return to increased progressivity in the tax system after enactment of the 1986 tax reform bill.

In the years since 1980, there have been major changes in business lobbying and in the Republican party, developments which are discussed in some detail in later chapters.

# Congress Turns Rightward

*Dissent,* Winter 1978

Reform, once seen as the vehicle to free the House of Representatives from the constraints of conservative leadership, is now serving increasingly to weaken the power of a liberal leadership at a time when pressures on the younger members come from the right. Working in tandem with basic shifts in the substance and style of district politics and with the growing perception that the country may face an economy of scarcity, the reform movement in the House has in part returned to one of the roots of reform in American history: a restrictive view in which corruption and a government of largesses become, if not one and the same, closely intertwined.

In the first session of the 95th Congress, there is abundant evidence of a shift to the right. Election-day voter registration, perhaps the most effective measure to increase the political leverage of the poor, is dead. Creation of a consumer-protection agency, acceptable even to the conservatism of Jimmy Carter, faces probable defeat or dilution in the House despite the presence of 289 Democrats. Common situs legislation expanding the right of organized labor to picket construction sites—a proposal passed in 1975 by a vote of 229 to 189—was defeated last year, March 23, by a margin of 217 to 205. Other votes include passage of antibusing amendments, a blanket prohibition of the use of federal funds for abortions, the denial of benefits to Vietnam War–era veterans whose discharges were upgraded under a presidential directive, and defeat of key minimum-wage amendments.

These votes are cast at a time when only token remnants of the once-powerful conservative Southern Democrats remain in power. Of the current roster of 22 committee chairmen, 15 had favorability ratings of 80 percent or more from the AFL-CIO in 1976. Carl Albert, one of the weakest speakers in history, has been replaced by Thomas P. "Tip" O'Neill, Jr., perhaps the quintessential Northern Democrat, and a politician who thrives on the manipulation of votes to build majorities.

This essentially liberal leadership is faced, however, with a growing body of younger members who are not only reform-minded but also conservative. To intensify the conflict, reform has clipped the power of the speaker and the committee chairmen to line up votes among the younger members and, despite portrayals of O'Neill's tenure as a return to the tradition of a strong speaker, his political muscle is highly fragile. "You know, there is nothing the leadership can offer me, really nothing," Richard A. Gephardt, Democrat of St. Louis and one of the stars of the freshmen class, noted with some pleasure during an interview.

Gephardt, to a large extent, personifies the difficulties facing O'Neill and the other, older Democratic leaders whose roots are in the Roosevelt coalition. Gephardt, who represents the white half of St. Louis and adjoining white suburbs to the South, was elected to the St. Louis City Council as a young Turk and now, as a member of Congress, he does not owe his election to any city organization.

This lack of a debt to any locally based political organization, which has become the rule among members elected since 1968, is one of the basic steps toward autonomy from the House leadership. One of the traditional mechanisms used by the leadership to reward or penalize new members was the granting or denial of pork-barrel projects: courthouses, post offices, roads. These projects allowed members to proclaim their personal power to the voters—but, more important, the projects provided jobs and contracts to the clubhouse politicians back in the district whose decision whether or not to endorse a new member for reelection often determined the outcome of the contest. Now, Gephardt pointed out, not only is there no traditional organization demanding that it be paid off, but "pork-barrel deals would hurt me in my district."

The local organizations, which could once make or break a junior member, have been replaced by institutionalized personal organizations available to any member once elected. In addition to the small district cadre that any candidate needs to get elected, Congress, in the name of reform, has granted each member a personal staff of 18, a computer service that is the envy of any direct-mail specialist, and the creation, by every agency of the executive branch, of a "congressional liaison" section, whose function is to grant a prompt response to every request from a member on behalf of district constituents.

These perquisites have been developed and are based on the argument that they provide the services essential for sound judgment on issues before the House. In terms of House politics, however, the critical fact is that these benefits are handed out on an entirely neutral basis.

For the members with a rudimentary sensitivity to their district, these perquisites guarantee reelection and have served to break critical dependency on the leadership for elective victory. New members can service their district and, through well-established public-relations techniques, project an image that is almost totally independent of committee assignment, passage of sponsored bills, or the award of public-works projects. Most important, the leadership cannot penalize any recalcitrant member by taking from him this machinery for reelection.

Although the House has progressively weakened the powers of the committee chairs and seemingly added to the procedural leverage of the speaker—giving him control over the Rules Committee, for example—the major development has been the rise of the Democratic caucus on which, ultimately, almost all the speaker's powers depend. This group, which now has a majority of members who have served three or fewer terms, gives final sanction to committee and floor rules, elects the leadership, and decides whether committee chairpersons will keep their jobs. The democratization of House Democrats has served to reinforce the independence of the membership. To a certain extent, power is the authority to make discretionary decisions, benefiting some and hurting others. The presence of the caucus and its demonstrated willingness to vote out of office four committee chairmen—Patman, Sikes, Hebert, Poage—acts as a major brake on the exercise of discretionary power.

O'Neill's talent as speaker has been to define the terms on which his own power is judged. He does not place the prestige of his office behind a bill until it is ready for floor action and the votes are counted. In this way, he has taken credit for the passage of a new ethics code, the federal pay increase, and the energy bill—while avoiding any liability for the failure of common situs, Election-day registration, and consumer protection. The measure for which he is given the most credit—the ethics code—was in fact critical to the establishment of his credibility as a leader; without it, he faced debilitating defections from the junior members. O'Neill, however, does not have the authority to be autocratic within the confines of congressional procedure or the power to either insure or seriously injure a member's chance of reelection.

The Rules Committee has become in large part an arm of the leadership, but it is generally obliged to send bills to the floor with rules permitting up-and-down votes on major issues within the legislation. O'Neill has the discretionary power to appoint special ad hoc committees, such as the Energy Committee, but he has had to guarantee adequate representation in its membership of all regional interests. (O'Neill's attempt to formally expand his procedural power by winning approval for the creation of a House "administrator" recommended by the Obey Commission and to be appointed by the speaker was overwhelmingly defeated: 252 to 160.) New members dismiss out of hand what in the days of Sam Rayburn was an accepted truth: that the leadership had absolute control over each member's congressional career. This weakness in the present Speaker's power was quietly reflected in O'Neill's decision to abandon any effort to keep Robert L. F. Sikes in the Appropriations Subcommittee chair. Had O'Neill tried to enter the controversy he would have faced a humiliating defeat at the hands of a collection of freshmen and sophomores.

Beyond the shifting power, reform is also serving to alter basic patterns of congressional behavior. In the past, a newly elected member from a farming district would seek a seat on the Agriculture Committee; from a city district, a seat on Education and Labor; from a district with military bases, a seat on Armed Services, etc. In these berths, members slowly acquired seniority and expertise in fields that would provide increasing benefits for their constituents. The development of procedural reform, as a separate terrain from which elective capital can be harvested, has provided a new, and quicker, avenue to congressional prominence. It is a guaranteed no-lose issue, risking none of the loss of voter support that advocacy of substantive legislation inevitably produces. No constituent group is against it. In addition, lack of congressional experience functions as a credential instead of a liability. Finally, reform coincides with the growth of elective politics based on the media, and it is one of the most accessible vehicles a junior member can use to get coverage in the home papers. The flood of inserts to the *Congressional Record* and of releases to the press gallery during the debate on the ethics code was equalled in the last session only during the debate on a congressional pay raise, and on the day of the demise of the B-I Bomber.

When Gephardt arrived in Congress last year, it was not the leadership who provided him with the most important post in his first term—an assignment that probably will be instrumental in his reelection. Instead, the freshmen caucus made him their reform chairman, a position that will give him the opportunity to try to put an end to the cheap meals, free flowers, lavish athletic facilities, and other side benefits that now go with membership in the House. From a purely political point of view, no freshman could ask for a better assignment, and no speaker could ever give it to a freshman.

With the near-elimination of "machine" districts, the style of campaigns in the past ten years has radically shifted in directions that further weaken the power of the House leadership to bargain for votes. The dominant forces in district politics have become a broad array of issue-oriented interest groups—chambers of commerce, civic-improvement organizations, branches of Common Cause, ethnic social clubs, PTAs, farmers' organizations. What unifies almost all these groups is their insistence that congressional candidates spell out their positions in detail on every conceivable issue. In the 1976 contest in Baltimore's Third Congressional District—where the winner used to be picked by a small handful of clubs and, if he wanted to stay in office, he did as he was told—five candidates issued position papers on everything from juvenile crime to deregulation of natural gas to abortion. The consequence is that each term a growing number of members begin locked into a set of positions: the bartering process characteristic of democratic legislating is ruled out, not only by middle-class constituents suspicious of the process, but also by a set of campaign commitments made well before the reality of the choice in committee or on the floor, and before the potential benefits of compromise are present.

A second major characteristic of current local-interest groups is that they are predominantly middle-class, and the pressure they apply is not for the creation of new, substantive programs, but for procedural reform or for the elimination and prevention of government initiatives. Common Cause and the League of Women Voters, whose concerns reflect the values and interests of their predominantly upper-middle-class membership, are often working for the reduction of power of the liberal leadership.

Business groups lobby against federal regulation, bills beneficial to labor, increases in the minimum wage. Neighborhood and civic groups, less interested in federal issues than in local government, echo, however, a recurring plaint against their tax burdens. These groups also share a deep distrust of traditional mechanisms in the congressional legislative process: log-rolling to build up majorities, patronage, and the distribution of pork-barrel benefits, the placement of a premium on personal and party loyalty as factors in making legislative decisions.

The increasing shift in balance of pressure on individual House members from the congressional leadership to organized local groups work, in turn, as a pull to the right. In any district containing an economic mix, the more affluent are far more likely to be organized than the poor, and far better equipped to make their position known to their representatives. Business organizations and their lobbying arms are demonstrating, in the current session, the most sophisticated use of constituent pressures, using lists of business people, conservatives, Republicans, and management personnel to create district opposition to consumer-protection, minimum-wage provisions and common situs.

The conflict between the pressures of district groups—to which the younger members are far more sensitive than those who first won election in a different era—and traditional congressional politics was embodied in the drive to oust Representative Robert L. F. Sikes from the Military Construction Appropriations Subcommittee chair he had used to increase the value of personal investments. A leader of the anti-Sikes forces was Leon Panetta, a freshman Democrat from Monterey, California. Ten years ago, the thought of the representative from Panetta's district challenging the chairman of Military Construction would have been inconceivable: the district includes Fort Ord, the Monterey Language School, and the naval postgraduate training school. There is no coherent party structure in the district, and Panetta won largely through his own work and organization. Panetta himself has minimal ties to the Democratic party: he was a Republican civil-rights appointee under the Nixon administration. In a reflection of the changing nature of district politics, Panetta noted after the Sikes defeat, his position was "not only morally right, it was politically right. If that means not returning favors and (not) getting the pork barrel, it is politically right and what my constituents want."

The Panettas and Gephardts of Congress—prototypes of the new generation of members—have changed the rules of the ball game. They argue, with some legitimacy, that the vehicle for the winning of votes, particularly among the younger members, now must be rational persuasion; logic, and not the offer of a job to a backer or the promise of a campaign contribution must prevail. This argument, however, works only for those with constituencies that coincide with the national middle-class majority and do not need exceptional benefits from government. The only way, for example, major revisions of the Food Stamp program were approved by the House was through a major vote-trading arrangement between farm and urban representatives, a process anathema to the constituencies of Panetta and Gephardt. Leading proponents of the use of vote-trading are representatives of minorities who, in an increasingly "rational" Congress, are going to find prospects of winning, or even maintaining, governmental benefits dimming.

Just as important as the changing forces in district politics is the shift in representation that will take place after the 1980 census, a change demographically foreshadowed by the 46 freshmen Democrats. The first-term members—those elected in '76—are representative of the population changes that will be integral to redistricting before the 1982 election. A solid block of them, 20, are from Sunbelt states—the tier of states extending across the Southern third of the country—which has been experiencing the sharpest population increase—and a majority, 29, represent the range of districts where the largest population shifts, up and down, are taking place: once rural areas now subdivided into surburban population centers; the edges of declining cities in the East and Midwest; well-established white bastions outside the cities that have high percentages of blacks.

These 46 freshmen are, as a block, more conservative on social and economic issues than any other class, a voting pattern that increases in importance with the recognition that these 46 are also a reflection of probable trends after redistricting. Analysis of their votes on the litmus issues that have surfaced in the first months of the 95th Congress shows: while Democrats as a whole backed the common situs bill by a margin of better than 2 to 1—191 to 88—the freshmen democrats gave only lukewarm support, 25 to 17; on a minor consumer-protection bill prohibiting debt-collection agencies from harassment of debtors, Democrats were in favor 158 to 105 while the freshmen among them opposed the measure, 15 to 27; an amendment prohibiting federal funding of Legal Aid-backed desegregation suits was opposed by Democratic members 150 to 101, but supported by the freshmen Democrats, 21 to 20. The pattern extends to proposals of shifting money to social programs, antibusing amendments, minimum-wage provisions and, to a lesser extent, to measures prohibiting federal funding of abortions. The difficulties facing the consumer-protection agency bill and the Election-day registration bill are in large part attributable to the lack of support among the first-term Democrats.

In writing about the two most recently elected classes in the House, there has been a strong tendency in the press to lump them together with an emphasis on their shared "questioning attitude" and "unwillingness to accept the status quo." This vantage point results in a dangerously inadequate perception of Congress: it glorifies the new members' "independence" without recognizing that changed district politics require independence as a prerequisite to election.

More important, the emphasis on shared challenges to tradition fails to recognize the dramatic ideological differences. The 75 Democrats elected in 1974 were by any standard statistical freaks, containing a disproportionate number of men and women with roots outside regular politics, from the peace and antipoverty movements, who used the lever of Watergate to win elections. What makes these Democrats unique is that they are more liberal—in the traditional sense of a commitment to social-welfare legislation, prolabor bills and income redistributing measures—than either their seniors or juniors. As a sample of long-term trends, however, the 46 Democrats elected last year are far more significant. They won election in a year when the remnants of the left-wing politics of the 1960s no longer had the adhesive of Watergate to hold together a dying coalition; the presidential candidates were not, except perhaps in the South, major factors at the congressional levels; geographically, the 46 were elected from districts that are likely to produce most change in the composition of the House after the 1980 census: the Sunbelt tier and suburbia.

The result of these political circumstances is a freshman class of Democrats that votes more conservatively on domestic social issues than any other class in the House. Their conservative votes reflect what might be described, more accurately, as rational representation of middle-class interests. While not insensitive to the needs of and pressures on minorities and the poor, the critical factor for these representatives in the casting of a vote is the protection of the economic and social gains of those who are not in poverty. This style of representation includes a strong commitment to procedural reform of the House, but, while the 75 Democrats of 1974 blended reform with the basic tenets of liberalism, the freshmen have an entirely different ideological undercurrent. To them, an integral, although largely unstated, element of reform is the curbing of major parts of the basic Democratic majority: demands from blacks, unions, and urban interests for increased spending and protective legislation. This joining of the reform drive with domestic conservatism among the youngest Democrats is probably the major factor in the seemingly exceptional strength demonstrated by the dwindling Republican minority during the 95th Congress.

In the short run, the consequences of the reform-conservatism of the freshman Democrats is already apparent in the opposition facing such bills as consumer protection, Election-day registration, and common situs. In the long run, particularly after the growth in suburban and Sunbelt representation following the 1980 census, the consequences are likely to prove both more subtle and significant. Still in the formative stages is the beginning of a major dispute over the distribution of funds, pitting the South and Southwest against Northeast and Middle West, and suburb against city. This dispute now takes place in the context of the continuing shift away from discretionary grant programs—urban renewal, model cities—to formula grant programs patterned in part on the principle of revenue-sharing. Discretionary programs have given cities the opportunity to take the litany of evidence of distress—percentages of decayed housing, number of unemployed, loss of small businesses—to federal executive branch agencies and there to corner all appropriations for housing or unemployment programs. More affluent suburban governments were often either out of the running or unwilling to compete for funds requiring that recipients provide housing for the poor.

In 1974, however, 11 of the major urban programs were consolidated into a formula program—Community Development—in a pattern followed by a number of lesser public-works and unemployment programs. Formulas guaranteed the distribution of money outside city limits to almost every governmental jurisdiction, no matter how affluent. More important, the creation of these formulas gave Congress the authority to determine precisely how the money for each of these programs will be distributed, down to the smallest county in the state. Debates on alternative formulas in the House are not conducted on the basis of need but of computer printouts showing dollar figures for each state, city, suburb, and county for the duration of an appropriation.

Over the past three years, however, the effect has been to shift all the new funds to jurisdictions, largely in the Southeast and South, that had been receiving no money under the old, discretionary system, and to maintain funds for the older cities in the Northeast and Midwest at essentially stagnant levels, despite inflation. Legislation passed in the current session prevented a sharp cutback in the housing-aid levels to the older cities, but it is highly questionable whether existing formulas can survive the shift in the balance of power in the House after the next census.

Although the prospect of redrawn districts is still three elections away, it is a growing force in the thinking of members of the House, particularly younger members who have the least leverage with the state legislatures that set the new district lines. The problem of redistricting is most acute for white members who represent urban districts that have been core bases of liberal support in the past.

In these areas the proportion of whites has been steadily declining, and the typical response has been to create black core districts while forcing white incumbents to compete for a declining number of seats that are being diluted with larger chunks of suburban wards and precincts. Gephardt, for example, noted in an interview that Missouri will probably lose one of its ten seats. The likely prospect is that his district will be pushed further out of St. Louis to the more conservative south, in a move to preserve the majority black district for the current incumbent, William Clay, in the northern half of St. Louis, and to prevent any court challenge based on discrimination.

The practice of creating black districts, characteristic of most northern cities—including St. Louis, Cleveland, New York, Detroit, Baltimore and Chicago—has cut two ways. It has guaranteed a solid block of black representation in the House but at the same time has served to create almost lily-white districts in the same communities, consequently eliminating from these districts what had been a source of pressure to support traditional Democratic programs.

The almost universal practice has been to effectively place all blacks in a city in one or more districts, depending on the numbers, so that the black voting majority ranges from 55 to 80 percent, and then to establish adjoining white districts with black populations of 2 to 20 percent. The consequence, in the politics of the House, is that the problems associated with central cities are reduced to the problems of the black congressional caucus, a group gaining in sophistication and seniority but increasingly isolated from many of their white, urban colleagues.

What appears to be happening, if the freshman Democrats do represent a long-term trend, is that, as congressional Republicans move further to the right and decrease in numbers, the vacuum in the center is being filled by Democrats, and that the majority party is itself moving to the right. On this assumption, the probability is that over the next three years the House will progressively recede from its public image as a force for continued deficit-spending and become at least a partial ally of the Carter administration's goal of a balanced budget, despite the grumbling from O'Neill and other House leaders that such a goal does not deserve a first priority from a Democratic administration.

The concept of a balanced budget coincides with the kind of reform impulse characteristic of the new member and of their constituencies, voters who see the placement of ethical restraints on members of Congress as an integral part of a larger constraint on the spending and regulatory practices of government, practices that were until now basic to the Democratic party and to the majorities it won among blacks, unions, and in city wards and precincts.

# Business Lobbying Helps Aid Effort

*Opinion polls consistently give foreign aid less support than any other federal program. Yet the plan survived attack in the House last year and passed critical tests this year. This is the first of two articles examining some reasons for its political resilience.*

The Sun, July 23, 1979

WASHINGTON—In the middle of last summer, 76 members of Congress received letters in support of the controversial foreign aid appropriation bill from a seemingly unexpected source—R. H. Malott, chairman of the board and chief executive officer of the FMC Corporation.

Traditionally, the strongest lobbying for the measure has been conducted by liberal organizations such as the League of Women Voters and the Leadership Conference on Civil Rights.

The letter from Mr. Malott, however, was from the head of a major manufacturer of industrial and farm equipment that last year had sales of $2.78 billion and ranked 97th on *Fortune* magazine's list of the top 500 industrial companies.

It was a part of a new lobbying strategy coordinated in part by the White House designed to demonstrate that foreign aid is not simply the transfer of money to overseas countries but in fact a source of at least $3.4 billion annually for United States interests, particularly American-based multinational corporations.

In the 33 years the U.S. has contributed to the World Bank and other international lending institutions, the total U.S. contribution has been $6.23 billion, but American companies have been paid a total of $8.34 billion from World Bank-financed projects.

"If one stands in front of a slot machine in Las Vegas and can put in $1 and take $2.50 out, one has to have a leak in the think tank to walk away from it," one congressional proponent of the program argued on the House floor last year.

The letters from Mr. Malott were directed to the 76 members of the House whose districts have FMC facilities. "We don't see foreign aid as a liberal issue, we see it as a part of world trade and we are a part of world trade. Clearly foreign aid is of interest to us," an FMC lobbyist commented.

The political mobilization of FMC and a number of other corporations has been a key factor in the continued survival of the foreign aid program. It has taken the edge off conservative opposition by demonstrating that aid abroad means export profits at home.

The success of this effort was shown last year. Conservative Republicans representing districts with factories producing heavy machinery—one of the major U.S. beneficiaries of foreign aid—unexpectedly switched from their critical stance of 1977 to cast key votes in favor of foreign aid, allowing the appropriation bill to pass relatively unscathed.

"By bringing in the corporations, we wanted to set a new note," Frederick Stokeld, chief of the international division of the Chamber of Commerce and a central coordinator of the drive, said. "I think many members of Congress are getting bored with the church groups," he said, referring to the traditional lobbying organizations.

In fact, however, the strategy of bringing in the corporate beneficiaries and placing strong emphasis on the domestic profits for foreign aid has been used repeatedly whenever the 31-year-old program has faced a serious threat in Congress.

It was an essential ingredient in the successful drive to reverse a 1971 Senate vote killing the program altogether when an unusual coalition of liberals opposed to the Vietnam War and fiscal conservatives joined together to form a 41 to 27 majority. Similarly, the same strategy served to defuse a 1953 congressional mandate ordering the program phased out by 1957.

The vulnerability of the foreign aid program is reflected in a series of polls by the Roper Organization. Taking 12 government programs including defense, welfare, education and environmental protection, the polling organization found that from 1971 to the most recent survey in 1977, the public consistently opposed foreign aid expenditures more than any other program.

In 1977, 69 percent said "too much" money was spent on foreign aid, compared to 4 percent saying "too little." The figures for welfare, which was second from the bottom, were, respectively, 58 percent against and 15 percent for an increase.

The current lobbying drive for foreign aid has a number of new ingredients growing out of basic shifts in the program toward indirect assistance through the multilateral development banks, instead of direct aid and loans—the increased emphasis on politically based aid in the Middle East; the development of more sophisticated lobbying techniques, and the increased political muscle of the exporting corporate community.

"Forgetting humanitarian reasons for the moment, we see a major marketing opportunity in the projects that are supported by the bilateral programs and the development banks," said the vice president and Washington representative of a major Illinois producer of heavy construction equipment.

There are at least 5,000 companies spread across almost every congressional district that were direct recipients in 1978 of contracts financed either through the direct foreign aid program or through the development banks. This figure does not include a host of subcontractors, a group so diverse that none of the foreign aid agencies have statistics on them.

In the fiscal year ending September 30, 1978, for example, the Agency for International Development (AID) financed purchases totalling $1.04 billion for goods and commodities from over 3,500 U.S. firms.

Of that amount, however, just under half—$504 million—went to 22 companies. These included the major grain exporters—$44.7 million to Continental Grain Company, $93.5 million to Cargill, Inc., and $42.8 million to Louis Dreyfus Corporation—and such heavy machinery producers as Caterpillar Tractor Company, $9 million; Massey-Ferguson, $13 million, and International Harvester Company $9.5 million.

In the same period, loans financed by the World Bank produced payments to American companies totalling $432.8 million, about 60 percent of the total of direct American purchases from multilateral banks.

The World Bank has just begun a program of breaking down disbursement figures for corporations within states as part of an indirect lobbying effort for the foreign aid program. The figures for 1978 do not represent total contracts, but only the amount disbursed in the fiscal year under what are often contracts for much larger amounts extending over a number of years.

The figures listed by the World Bank show the major recipients of disbursements last year to be Brown and Root, a Texas construction firm, $62.9 million;

six divisions of Caterpillar Tractor, $18.6 million; Alcoa Conductor Products Company, a Pennsylvania electrical manufacturer, $6.4 million; Pullman Kellogg, a Texas consulting firm, $8 million, and Hohenberg Brothers Company, a Tennessee manufacturer, $6.9 million.

"I think the mood of the country is that it's tired of being sugar daddy and wants to know what's in it for us," said a World Bank official involved in the effort to increase business support for the program. "Our interests are represented by these companies."

Carol Stitt, who is in charge of business liaison for the World Bank, said she gets numerous calls from members of Congress looking for economic justification to vote for the aid program—a need the detailed breakdowns of benefits to corporations state-by-state are designed to fill.

From this vantage point, the contribution of the U.S. to the international banks can be shown to have been more than equalled by the dollar value of the bank-financed contracts going to American corporations.

Treasury Department statistics show that payments to U.S. corporations from projects financed by the international banks exceed the total U.S. contribution to the World Bank and three regional development (Inter-American, Asian and African) banks by $2.11 billion.

These figures have become increasingly important to segments of the American business community as corporate dependence on exports as a source of revenues grows and as competition from multinational corporations based in other countries—particularly Japan and Germany—intensifies.

"We are providing financing for them [the U.S. companies] to export," Mrs. Stitt pointed out.

In addition to the administration-inspired lobbying in Congress for the foreign aid program, many exporting corporations actively supported the program without any prodding from the executive branch.

Richard Goodman, Washington representative for Continental Grain, said he independently made "two or three calls [to members] on the GOP side. It's not a very popular program [with the general public]; it doesn't have many constituents in the U.S."

A representative of Fiat-Allis Construction Machinery Company complained that he had never been contacted by the administration to see if there were any members he could help persuade to support the program. Despite this, he said he views foreign aid as in the interest of his company and called a number of members of Congress to seek their support.

In other cases, however, the lobbying effort was initiated and coordinated by agencies of the executive branch and by a network of trade organizations financed by corporations seeking improved opportunities for exports and expanded markets among the less developed nations.

On July 28, 1978, just days before the foreign aid appropriation bill was to go to the House floor, the White House called in the Washington representatives of ten major exporting companies to encourage them to lobby for the program.

Among the corporations represented were General Motors, Ford, General

Electric, E. I. du Pont de Nemours & Co. and FMC. Together, their sales last year amounted to $144.2 billion and their total workforce was 2.37 million persons.

Some agreed to take up the banner for foreign aid and, in the view of administration lobbyists, provided essential help in the fight for the program.

"Conservative attacks on the 'giveaway' program began to pale in the minds of a lot of congressmen when they started getting letters not only from the Chamber of Commerce but also from big companies with factories in their districts," one lobbyist said.

While FMC conducted a carefully targeted campaign, the more common practice among the firms, according to several corporate lobbyists, was to pass the word in casual conversations with members of the House that they backed the legislation and opposed restrictive amendments.

At the World Bank, the position held by Carol Stitt—business relations adviser—was created in part to encourage business support for the multilateral program.

Another key lobbying vehicle for the program is the set of organizations that promote international trade and cooperation, including the Chamber of Commerce, the United Nations Association, New Directions, the Overseas Development Council and the Emergency Committee for American Trade.

These groups, often armed with detailed lists of contracts and other economic benefits flowing into the U.S. from the foreign aid program, buttressed the campaign for the program.

Corporate support of the foreign aid program has been a key element in current and past controversies, but in recent years this involvement has taken on an added dimension as an increasing number of companies have been persuaded that the aid program is not just a potential market, but also an integral part of the entire export arena.

Many of the major companies called into the July 28, 1978, White House meeting are by no means dependent on what they make from sales through AID or through World Bank financed loans—General Motors' sales in 1978 were 63 times larger than total AID business procurement that year, for example—and consequently they were not going to be persuaded to back the program on a direct self-interest argument.

"The contracts are just a drop in the bucket for these big companies," said a State Department official who helped organize legislative strategy. "What's important to them is the growth of the international marketplace and foreign aid both encourages development and, if it works, helps to reduce hostility to the United States, and perhaps its corporations."

The rate of growth in revenues for American companies from export sales has more than doubled the rate for domestic sales—manufacturing for export grew by 127 percent between 1972 and 1976 while manufacturing for domestic consumption grew only 57 percent—and consequently there is a vital interest in the development of foreign markets.

The argument linking foreign aid with export is being taken up as a central theme of proponents of the program on the House and Senate floors:

Senator Frank Church (D-Idaho), chairman of the Foreign Relations Committee, told his colleagues last month when he brought the foreign aid authorization bill to the floor: "We sell more American goods and services to developing countries than to Europe and Japan combined. Without these markets, our balance of trade deficit would be much greater and unemployment much higher."

# Constituents' Economic Interests Lead to Conservative's Switch on Foreign Aid

*Opinion polls consistently give foreign aid less support than any other federal program. Yet the plan survived attack in the House last year and passed critical tests this year. This is the second of two articles examining some reasons for its political resilience.*

The Sun, July 24, 1979

WASHINGTON—Between 1977 and 1978, Rep. Henry J. Hyde, an Illinois Republican with unassailable conservative credentials, underwent a conversion on key foreign aid questions.

A huge man—6-feet 3-inches tall and 265 pounds—Mr. Hyde won his ideological stripes with the sponsorship of the Hyde amendment, a prohibition on federal aid for abortions, one of the litmus test issues for the right wing.

But August 3, 1978, he unexpectedly took the floor of the House and emerged as a leading proponent of the foreign aid appropriations bill, a burden traditionally taken on by liberal Democrats.

Not only did Mr. Hyde present some of the most forceful arguments in support of the bill, but his presence on the floor functioned to alter the political-moral equation that links conservatism with opposition to foreign aid.

In lengthy remarks to the House, Mr. Hyde touched on most of the reasons traditionally used in support of foreign aid: "The Biblical admonition, I would suggest to my friends, to give food to the hungry and to clothe the naked does not end when we enter this chamber."

The core of the Hyde conversion, however, may have been reflected in a brief phrase he also used on the floor: "I listen to the entrepreneurs in my district."

Mr. Hyde represents a district that is a part of the industrial heartland of the Midwest, a section where the factories of Caterpillar Tractor, International

Harvester, FMC Corporation, General Motors and John Deere are an integral part of the landscape.

For these companies, foreign aid is not a giveaway program; it is a major source of revenue.

Illinois firms, as a case study, sold $63.3 million through contracts financed by the Agency for International Development (AID), received payments of $48.8 million from foreign contracts financed by World Bank loans and, in 1976 and 1977, received $29.8 million from Latin American contracts financed by the InterAmerican Development Bank.

In a watershed for the foreign aid program, rock-ribbed Illinois Republicans like Representatives Hyde, Robert Michel, Edward R. Madigan, and George M. O'Brien all switched their 1977 votes in 1978.

In the crunch between ideological conservatism and economic interest, these members, all of whom represent districts with major corporations selling goods through foreign aid, provided the essential margin of victory—the vote was 203 to 198 on the critical test facing the foreign aid bill. Each voted in favor of allowing United States taxpayers' dollars to be used to give aid to the Communist countries of Cambodia, Vietnam, and Laos.

These and other votes in favor of the foreign aid program have created bitter frustration among such hardcore conservatives as Rep. Robert E. Bauman (R-1st, Md.), chairman of the American Conservative Union.

Mr. Bauman, whose Eastern Shore district does not benefit in any substantial way from the foreign aid program, complained, "It is the big business Republicans who are making the difference" allowing foreign aid to pass relatively unscathed, despite growing pressures for fiscal conservatism.

Ideological purity is, however, an almost impossible demand to place on conservative members of the Illinois delegation. The state epitomizes the domestic economic underpinnings of the foreign aid program, an interrelationship between a highly controversial federal program on the one side, and a market providing contracts and jobs for American corporations on the other.

"We are a big exporter," said Mr. Michel, the Republican whip whose Peoria district includes the headquarters of Caterpillar Tractor. "We just recognized the importance [of the program] to our balance of trade and our exports," he said about the switch in the voting between 1977 and 1978.

Henry Holling, chief of government relations for Caterpillar, said no effort was made to lobby the members of the Illinois delegation. "We don't have to walk into Bob Michel's office and say, 'Hey, the World Bank appropriation is important,' " Mr. Holling said. "If there is a bottom line, it is that our legislators know how this company ticks."

While not the only logic used to sway votes on Capitol Hill, the financial benefits that flow directly to a host of American interests from the foreign aid program are a key, if not critical, factor in preventing conservative critics from making a serious dent in the program.

With the intense pressure on members of the House to vote for budget-cutting proposals, lobbyists, both in the Carter administration and in the private sector, have found that the economic benefit argument has worked not only to reverse the stands of some conservatives, but also to quiet the fears of moderate junior members concerned that a vote for foreign aid will be held against them in the next election.

"If we can show a freshman that his district gets money out of the program, he's a lot less scared to vote for it," an administration lobbyist said. "If some constituent complains about the vote, he can say, 'Look, there's a GE plant here that employs 1,200 people, a lot of those jobs depend on exports and the plant got $2 million from AID last year.' Once we show him that, then he'll start listening to the merits of the program."

To back this claim up, all the agencies providing foreign aid have developed increasingly sophisticated statistics to demonstrate the benefits to each state.

The Treasury Department has drawn up a set of five, multi-colored maps showing each state's dependence on the $31 billion annual export market to poor countries, the distribution of $2 billion in AID goods and commodity contracts, $786 million in AID service contracts, the allocation of $375 million in U.S. purchases financed through World Bank loans and the $166 million from Inter-American Development Bank loans.

Following a tactic originated by the Agency for International Development, both the World Bank and the Inter-American Development Bank are producing detailed state-by-state breakdowns which show not only how much goes to each state, but also how much goes to each corporation within the state.

To take Illinois as an example, these agencies show contracts totalling $7.9 million for International Harvester in Chicago, $5.8 million for Fiat-Allis Construction Machinery Company in Deerfield, $5.4 million to General Motors in La Grange, $12.1 million to Tabor and Company in Decatur, $36.5 million to Caterpillar Tractor in Peoria and $9.2 million to Deere and Company in Moline.

These detailed maps and charts are making their way into congressional offices in growing numbers, along with lengthy position papers put out by the Treasury Department and the World Bank showing how the U.S. contributions to the international financial institutions are helping to both reduce the trade deficit and to create new markets for American companies.

In a letter to freshman Senator Donald Stewart (D-Ala.), for example, W. Michael Blumenthal, then Secretary of the Treasury, wrote:

"Since the inception of the World Bank in 1946, the total value of project-related procurement of U.S. goods and services financed by all of the banks is more than $8.3 billion, which exceeds our total paid-in contribution to the banks by $2.2 billion.

"I might add that Alabama benefited from $14,593,578 in procurement projects financed by the World Bank and the InterAmerican Development Bank over 1976–1977. . . ."

Because of the interrelationship between foreign policy and the export market, political decisions on the distribution of foreign aid take on added significance to some U.S. companies.

The current debate, for example, over aid to Turkey is publicly cast in terms of the need to maintain an ally in the politically volatile Middle East versus the moral and political pressure of the Greek community against giving Turkey additional assistance until it actively supports a settlement on Cyprus. The market potential in the aid adds, however, a far less publicized dimension to the issue:

"Right now there is a proposal before Congress to give $150 million in supplemental aid to Turkey," the lobbyist for a major Illinois manufacturer said. "Turkey is important to us now that we've lost Iran, especially if this administration wants to maintain a critical alliance with a country sharing a long border with the Soviet Union.

"But for us, Turkey has the potential to be a hell of a market, a market for heavy capital goods. That country needs major construction, but the aid package is being held up in the House.

"The only member of the House really fighting for the package is Paul Findley [(R-Ill.]). Paul is our congressman. He knows the importance of Turkey to the United States and he is not unaware that there is a plant in Springfield [(Ill.]) that employs seven to eight thousand people. Paul is enlightened."

This economic benefit argument is substantiated when the financial consequences to U.S. companies of the 1975 policy decision to grant aid to Syria are examined. In an effort to promote stability in the Middle East, the U.S. approved specific expenditures of $87.6 million for goods to be shipped to Syria between February 28, 1975, and May 30, 1979. The recipients of awards larger than $1 million were:

• International Harvester, $1.6 million; Fiat-Allis Construction Machinery, $7.6 million; Wabco Trade Company, $4 million; Caterpillar Tractor, $34.9 million; Mack Trucks, $11.8 million; Elucid Co., $4.5 million, and Clark International, $3.5 million.

The foreign aid to many of the Middle Eastern countries is one area where there is a sharp conflict between the humanitarian supporters of foreign aid, who contend the supported projects should directly aid the poor, and the major American manufacturing companies, which profit more from such capital intensive development as the construction of airports, dams and power plants.

This conflict has been a running internal dispute within the Agency for International Development. In the early 1970s, in part in reaction to the Vietnam war, the so-called light capital technology, or "hoes and rakes," humanitarian view, was temporarily dominant, although more recently there has been a swing back towards major projects.

The backing of major roads, power plants and airports has been criticized by such members of Congress as Rep. Clarence D. Long (D-2d, Md.) as benefiting the elite of a foreign country while doing little or nothing for the poor.

In dollar terms, however, the direct aid given out by the United States has been going increasingly to Middle East countries where it is used for capital intensive development. The grants and loans are made largely for political reasons, and the U.S. has been unwilling to try to impose guidelines requiring that benefits go directly to the poor.

The House foreign operations subcommittee, which is dominated by such humanitarian supporters of foreign aid as David R. Obey (D-Wis.), Louis Stokes (D-Ohio) and Matthew McHugh (D-N.Y.), has been particularly critical of the way Egypt has been spending the $2.5 billion it has received from the U.S. over the past three years. A subcommittee report found:

"As long as the U.S. continues to put priority on large infrastructure projects, a perception may be created among the Egyptian people that the major beneficiaries of foreign aid are not the poor. . . .

"The committee is of the belief that instead of expensive, labor displacing agricultural mechanization, AID should be encouraging the development of small scale industries which can design and manufacture capital saving technologies in the rural sector."

It is, however, the Egyptian type of development that has produced, for example, contracts totalling $11.3 million for Ratheon & Company, of Waltham, Mass., for microwave relay equipment for the Cairo telephone system; $17 million for Massey Furguson for tractors; $5.5 million for General Motors for trucks and trailers; $8.1 million for Mack Truck for tractors and other vehicles, and $54.9 million for Ward Industries for buses.


# Business Learns to Play New Politics

*First of three articles*

The Sun, February 25, 1980

WASHINGTON—In recent years, the business community has been demonstrating exceptional political muscle, regaining leverage in what had been perceived as a hostile Congress.

This influence has gone beyond the ability to defeat liberal legislation—consumer protection, labor law reform and expanded powers for unions to shut down construction projects.

With the abandonment of competitive instincts in favor of industry-wide coalitions, the development of improved fund-raising mechanisms and the mobilization of both employees and stockholders, the business community has gained the ability to take the initiative to weaken regulation of commercial activities and to shift the tax burden away from corporations.

Adopting the tactics of organized labor and liberal organizations, corporations—of all the institutions in the United states—are proving to be the best equipped to respond to the changes that have affected the style and substance of American politics during the last decade.

By any standard, the business community in 1974 faced what appeared to be overwhelming odds.

Business leaders perceived the scandals that grew out of Watergate—massive and often illegal campaign contributions from corporate executives and disclosures of foreign bribery—as weakening their political influence.

In November 1974, 77 new Democrats were elected to the House, and George Meany, president of the AFL-CIO, was boasting of a "veto-proof Congress."

Even under Richard M. Nixon and Gerald R. Ford, the consumer and environmental movements had won the creation of the Occupational Health and Safety Administration, the Environmental Protection Agency and the Consumer Product Safety Commission.

The public's confidence in business fell more rapidly than its confidence in any of the other nine major institutions, public and private, examined annually by the Louis Harris poll. By 1973, trust in the leaders of large corporations had dropped to the level of confidence placed in members of Congress, and the next year public support of corporate leaders fell another 8 points, to 21 percent.

"The danger had suddenly escalated," Bryce Harlow, special counsel to President Nixon and, as Washington representative for Procter and Gamble, one of the most senior and respected members of the corporate lobbying community, recently recalled.

From this predicament, the business community has rebounded, running up a string of exceptional and unexpected legislative victories that go well beyond the simple defeat of such liberal initiatives as labor law reform or consumer protection. The victories include major changes in the regulatory system, most notably the Federal Trade Commission.

This development did not result from any alteration of the partisan balance in the federal government. Democrats have retained their control of both the House and Senate, and, in 1976, they took over the White House with a president committed to most parts of the now-defeated liberal agenda.

In addition, public opinion has not swung back in favor of business. On the contrary, by 1979 voter trust in business had fallen to 18 percent. The decline has been compounded by what Republican polls show to be intense public suspicion of the major oil companies.

Instead, one of the key factors in the radical shift in the mood of Congress over the last six years was the ability of the business community to recognize vacuums in congressional leadership and move quickly to influence their filling.

Most of these vacuums were generated by the liberal-moderate wing of the Democratic party in what it considered an effort to eliminate abuses of power and to control the influence of special interests.

The theory, rooted in the thinking of such groups as Common Cause and the "New Democratic" clubs that sprang up in the early part of the last decade, was that a more open government would give the public the ability to govern the political decision-making process for the benefit of the common good.

The methods used to open the system have proved, however, most beneficial to those groups whose interest in the outcome of governmental decisions is a sustained economic one.

Business interests have capitalized on the elective tensions of representatives and senators no longer able to depend on the backing of political organizations, and on the diffusion of power resulting from congressional reform. The achievements of what can loosely be described as the business-trade association lobby include the following:

• Fund-raising tactics have been developed to the point where they can now overwhelm the efforts of organized labor. In 1976, corporate and trade association political action committees (PACs) gave $10.7 million to congressional candidates; organized labor committees gave $7.4 million. Two years later, labor contributions grew to $9.9 million, but those of the business and trade association PACs reached $20.8 million.

In addition, business and trade association PACs have taken a page from labor, and increasingly are directing money to conservatives, particularly Republican challengers, rather than to influential Democratic incumbents. In 1976, corporate and trade association PACs almost split their money evenly between the parties. By 1978, Republicans got $12.5 million compared to $8.1 million for Democrats, and the trend is continuing.

• Grass-roots lobbying by corporations and trade associations has become a computerized science. The more aggressive firms have prepared lists by congressional district of managerial employees, production statistics, employment figures and suppliers and distributors. Small business associations have developed comparable techniques that make it possible to target lobbying to key members of a specific subcommittee or to all wavering members of the House before a floor vote.

• In what may be the most important development, competitive instincts have been submerged in favor of forming broad coalitions and alliances among seemingly competitive corporations.

The capacity of businesses to join forces in the legislative arena appears, at present, to equal, if not exceed, that of organized labor. In addition, business appears to have developed far better capacities for anticipating the areas where political decisions will touch on the profit margin, particularly tax legislation.

The results of the political mobilization of the business community, along with the deterioration of the union movement and the waning of the influence of consumer advocates, have been striking:

• All of the major initiatives on the Democratic agenda that business opposed when Jimmy Carter took office have been defeated—labor law reform, common situs picketing, the Consumer Protection Agency, election day registration.

• Majorities in the Senate and House have abandoned the traditional Democratic view that the tax system should be used to reduce the financial burden of the poor and lower-middle class. Instead, an essentially Republican "trickle down" approach, which focuses on establishing business tax incentives and encouraging capital formation, has been accepted.

In this respect, the 95th Congress marked the first time since Democrats took over in 1955 that a tax-cut bill was skewed in favor of the upper-middle class. The bill featured a tax reduction on capital gains—a form of income limited almost exclusively to the upper brackets—and a lowering of the corporate income tax from 48 percent to 46 percent.

The major tax initiatives of the current Congress include a bill that would eliminate a 1976 measure to tax capital gains on inherited wealth and would give businesses an accelerated depreciation rate that would, within five years, mean a tax break in excess of $50 billion a year.

• The regulatory structure created to protect the consumer, the worker and the environment is under sustained attack. There is no question that this session will produce a major reduction in the powers of the Federal Trade Commission. A drive to reduce the inspection powers of OSHA is gaining momentum. Recognizing the strength of the assault, regulatory agencies ranging from the Securities and Exchange Commission to the Environmental Protection Agency are quietly postponing or modifying new initiatives.

The ability of the business community to take advantage of reforms initiated largely by Democratic liberals was reflected in the results of 1974 changes in the federal election code.

The revision in the election laws came in direct response to Watergate. The purpose of setting limits of $1,000 on individual contributions and $5,000 on contributions by political committees was to prevent a repetition of the massive, and often illegal, gifts to political campaigns, almost all of which were donated by corporate executives.

In practice, the 1974 law has become the vehicle for an extensive political mobilization of the corporate community. The legislation, and subsequent court and administrative rulings, in effect codified and placed a stamp of legal approval on the massive growth of political action committees.

By its very nature, the political action committee, once the instrument of the labor unions, lends itself to use by corporations. The chief executive officer of a company can, subject to review by the board of directors and stockholders, order the financing of a political action committee to be picked up by the company.

In addition, in any large firm there is a ready-made constituency of middle- and upper-level management available for solicitation, and the corporation has the ability to collect the money through payroll deduction systems.

The Amoco Political Action Committee, for example, has a payroll deduction system to which over 650 employees make monthly payments ranging from $8 to more than $40, with the result that last year, a non-election year, the PAC raised $167,274.

A similar system at the Eaton Corporation last year raised $75,380 in bi-monthly deductions ranging from the $45 payments by James R. Stover, president and chief executive officer at the firm's Cleveland headquarters, to the $2.99 payments by John S. Rodewig, vice president for trucking operations at the firm's plant in Hounslow, England.

The result of the 1974 law has been more than a tenfold increase in the number of corporate PACs—from 89 to, at last count, 942.

Although money is the most obvious and most easily documentable aspect of the growth of business's political influence, it is not necessarily the most important.

One of the key factors affecting changes in business's political style, both in campaigning and in the legislative process, has been the severe weakening of the power of committee chairmen, political clubs and machines, party organizations and the leadership of the House and Senate.

The attack on these centers of power was largely initiated by those opposed to the Vietnam War: the civil rights movement seeking to force legislation out of committee onto the floor for votes, party activists angered over their denial of rights in the 1968 Democratic convention, the environmental movement seeking to break the ties it perceived between polluting industries and elected officials and reform groups seeking procedural mechanisms to prevent a recurrence of the corruption of the Nixon administration.

While the issues of importance to these groups were admittedly at the top of the public agenda, the groups demonstrated remarkable ability to win a series of legislative victories paralleling those more recently won by the business community. But in gaining the victories, these groups helped alter the methods of winning in Congress; as the interest of these groups has waned, their tactics have been taken over by their adversaries.

The attack by the reformers of the late 1960s and early 1970s on the power of party organizations, committee chairmen and the congressional leadership had the effect of shifting political muscle, both in Congress and in congressional districts, to the groups that were best equipped to make their views known.

In this competition for the attention of elected officials, corporations have demonstrated a far better ability to respond to the changing system of influencing votes.

R. Heath Larry, president of the National Association of Manufacturers, said, in identifying the most important factors behind the resurgence of business's political strength: "First was the decline in the role of party, yielding a new spirit of independence among congressmen—independent of each other, of the president, of the party caucus."

In fact, however, this newfound independence replaced vulnerability to pressure from party and congressional leaders with vulnerability to organized district-based pressures. These were pressures that the consumer, environmental, anti-war and reform movements were initially better prepared to apply—until the business community began to recognize the potential of its own resources.

Describing the new style of lobbying, Wayne H. Smithy, vice president for Washington Affairs for the Ford Motor Company, said: "As long as you could go and get the cooperation of the committee chairman and the ranking member, and maybe a few others, you didn't have to have the vast network we are talking about now."

The vast network to which Mr. Smithy referred includes the mobilization of employees and stockholders, the formation of alliances with suppliers and distributors, and the development of coalitions with competitive industries that share an interest in the defeat or passage of legislation.

When there is legislation before Congress that provokes a broad, shared interest within the business community—either for or against the proposal—the ability to apply pressure has become a developed art form.

In fights over such legislation as that involving the Consumer Protection Agency, common situs picketing or Federal Trade Commission authorization, business can marshal letter-writing campaigns that produce 200,000 or more letters and postcards, although many are form letters, which are given less credence by members of the House and Senate.

More complex methods involve the identification of key businesses and industries within each senator's state or representative's district. The Chamber of Commerce calls letter-writing the "shotgun approach," while the use of a local business leader with a large workforce to whom a member of Congress feels compelled to listen is called in the trade using a "golden bullet."

One of the business community's most successful "golden bullets" this year was the use of Ernst Pepples, vice president of the Brown and Williamson Tobacco Company, of Kentucky, to present the industry case against the use of broad, investigative subpoenas by the Federal Trade Commission.

The chairman of the subcommittee with jurisdiction over the FTC is Senator Wendell H. Ford, a Democrat from Kentucky to whom the tobacco industry in general and Brown and Williamson in particular are key elements in the political landscape. The committee included an amendment in the FTC bill severely restricting the agency's subpeona power.

Some of the more sophisticated companies are, in effect, attempting to invest many of the functions that had been performed by political parties in programs of their own.

The best known of such programs is run by Atlantic Richfield (Arco). The company now spends about $1 million annually for a program in which 15,000 of the firm's 50,000 employees are members of politically active committees, and almost 80,000 stockholders, suppliers and distributors are on a mailing list for company newsletters and publications on political and public policy issues.

Although separate from the firm's fund-raising PAC, the program had its roots in the realization that federal law had, in effect, endorsed certain types of corporate political activity:

"The organization of our whole program started with the idea that we could have a PAC . . . ," Robert P. McElroy, the director, said. "A natural extension of that involvement is personal involvement."

At a time when politics has become an increasingly discredited activity, the

Arco program is attempting to encourage the employees on the committees—most of whom "agree with the things the company agrees with," according to Mr. McElroy—not only to increase political contact, but also to run for office or to become campaign officials.

At another level, the formal legalization of corporate political activity through PACs, along with the discovery of corporate resources to fight legislative battles, produced a reborn aggressiveness among some business leaders, a willingness to engage openly in the political fray.

Although Watergate temporarily prompted many business executives to shy away from comment on politics, the times have now changed. Justin Dart, chairman of Dart Industries, reflected the new mood when he told a reporter in 1978 that talking with politicians "is a fine thing, but with a little money they hear you better."

Similarly, when Kaiser Aluminum decided to initiate a major program involving advertising and the mobilization of employees and stockholders, the chairman, Cornell Maier, declared in a speech: "This is war. The battle is not over our economic system. The battle is over our political system."

# Business's Winning Way with Democrats Shows in Battle over Authority of FTC

Second of three articles

---

The Sun, February 26, 1980

---

WASHINGTON—The recurrent congressional fight over legislation determining the powers of the Federal Trade Commission has become the strongest reflection of the newfound strength of the business community, not only with its traditional ally, the GOP, but also within the Democratic party.

As the legislation wends its way through the House and Senate this session, its course has been marked by the following:

• Sen. Birch Bayh (D-Ind.), a stalwart of the Democratic liberal wing, threatened to sponsor an amendment prohibiting the FTC from regulating the trailer industry, until the agency assured the senator that no final regulations would be issued for at least a year. Elkhart, Ind., is the national center of mobile home manufacturing.

• Sen. Howell Heflin (D-Ala.), who campaigned on behalf of small business, proposed legislation eliminating the FTC's power to order divestiture as a remedy in antitrust cases. The measure was backed by such industry giants as General Mills, Inc., and General Motors Corporation and was killed only after small-business representatives testified that it would eliminate a key source of protection in fights with major corporations for a share of the marketplace.

• Rep. Andrew Maguire (D-N.J.), a staunch proponent of reform voted in committee in support of a proposal to cut off all FTC funds used in generic trademark cases. The amendment was designed to kill a current FTC inquiry into whether the trade name Formica has become an anticompetitive factor in the plastic laminate market. Formica is owned by American Cyanamid, whose headquarters is next door to Mr. Maguire's district.

• As soon as Sen. Wendell H. Ford, chairman of the Senate consumer subcommittee, announced, in effect, that he had given up his fight against amendments restricting the FTC, his office was swamped with more than 200 requests to discuss the legislation, almost all from industry lobbyists.

The industries regulated by the FTC have become a growing element in the sources of money for congressional campaigns, including the fiscally strapped Democratic House and Senate campaign committees.

More than 20 percent of the money raised last year by these committees came from corporate and trade association political action committees, and at least half those PACs have a direct interest in weakening the FTC.

The result of the lobbying has been an exceptionally successful whipsaw effort between the House and Senate.

"We are now going into a conference committee with a pat hand. I don't see how we can lose," a Chamber of Commerce lobbyist said.

"It's as if we were making a fruit salad and the House is bringing the apples and the Senate is bringing the oranges," Jeffrey H. Joseph, head of the Chamber's Regulatory Action Center, said.

The "apples" in the House version include:

• A prohibition against the FTC initiating antitrust cases against agricultural cooperatives, through an amendment specifically designed to kill a current case against Sunkist Growers, Inc. If included in the enacted law, the amendment would represent an unprecedented congressional killing of an ongoing antitrust case in which the FTC has accused the California cooperative of using anticompetitive tactics to corner 75 percent of the Western market in oranges and lemons.

• The commission would be barred from denying exclusive use of trademarks that have become the generic name for a whole line of competitive products, such as Formica or Scotch Tape.

• The funeral home industry would be protected from any efforts by the FTC to establish industrywide regulations governing sales practices.

• All future FTC regulations would be subject to congressional veto. By majority vote, either the House or Senate could independently kill the regulation, and the action would stand unless affirmatively overruled by the other branch of Congress.

Similarly, the Senate "oranges" included:

• A flat prohibition against FTC regulation of the insurance industry.

• A prohibition against FTC regulation of private industry boards such as Underwriters Laboratories that establish standards for consumer products. The groups, often dominated by the corporations already controlling the market, have a major influence over the type of new products that obtain access to retail outlets.

• The FTC would no longer be able to set rules governing advertising based on the standard of "unfairness." Instead, the FTC would be restricted to the standards of "false and deceptive," a limitation that would function to kill the current proposal to set rules governing television advertising aimed at children.

• The FTC would be barred from issuing broad, investigative subpoenas. Instead, the agency would be required to tell the company under investigation "the nature of the conduct of the alleged violation . . . describe the class of documentary material to be produced with definiteness and clarity." Both the tobacco and automobile industries have complained bitterly in the past about broad subpoenas issued by the FTC.

• There would be a flat ban against the FTC ordering used car dealers to inspect cars for sale or to issue warranties on the cars.

The scope to which the business community touches the fiscal nerves not only of the Republican party, but also of the Democrats is reflected in the campaign reports of the Democratic Congressional Dinner Committee.

The dinner committee last year was the key vehicle to raise money for the House and Senate Democratic campaign committees, providing a total of $1.49 million.

Of that amount, $312,825 was raised from corporate and trade association PACs, or about $1 out of every $5. In the case of the FTC, almost every one of those PACs had an indirect interest in placing a leash on the agency.

About half, however, have a very direct interest in the FTC, including, for example, the National Association of Life [insurance] Underwriters, which gave $10,000; agricultural interests seeking exemption from antitrust regulation, $44,600; car manufacturers and dealers, $9,000; savings and loan and other credit interests, $17,000; corporations opposed to either the FTC's attempt to regulate industry-standard groups or trademarks, more than $20,000.

The total amount given by political action committees associated with organized labor or other employee groups to the congressional dinner committee last year was $159,000.

The ability of the business community to reward members of Congress for "correct" voting was overwhelmingly demonstrated after the 1977 House defeat of common situs picketing legislation giving construction unions additional leverage to close down projects through strikes.

The bill was an essential part of organized labor's legislative package, and of particular importance to the beleaguered building and construction trades unions that have seen a steady decline of membership and a steady growth of non-union construction.

It was considered almost certain of passage at the start of the 95th Congress in January 1977. But by the time the vote was taken on March 23, what had been solid majorities in the House collapsed and the bill failed 205 to 217.

Between 1975, when the last prior vote had been taken, and March 1977, 11 Democrats switched from support to opposition. Those changes particularly angered organized labor which, in the case of many of those 11 members, had provided large sums of money and manpower in the 1976 election. In 1978, there was a sharp reduction in labor support for the 11, dropping from a total of $166,987 in 1976 to $97,820.

Rep. Harold E. Ford (D-Tenn.), for example, saw a decline in organized labor financial backing from $28,750 in 1976 to $10,990 in 1978. For James D. Santini (D-Nev.) it fell from $26,517 to $12,100. John R. Breaux (D-La.) went from $6,600 to $430 and Mike McCormack (D-Wash.), from $23,900 to $12,100.

But, in every case except one, Albert Gore (D-Tenn.) who had no 1978 opponent, the loss of labor backing was more than made up by additional business and trade association PAC contributions.

From a 1976 total from business and trade associations of $177,208 the group shot up to $346,293 in 1978, or $2,098 more than their combined total of $344,195 from business and labor in 1976.

Mr. Breaux, for example, lost a total of $6,170 in labor contributions, but business and trade association PAC gifts shot up from $21,600 in 1976 to $41,350 in 1978. For Mr. Ford, the increase was from $4,100 to $29,750. Mr. McCormack went from $18,375 to $42,675 while Mr. Santini went from $39,308 to $58,449. The tactic of targeting money to persons considered sympathetic on key issues is used by both organized labor and by business groups.

The phenomenal growth of corporate and trade association PACs, while significant, it equaled in importance by the extensive politicization of company officials running the gamut from small-town car dealers through the middle- and upper-echelon executives of multinational corporations.

*Hardware Age,* for example, was, a few years ago, one of a multitude of trade publications, in this case a vehicle for articles on marketing, storing and promoting new products.

In a reflection of the change in tone endemic in almost all industry trade associations, the publication is now running articles on such issues as "CLOUT: How To Get It" and editorials on "Grass roots politics—corporate style."

In September 1978, the *Savings and Loan News* put out an entire issue not just on federal legislation, but also on the political mobilization of employees of savings and loan institutions.

W. Dean Cannon, Jr., executive vice president of the California Savings and Loan League, suggested that savings and loan officials give employees "specific assignments to work in politics" and added that salary hikes "might well be tied directly to his involvement in the political assignment you have given him."

The politicization of some businesses extends to almost all commercial activities that touch on the federal government. The scope of this is reflected by some of the firms and associations that have formed fund-raising political action committees: Dr. Pepper, Avon Products, the American Fishing Tackle Manufacturers and the Association of Corrugated Converters.

Major corporations and some branches of the Chamber of Commerce have tried to institutionalize this political activity through the formation of congressional action committees or various types of employee and shareholder efforts generally run under the imprimatur of "civic action programs."

Intertwined, but separate from their fund-raising PACs, such firms as Dart Industries, SmithKline Corporation, Kaiser Aluminum & Chemical and General Electric Company have initiated expensive advertising campaigns and efforts to mobilize employees in support of positions adopted by the companies.

In the case of the Atlantic-Richfield Company, the employee and stockholder programs cost the firm about $1 million a year. Mobil Corporation's advertising program costs about $3.5 million.

There are no accurate estimates of the total cost of this corporate activity, although one House subcommittee has made an estimate of at least $1 billion a year.

The Barry Wright Corporation, of Watertown, Mass., for example, claims to have generated 3,800 letters from stockholders to members of Congress in favor of the reduction in capital gains taxes that was finally included in the 1978 tax bill.

Using a newsletter called *Point of View,* the firm also claimed to have produced more than 350 letters to senators in favor of the 1978 filibuster against the Labor Law Reform bill.

# Business Coalitions Form
# to Win Congressional Clout

### Last of three articles

---

The Sun, February 27, 1980

---

WASHINGTON—Early last year, a coalition of such seemingly diverse groups as the American Bankers Association, the National Forest Products Association, the National Association of Realtors and the Authors' League of America began to form around an obscure provision in the tax code known as "carryover basis."

Meeting first in the bankers' association Washington office, the group soon grew so large that sessions were shifted to the Chamber of Commerce Building, as the National Association of Manufacturers, the Independent Oilmen and the National Association of Home Builders joined the alliance.

The alliance was one of many that have begun to dominate Washington lobbying, as business and trade associations abandon competitive instincts to form cooperative efforts for the benefit of all the participants.

The coalition's goal was repeal of a section of the 1976 tax reform act that attempted for the first time in a generation to increase taxes on inherited wealth.

Opponents claimed the law was cumbersome and impossible to administer, although there was also the private fear that it represented the first step toward capital gains taxation at death, a major expansion of tax liability for large estates.

Each of the groups in the coalition mobilized its members. Congressman began to hear from local bankers vehemently opposed to the tax provision. Many of the bankers not only had estates affected by the law, but also, as trust officers, had to administer the law for some of their best clients.

The bankers were joined by oilmen, cattlemen and the Farm Bureau, forming a nonprofit corporation to win repeal of the carryover basis provision. The group, called FAIR (Families Associated for Inalienable Rights) hired as its chief lawyer former Senator Carl T. Curtis of Nebraska, recently retired as the top Republican on the Senate Finance Committee.

Even though the carryover basis, in revisions proposed by the Treasury Department, would have affected only the top 2.6 percent of estates—a tiny and generally Republican constituency—the tactics of the alliance have been remarkably successful with legislators of both parties.

Last November 19 the Senate voted 81 to 4 to repeal the carryover basis and blocked a threatened veto by President Carter by attaching the amendment to the windfall profits tax bill, Mr. Carter's top priority for energy legislation. It is almost guaranteed to become law.

This lobbying-by-alliance now follows almost a casebook procedure:

A lobbyist spots a bill in a subcommittee that could threaten his company and seeks to broaden the counterattack by recruiting other lobbyists whose employers' interests are affected.

The process is facilitated by the Chamber of Commerce, which conducts regular breakfasts for Washington corporate and trade association representatives, with more than 400 persons in attendance. The lobbyist is apt to find an informal coalition already in existence—more than 55 such strategy groups have been organized so far, running the gamut from a Securities and Exchange Regulations Committee to a Water Strategy Group.

If the issue appears to have the potential of moving through committee and onto the floor, two steps are often taken: hiring a major lobbyist to coordinate legislative strategy and beginning to marshal the troops in the boondocks.

The major lobbyists most often hired include:

• Timmons and Company, run by William E. Timmons and Tom Korologos, both legislative strategists for former presidents Richard M. Nixon and Gerald R. Ford, whose clients include the American Petroleum Institute, H. J. Heinz Company, G. D. Searle and Company, and Standard Oil of Indiana.

• The firm of Patton, Boggs and Blow, of which Thomas Hale Boggs, Jr., son of the former Democratic House majority leader, is a partner. The firm's 99 legislative clients include Atlantic Richfield Company, General Mills, Inc., General Motors Corporation, Lehman Brothers, Montgomery Ward & Co., and the Nestle Co., Inc.

• Charls E. Walker Associates, whose namesake was deputy secretary of the treasury under President Nixon. The firm's clients include the Bechtel Corporation, American Airlines, Bethlehem Steel Corporation, Ford Motor Company, General Electric Company, Procter & Gamble Company and the Weyerhaeuser Company.

The lobbyists' specialty is identification of wavering members of Congress on any given issue and the ability to determine the best means for persuasion. For example, a legislator suspects that the bill would benefit big business only, so he needs pressure from operators of small firms; he wants a detailed, but simple, economic justification of the legislation to legitimize the vote to constituents; he needs to be shown how the bill will help (or hurt) employment and specific businesses in his district.

The practice is called "grass-roots lobbying" and consists of organizing constituent support in a highly sophisticated fashion involving the use of computers. Natural bases of this support are a corporation's executive and managerial level employees and stockholders, and members of local Chambers of Commerce, the National Association of Manufacturers and a host of such smaller trade associations as the Restaurant Dealers, Automobile Dealers or the Trailer Manufacturers Association. They are among the more than 1,400 such groups which have blossomed in recent years in response to increased governmental regulation.

When the issue cuts a wide swath across the business community, the potential of this alliance is enormous. More than 250,000 letters and postcards to the Congress have been generated and countless Rotary and Kiwanis club meetings have been turned into angry forums demanding congressional action.

Combined with another key ingredient—money—these seemingly simple tactics, which in fact require a concentrated effort approaching the doggedness of an East Baltimore political leader trying to guarantee a solid turnout, have succeeded in altering the ideological balance in Congress in less than eight years.

To a certain extent, these developments reflect other factors: a public wariness of governmental regulation and intrusion, and an economy troubled by escalating inflation and declining productivity which has made Congress more sympathetic to pleas for regulatory relief by business.

But the conversion of these economic trends and public doubts into a massive shift in congressional ideology required a coordinated effort to politicize the business community.

Essential elements of this politicization were the formation in 1972 of the Business Roundtable, the revitalization of the Chamber of Commerce and the conversion of the National Federation of Independent Businessmen into an effective lobbying arm.

In terms of dollars alone, the Business Roundtable (BRT) represents the elite of the corporate community. Of the 195 members, 112 are in the top 200 of the Fortune 500 list of the top industrial corporations. Thirty-seven others are among the 50 largest banks, life insurance firms, diversified financial companies, retailers, transportation companies and utilities.

With a professional staff of 20 split evenly between New York and Washington, the BRT—whose members are limited to chief executive officers—operates with an annual budget of $3.5 million. But that figure in no way reflects the corporate resources available, for example, to Reginald H. Jones, chairman of General Electric, in lobbying on tax legislation, or to A. W. Clausen, president of the Bank of America, in opposing proposed Securities and Exchange Commission regulations.

More important, the multiplicity of almost all the BRT members' plants, suppliers and distributors gives the organization a network of avenues for direct access through every congressional district in the nation.

During the 1978 lobbying against the consumer protection bill, a superficial reflection of the scope of this influence was shown in the following conversation between two BRT staff members discussing strategy regarding specific members of Congress, as recorded by *Fortune:*

"Henry Gonzalez of San Antonio . . . Should we use Sears? We have problems with Jake Pickle on this, I'm not sure we can get him. . . . Let's ask Sears about Gonzalez.

"Delaney of Long Island . . . Bristol Meyers is close to Delaney, let Bill Greif handle that. . . .

"Gaydos of Pennsylvania. . . . Ask Alcoa if they'll do it, John Harper was very enthusiastic about this one. . . . Hatfield of Continental could do it, but I hate to ask him.

"Marks of Sharon, Pennsylvania. . . . Ask Ferguson of General Foods to call Kirby of Westinghouse about Marks. . . .

"Gore of Tennessee. . . . Carrier Corporation and TRW. . . . Do we really have a chance with Gore? We really think we do. Ask Lloyd Hand of TRW."

The chief function of the Business Roundtable, however, has been to provide big business with a forum within which to establish common policy on such issues as antitrust, taxation, pension law, occupational health and labor legislation.

In addition, active participation by the chief executive officers has not only provided an invaluable lobbying tool, but it has also helped the larger process in which political participation, both the making of contributions and active involvement in legislative fights, is becoming an integral part of the responsibilities of corporate executives.

In both public and private, representatives of other business organizations are often critical of the BRT, although it is difficult to tell whether the criticisms are based on envy of the extraordinary access available to BRT members to the executive and legislative branches or on actual failures in lobbying.

In addition, there is a widespread suspicion, based in large part on the BRT's private negotiations during Senate consideration of antitrust legislation, that the chief executives of the major corporations will abandon alliances with smaller companies and even the Chamber of Commerce when they can cut a private deal to their benefit.

When the 1978 tax bill went to a House-Senate conference committee, James Mike McKevitt of the National Federation of Independent Businessmen said "the 'bigs' lobbied against us and squashed us," acknowledging that small business lost key provisions while big business came out far ahead in the tax fight that year.

Mr. McKevitt's organization epitomizes the tactics of computerized grass-roots lobbying.

Unlike most business organizations which serve a variety of communications and social purposes in addition to lobbying, the NFIB exists entirely to exercise political influence.

Its 596,000 members contribute between $35 and $500 based on each firm's willingness to pay, exclusively for political leverage in Washington and some state capitals.

Information about each of the members is coded into a computer through two key systems: a three-digit standard industrial classification that, for example, breaks down food stores into groceries, meat markets, fruit stores, candy outlets, dairy products and bakeries, and then by congressional district.

The entire membership is regularly polled on issues before Congress. Each member of Congress receives not only a tabulation of the results of these "votes," but is given a computer printout of how each member of the NFIB living in his district cast his ballot.

The twofold system gives the NFIB the ability to target pressure by specific congressional district and to identify its members affected by a particular bill.

In addition, the NFIB is attempting to computerize information already developed by such established lobbies as the American Bankers Association or the chamber: the identification of organization members who have strong political or personal ties to incumbent members of Congress.

The ABA claims to have a network of 1,200 "contact backers" who have served as campaign treasurers or chairmen or are particularly close to specific members of Congress. Those contacts provide a means of direct access.

Mr. McKevitt claims to have an "action council" of 10,000 NFIB members who attended school with their congressman, worked on campaigns or have some other means of guaranteeing direct access.

In fact, however, many of those on the NFIB's action council are those who, when they first joined, simply indicated a willingness to make an extra effort to contact their congressmen. Many of them do not, in fact, have close ties to the incumbent.

Despite this, the NFIB has gained a reputation on Capitol Hill and among fellow lobbying groups as one of the more effective organizations.

"A congressman is impressed when Reg Jones (chief executive officer of General Electric) makes a personal visit," one aide commented, "but he may say to himself, 'Jones thinks this bill is important but he doesn't vote in my district.' When he sees a list of actual small businessmen who are active in their churches and Kiwanis, he has to think twice."

The group is more often faulted, mostly in private, for occasional failures to recognize and protect the interests of small businesses as opposed to larger, capital-intensive large corporations.

Along with the acknowledged drubbing on the 1978 tax bill, the NFIB is currently supporting an accelerated tax depreciation bill known as 10-5-3, which some other representatives of small business contend would give a disproportionate share of the benefits to large corporations.

The 10-5-3 bill was created by a coalition of organizations including the NFIB, the Roundtable, the Chamber, the National Association of Manufacturers and the American Council for Capital Formation, an alliance in which major corporations outweigh smaller firms.

Operating somewhere between the Roundtable and the NFIB, although with ties that are generally conceded to be closer to big business, the Chamber of Commerce has shifted in the past decade from decaying grande dame of the business community to a clearinghouse and catalyst for much of the revived political activity taking place.

A critical juncture for the Chamber occurred in the mid-1970s.

The potential for legislative disaster was recognized by the elite of Washington's lobbying community—Bryce Harlow of Procter and Gamble; William Whyte, of United States Steel Corporation; Albert D. Bourland, Jr., of General Motors; Don A. Goodall, of American Cyanamid Company—many of whom turned to the Chamber as the best vehicle, along with the newly created Roundtable, to begin a business counterattack.

"I had the strong feeling we had to prevent business from being rolled up and being put in the trash basket by that [the 94th] Congress," Mr. Harlow recalled.

Since then, the Chamber has about doubled its membership to 90,000 and now has an annual budget of $30 million. The Chamber has been the most active promoter of developing corporate political action committees, cultivation of mass-mailing lobbying campaigns from the "grass roots," the formation of both local Chamber-based "congressional action committees" and "corporate action committees," and, most recently, of concerted business opposition to the establishment of new federal regulations.

The Chamber refused to give out a list of all the corporations with action committees, but a check of a small sampling of the firms the Chamber would identify suggested that the figures may be inflated. Richard Kopke, who directs the General Motors Political Action Committee, said, for example, that the corporation has done little or nothing along the lines of the ARCO program, and that most of its political work is restricted to fund-raising.

While some members of Congress dismiss the Chamber and the organization has been accused of distorting facts, exaggerating the influence of its membership and encouraging letter-writing campaigns that have little relationship to the views of the general public, there is no question that the Chamber has helped create a number of almost institutionalized mechanisms for influencing Congress.

As members of the House and Senate are increasingly unable to depend on local political organizations for direction on key issues before Congress, the ability to persuade even a small percentage of the business community to make its view known carries enormous weight and is a key factor in the changing of the ideological tone of Congress.

# The Battle of the Budget

*The Nation,* May 10, 1980

The decision of Democratic Congressional leaders to adopt a balanced budget for 1981 reflects a recent major shift in American politics, the emergence of a politics of scarcity, replacing what has been a three-decade-long assumption of continued growth and abundance. Signs of this shift have grown more evident since the Vietnam War ended and OPEC imposed its oil embargo in 1973. Yet as push comes to shove in the halls of Congress, the Democratic party has shown that it is ill-equipped for the escalating legislative battle for the federal dollar and the federal tax break. As a result, Democrats face the prospect of an increasingly divided party, as factions on the left, particularly organized labor and blacks, disassociate themselves from the majority. Republicans, for their part, are placed in the quandary of whether to accept what amounts to their own fiscal policy offered by the majority party or to demand additional concessions and champion a more stringent—but certifiably Republican—austerity.

As the debate in Congress shifts from the relatively peaceful arguments over the cutting up of a growing pie to a bitter fight over which groups will be forced to take smaller shares, the Democratic majority is being threatened on at least three fronts: (1) the business community, which is far better prepared not only to protect its interests but to capitalize on the situation than organized labor, blacks or any current coalition on the left; (2) advocates of increased defense spending, who have won the day politically, and (3) the Democrats' own leadership, which is unable to devise a strategy of austerity that protects the party's traditional constituencies—a failing that is working to undermine, if not to eliminate, the fragile resurgence of a partisan loyalty during the past year in the House of Representatives.

Throughout the last six years, the business community has displayed an extraordinary array of political skills, moving from a post-Watergate nadir to a peak of influence from which it now, in effect, dictates the nation's tax laws. Business has also demonstrated an ability to block Democratic social initiatives—labor law reform, consumer protection, Election Day registration, common situs picketing. On top of that, it is effectively pushing for a major rollback in the powers of the Federal Trade Commission, the one Federal agency with a combined mission of insuring competition in the marketplace and protecting the consumer, and mounting a substantial attack on the Occupational Health and Safety Administration.

This business resurgence stemmed from an astute recognition of the important changes that have recently taken place in the structure of Congress, in Federal election law, in the techniques of winning Congressional elections and a recognition of the importance of having intellectual and academic endorsement of economically advantageous positions.

The large majority of members of Congress are no longer allied with any political organization. While theoretically this may increase the independence of each Congressman, in actuality it has eliminated a source of dependable electoral support which had encouraged greater voting independence. To capitalize on the reelection anxieties and hypersensitivity to murmurs of discontent from constituents that members of Congress now feel because of their enhanced vulnerability, the business community has turned to "grass-roots" lobbying and has made it a computerized science. National groups like the Chamber of Commerce and the National Federation of Independent Businessmen have developed smoothly operating machinery that will generate mail and personal lobbying on behalf of member businesses affected by specific legislation, whether it be restaurant owners worried about higher minimum wages or nonunion contractors in need of Davis-Bacon repeal, all targeted with pinpoint accuracy on undecided, swing-vote members of key subcommittees. Similarly, corporations tap constituencies of management-level personnel and stockholders for protests against impending legislation that management has flagged as harmful.

The Federal election "reforms" of 1974 not only spawned a plethora of corporate political action committees, they also altered the fundamental motivation behind political contributions. The old system encouraged businessmen to contribute to advance their own competitive position against other businesses; thus the host of corporate donors to President Nixon's Committee to Re-Elect the President sought favorable treatment in tax, antitrust or regulatory proceedings. But PAC contributions encourage business to act as a class, exerting combined financial leverage on Congress to win a lower capital gains rate, for example, or to weaken the subpoena power of the Federal Trade Commission or to exempt most industries from OSHA inspections. Of all the institutions in the United States, the corporation is the one most ideally suited to use the political action committee as a vehicle to raise money. Establishing a committee is an act of company policy and members of management know that their financial contribution goes with the job—and the corporation will be happy to arrange a convenient system of payroll deductions.

The original impetus behind the revitalization of the business community was a pervasive fear that the corporate scandals growing out of the Watergate proceedings and the major gains by Democrats in the 1974 elections would achieve just what George Meany was calling for, a "veto-proof Congress." As Bryce Harlow, former special counsel to President Nixon and, at that time, a key strategist for business interests in his capacity as lobbyist for Procter and Gamble, recalled, "The danger had suddenly escalated." Similarly, Jeffrey Joseph, head of the Chamber of Commerce's regulatory division, said, "Even under Nixon and

Ford we had seen the creation of OSHA, EPA [the Environmental Protection Agency] and the Consumer Product Safety Commission. We didn't know what to expect next."

As it turned out, however, the Democratic party, particularly in Congress, failed to revive as a coherent force. Although the divisions created by the civil rights and anti-war movements had begun to heal, a new split emerged. The new Democrats elected in 1974 and 1976 represented largely white middle-class suburban districts. Their interest lay less with substantive legislation than with procedural reform of Congress. These reforms coalesced into a concerted attack on the institutional power of committee chairmen through such measures as requiring their election by the full caucus, diffusing authority through the establishment of semiautonomous subcommittees and restricting the ability to horse-trade by requiring open sessions and recorded votes. For the junior members, many very aggressive and very bright, procedural reform was the route to quick prominence; seniority was a liability and solid results could be achieved by a freshman or sophomore.

But when it came to substantive legislation, the reformer–old-guard conflict served to maintain splits within the party. The old guard was no longer the collection of Southern conservatives who had used their power to prevent legislation from going to the floor. Instead, the committee chairmanships were in the process of shifting to a generation of politicians with ties to organized labor, many of whom represented urban, or Northern, or both, constituencies: on Judiciary, Peter Rodino, Jr., of Newark; on Rules, Richard Bolling of Kansas City; on Interior and Insular Affairs, Morris Udall of Tucson; on House Administration, Frank Thompson, Jr., of Trenton. The accession to power of these chairmen closely coincided with the replacement in 1977 of Carl Albert by Thomas (Tip) O'Neill, Jr., as Speaker, a shift that marked the high tide of Northern, big-city dominance, which, as the 1980 census produces a shift in power in the House to the Sunbelt and to the suburbs, will soon begin to recede.

The pre-eminence of the reform issue, coupled with the legislative incompetence of President Carter, transformed the Democratic agenda for the 95th Congress of 1977–78 into a farce. The business community capitalized on the resultant diffused authority and used its increasingly sophisticated lobbying tactics to defeat every major domestic initiative. The House defeated consumer protection and common situs picketing [see Thomas Ferguson and Joel Rogers, "Labor Law Reform and Its Enemies," *The Nation*, January 6–13, 1979], and the head count on Election Day registration was so unfavorable that its sponsors didn't bother bringing it to the floor. Legislation that passed the House was either filibustered by the Senate (e.g., labor law reform) or completely revised there (e.g., the energy program of 1977).

When the 96th Congress was seated in 1979, however, a new tone was discernible. One of the first signs that O'Neill's patient cultivation of partisan loyalty was beginning to bear fruit was a vote by the Democratic caucus to consider the case of Michigan Democrat Charles Diggs, Jr., in closed session.

Diggs had been convicted of taking kickbacks from Government employees and the issue was whether he should continue to hold his chairmanship of the District of Columbia Committee. The decision to bar the press and the public would not have been possible two years before, and it reflected a willingness to treat the controversial issue as a party matter, not as a subject for grandstanding to the media. At the same time, the freshman Republicans inadvertently worked to heal Democratic wounds by themselves taking up the banner of procedural reform and converting the maneuvers in the House from an intra-Democratic party dispute into a partisan debate, with the Republicans assuming their customary role as critics of the majority party. Further enhancing the prospects for stronger Democratic unity was the fact that key Democrats elected in 1974 and 1976 had taken their first steps up the seniority ladder. Richard Gephardt of Missouri, Anthony Toby Moffett of Connecticut, Timothy Wirth of Colorado and Leon Panetta, Henry Waxman and Norman Mineta of California had all gained subcommittee chairmanships or seats on the Ways and Means or Budget committees, and in the process had become more interested in substantive legislation than in procedural change.

The most significant development was the retirement of James Delaney of Queens, New York, and his replacement as Rules Committee chairman by Bolling. Bolling's ideological allegiance lay with the leadership and, through the Rules Committee, he began to use the panel's power to delineate the scope of floor debate and the range of amendments permitted on key bills. The importance of this rather arcane power cannot be overestimated. When welfare reform legislation came under consideration, for example, the Rules Committee barred most Republican "workfare" amendments which many Democrats would have found it politically difficult to vote against, but which also would have made the legislation unacceptable to the Carter Administration. The use of this parliamentary technique known as the "partially closed rule" to set limits on floor consideration is still in the embryonic stage, but it has already played a key role in the House's passage of a measure to restrict contributions by political action committees and of the windfall profits tax. Under this process, the critical vote becomes whether or not the House will approve the "rule," a vote that tends to encourage partisan, rather than ideological, divisions. On these votes, as well as on past budget resolutions, Speaker O'Neill had begun to fashion a slim majority composed exclusively of Democrats, who range from members of the Black Congressional Caucus on the left to some of the moderate to conservative Southern Democrats on the right. This new majority was one of the first concrete manifestations of a revived sense of unity within the party.

The coalition is a fragile one, however, and will almost certainly be shattered by the drive to balance the budget. All fifteen black Congressmen oppose the move for a balanced 1981 Federal budget, and they are sure to be joined by fifty to seventy liberal whites. With the budget unquestionably the dominant issue this year, the O'Neill majority, already operating on a paper-thin margin of fewer than five votes on many issues, will have to be reshaped, probably to include

Republicans; in that case, it would no longer be the O'Neill majority.

Equally important, the Democrats advocating a balanced budget make two essential assumptions: (1) cutting tax "expenditures" by closing tax loopholes must not be used as a means of expunging budgetary red ink, because that opens up the Democrats to the charge that they are raising taxes to balance the budget and (2) the defense budget must be increased, the only question being by how much. Refusal to close tax loopholes in order to capture more revenue inevitably favors the business community, which is the beneficiary of most politically vulnerable tax expenditures. On the opening day of the House Budget Committee hearings, one of the first requests of Richard Lesher, president of the U.S. Chamber of Commerce, was that the panel leave tax expenditures untouched. As for the inviolability of the defense budget—about 24 percent of the total—the net result can only be that a larger share of the cuts will have to fall on domestic programs.

In the short term, the political consequences of the majority party's inability to make a plausible case for austerity, one that key voting blocs such as blacks and labor will accept as equitable, may have been visible in the Pennsylvania primary, in which Senator Edward Kennedy captured both blocs. The black vote alone was essential to Carter's 1976 victory, providing the margin in the South and in his 51 percent victory in New Jersey and 52 percent success in New York. The 1976 Presidential election marked, in sharp contrast to 1972, a partial return to earlier voting patterns that were closely correlated with income. While George McGovern's support had little or no relationship to economic status, Carter consistently did best among the lowest income levels in every major geographic or ethnic group, from blacks to Catholics to white Southern Protestants. An economic policy that fails to honor this election debt risks serious repercussions at the polls in November.

In the longer run, a policy of continued fiscal restraint will force Democrats to abandon the basic tool the party has used to reward loyal constituent groups: expansion of existing programs (the Comprehensive Employment Training Act, countercyclical aid, summer jobs for youth) and the initiation of new ones—in effect, the outlay side of the budget. If Federal spending remains stagnant, the political fight will shift to the redistribution of the tax burden, a technique of rewarding supporters and punishing opponents that cuts across the entire economic spectrum. It is in this arena that the liberal wing of the Democratic party is at its weakest.

Of all the committees in the House, O'Neill's influence is probably least on the Ways and Means Committee, where all tax legislation must originate. The panel is already controlled by a coalition of conservative Democrats and Republicans who demonstrated their strength in 1978. That year marked the first time since Democrats took over Capitol Hill in 1955 that a major tax cut, the Revenue Act of 1978, was skewed in favor of the upper-middle class. The minority liberal faction will be further weakened by the retirement of Charles Vanik, Democrat of Ohio, and by the likelihood that James Corman, Democrat of California, will be defeated.

In the ongoing battle over the apportionment of the tax burden, business interests have been quietly winning a series of major concessions on one of the least studied sources of revenue—wealth. In contrast to income, wealth is far less equally distributed throughout the population: in 1976, the top 5 percent of the population received 15.6 percent of the income; the most recent study by the Internal Revenue Service of wealth in 1972 showed that the top 1 percent of the population held 30 percent of the wealth. While the income tax rate structure has remained relatively constant, Congress has done the following over the past five years to lessen the tax burden on wealth: In 1976, the maximum inheritance tax was lowered from 77 to 70 percent and the basic exemption nearly tripled from $60,000 to $175,000. Two years later, the amount of capital gains excluded from regular taxation was raised from 50 to 60 percent. Of the $2.2 billion reduction, about 80 percent went to those making more than $50,000 a year, who in turn make up less than 1 percent of the nation's taxpayers. This year, Congress has enacted legislation repealing altogether a provision known as carry-over basis, which was the first attempt in a generation to tax the increase in the value of inherited property and securities that occurred before the benefactor's death—an extension of the principle that a living person must pay taxes on capital gains. Although carry-over basis was designed to close this loophole for only the richest 2.6 percent of the population, a largely Republican constituency that owns about 75 percent of the wealth, it was repealed by strong majorities in both House and Senate, despite Democratic control.

On a broader, theoretical level, Congressional Democrats, unable to shift to the left and come to grips with the possibility that some of our current economic problems may result in part from the shape of the private marketplace—the share of industrial assets owned by the largest 0.1 percent of manufacturing corporations grew from 41 percent in 1950 to 63.1 percent in 1976—have been overwhelmed by Republican "supply-side" economics. This theory, a trickle-down approach, holds that the answer to the failure of American corporations to keep pace in productivity and capital investment is to provide tax relief. It was the basis for the capital gains reduction in 1978 and it is the ground for the widespread Congressional support for granting business a sharply accelerated capital depreciation schedule starting this year. The strength of the pro-business advocates among taxwriters in Congress was reflected in the willingness of the Chamber of Commerce to sacrifice the goal of a balanced budget if, instead, a tax cut were to be enacted. At this stage in the process, the drive to achieve both a tax cut benefiting business and a balanced budget has a majority behind it in both houses of Congress, a development that, at least in the next election, will make it very difficult for the Democratic party to hold together what remains of the New Deal coalition.

# House Majority Leader Wright
# in for Tough Election Fight

---

*The Sun,* September 24, 1980

---

FORT WORTH—In this city where the railroad once ended and the West began, Jim Wright took a first step into politics 34 years ago with a demonstration that he might be a liberal but he was not a "damn sissy."

At a breakfast meeting of the American Legion back then, a half-drunk Dub Tucker bumped into the 22-year-old firebrand of the left and called him both a damn sissy and "a Commie sonofabitch."

Mr. Tucker then, according to Representative Wright, "swung a haymaker, a club-handed left hook. I saw it coming, rolled with its motion just as it impacted on my face, pivoted, dug my left fist as hard as I could into his ample midriff, and then my right. As he backed away, I followed in step and hit him six more times before he fell, crumpled like a sack of wet laundry."

The incident, Mr. Wright suggests, "may have been the best thing that happened in my race for the legislature from Parker county that year. Word spread, and the episode won me a begrudging acceptance from many of those" who eyed his adamant opposition to censorship at the University of Texas with suspicion.

This year, Mr. Wright, now the 57-year-old Democratic majority leader of the House, is in a tough political fight, nasty by even Texas standards. It is a fight in which there is no Dub Tucker, and Mr. Wright is no longer the young reformer, but a Democratic politician whose aspirations to leadership are caught in increasinglycomplextrendsinhisdistrictandthecountry.

A born-again evangelical political movement is questioning his "Christianity," a multimillionaire is running ads in the local paper telling him it's time "to hang up your spikes", and a well-financed Republican challenger in this heartland of Pentagon spending is telling voters Mr. Wright is soft on defense.

Compounding these problems are contrasts between Representative Wright's current circumstances and his image as a man with populist roots. He won that image as a young politician who advocated guaranteed jobs for everyone and a direct tax on oil and gas production.

The tarnishing on the image has come from recent news stories disclosing controversial gas well investments. These opportunities for profits were provided by Texas oil barons whose international interests Mr. Wright has advocated in Washington, including an attempt to get Egyptian President Anwar el-Sadat to help out one of the firms.

Mr. Wright finds himself in a similar, if not quite parallel, bind on the direction of his politics today.

He feels his constituents are moving to the right on a number of issues, but his main concern in recent years has been to solidify his position as majority leader and to protect his chances of becoming speaker.

The only threat to Mr. Wright's House leadership position would come from the left—in 1977 he defeated Rep. Phillip Burton (D-Calif.), a very liberal representative, by just one vote to win the majority leadership. Since winning the post he has moved from the right of his party toward the center, reversing his increasingly conservative movement before 1977.

Meanwhile, his district has become, if not more conservative, more deeply divided. It contains strong labor, Mexican-American and black voting constituencies, but at the same time conservative businessmen have been moving out of the Democratic party and into a growing Republican movement, and the district is fertile ground for growing role of evangelical Christians in right-wing politics.

"You know, of all the things I have to do—majority leader, helping my colleagues get elected, family—I find the most tiring of all is campaigning," the former World War II aviator commented at the end of a long day in the district.

Despite the fatigue, however, a sharp edge of anger takes hold of Jim Wright's voice when he talks of one political element—the influence of the Rev. James Robison, an evangelical minister affiliated with the First Baptist Church of Euless, just outside Fort Worth.

"It is a potentially dangerous thing for anyone to assume to himself the self-righteous presumption to announce the will of the Almighty," Mr. Wright comments.

Mr. Robison is a leading figure in the "new right" Christian movement. He has given Mr. Wright's voting record a very low morality "rating."

"Jim Wright has hurt this country. Last year, he voted wrong 99 percent of the time and sold the country down the river," Mr. Robison says.

His "wrong" votes, according to Christian Voice, the organization that compiles the rating, include opposition to the lifting of sanctions against Rhodesia, a "no" vote on a 1979 amendment to retain the language of the mutual defense treaty with Taiwan and opposition to an amendment that would have barred federal employment payments to "persons named by the General Accounting Office as violators of the law."

Another relationship that ended in adversity surfaces when Mr. Wright talks about H. E. Chiles, president of the Western Company and majority owner of the Texas Rangers baseball team:

"I guess Eddie Chiles feels anybody who has a baseball club ought to own at least one congressman."

Mr. Chiles, once a loyal Wright backer whose interests, including federally supported loans on oil rigs in the North Sea, have been looked after by Mr. Wright in Washington, is now the major angel behind the GOP challenger, Jim Bradshaw.

A politician used to taking the offensive and unaccustomed to a challenge in his home district, Mr. Wright appears to have been pushed back on his heels, slightly off balance, by the sudden emergence of vehement opposition in this Fort

Worth district he has dominated since 1954.

Early on in the election, the Wright-Bradshaw race was targeted by the Republican Congressional Campaign Committee and by a host of conservative organizations. They sensed, in the words of one National Conservative Political Action Committee staff member, "a major coup if we could knock off the Democratic majority leader."

This was based on an initial assessment that Mr. Wright was highly vulnerable, a view that produced a steady flow of money to Mr. Bradshaw's campaign. By June 30, the most recent reporting date, the GOP challenger had raised $203,172, and the figure has grown considerably since then.

Under challenge, however, Mr. Wright has put together a formidable campaign organization and more than doubled Mr. Bradshaw's fund-raising. By June 30, the incumbent had $499,697. As a result, Mr. Bradshaw's backers are now talking less of defeating Mr. Wright than of throwing a conservative scare into the majority leader, and of preparing Mr. Bradshaw for another congressional bid in 1982, when redistricting is likely to produce a new seat in the Dallas–Fort Worth areas.

By any standard, and particularly by Texas standards, Mr. Wright ought to have a safe seat this year.

He is the majority leader and, barring a major shift in the politics of the House, the heir apparent to House Speaker Thomas P. O'Neill, Jr. (D-Mass.), who may retire in two years. Texas is a state that honors congressional seniority. "We send them there and we keep them there," Sam Rayburn, the last Texas speaker of the House, said about his state's strategy in gaining power in Congress.

In addition, Mr. Wright's district is suffering none of the unemployment endemic in most of the rest of the country. Fueled by defense contracts to General Dynamics, Bell Helicopter Textron and nearby LTV Vought, the district gets more money from the Department of Defense than any other in the country. Campaigning in blue-collar areas near General Dynamics on a Saturday is tough because half the adults are working overtime on the F-16 production line.

If that were not enough, Amon G. Carter, Jr., publisher of the *Fort Worth Star-Telegram*, not only backs Mr. Wright, he is chairman of the congressman's fund-raising committee, the Jim Wright Congressional Club. The newspaper's editorial page, a local magazine noted, has "come to read like a Jim Wright fan club newsletter."

Although the Wright campaign has emphasized claims of his power in Washington, he has not demonstrated an ability to develop the kind of legislative muscle associated with such past Texans as Sam Rayburn or Lyndon B. Johnson.

This results largely from changing political standards—few, if any, congressmen owe their seats to the leadership anymore—and from Mr. Wright's style. He is more of an orator than a politician who knows how to gain absolute loyalty from colleagues.

Of the three House leaders, Mr. O'Neill, Mr. Wright and Rep. John Brademas (D-Ind.), the majority whip, Mr. Wright does have a group of Southern and conservative members upon whom he can call periodically for support on key votes.

These votes, however, are almost always on issues where the Democratic majority needs every "yes" it can get in the face of Republican opposition (the budget resolution, for example). The use of this kind of leverage in the House does not win plaudits from conservative Texans.

Mr. Bradshaw, the 39-year-old former mayor pro tem of Fort Worth and Mr. Wright's challenger, is not opposed to using any opening to put Mr. Wright on the defensive. "This race is a barn-burner, and there is no question it's going to get rougher," he boasts.

He has attacked Mr. Wright from the left—"Jim Wright hasn't hired any blacks on his staff"—and from the right, releasing a statement from Adm. Thomas H. Moorer, former chairman of the Joint Chiefs of Staff, charging: "Jim Wright bears a major part of the blame for the weakened condition of the United States."

Coping with the Bradshaw offensive alone might not have been a major problem for Mr. Wright, but the campaign has been marked by a series of developments that have made it difficult for the incumbent to maintain control.

The entry of right-wing religious groups under the banner of the "Moral Majority" has thrown a wrench into traditional political tactics.

"If you get attacked by this Reverend Robison, what do you do?" a Wright backer complained. "You can't get involved exchanging charges with a Baptist minister in Fort Worth, and how do you explain to voters that a moral rating is just a collection of right-wing positions on abortion, busing and prayer in the schools?"

The evangelical political drive has politicians in numerous districts worried because, they contend, it is impossible to anticipate its strength. They cite the defeat of Rep. John H. Buchanan, Jr. (R-Ala.), who appeared strong in preelection polls, but lost in a primary to a Moral Majority-backed candidate.

"There were a lot of voters who had no idea how they were going to vote until they heard a sermon the Sunday before the election," a person familiar with the Buchanan contest said.

Similarly, along with the conservative religious groups, Mr. Wright is under attack from Mr. Chiles, who, over the last year, has run harshly critical avertisements in the paper.

On October 9, 1979, a Chiles ad declared in boldface headlines: "Jim Wright, About your pay raise . . . you're WRONG, WRONG, WRONG." After Mr. Wright, voting in support of President Carter, saw his ratings by petroleum industry groups fall to 14 percent, Mr. Chiles asked "WHAT NEXT, JIM WRIGHT?"

Energy has been just one of a number of issues where Mr. Wright's role as majority leader has conflicted, at least partially, with the way most members of the Texas delegation have seen their interests.

In addition to voting against deregulation of natural gas, Mr. Wright backed

Mr. Carter by voting to stop production of the B-1 bomber. In the case of the windfall profits tax, he backed a version considered least harmful to energy interests, but in many quarters of Texas, no version was acceptable.

To defend this voting record, Mr. Wright has placed himself in the peculiar position of indirectly blaming his responsibilities as majority leader for ballots he has cast. As part of a detailed explanation to voters, his campaign staff wrote:

"While Congressman Wright does have some extraordinary responsibilities as majority leader, and while these responsibilities obviously involve a certain degree of loyalty to the president, particularly on international matters, the fact is that Wright has voted with the majority of his Texas Democratic colleagues 90.6 percent of the time."

One area where Mr. Wright has shown no reluctance to use the stature of his position in the House is in fund-raising. Last month, after learning that Republican Senator John G. Tower had sent out a letter to business political action committees suggesting they give to Mr. Bradshaw, Mr. Wright on September 2 sent out a counter-letter to the PAC organizers which read, in part:

"Whatever happens in the next elections, most people agree that the Democrats will quite likely retain control of the House. Who occupies the position of majority leader is a matter of considerable importance to the nation. . . .

"The one thing my opponent does not need is money. I'll be coming back to Congress, but anything you give to my opponent just makes it that much more costly for me."

The letter read, in some quarters, like a veiled threat, although the Wright campaign contended that the letter merely states facts apparent to everyone but "wishful-thinking Republicans."

In Texas, however, allegations of veiled threats do not carry the political liability that might occur from a similar letter in other states.

The same appears to hold true from the recent controversy over Mr. Wright's investments in gas wells. The Moncrief family, of the Moncrief Oil Company and part owners of the Neptune Oil Company, last year sought out Mr. Wright to help in dealings with the Egyptian government.

Neptune Oil had invested $102 million in 1976 in an oil project then on Israeli soil, but which was to be turned over to the Egyptian government.

At a meeting in Washington, Mr. Wright personally gave President Sadat a letter asking him to help out Neptune's interests, which were threatened by Egypt's plans to turn the land over to the Amoco International Oil Company for development.

During these negotiations, the Moncrief family allowed Mr. Wright to join in on two domestic gas well investments. "I had been talking with Jim Wright for over two months. This little well in East Texas happened along in February. We contacted Jim about it and he said he wanted in on it. That's all there was to it," Dick Moncrief told the *Fort Worth Star-Telegram*.

The *Dallas Times Herald* went after the story with considerable intensity. The Forth Worth newspaper, however, has been less aggressive, headlining one story "Jim Wright Gets 3-way Oil 'Lesson'—Millionaires Are Trying to Alter his Philosophy." The newspaper quoted W. A. Moncrief, Sr., saying: "I concluded that I should work with him and try to cultivate a change in his philosophy."

This is a town where press conferences are held in the Petroleum Club and gas ventures are a commonplace among the wealthy. As a result, most observers believe Mr. Wright will survive the Bradshaw challenge, although he is likely to win with less than 60 percent, a victory margin that does not help the stature of a candidate for the speakership.

However, just as redistricting may produce a new seat for Mr. Bradshaw in 1982, it is also likely to give Mr. Wright the opportunity to shed some of the more Republican sections of his district, and to take the edge off potential future challenges.

# Money, Technology
# Revive GOP Force

*First of two articles*

*The Washington Post,* June 17, 1984

Over the past decade, the Republican Party steadily has used money and technology to build a national organization superior to anything previously known in American politics.

In the process, the GOP has transformed the nation's political structure and revived the party as a powerful force in the election process.

The Republicans also have moved far ahead of the Democratic party in the targeting of money and resources on close House and Senate races, in capitalizing on the increasingly technical and computerized nature of campaigning, in maintaining party loyalty and providing jobs to supporters.

There is no absolute scientific evidence that money or technology determines the outcome of elections. However, there is a growing body of evidence developed by such political scientists as Gary Jacobson of the University of California and David Adamany of Wayne State University that effective allocation of cash and resources to key marginal races can alter results.

"Had the 1982 [House] elections followed the pattern of previous postwar midterms, the Republicans would have lost between 40 and 60 seats," Jacobson and Samuel Kernell, also of University of California, wrote recently. "The economy was in its worst postwar recession, and [President Reagan's] job performance rating . . . was lower than that of any president since Truman in 1946."

But as it happened, the Republicans lost only 26 House seats.

Defying the notion that the political parties are dead or dying, the GOP has capitalized on its unprecedented fund-raising ability to finance an extraordinary, ten-year revival of its formal party structure: the Republican National Committee (RNC), the National Republican Senatorial Committee (NRSC) and the National Republican Congressional Committee (NRCC).

The scope of the GOP financial advantage is reflected in these facts:

• The party and its major candidates have developed such a strong fund-raising base, particularly in direct mail, that the Reagan-Bush '84 Committee raised the maximum amount allowed in the presidential primaries—a total of $24.04 million, in just 7½ months, from October 17 to May 1. No other candidate has come close to this record since the enactment of the 1974 election law.

• Last year the three Republican committees raised $93.3 million, mostly from direct mail and major donors; this was nearly six times as much as the $16.4 million raised by their Democratic counterparts, which are much more dependent on "special-interest" money from political action committees (PACs). In the first three months of this year, the GOP committees raised $41.3 million, with all indications pointing toward a record $150 million for the year.

• In 1983, the RNC's postage bill alone—$7.5 million—was almost equal to half the entire operating budget of the Democratic National Committee (DNC), $15.5 million.

• The total raised in 1983 by the Democratic Congressional and Senatorial Campaign committees was $4.4 million—a fraction of what the two parallel GOP committees have budgeted for the coming elections for direct candidate support ($17 million), polling and other research ($8.3 million), long-range development ($12 million) and candidate services ($10.9 million).

In 1981–82, money from the nation's 3,371 PACs—representing labor unions, corporations, trade associations, ideological groups and the like—totaled $199.2 million. Democratic committees raised $39 million. Republican committees, primarily the three national bodies, raised $214.9 million, nearly as much as PACs and Democrats combined.

"I once listened to one of my GOP counterparts outline their 1981–82 budget," said Martin D. Franks, DCCC executive director. "Just doing it on the back of a napkin, in 1981 and 1982, I think they made more in interest on their certificates of deposit than we raised."

In short, the GOP has become the single most important source of money in the American political universe. Dwarfing the Democrats' world, the GOP money machine provides sustenance not only to candidates, but also to a bureaucracy of 600, a network of consultants, out-of-office loyalists, polling firms, stationers, media specialists, direct-mail firms, computer companies and Madison Avenue advertising specialists.

The GOP's advantage is particularly telling in direct candidate support.

Although the GOP spends far more money than all the PACs on such indirect campaign expenses as surveys, voter registration, political party television advertising and staff, it still has enough left over to be the major source of cash for its House and Senate candidates.

In the 1981–82 cycle, GOP House and Senate candidates got $19.3 million from national party committees, compared with $18 million from corporate PACs, $12.4 million from trade and professional association PACs and $1.1 million from labor PACs.

In contrast, Democratic party committees were the least important sources of money for their congressional candidates. They got $19.1 million from labor PACs, $9.4 million from corporate PACs, $9.3 million from trade and professional association PACs and $4.6 million from the party committees.

By concentrating fund-raising within the party, channeling its own and outside money into key races and avoiding free-for-all competition for funds by individual candidates, the Republican party has made far more effective use of its resources than has the Democratic party.

Democratic candidates on average have no problem raising money. In 1982 House Democratic candidates raised an average of $216,000 each and Republicans raised an average of $230,000.

But the financial key to victory is the provision of adequate funds to challenge Democratic incumbents or seek open seats. In these 30 to 90 races—not those of GOP incumbents—involving challengers to incumbents or open-seat contests where the outcome is in serious doubt, the Republican party structure has flexed its muscles, targeting cash and resources.

"The average winning challenger in a marginal district in 1982 spent about $225,000," said the DCCC's Franks. "We can offer them about one-ninth of their budget; the Republicans can offer them about a third of their budget."

The striking differences in distribution in close races were apparent in the 1980 and 1982 House elections:

In 1980, when polls favored the Republican party, 27 largely unknown GOP House challengers had significantly more money to spend than their incumbent Democratic opponents, averaging $341,499 to $285,686, and went on to win their elections. The defeated Democrats included such House powers as Ways and Means Committee Chairman Al Ullman (D-Ore.), Public Works Committee Chairman Harold T. (Bizz) Johnson (D-Calif.) and Democratic whip John Brademas (D-Ind.), all of whom had the leverage to raise large amounts of money.

But two years later, 1982, when public opinion turned toward the Democratic party, the GOP shifted gears to protect its incumbents. The 55 who won close races financially overwhelmed the Democrats, spending an average of $361,-295 each compared with $182,232 for their challengers. Even the 26 who lost close races outspent their challengers, $465,027 to $292,781 each.

Much of the Democratic money is wasted on incumbents who hold safe seats but still receive far more money than needed.

In 1982, 42 Democratic incumbents who won with more than 80 percent of the vote received more than $100,000 each in contributions. They included Ways and Means Chairman Dan Rostenkowski (D-Ill.), who raised $516,438, and Reps. W.J. (Billy) Tauzin and Charles E. (Buddy) Roemer, both Louisiana Democrats, who raised $415,797 and $480,173, respectively.

By contrast, only seven Republicans who won by more than 80 percent in 1982 received more than $100,000 each, and at least 20 close House contests possibly were decided by the Republican party's superior resources.

In one, Democratic challenger Billy Joe Camp raised only $145,213 but came within a percentage point of defeating Rep. William L. Dickenson (R-Ala.), who had $300,183. G. Douglas Stephens, who came within 2 percentage points of defeating House Minority Leader Robert H. Michel (R-Ill.), raised $174,556 to Michel's $697,084. David A. Geisler raised $109,635 in a 1,842-vote loss to Rep. Gene Taylor (R-Mo.), who had $222,772.

Without a change in Democratic tactics, the parties' differences in allocating money could have major long-range consequences. The Democrats' severe tilt toward safe incumbents tends to protect the partisan status quo but fails to encourage the winning of new seats by unknown challengers and leaves marginal incumbents particularly vulnerable when the voters turn against the party. The Republicans' focus on close races—financing strong challenges when opinion favors the party and protecting incumbents in hard times—changes the status quo wherever possible and guards incumbents facing tough challengers.

The once hostile relationship between the Republican party and the conservative movement has been replaced by a de facto alliance, with strong evidence that the GOP has gained power and legitimacy in the nation's right wing.

The indirect bonds between the Republican party and such groups as the National Conservative Political Action Committee (NCPAC), the Conservative Victory Fund and the Fund for a Conservative Majority are most apparent at the elite level of major donors:

Richard DeVos, founder of the Amway Corp., was finance director for the RNC and is now on NCPAC's policy advisory council. In the 1981–82 election cycle, Roy Guffey, a Dallas oilman, and his wife gave $8,650 to Republican committees and $19,100 to major conservative PACs. T. Boone Pickens, chairman of last year's RNC Eagles ($10,000-a-year donors) campaign, gave NCPAC $1,500 in the 1981–82 cycle. Eddie Chiles, a GOP Eagle and owner of the Western Company of North America in Fort Worth, gave NCPAC $5,000.

The two men given most credit for providing the technical expertise in turning the GOP into a fund-raising machine, Wyatt A. Stewart, III, and Stephen Winchell, both were vice presidents in the firm run by the dean of conservative fund-raisers, Richard A. Viguerie. More recently, another former Viguerie vice president, Ann Stone, has become increasingly involved in Republican fund-raising.

This year, Joe Rodgers, finance chairman for the Reagan–Bush '84 Committee, is seeking to cement the GOP-conservative nexus with a fund-raising drive tapping major Republican givers whose cash will be funneled to conservative organizations across the country for voter registration.

While money in the GOP has helped unify the party around conservative positions and to encourage party loyalty, money in the Democratic party is often a divisive force.

Insofar as PAC money provides guidance on votes, and insofar as the goals of labor PACs conflict with those of corporate and trade association PACs, Democrats often find themselves at cross-purposes. In 1982 they got almost the same amount from labor PACs ($18.3 million) as from corporate and trade association PACs ($17.5 million). For Republicans, in contrast, corporate and trade association contributions overwhelmed labor contributions by 29 to 1, $29.3 million to $1 million.

The Reagan administration has capitalized on conservative Democratic donors to help win passage of major legislation. In 1981, key White House officials used computers to identify all persons and PACs who had given to both the President Reagan and to Southern Democrats. These donors were then asked to lobby Southern Democrats in favor of the administration's budget- and tax-cut legislation. Southern Democrats—the "boll weevils"—provided the margin of victory for the White House.

GOP cash also has turned traditional U.S. organizing on its head.

In a stark departure from a party built on neighborhood and local political organizations run by old-line bosses and volunteer civic leaders, the national GOP has become highly centralized, with the hub of power and money in the nation's capital, filtering resources down to state and county groups.

Its cash and resources equip the GOP to nurture candidates through the entire electoral process: initial ticket selection, preliminary organization, training, fund-raising, polling, hiring of consultants, analysis of the opposition, manipulation of the media, computerized phone banks, advertising, direct mail and last-minute, get-out-the-vote drives.

"It's a whole new world out there," said NRCC's Steven Lotterer. "With all these services, we are able to guide them [GOP candidates] down the right path. . . . We're able to make sure they don't get led astray."

Money also has allowed the Republicans to gain the edge in the new world of voter mobilization—using not ward captains and precinct lieutenants but television, direct mail, surveys, demographic consultants, telemarketing and computerized precinct analysis.

From January through April, for example, the RNC spent $983,000 for surveys by Decision Making Information, the polling firm headed by White House pollster Richard B. Wirthlin; the Democratic National Committee could afford no surveys.

Similarly, the Democratic party is depending almost entirely on "nonpartisan" groups for voter registration, hoping to add 5 million to the rolls; the RNC and the Reagan-Bush '84 Committee are spending $8 million to $10 million to put two million GOP loyalists on the rolls by using the most advanced telephone marketing techniques combined with sophisticated manipulation of voter and census lists.

Perhaps most important, the revived GOP has encouraged the development of a highly disciplined political party, with far less dissent than the Democrats and with an exceptionally high degree of ideological agreement, at least when tested in critical congressional votes.

This discipline was reflected in the remarkably uniform GOP support of the president's highly controversial 1981 budget- and tax-cut program throughout a sequence of votes which, in many cases, created severe political difficulties for Republican incumbents in the subsequent 1982 election.

In a series of three budget- and tax-cut votes in the Senate, the GOP majorities in favor of the legislation were 41 to 1, 50 to 2 and 51 to 2; in four parallel House votes, the GOP majorities were 190 to 1, 188 to 1, 189 to 0 and 190 to 1. The cumulative total was 899 to 6.

"The fact that the party is strong and the party is out there working for all candidates is something that would lead to more unity among Republican officeholders," said RNC chairman Frank J. Farhenkopf, Jr.

The discipline remained firm through the 1982 election when, despite the worst recession in 40 years and declining popular support for Reagan, GOP House and Senate candidates limited their dissent, never crossing over the boundary to disloyalty, in sharp contrast to traditional Democratic chaos.

"We were able to persuade House candidates that it was all right to discuss how they differed from President Reagan, but not to break with the president. We convinced them that blood in the water would just draw sharks, not win elections," said a strategist for the NRCC.

The argument for loyalty was made all the more convincing by the fact that the NRCC was armed with $48.9 million in that election cycle, compared with $6.5 million by its Democratic counterpart.

# Donors, Voters Pinpointed

## GOP Purchasing Technological Edge

*Second of two articles*

---

*The Washington Post, June 18, 1984*

---

As political campaigns move ever closer to the realm of Madison Avenue marketing, the National Republican Senatorial Committee (NRSC) has hired the New York advertising research firm of McCollum/Speilman to develop "psychometric" analyses of GOP strategies.

The goal is to provide each candidate with a "copy platform," the carefully developed combination of messages, conscious and subliminal, that is regarded as essential to a winning advertising campaign, whether for a soup or a senator.

"It's very close to the work we've done in corporate imagery," said Elaine

Morgenstein, vice president and research director of McCollum/Speilman. "You try with a corporation to give it personality."

The McCollum/Speilman project is one small part of a broad and intense effort by the three major Republican party committees to keep extending the outer edges of political high technology, exploring new uses of computers, electronic fund transfers, telemarketed voter registration and contribution solicitation, highly targeted direct mail and even ways to mix fund-raising with money market and mutual funds.

"We see research and development as one of our basic functions," said Mitchell E. Daniels Jr., executive director of the NRSC.

The Republican technological advantage over the Democrats lies not in secret techniques but in having the money to pay for the latest advances, most of which are developed for the commercial telemarketing and direct-mail world or by computer specialists producing programs for the political arena.

In the long run—as the precise targeting of voters, contributors and key interest groups grows in importance—the GOP technological advantage could prove at least as significant as the Republican advantage in providing direct cash to candidates.

In the case of McCollum/Speilman, the firm uses a campaign's polling data to determine which demographic groups—such as women, abortion opponents, Hispanics, blue-collar workers—are key to the election and are "leverageable," meaning that significant numbers can be persuaded to change their positions.

The firm then picks a sample of about 200 people in each key target group to test marketing strategies—a process the company calls "magnitude estimation."

Morgenstein said, for example, that "generically, Republicans are less likely to be perceived as tuned to the needs of women." A GOP candidate could look foolish suddenly advocating women's rights, she said, so the goal is to "find a way to see how you could connote" that position without stating it directly. The candidate might stress his concern for "the little guy," suggesting sympathy for the underdog in society which, in turn, could be used to imply support for women struggling for parity in the marketplace.

Morgenstein has done "a lot of work with imagery products"—perfume, liquors, cigarettes and the like. "One brand is not particularly different from another," she said, "and you have to give the client's brand a specific personality," a process similar to helping a first-time candidate develop "an image from scratch."

So far this year, the NRSC has spent about $50,000 on the McCollum/Speilman contract. It is not yet clear whether "psychometrics" is advertising hype or a real political tool. But for the GOP, the fee is a tiny and affordable gamble.

Three years ago, Ron Charnock left his job as director of computer services at the Republican National Committee (RNC) to start National Political Resource Inc. (NPRI) with a number of RNC colleagues.

NPRI, in turn, developed a telemarketing computer software program that has substantially altered telephone fund-raising. The program leaves telephone solicitors—known as "communicators" in the business—free to focus their attention on the potential giver, known as a "prospect."

The computer automatically dials the number of a prospect. As the phone rings, the prospect's name, address and history of contributions appear on the computer screen. The caller then asks the prospect for support, perhaps noting that he or she usually contributes every six months and that it has been seven months since the last donation.

If the prospect agrees to contribute, the caller presses certain keys and punches in the promised amount. A personalized letter and return envelope are automatically mailed by another computer.

If someone other than the prospect answers the phone and says to call back, the communicator presses certain keys—E, for example, to indicate an evening return call. Sometime after 6 P.M., the computer will dial the number for a second try.

The program is being used by the RNC and by a private company, the Campaign Marketing Group, run by Bruce McBrearty, former deputy finance director of the RNC and the National Republican Congressional Committee (NRCC), whose clients include all three GOP committees.

"What we have tried to do is set up a system that is void of paper," McBrearty said.

Most advances in political "high tech" involve the application of computers to various types and combinations of lists: census data, voter registration records, precinct voting histories, patterns of television watching, magazine subscription records and a wide variety of other materials available in the commercial market.

It is extremely expensive terrain, and the parties are only beginning to explore it. But it has the potential of affecting almost every aspect of political life, from fund-raising and direct mail to voter registration and mobilization and even post-election challenges of questionable vote tallies.

At the Democratic National Committee (DNC), direct-mail specialists have bought the services of the Claritas Corp., which has "geocoded" all 35,000 ZIP codes in the United States into 40 clusters based on income, race, neighborhood, class, life style, homeownership and a host of other demographic characteristics.

The clusters have nicknames ranging from "blue-blood estates" and "furs and station wagons," for such upscale communities as Beverly Hills or the River Oak suburb of Houston, to the "sharecropper" areas of rural black poverty or "Hispanic mix" sections of east Los Angeles and east San Antonio.

The DNC applies these classifications to donor lists to determine which kinds of clusters have produced profitable returns in direct-mail campaigns. Armed with this information, the committee takes lists of registered Democrats and, through a computer process known as merging and purging, pinpoints Democratic voters who, according to the cluster system, are likely donors.

"When you lay Claritas over the voter lists, you can mail 40 to 50 percent of the list," said Frank O'Brien of the DNC.

While Democrats are working with ZIP codes—units of 2,250 households, which can be extremely diverse—the NRSC has purchased a similar service from a corporation, CACI Inc., that analyzes donor lists at far more detailed, and far more expensive, levels.

CACI uses what it calls ACORN (A Classification of Residential Neighborhoods), which divides America into 44 types of areas, from "wealthy, established suburbs" to "very poor blacks, low-rent housing." The groupings are similar to the Claritas clusters. But the NRSC is paying for breakdowns to the census-block level, units of about 260 households, which allows far more accurate targeting to income, race or age groups.

The National Republican Congressional Committee has computers so sophisticated that, instead of buying such services from a company, it has acquired a complete set of census tapes, down to the census-block level.

"We have it right here, and we can tell any candidate the demographics of any block in his district," NRCC political strategist Stephen Lotterer said. "[We are] able to focus on almost any specific block and tell you who lives in that house and what they do for a living, how many kids they have and what their income is."

In one area—the production of radio and television commercials—the Democrats have begun to catch up with the GOP with the recent opening of the Democratic Media Center, which will reduce costs for candidates. But in terms of financing advertisements promoting their party, the Democrats remain far behind. In 1980 and 1982, for example, the GOP, which has highly sophisticated media production facilities, spent $20 million on commercials seeking to persuade voters to support Republicans, while the Democrats hardly spent anything.

Charnock's NPRI has the franchise, in its dealings with Republicans, to represent Metro Mail, a company maintaining perhaps the most comprehensive list of households in America.

Metro Mail regularly computerizes phone books, lists of driver's licenses, census data, information from insurance companies and other data. It can provide a basic list of most residents in any state or congressional district, characterizing individual households or neighborhoods by wealth, income, race, age, education, number of children, length of residence and other factors.

This list, in turn, can be run against a list of registered voters. The names that "fall out" provide not only a list of the unregistered, but also some basic indicators of their likelihood of voting Republican or Democratic. The process also can be taken an expensive step further, matching unregistered voters with precinct voting histories to aid a partisan voter-registration drive.

This combination of computerized lists forms the core of the Republicans' $8 million to $10 million voter-registration drive. The tool is far more important to the GOP than to the Democrats because Republican supporters are spread diffusely and are difficult to pinpoint, while Democrats can register successfully in almost any poor, working-class, black or Hispanic neighborhood.

As a side benefit, Charnock said, the melding of a Metro Mail list with a list of registered voters can identify persons who apparently have moved away but whose names remain on voter rolls. If persons using those names try to vote, the losing side could use the list to challenge the results.

Detailed demographic information, the NRCC's Lotterer said, can be critical in attempting to persuade voters. "Now it's gotten to where a candidate may have eight or ten different direct-mail pieces," each tailored to a different group: Roman Catholics, veterans, the elderly, Hispanics, suburbanites. "You can really pinpoint it down so that the letter that person gets is going to touch them directly," Lotterer said.

Computers also are being used to keep an eye on the opposition. The NRCC has computerized the contribution history of each political action committee (PAC). Anytime an incumbent Democrat votes against the interest of a PAC that has contributed to him or her, the NRCC informs the PAC. "Here's how your guy voted in the last six months, and are you really sure you want to give him $5,000 the next time around?" it asks, in effect.

Similarly, the House Republican leadership has purchased a computer program for "monitoring member behavior." For each House member, Republican or Democrat, it provides a list of "economic influences," including major campaign contributors, voting histories, electoral vulnerability ratings and even a rating of the reliability of a member's promise on specific votes.

There is disagreement in the GOP on the value of various high-tech systems. Phil Smith, the RNC's finance director, said Claritas or CACI demographic analysis may prove very useful in voter mobilization, but added that it is not worth the cost in direct-mail fund-raising, at least for the RNC.

The RNC, however, is, exploring other tactics, including automatic electronic transfers from donors' bank accounts into the RNC's checking account. After each donation, the computer would send the contributor a "thank you" letter.

At a more complex level, the RNC, which has developed a list of affluent donors, is working on a plan to cooperate with a brokerage firm seeking investors in money markets, mutual funds and individual retirement accounts. The firm would use the RNC donor list to solicit investors, who, according to Smith, would be guaranteed competitive returns.

In return for use of the donor list, the brokerage firm would pay the RNC a monthly "finder's fee" of .03 percent on the amount invested. A $10,000 investment in a money-market account would bring the RNC $30 a month at no cost to the investor.

# CHAPTER THREE

# THE EARLY YEARS OF THE REAGAN ADMINISTRATION

T HE CONSERVATIVE FORCES that had been building throughout the 1970s swept Washington like a tidal wave in 1981. The drive to cut taxes submerged the fifty-year commitment to an expanding federal government—a commitment to domestic spending that had survived three previous Republican presidents, Dwight Eisenhower, Richard Nixon, and Gerald Ford, and even the Republican-controlled Congress of 1953–54, when the GOP held majorities in both the House and the Senate. The election of Ronald Reagan and the GOP takeover of the Senate fundamentally altered the national debate in ways that continue to shape the political and economic strategies of both the Democratic and Republican parties.

Considerable damage has been done over the past seven years to the dominant members of the Republican coalition that put Reagan in office and provided the momentum for his budget and tax cuts in 1981, but that year produced a degree of success for the affluent and for business unseen in two generations. From the Occupational Safety and Health Administration to the Civil Rights Commission to the Federal Trade Commission, a policy of deregulation was initiated that in large part has remained in force throughout the Reagan administration. Taxes were cut so deeply that the national debt reached $2.4 trillion by the end of 1987, insuring that deficit politics would dominate not only Republican campaigns, but those of Democrats for years to come. Rejecting the use of the tax system to progressively redistribute income, the Reagan administration achieved an antithetical goal: from 1980 to 1984, the federal income and Social Security tax burden of everyone making less than $75,000-a-year grew, while those making $200,000-a-year or more saw an average $17,403 tax cut. The provisions of the 1981 tax bill cutting corporate taxes were written by business lobbyists; as a result, the tax rate on profits from some corporate investments fell below zero—meaning that the federal government effectively subsidized corporate purchases—and businesses paying little or no taxes were allowed to sell useless investment tax credits to companies paying high tax rates in need of additional breaks.

The articles in this section only touch on the radical transformation of the balance of power between Republicans and Democrats, rich and poor, business and labor, that reached its height in 1981. In the years since then, none of the forces on the left have recovered. A central issue in American politics by 1988 is whether the Reagan coalition, or a version of it, can survive as the dominant force in presidential and state politics. Clearly, the 1984 election demonstrated that Reagan, at least individually, contributed to the shaping of a new presidential majority. The next two chapters explore in more detail not only the strengths of that coalition, but some of the divisive pressures on it, including the splitting of the business community, the profiteering from political connections by Reagan loyalists, the emergence of growing inequity in the distribution of income, and the increasing economic difficulties of those with middle-level incomes in financing housing, education and all that has been associated with a middle-class American life.

# Reagan Wins May Be Far-Reaching

## Tax and Budget Cuts Could Transform Nation's Political Balance

*The Washington Post,* August 13, 1981

In the largely unexplored terrain where economic policy alters the partisan political balance, President Reagan may turn out to have won a lot more from the Democrats than some tax and budget cuts.

The federal tax and benefit structures have both been altered by the 97th Congress in ways that could have enormous long-term political consequences.

• First, with surprisingly little debate Congress took a revolutionary step long advocated by Republicans; it voted to limit government growth through what amount to permanent tax cuts out into the future. For the next three years individual income tax rates will be reduced 25 percent in every bracket; thereafter the tax code will be indexed or adjusted automatically each year to offset the tax-increasing effect of inflation. Unless the Reagan economic program produces a revival far exceeding the forecasts of even the most optimistic supply-siders, this tax bill will thus eventually force a deficit-minded Congress to make even more spending cuts than it already has, not put programs back as some Democrats hope. In effect, the administration has succeeded in placing a fiscal noose on Democrats that will not be loosened even if the party regains control of the federal government.

• Second, Congress significantly narrowed the base of the federal tax structure. In a bill that heavily rewarded traditional Republican constituencies, it sharply reduced and in some cases nearly eliminated federal taxes on such forms of income as business profits, capital gains, interest income and oil revenues, as well as on inheritances. In doing so, it left the government more dependent than ever on taxes on ordinary wage and salary income. This could put the Democrats in a quandary if they move to increase taxes to restore spending programs in the future. To build back programs for some of their constituents, they will have to increase taxes on others. Unless they can revive some of the taxes that Congress nearly wiped out this year to help welfare mothers they will have to tax factory workers. There is no political joy in that.

• A third point has to do with middle-income taxpayers, those in the $25,000 to $40,000 range. This is a swing group to which Democrats have primarily appealed in the past. But in this year's bill the Republicans appealed heavily to such taxpayers, whose incomes and tax brackets have risen with inflation, claiming, in effect, "We can match Democrats." The Republicans moved to supplant the Democrats as the tax champions of the middle class. The ability of the GOP to translate tax policy into voter allegiance is unknown.

• Fourth, the cuts in social programs not only reduce federal spending for the poor, an essentially Democratic constituency; the people running these programs who stand to lose their jobs are also largely Democrats, in many cases active supporters of the party.

Some liberal to moderate Democrats have professed to be happy they lost on the tax and spending votes. Reagan is now responsible for the economy, and these Democrats believe the Reagan economic policy will fall flat on its face. In the subsequent rising unemployment and continuing inflation, according to this scenario, voters will return to the Democratic fold.

In the words of Sen. Thomas F. Eagleton (D-Mo.) during the Senate debate on the tax cut: "This bill keeps the Democratic party alive. It is so inherently inequitable, so inherently unbalanced, so inherently unfair that it will stand as a bedrock for the rebirth of the Democratic party."

This strategy was advocated on the budget side by Rep. David R. Obey (D-Wis.), who contended that instead of putting up a fight, the Democratic-controlled House ought agreeably to give President Reagan what he wanted. Democrats could then sit back as the political time bombs in the budget—fewer college loans for middle-class students, costlier school lunches, no more Social Security minimum benefits, to name a few—began to explode inside the Republican lines. Eventually, so the theory goes, this will help revive the fundamental Democratic belief that government has an essential role in maintaining the general welfare.

This view of the future fails, however, to recognize an alternative scenario in which, even if Reagan economics does collapse, the altered tax structure, and to a lesser extent the substantive changes in spending programs, will make it very difficult for a hypothetically revived Democratic party to reassert its support for programs important to the Northeast and the Midwest, where loyalties remain strongest.

For the Republicans, the tax and budget bills were remarkable political accomplishments.

Not only did the $749 billion tax cut—particularly indexation starting in

1985—go a long way toward the Republican objective of restricting future federal growth, but the tax legislation significantly altered the tax burden in a fashion furthering GOP partisan interests.

The tax bill will accelerate a longterm trend toward what is almost a phase-out of the corporate income tax. In 1940, this tax on profits provided 30.5 percent of federal revenues; in 1950, 34.3 percent; in 1960 it dropped to 22.3 percent; in 1970 it was 16 percent and this year 12.4 percent.

With the passage of the tax bill and the provisions effectively ending taxation on income from new investments, the administration foresees revenues from the corporate income tax remaining basically static through 1986, while total federal revenues increase from $520 billion in 1980 to $923 billion in 1986. This would leave the corporate income tax providing 8.1 percent of federal revenues.

While there is an extensive debate among economists over who ultimately pays the corporate income tax (consumers, shareholders, employees in lost wages, or others), it is first felt by the corporation and its stockholders, who tend to be among the well-to-do.

Similarly, aside from the across-the-board rate cuts, most of the "sweeteners" added to the tax bill are directed to the rich. Oil tax breaks total $11.7 billion through 1986; new savings certificates and new interest exemptions, which are advantageous only to those in high tax brackets and with large amounts of money earning interest, total $7.6 billion; the near-elimination of the estate tax, which will exclusively benefit heirs to very large estates, will amount to $15.3 billion. The reduction of the maximum rate on unearned or investment income, and the associated cut in the capital gains rate, will also benefit almost entirely those with incomes above $50,000, at a cost to the Treasury of about $15 billion.

Translating these fiscal shifts into political terms, the Reagan tax bill targets benefits to predominantly Republican constituencies. Taking just persons with incomes above $35,000, a May 1981, Associated Press-NBC poll found that 53 percent were Republican, compared with 31 percent Democratic. The figures are even higher above the $50,000 mark. (In contrast, the poll found that persons earning from $8,000 to $15,000 were 43 percent Democratic and 39 percent Republican.)

At the bottom end of the income scale, figures compiled by the Joint Committee on Taxation show that—when already scheduled Social Security tax increases are taken into account, plus inflation's effect in pushing taxpayers into higher brackets—those earning $20,000 or less, a majority of tax filers, will face a net tax increase in 1984.

This group of tax filers, who are also the strongest supporters of the Democratic party, is expected to submit 42.5 million returns to the Internal Revenue Service this year out of 77.2 million, or 55 percent of the total. According to the joint committee, persons in these low (and largely Democratic) income brackets will end up paying $4.5 billion more in taxes in 1984 when inflation and Social Security increases are taken into account.

By the same accounting standard, the tax savings for those making more than

$20,000 will be $16.2 billion in 1984. These totals do not reflect the distribution to income groups of the changes in the estate tax, savings certificates, exclusions on income earned overseas, the oil tax cuts and the interest exclusions, all of which directly or indirectly (some are not part of the income tax) function to increase the disparity in the distribution of the breaks in the tax bill.

Again, translating these statistics into political terms, the Reagan administration has succeeded in keeping what might be described as tax pressure on the income group from which liberal and moderate Democrats must receive maximum support in order to win elections. The group this wing of the Democratic party must persuade to go to the polls in support of candidates advocating restoration of social programs is precisely that part of the electorate receiving little or no tax relief.

In effect, there will be a tax disincentive to support restoration of social programs among those making less than $20,000 a year. In contrast, those from upper-income groups that have generally supported the GOP in the past will have received a tax reward for that support, further reinforcing the partisan tie.

For those in the middle ground—$20,000 to $35,000—the Reagan administration has succeeded in blurring, if not blunting, the traditional appeal of the Democrats. They do achieve a net tax reduction after the effects of Social Security and inflation are taken into account, although it is not as significant as the net cut for those in the upper brackets.

In coming elections and in future legislative strategies, these tax shifts will be one of many factors. Another major element will be the political consequences of the budget cuts.

Democrats are already attempting to develop maximum political capital out of the GOP proposal to end the $122 minimum Social Security benefit, the danger of which President Reagan has recognized and now appears ready to lessen through compromise. Other cuts with strong political potential for the Democrats are in the college loan program and school lunches, both of which will place additional burdens on the middle class, the swing group in elections.

At the same time, however, most of the cuts are not only in programs that provide services to the poor, a largely Democratic group with a poor turnout record on Election Day, but also in programs whose employees are largely Democrats. Not many Republicans are on food stamps; that is the political shorthand of the budget cuts, and both parties know it.

Not only in Frostbelt cities from Baltimore to Los Angeles, but throughout the Sunbelt, these programs provide employment for Democratic party activists, the men and women who ring doorbells, pass out leaflets and run telephone banks before election. In the middle of the budget fight, Sen. Pete V. Domenici (R-N.M.) went back to the Zapata Club in Albuquerque to meet with 50 of the workers in the programs facing reductions. "There might have been one Republican out of 50 there," Domenici noted. Although it is not possible to determine the number of workers who will be put out of work as a result of the cuts, it is clear that they will include far more Democrats than Republicans.

# Three Who Sowed Tax Provision
# Reap Its Business Bonanza

*Ex-Treasury Aides Profit from Their Handiwork;*
*Three Are Guides Down Tax Path They Cleared*

*The Washington Post*, October 5, 1981

A controversial provision in the 1981 tax bill allowing corporations in effect to sell tax breaks they cannot use was engineered in large part by three former Treasury Department officials who now represent companies standing to reap significant shares of the $27 billion bonanza over the next six years.

Their success in winning approval of what amounts to a backdoor federal tax subsidy to unprofitable companies reflects the power exercised by the business community in the development of the administration's $749 billion tax bill.

The new provision permits corporations to enter into lease transactions existing more on paper than in fact—a kind of fiscal netherworld in which businesses with low profits, or none, can "sell" unusable tax credits and depreciation deductions to profitable firms.

The Treasury Department estimates that this one section of the bill will result in lost revenues totaling $27 billion through 1986, although many business executives and lawyers in the field believe the figure will be far higher.

The key figures behind the administration's decision to adopt the provision, each of whom considers it to be an economically sound way of encouraging investment and of spreading the tax breaks evenly in the corporate community, are the following:

• Ernest S. Christian, Jr., a partner in the lobbying firm of Patton, Boggs and Blow whose clients include the Chrysler Corp., which is already planning to "sell" its tax credits. Christian, legislative counsel for the Treasury in 1973–74 and deputy assistant treasury secretary for tax policy in 1974–75, said he has been working overtime since the passage of the legislation, putting together deals in which low-profit firms or those running in the red will "lease" investments exceeding $1 billion to profitable companies.

These leases, he said, really amount to the selling of $560 million or more in tax breaks over the next five years, of which $190 million translates into tax breaks for the current year.

• Charls E. Walker, of Charls E. Walker Associates, whose status among Washington lobbyists has reached its zenith with the election of President Reagan. Walker, undersecretary of the Treasury from 1969 to 1972 and deputy secretary of the Treasury in 1972 and 1973, includes among his clients such capital-intensive companies as Ford Motor Co., Bethlehem Steel Corp., American Airlines and Trans World Airlines, all of which would be unable to profit fully from the basic elements of the business tax cuts without the ability to "sell" tax breaks.

Frederic W. Hickman, assistant Treasury secretary for tax policy from 1972 through 1975. Hickman is widely credited by colleagues with coming up with the basic leasing concept adopted. A partner in the Chicago law firm of Hopkins, Sutter, Mulroy, Davis and Bacon, Hickman said he was putting together deals on a scale similar to that of Christian, about $1 billion.

These three men played critical roles in the leasing tax provision: Hickman producing the idea, Walker and the chief executive officers of his corporate clientele "softening up" Treasury officials reluctant to take a provision that might appear to be a federal subsidy, and Christian nurturing the provision through the complex paths from the Senate Finance Committee to the Senate floor into the House version and finally through the House-Senate conference committee.

The drive to create the new mechanism grew out of the fact that the basic business tax cut was larger and offered more benefits than many companies could use.

The basic cut took the form of a depreciation speedup, allowing companies to depreciate new investments at a rate significantly faster than the actual useful "life" of the machinery, buildings, cars, trucks purchased. But for companies with little or no taxable income, these accelerated deductions, along with the existing ten percent investment tax credit, were of no use: They had no income against which to write off the investments.

Christian said experts knew from the outset that not all companies could take full advantage of this basic tax cut.

Walker, who has been representing a group of companies operating in the red or with only marginal profits—airlines, mines, Ford Motor Co., steel companies—had, as a member of the Reagan task force on taxes, unsuccessfully pressed for a concept of "refundability" to help such companies.

Under refundability, a low- (or no-) profit company that makes an investment would get a direct payment from the federal government in place of the unusable ten percent tax credit. The idea would not sell in Republican circles, where it looked like a subsidy to companies unable to make it in the free market.

A political strategist of no small will or influence, Walker engineered a meeting in March between the chief executive officers of what had become known in the lobbying world as the "refundability group" and Treasury Secretary Donald T. Regan. The administration was still unwilling to go the route of refundability, but a task force was appointed, ultimately headed by William S. McKee, tax legislative counsel at Treasury.

A key argument Walker and his clients used was that the massive new tax breaks created by the legislation posed the danger of encouraging a breakout of corporate takeovers: profitable companies would find it worthwhile to buy unprofitable companies just to pick up the tax breaks.

During this period, Hickman, who shares a number of clients with Walker, began to press for the concept of "leasing" as an alternative to refundability.

Leasing, Hickman suggested, offered a way to create a corporate marketplace in tax shelters without the "emotional excess baggage" of appearing to be federal subsidies. "This was a way to sort of sweep the slate clean," Hickman said.

As an example: an automobile company, hypothetically called Chryford, spends $100 million for new equipment to retool its plants. Chryford has been operating in the red and consequently cannot use the investment tax credit, worth $10 million, or the accelerated depreciation, worth $46 million over five years to a profitable company.

Under the new law, Chryford could, within 90 days of buying the equipment, go to a profitable company—a computer or oil company, for example—and in effect "sell" the equipment to the profitable company.

The profitable company has absolutely no interest in owning the equipment, except for the resultant tax advantages. In fact, under the exceptionally loose law governing this transaction, the profitable company does not even have to take legal title to the equipment, just something called "tax title," according to congressional aides. Ownership, property tax liability, responsibility for upkeep, insurance coverage and everything else stays with Chryford.

Using a model developed by Peter K. Nevit, president of Bankamerilease, the "lease" between Chryford and the profitable company could be structured as follows:

The profitable company buys the equipment from Chryford and gives a down payment of $15 million for the equipment, effectively reducing Chryford's purchase cost by that amount. At the end of five years, the profitable company agrees to "sell" the equipment back to Chryford for one cent.

The profitable company would immediately claim the investment tax credit of $10 million and the first year of depreciation, or $6.9 million, for a total tax break of $16.9 million. Chryford would be ahead by $15 million and the profitable company is ahead by $1.9 million.

For the next five years—the accelerated-depreciation period for the equipment—the profitable company would "pay" Chryford annual payments of $25,356,820 (principle and interest at 15 percent on the $100 million) and Chryford would pay a "rental" or "lease" fee back to the profitable company of exactly the same amount. These payments would cancel each other.

Until the last of the five years, the profitable company would be able to deduct depreciation on the equipment, reducing its tax liability by a total of $10,143,200 over four years. The profitable company would owe this same amount to the federal government as a tax liability in the fifth year, but the money for those four years would function as the equivalent of an interest-free loan of $10,143,200.

In sum, Chryford gets to buy the equipment at a $15 million discount, and the profitable company gets $1.6 million out front and a four-year interest-free loan totaling $10,143,200.

Asked about his interest in the provision at this point, Christian said that until the concept was adopted by Treasury he had no clients with a direct interest in leasing as a way of shifting tax benefits.

But soon after the approach was accepted, "it was at that stage that I had from then on a very substantial interest in the matter and spent a lot of time working on the subject," he said.

Christian contends that the leasing provisions of the 1981 tax bill are "marvelous" and will emerge as "one of the most important developments in the tax law."

As for providing the legal work for lease arrangements, he said, "In one form or another, I'm probably involved in close to a billion dollars. . . . I've been working hard, that's all I can tell you."

Hickman said he had picked up about the same amount of business. "I think that our office and Christian's office, because of the fact that we were involved in the genesis of the thing, . . . undoubtedly we are heavier in it than the normal office."

# Why the Republicans Can't Lose
## No Matter How Well the Democrats Play, It Will Still Be the Reaganauts' Game

*The Washington Post,* January 17, 1982

On the surface, these appear to be days for Democratic rejoicing.

The Reagan economic program, at least for the moment, is not working. The tax bill has produced none of the claimed massive increase in corporate capital investment. Instead, after accounting for inflation, the rate of investment has been negative. Worse, while only token individual rate cuts have reached the average taxpayer, the major beneficiaries of the tax cut, corporations, appear to be using this money not to rebuild the nation but to buy each other, to acquire their own undervalued stock, or to buy and sell their own tax breaks. All this has rekindled the flame of distrust in corporate America.

On the budget side, the cuts have been so swift, deep and lacking in concern for consequences that even conservative Republican senators and governors are calling for a halt. Instead, a rediscovered interest in the tax system to counter deficits approaching $200 billion by 1984 has emerged not only among Democrats but within the GOP.

If this were not enough, the Reagan administration is sending out contradictory signals on gut Republican questions, the most sensitive of which has been the importance of federal deficits. These conflicting messages have prompted a gleeful Sen. Daniel Patrick Moynihan (D-N.Y.) to warn his Republican colleagues that such differing portrayals of reality has been shown to cause catatonia in white rats.

Despite these developments, however, there are forces suggesting that a rebirth of the Democratic party agenda is not at hand. These forces are present in addition to the outside possibility of a major economic revival and a consequent firm entrenchment of the GOP.

Start on the extremes with the familiar Democratic division between conservative Southerners who, in the main, have weakened ties to populism, and urban liberals representing largely poor districts in Northern cities from San Francisco to Boston.

Then go to the deeper and continuing split between Democratic constituents dependent on Great Society programs—food stamps, medicaid, broadened welfare benefits—and those blue-collar workers who were drawn in (or whose parents were drawn in) to the fold during the New Deal. This is the conflict that is repeatedly encapsulated in the story about the steelworker and his wife who wait with mounting anger in the supermarket checkout line as a woman—in most recountings, black—pays for six bags of groceries with food stamps.

The depth of this conflict cannot be underestimated—and Democrats have shown no talent for resolving it. They evidently prefer to participate passively in a new economic debate whose terms have largely been defined by Republicans.

The Republican party, in contrast, has for the moment found a set of policies benefiting its own basic constituencies. Put aside for now the question of whether the Reagan tax bill is the legitimate expression of a new concept for reviving the economy or simply an extreme recycling of trickle-down policies disguised by the phrase "supply side." The measure unquestionably has benefited the core of the Republican party.

The wealthy have seen the top rate on unearned income drop from 70 to 50 percent and the capital gains rate fall from 28 to 20 percent. The savings incentives (IRAs and All-Savers certificates) are far more favorable to those in upper brackets, because they are deductions from income (a $2,000 deduction means $1,000 to a person in the 50 percent bracket and $400 to someone in a 20 percent bracket) rather than tax credits.

The same is true of the whole subnetwork of less publicized breaks in the Reagan bill, including incentive stock options, the $75,000 exemption on foreign income and the effective elimination of the estate tax so that it will apply only to the top 0.3 percent of estates, which in turn will pay lower rates.

Similarly, the business community received a tax cut which, in some cases, will not only mean the elimination of all federal taxation of income from new investments, but an actual negative income tax allowing corporations to shield income from past investments.

While the tax benefits flowing to lower- middle-class Democrats who defected to the GOP are negligible—and are likely to be eaten up by inflation, bracket creep and Social Security levies—the demand of many in this group for a cutback in social welfare spending has been met. Proposed additional cuts for 1983 and 1984, moreover, would further meet this pressure for reductions in benefits for the poor.

In calculating political strategies, the longrange question is whether wavering

Democrats—who generally fall into households earning $15,000 to $35,000 a year—will continue to identify "welfare" as the key source of economic deterioration. The possible alternative is a return to placing more blame on corporations that escape taxation and on the lessened share the wealthy contribute to the operation of the government.

The potential for this kind of political shift is reflected in the fact that the group that considers the tax system to be most unfair is made up of union workers. The outcome of this delicate balance between anger at welfare and anger at inequitable taxation is perhaps the key to the politics of the current decade. In this context, the second key factor becomes the ability of the extraordinarily well financed Republican party to maintain control over the terms of the public debate.

While continued failure of the economy would be a major blow to the GOP drive for majority status, the power to define the political agenda cannot be underestimated. It is, for example, quite possible that the GOP will make no real headway in November, even lose seats in the House and Senate, but still have the power to determine the way Congress approaches the economic issues.

This power obviously has been present during the past session of the 97th Congress, but it was also the case in the 1978–1980 period under a Democratic president and Democratic control of both branches of Congress. From this vantage point there are three factors that have stood out, and all continue to be overwhelmingly favorable to the Republican party.

The first, and simplest, is money. In 1981 alone, the Republican National Committee, the Republican Senatorial Committee and the Republican Congressional Committee raised a total of about $73.6 million. Their Democratic counterparts, despite a revived fund-raising effort, gathered a total of only $9.9 million.

GOP fund-raising has reached a level of sophistication at which the party not only can provide seed money to House and Senate candidates, but also performs much broader functions. In addition to its own resources, the GOP has gained considerable leverage over the money flowing from corporate and trade association political action committees—cash that is even more important than party funds to congressional candidates. The knowledge of this party leverage, which works to maintain party discipline, was one of the unstated bases for the exceptional party-line voting by Republicans in the budget and tax fights last year.

Perhaps more significant, however, is the Republican realization that the money it has raised can be used for TV promotion of GOP ideology and legislative positions, distinguished from promotion of specific candidates and elections. The party has already started using commercials to advocate the virtues of the GOP and the weaknesses of the Democrats (the most memorable of which was the caricature of Tip O'Neill running out of gas), and it has tentatively explored the use of commercials to promote specific measures before Congress, including the Reagan tax and budget bills.

The second factor has been the politicization of American corporations. The growth and expanded financing of corporate and trade association PACs—$6.7

million from 450 committees in 1976 to $67.7 million from 1,885 committees in 1980—has become a cliché of political reporting. This in good measure testifies to the fact that the corporation is an almost ideal fund-raising vehicle.

The chief executive officers define the giving of contributions as formal policy for all management level employees—while maintaining the appearance of voluntarism. The money can be collected through payroll deduction. Distribution of the funds is carried out by individuals whose function is to advance the corporation's political and legislative interests (except in the cases of PACs that receive primarily "earmarked" money, specifically designated for a candidate by the individual donor).

These same factors make the corporation an ideal lobbying vehicle. In addition to the power to encourage all management-level personnel to contact their congressmen and senators on specific issues, large corporations or trade associations can (and almost all do) computerize the entire process by correlating all plants and employees with specific members of Congress and providing each with specific information of the importance to every state and district of the company's spending and payroll.

Although there is no disputing the widespread public support Reagan received for his tax and budget bills, there is also no question that corporate-induced lobbying, coordinated by the White House and supportive organizations ranging from the Chamber of Commerce to the Securities Association, contributed enormously to the outpouring of telephone calls and telegrams that inundated the last Congress.

At a more subtle level, the politicization of corporations has resulted in the massive expansion of financing for such groups as the American Enterprise Institute, the Hoover Institution and the Heritage Foundation, along with the concentrated effort by these groups to influence discussion of issues in the media. Coinciding with this has been the financing of growing numbers of public TV programs that attempt to discuss broad and specific economic questions. Both these efforts function to define the nature of the political debate on economic issues.

The politicization of corporations reflects two other important developments. Business recognized that in the political arena, competitive interests should be submerged in favor of broad, cooperative coalitions. The effect was to give this segment of the American political community far more strength, particularly in contrast to the divided constituencies of the Democratic party. Secondly, business as a class realized that policies affecting their interests are the result of discretionary decisions on tax, regulatory and budget questions by both Congress and the executive branch.

Democratic politicians and their constituencies, in contrast, failed to take any parallel steps. The lower-middle class saw fewer and fewer benefits from Democratic policies, and union workers felt a steady decline in their economic position. Union leaders, apparently distrustful of the McGovern wing of the party, did little or nothing to draw their membership into the political process in the same fashion that middle-level management has been drawn into the fray. Party leaders, in turn, failed in their efforts to broaden the franchise among the most loyal Democratic voters, the poor, by winning approval of some form of Election Day registration.

In addition, it may well be that the creation of "entitlement" programs— food stamps, medicaid—functioned to create the false belief that these benefits are permanent rights and discouraged political participation to protect these programs. It may be that the Reagan administration's demonstration that these programs are subject to discretionary, political decisions will alter this attitude.

The third and most complex force functioning to benefit the GOP is television. The medium, which has come to dominate political campaigning, is in many ways antithetical to traditional Democratic campaign tactics.

In the pre-TV period, strategy amounted to multiple campaigns among often conflicting groups in a delicate process of converting a collection of minorities into an Election Day majority. The essence of Democratic politics was to piece together a diverse collection of minorities—union members, blacks, Southerners, Jews, city pols—into a loose majority, through a collection of separate promises and campaign commitments. If these campaign promises were often contradictory and newspapers raised questions, the response would be some version of the argument that America is a pluralistic society and strict logic cannot be applied to the campaign process.

Television, however, precludes this kind of campaigning. The prime-time audience (except on certain marginal channels) has no coherent racial, ethnic, religious or class identity to which an appeal can be made. A commercial making specific promises to blacks or union members, for example, is likely to offend as many or more viewers as it appeals to. The old-style Democratic appeal becomes a zero-sum game, or worse.

Republicans, in contrast, historically have targeted their campaigns to the Protestant middle and upper class. The interests of this group are most often the protection of the status quo, and consequently do not involve a direct challenge or threat to other groups.

In addition, the basics of Republican economic thinking as reflected by members of Congress—balance budgets, eliminate excessive spending and eliminate government impediments to business success—are simple enough to translate easily to TV.

In effect, television turns the Democratic mix into a cacophony of voices, while Republicans mesh easily into the centrist medium.

In this respect, the rightward shift of the GOP has become an elective benefit, rather than the liability it proved to be in the 1964 Goldwater campaign. In recent history, the major conflict within the Republican party has been between the moderate Eisenhower-Rockefeller wing and the conservative faction that emerged in full strength in 1964. The effective takeover of the party by the right has, however, functioned to almost eliminate this conflict.

As a result, the party can present on television what amounts to a single voice, even when multiple leaders are speaking. That voice may be significantly further to the right than the general public, but it speaks in the soothing tones of a Walter Cronkite. And the image of internal harmony may well be more important than position and substance in the politics of television campaigning.

There are developments that could cut across these trends and significantly alter the course of politics. U.S. involvement in El Salvador is the most obvious in the area of foreign affairs, but the internal potential of the Reagan administration for creating an external conflict on almost any continent cannot be underestimated. Similarly, no one really anticipated in the early Eisenhower years the emergence of the civil rights movement that both changed the face of society and, over a decade, gave the Democrats an issue of pervasive moral consequence.

But without this kind of wild card, Democrats face extremely difficult problems in regaining control of the political agenda. The perceived inequities of the Reagan economic program may do more for the Democrats than they can do for themselves, particularly in the tax arena.

The key group of swing voters—the 34.6 percent of the population from households making $11,500 to $22,900—will realize a tax cut of $4.7 billion this year, most of which will be eaten up by bracket-creep Social Security increases. The 6.8 percent of the population making more than $47,800, however, will realize a tax break of $12 billion.

Union members, who gave nearly half their votes to Reagan in 1980, are going to see their tax rates remain effectively the same and their incomes remain stagnant or decline with the growing "givebacks" in current negotiations. In contrast, the tax rates of their employers, both the chief executive officers and the corporations themselves, will drop radically, and these workers will continue to be regaled with stories of corporations buying and selling their tax breaks. This may well function to shift the focus of anger away from the food stamp recipient to the Fortune 500.

Even if such a shift in mood develops, the Democratic party retains the substantial, and perhaps irreconcilable, problem of the South. Democrats in the South are under little or no pressure to remain loyal to the national and congressional leaders of their party. The threat to their futures is a highly conservative GOP.

The gut populism of many Southern Democrats, which gave them at least rough areas for agreement with Northern colleagues on some economic issues in the past, has been replaced by a deep anxiety. Not only does the GOP have a strong foothold in all the confederate states, but the last election saw the defeat of such senators as Herman Talmadge (D-Ga.) and Robert Morgan (D-N.C.) by well financed nonentities, Mack Mattingly and John East, respectively.

In the face of this kind of threat, there is little the Democratic leadership can do to bring Southern dissenters back into the fold. The attempt by Tip O'Neill to buy off this wing of the party by giving them key seats on major policy and standing committees only resulted in placing Rep. Phil Gramm (D-Tex.) on the Budget Committee, where he became the principal sponsor of the Reagan budget cuts, and in putting Rep. Kent Hance (D-Tex.) on the Ways and Means Committee, where he became the Democratic sponsor of the Reagan tax cut.

Despite protestations of renewed intellectual vigor, Democrats have not demonstrated a capacity to regain the status of politicians equipped to direct the course of events. Incapacitated by internal splits, they have become increasingly like Republicans of the past generation: passive actors on the periphery of the main event. And the main event has become a debate between proponents of supply-side economists and traditional Republicans who consider elimination of the deficit to be the first priority.

While the Republican shift to the right has, to date, not proved fatal for that party, an attempt by the Democrats to develop more coherence, left, right or center, does not appear to be an option they are institutionally prepared to take. Instead, the party continues, in a strangely second-hand way, to try to be everything to everybody. Its current appeals to such diverse groups as the poor, the union movement and environmentalists are not based on positive programs; they are simply attempts to capitalize on the damage to these groups by the Reagan administration.

Faced with a growing shift of corporate and trade association money to the GOP, Democratic fund-raisers are pleading with PAC officials for a return to the policy of giving to both parties. Two key steps that were available to the Democrats in the late 1970s to counter the politicization of corporations—labor law reform designed to permit organized labor to make gains in the South and West, and Election Day registration designed to sharply increase turnout among the poor—failed, in part because of the lukewarm backing of President Carter.

Instead of major initiatives by the Democrats, the coming years are likely to be dominated by the Republican agenda, even if the GOP does not gain a plurality of voters. The vitality of the debate will probably remain within the GOP, just as Democrats were the focal point of fundamental political choices over the past 50 years on a sequence of issues including government intervention in the economy, the postwar rebuilding of Europe, the civil rights movement, and the Vietnam War.

Republicans are now engaged in a national debate between proponents of radical tax cuts and those who advocate the elimination of government red ink; between those who see government intervening to define sexual, and to a lesser extent religious, behavior, and those who consider this a violation of the constitutional role of the state; between those who see communism as an unrelenting threat and those who see the world as one large marketplace where political disagreement is to be submerged to economic gain. In these debates, Democrats have relegated themselves to the sidelines, dependent either on some degree of economic collapse or another unforeseen external development to restore them to center stage.

# How a Lobbyist Group Won
# Business Tax Cut

*Victory Raises Policy, Economic Issues;*
*Business Tax Cut Raises Critical Public Policy,*
*Economic Issues*

*The Washington Post,* January 17, 1982

In late 1978, a small group of elite tax lobbyists began what were to become weekly Tuesday morning breakfast sessions in the Sheraton Carlton Hotel on Sixteenth Street.

Such meetings have become a commonplace in Washington as business groups, with growing sophistication, have formed alliances and coalitions in preparation for legislative battles.

Similar groups defeated labor law reform legislation and won approval of a measure weakening the powers of the Federal Trade Commission, and an ad hoc coalition has been organized around the reauthorization of the Clean Air Act.

In this case, however, there were some differences. Among them:

• The tax coalition, which would come to be known as the Carlton group, first wrote the basic structure of the business tax cut known as 10-5-3, a system giving companies much faster depreciation write-offs on new investments that went into effect January 1, 1981. The coalition rounded up enough co-sponsors in the House to give the measure majority support and then persuaded the Reagan administration to adopt the measure as its own. But this was no ordinary bill: it would end up costing the Treasury $536 billion through 1990, according to estimates by the Joint Committee on Taxation.

• Not only would the measure represent the largest business tax cut in history, but also it would set new standards for any group seeking to lessen its tax burden: for most new capital investments, the tax break would more than equal the tax liabilities on profits from the investment, creating a situation in which corporations have a stronger incentive to invest than if there were no corporate income tax at all. This effectively created an indirect federal subsidy—or negative income tax—on corporate profits from new investments.

• In gaining the backing of the Reagan administration, the Carlton group had certain advantages. The lobbyist considered the "father" of the Carlton group, Charls E. Walker, was also chairman of President Reagan's tax policy task force. Other members of the task force who also were members of the Carlton group were Ernest S. Christian, Jr., who wrote the first three versions of 10-5-3 and whose clients include the American Retail Federation; Richard Rahn, formerly chief economist for Walker's American Council for Capital Formation and now for the U.S. Chamber of Commerce; and Mark Bloomfield, who has Rahn's former job at the American Council.

• At one point in the legislative consideration of the tax bill, the administration and the business alliance briefly split. The administration momentarily decided the measure was too expensive and would severely hamper its ability to balance the budget. But when the administration proposed specific reductions, the business community flexed its muscles in what would become known as the "Lear Jet weekend." Over that June 7–8 weekend, when chief executive officers from across the country flew into Washington to voice their protests, the Treasury Department not only backed off most of the reductions, but also actually added provisions raising the cost of the measure by $41 billion over the next decade.

• One of the key concessions by the Reagan administration to keep the business community fully behind the Reagan tax bill on that June weekend was the addition of a section that would become one of the most controversial tax concepts in recent memory. A superficially innocuous change in the rules governing leasing procedures, the new provision allowed corporations to buy and sell their tax deductions and credits. This provision would end up deeply embarrassing a number of congressional Republicans, who saw this as indirect welfare for business—"corporate tax stamps," in the words of one economist.

• There is a serious and substantive debate over the whole question of the corporate income tax. A number of conservative and liberal thinkers believe the tax, combined with levies on dividends, amounts to a form of double taxation. But the measure written by the Carlton group and amended by the administration created an entirely new twist to the argument. For a broad range of corporations, the combination of existing deductions and credits, the new depreciation schedule in 10-5-3 and the leasing (tax sale) provisions mean that they will actually make money out of the tax system, not pay into it. For these companies, the tax system amounts to a subsidy and functions to give them a competitive edge in the marketplace. As a consequence, rational lobbying strategy would call for these companies to pull out the stops and fight any effort to eliminate the corporate income tax.

• The administration's initial intent was to win approval of a "clean" tax bill containing only the Kemp-Roth individual rate cuts (30 percent spread over three years) and the 10-5-3 business cuts. Part of the tacit agreement with the key business lobbyists was that in return for the very generous 10-5-3 bill, the business community would back the "clean" bill. In effect, under the deal business would have to postpone pressure for a number of more specific breaks. In fact, however, key members of the Carlton group ended up as full participants in what became known as the bidding war between the administration and House Democrats.

This bidding war resulted in the addition of a host of new breaks benefiting the oil industry, financial institutions, truck company owners and the heirs of very large estates. Among the most prominent lobbyists for some of these additions were members of the Carlton group, including Charls Walker. Walker's clients, for example, included a number of multinational corporations seeking an exemption on foreign earned income, a provision that was added in the middle of the bidding war at a cost through 1986 of $2.7 billion.

The creation of 10-5-3, which really amounts to a simplfied and sharply accelerated system for corporations to depreciate the cost of new investments, was not carried out in a secret cabal. Members of the Carlton group generally talk openly about what took place, and the general outline is as follows:

During the passage of almost every tax bill over the past two decades, the business community had been bitterly split. This phenomenon continued through the 1978 tax bill, despite the fact that the congressional mood had swung from tax reform to strong support of business interests.

As one key lobbyist who successfully fought for the halving of capital gains rates from 46 to 28 percent in 1978 said: "Small business had been fighting for other things, but we whipped them."

In the aftermath of the 1978 bill, the two architects of the cut for capital gains, Reps. James Jones (D-Okla.) and the late William Steiger (R-Wis.), both members of the Ways and Means Committee, began to meet with key representatives of business and gave them a mandate: agree on a new tax bill and we will sponsor it. After Steiger's death, he would be replaced by Barber B. Conable (R-N.Y.) as the leading congressional proponent on the GOP side.

The mandate was irresistible. An industry group that had been meeting under the direction of Cliff Massa, IV, vice president for taxation at the National Association of Manufacturers (NAM), was converted into what would become the Carlton group.

The members would include the following: Massa, of NAM; Rahn, of the American Council and later of the Chamber; Christian, of the American Retail Federation, and whose firm, Patton, Boggs and Blow, has at least 140 clients ranging from Armco Inc. to Westinghouse Electric; Phillips S. Peter, of General Electric; John Post, executive director of the Business Roundtable, an organization representing most of the nation's largest corporations; various representatives of Walker's lobbying arm, Charls E. Walker Associates, whose 65 clients range from the Aluminium Co. of America to Weyerhaeuser Co.; John M. Albertine, director of the American Business Conference, an organization of mid-sized, high growth companies; William K. Condrell, a partner in the law firm of Steptoe and Johnson and representative of the Committee for Effective Capital Recovery; and both James D. McKevitt and John J. Motley of the National Federation of Independent Business.

"Those of us who represent the business community thought about what we might do about capital cost recovery," Rahn said. The group considered a number of options, including indexing depreciation, shifting to a system based on the replacement cost of investments instead of the purchase price, immediate expensing (writing off) of the entire investment in the first year, corporate rate reductions, and some form of reduction or elimination of taxation of both dividends and corporate profits.

"There finally developed a sort of consensus that the thing that made a combination of the best economic and political sense was 10-5-3," Rahn said.

Under 10-5-3 as introduced by the administration, the system by which corporations depreciate investments would have been reduced to basically three categories. Instead of the old system of 132 categories based on the "useful life" of an investment, all automobiles, light duty trucks and research and development equipment would be written off over three years, all other equipment over five years, and certain public utility, owner-occupied factories, stores and warehouses over ten years.

Shortening the depreciation period is of great tax advantage to the investor because the money is available much more quickly. The value of a dollar today is more than its value next year. Some factories, for example, would have seen their depreciation "life" shortened from 60 years to 10 years and some types of equipment from 36 years to 5 years.

The 10-5-3 bill raises a host of critical public policy and economic questions:

• Will it, as some contend, exacerbate, rather than lessen, existing distortions in investment patterns because the tax advantages for some industries will be far larger than for others? A May 1981, study by the Joint Committee on Taxation, for example, showed that the share of the tax break going to the petroleum and refining industry will be 320 percent larger than its share of total national investment in 1982; while for the airline industry, the share of the tax break will be only 40 percent of its contribution to total national investment, and for the telecommunications industry the share amounts to only 20 percent.

• On a larger scale, should the federal government remain dependent on the corporate income tax as a major source of revenue? Because of past business tax cuts, the proportion of the federal tax burden paid by corporations has been steadily falling, from about 22 percent of the total in 1960 to about 12 percent in 1980. The 10-5-3 bill does not directly address this question, but it does function to speed the process: by 1986, the corporate income tax is expected to provide 7.7 percent of federal revenues.

• What is the appropriate size of the tax cut? This was determined, to a large extent, by the Carlton group and later lobbying pressure. The administration did slightly modify the proposal when it was first introduced as H.R. 2400 in 1981, and later tried to back off from some of the cost in June. The early June cutbacks were, however, restored in less than six days, after the Lear Jet weekend.

Now, however, the administration and Congress are in the midst of a debate on whether or not to raise taxes this year, the first time in recent memory that taxes would be raised in a period of recession. One of the main reasons for the pressure for a tax increase is the deficit, which, in turn, has grown because of the size of the 1981 tax cut.

• Perhaps most important, is 10-5-3 the best vehicle to spur investment and to improve the nation's productivity? Because of the overwhelming and unflinching business support for 10-5-3, other proposals were never given serious political consideration. A system designed by two Harvard economists, Dale Jorgenson and Alan Auerbach, which placed all depreciation benefits in the first year to prevent the distorting effects of inflation never got off the ground in the congressional debate, as the one driving force became a competition between Democrats and Republicans to outbid each other for business backing.

Democrats on the Ways and Means Committee ultimately decided to match the administration dollar for dollar with a combination of corporate rate cuts and a system of depreciation called expensing: 100 percent of the cost of an investment could be written off in the first year, although the investment tax credit would be eliminated. Expensing had long been the goal of the business community, and it even received the backing of the Institute for Research on the Economics of Taxation, the consulting firm formally run by Norman Ture, Treasury undersecretary for taxation and a leading proponent of supply side economics. But, in the politics of the debate, a shift of support to expensing would have become a defeat for the Reagan administration, and the business community remained firm behind 10-5-3.

The final test of the bill will be economic results. To date, the measure has not produced the wave of business investment predicted by the administration. Instead, a survey by the Commerce Department showed that business this year expects total investment to decline by 0.5 percent and last year, with the tax cut fully effective from January 1, 1981, investment increased by only 0.3 percent.

# GE Gets Tax Refund on Billions Profit

## Two Firms' Annual Reports Illustrate Benefits of "Leasing"

*The Washington Post*, March 16, 1982

General Electric, which had pre-tax earnings of $2.66 billion in 1981, capitalized so successfully on the bill Congress passed last year which allows corporations to buy and sell tax breaks that it will get a net tax refund of $90 million to $100 million from the federal government.

A second highly profitable firm that bought up tax breaks last year, Amoco, which had a pre-tax income of $3.46 billion, was able to reduce its federal liability by $159 million through tax "leasing," although the oil company did still pay several hundred million dollars in federal taxes.

These figures emerged from annual reports for 1981 that are just being released and from interviews with company officials.

GE and Amoco are generally believed to have been among the most active firms buying up tax breaks. They bought the credits and depreciation write-offs from such companies as Chrysler, Pan American, Cleveland Electric, Commonwealth Edison and Phelps Dodge.

The benefit was most dramatic in the case of GE, which went from $426 million in tax payments in 1979 and $330 million in 1980, to its refund of $90 million to $100 million.

The company was able to achieve this negative tax situation largely through the purchase of tax credits and depreciation write-offs by a subsidiary, General Electric Credit Corp. GECC bought tax breaks from at least nine different companies and utilities through paper transactions called "leases" on about $1.4 billion worth of equipment.

The 1981 tax bill allowed companies to buy and sell tax breaks through leases; a company "leases" a piece of machinery and acquires the tax breaks associated with its cost. The provision was sold to Congress as a benefit for weaker companies. It has become highly controversial largely as a result of disclosures that profitable firms, like Occidental Petroleum, are also selling their unneeded tax breaks.

Sen. Robert J. Dole (R-Kan.), chairman of the Senate Finance Committee, has warned that he intends to seek repeal of the leasing provisions retroactive to February 19.

On the surface, the GE report indicates the company was preparing to pay $529 million in federal taxes for 1981. In the more detailed notes, however, the firm pointed out that the credit company subsidiary, GECC, produced "provisions for taxes recoverable" of $633 million for 1981.

This $633 million, about one third of which resulted from buying tax benefits, was used both to reduce the 1981 tax liability and to get a refund on prior year's taxes, according to John F. McCoy, the firm's tax manager.

Although GE did not spell out the process, McCoy noted that federal law restricts the use of investment tax credits, the major first-year benefits from tax sales, so that a company can only eliminate 80 percent of its federal liability by this means.

As a result, he said, the firm had to pay 1981 taxes of between $50 million to $60 million—he would not provide precise details—but then it was able to turn around, and by virtue of the same leases, collect a refund on past years of about $150 million, for a net gain of $90 million to $100 million.

McCoy noted that "even though we have reduced our 1981 liability and have generated credits," GE's benefit was not the full amount of the tax savings because it had to pay out significant amounts of cash to buy the tax breaks.

Amoco—Standard Oil Co. (Indiana)—said directly in its annual report that "income tax expense for 1981 has been reduced by $159 million, reflecting the effect of tax benefits purchased."

The company said it expects to pay $390 million in federal taxes in 1981, compared to $433 million in 1980, although it was not clear whether the reduction resulted primarily from buying tax breaks.

Amoco did, however, note that investment tax credits for 1981 increased sharply from 1980, going from $106 million to $334 million, although no breakdown was provided to show how much of the credits resulted from investments for the firm and from purchased credits.

The effective tax rate when all state, local, foreign and federal taxes are calculated dropped from 46.7 percent in 1980 to 44.4 percent in 1981 "primarily due to higher investment tax credits associated with tax leasing arrangements," Amoco said in its report.

# Democrats Find Budget Fight Waged on Republican Terms

## Tax Cuts Put Party on Defense

*The Washington Post,* May 2, 1982

As Republicans and Democrats resume their trench warfare over the budget, one basic fact remains: the substance of the debate continues to be defined in Republican terms.

Partisan rhetoric to the contrary, the stereotyped big-spending Democrat has all but vanished from the scene. Despite a recession and nine percent unemployment, there is no serious consideration in the Democratic House of a jobs program to put people back to work. The Federal Reserve's tight money policy has come under modest fire, but nothing like the attack that could be expected from liberal Democrats in their prime.

Instead, one of the fundamental budget conflicts last week was whether to cut non-defense programs by $35 billion (the Democratic stance) or by $60 billion (the administration position).

For House Speaker Thomas P. (Tip) O'Neill, Jr. (D-Mass.), the starting point in the bargaining was the acceptance of $35 billion in reduced federal spending for social programs over three years.

O'Neill, the quintessential Democratic liberal with the Boston accent and wheel-horse physique, who has been characterized in Republican political commercials as the symbol of deficit spending, had accepted a basic Republican tenet: that federal spending for social programs had to be cut.

This remarkable situation results from the key victory of the Reagan administration: the $749 billion tax cut enacted last year.

The supply-side theories behind the tax cut may be in disfavor among many legislators, but the consequences of the tax cut remain the dominant factors in the debate.

The 1981 Economic Recovery Tax Act effectively mandates that legislators seek additional ways of cutting federal spending to avoid economically and politically disastrous deficits. The tax cut will result in a growing erosion of federal revenues—$37.7 billion in the current fiscal year, $150 billion in 1984 and $267.7 billion in 1986.

This erosion represents the fulfillment of conservative dreams. The tax cut explained why the debate has stayed within the terms defined by Republicans, despite the deterioration of President Reagan's popularity in public opinion polls.

And that is the reason Reagan has remained so firmly behind the third year of his individual tax cuts. "We had to reduce the share of the people's earnings the government was taking in taxes," the president said in his televised speech Thursday night. "Because government always finds a need for whatever money it gets, the cost of government continues to go up."

While making concessions in the budget negotiations on the need to raise new revenues, administration representatives generally sought temporary taxes on energy or on individuals, which would not permanently set back the reductions mandated by the 1981 legislation.

In addition, Reagan is now strongly pressing for enactment of a constitutional amendment to balance the budget. This would function not only to deflect some of the political embarrassment resulting from the record deficits during his own administration, but also to protect the strategy of forcing continued reduction of the federal government:

"With the stick of a balanced budget amendment, we can stop government's squandering, over-taxing ways and save our economy," the president said in his speech.

While Reagan is working to keep the economic debate structured in essentially conservative terms, Democrats are having difficulties in substantially capitalizing on what is emerging as their best issue: fairness.

As public opinion polls have shown growing voter perception of the Reagan administration as favoring the rich and disregarding the poor, Democrats have repeatedly mounted verbal attacks on alleged inequitable policies.

But one of the key sources of public discontent has been the Reagan tax bill, particularly provisions that are seen as giving excessive benefits to corporations and the very wealthy. Whether or not the complaints are justified on economic grounds, public opinion polls show opposition to the breaks for oil companies and to corporate tax leasing running well over 75 percent. Support for a tougher corporate minimum tax runs over 80 percent.

In the case of the corporate tax leasing and minimum tax, however, the initiative has been taken by, of all people, a Republican—Sen. Robert Dole of Kansas, chairman of the Finance Committee.

Not only has Dole taken these issues for his own, despite the fact that they would appear to be gold mines for Democrats, but he also has seized the tax reform issue generally, developing a multibillion-dollar list of loopholes largely benefiting the affluent, many of which he plans to propose to his committee for closing in coming weeks.

In contrast, Rep. Daniel Rostenkowski (D-Ill.), chairman of the House Ways and Means Committee, has remained silent on specific tax initiatives. He has, in fact, indicated that he will defer to Dole, apparently calculating that the political liabilities of initiating new taxes outweigh the benefits of taking the lead at a time of public discontent.

Rostenkowski is giving serious consideration to closing the committee sessions when final decisions are made, to focus attention on Democratic opposition to the administration.

In addition, the Chicago Democrat has indicated that he may support repeal of the third year of the tax cut for individuals. This would help the deficit situation, but it does not necessarily address equity issues.

The 10 percent rate reduction scheduled to go into effect on July 1, 1983, is the least beneficial to the very wealthy, who have already benefited from first-year features of the act—the reduction in the capital gains rate from 28 to 20 percent, and the reduction of the maximum rate on unearned income from 70 to 50 percent.

For those making over $200,000 a year, repeal of the 1983 tax cut would mean the loss of only 5 percent of the total benefits from the act. For everyone else, particularly the working class and middle class, the Democrats are attempting to bring back into the fold, loss of the third year means the loss of about 40 percent of the total tax break.

In another quirk of political strategy and tax distribution, most Democrats have been strongly opposed to indexation of the system—adjusting rates to compensate for inflation.

If, however, indexation were limited to a one-year experiment, and substituted for the 1983 individual rate cut, it would result in a more progressive distribution of the tax cut as well as a significant reduction of the revenue loss. Both of these results should appeal to Democrats.

This proportion of the cut going to the lower-middle class would increase by about 3 percent, the share to the middle class would stay the same, and for the wealthy it would drop by about 4 percent. This shift results because indexation also increases the standard deduction and personal exemption, both of which function to give more of a tax break to the working poor and lower-middle class.

It is clear that the current debate over tax policy will in large part define the future political posture of Republicans and Democrats, because of the magnitude of the tax revenues that must be raised to reduce budget deficits; both sides agree that more than $110 billion must be raised over the next three years.

While there is no coherent tax strategy among Republicans or Democrats, the stance among Democratic leaders in Congress has been conspicuously more negative and passive than Republican leaders. Sen. Pete V. Domenici (R-N.M.), chairman of the Senate Budget Committee, who has joined Dole in seeking closure of a number of tax loopholes, is exploring ways to place controls on tax "expenditures" or tax preferences, many of which benefit the wealthy.

If this continues to prove the case, Republicans will have co-opted an issue most readily available to the Democrats.

# How Democrats Sold Out—
# for Nothing

## *Business Keeps Giving Cash to Republicans Despite Hefty GOP Tax Increases*

*The Washington Post,* August 1, 1982

To judge by the spectacle last week when Democrats in the House gave up on trying to write a new tax bill, the Democratic party is frozen—stymied by political anxieties and the fear of interest groups aligned with their Republican rivals.

Last week, big business and the independent oil lobby helped scare the Democrats out of making any attempt to exploit what ought to be their best issue in 1982, the apparent "unfairness" of the Reagan economic program. Instead, House Democrats allowed the Republican Senate to take full credit for a tax bill that by any standard is anti-business and anti-rich.

Curiously, the interest groups the Democrats think they are courting by their failure to act on tax increases are, almost without exception, determined to help Republicans beat Democrats next November. Just as curiously, the corporate lobbies that Senate Republicans offended with their tax bill appear willing, even eager to turn the other cheek, and continue giving most of their political contributions to Republicans.

To be fair, the Democrats' inability to act on taxes was more than an effort to curry favor with corporate interests. Many Democrats in the House believed that if they tampered with the Republican tax bill, they would be blamed for the substantial tax increases—$98 billion over the next three years—that it contains. Better, these Democrats reckon, to give the Republicans their entire program, then blame the economic consequences on the GOP.

But by itself, this political consideration would not have been sufficient to block House action on a Democratic alternative to the Republican Senate's tax bill. House Democrats flinched when a proposal to increase taxes on independent oil producers was raised by Rep. Daniel Rostenkowski (D-Ill.), chairman of the Ways and Means Committee.

Rostenkowski was echoing majority opinion on his panel; the betting on both sides of the aisle was that if the Ways and Means Committee had written a tax bill, new oil taxes would have been part of it. But powerful Democrats wanted no such tax.

The issue became a quiet conflict within the Democratic leadership. The failure to act was a defeat for House Speaker Thomas P. (Tip) O'Neill, Jr., (D-Mass.), whose Republican opponent has received strong backing from oil interests in Texas and Oklahoma, and a victory for Rep. James Wright (D-Tex.), the majority leader, who has been struggling to maintain oil support for Democrats in his home state as the Republican party there grows in strength.

Wright was supported by a number of pro-oil Democrats, notably Rep. Tony Coelho (D-Calif.), who happens to be chairman of the House Democratic Campaign Committee. Coelho's district includes oil lands, and he acknowledges that he is trying to get independent oilmen to give more money to his campaign committee.

"I've said openly that independent oil in the past has been actively Democratic," Coelho argued. "They should be back in."

But independent oil has other ideas. It not only played a significant role in the defeat of at least eight Northern Democratic senators in 1980, along with such House members as former Democratic whip John Brademas (D-Ind.), but it is now leading the charge against vulnerable Democrats and in support of marginal incumbent Republicans.

Examination of the reports of such key independent oil political action committees (PACs) as the Dallas Energy PAC, the Louisiana Energy National PAC and the Houston PAC shows an overwhelming preference for Republicans. Through April of this year, the Dallas PAC, for example, handed out $71,000, every cent of which went to Republican candidates, all in amounts of $2,000 to $5,000.

In other words, Democrats were unwilling to go after an industry that in large part is committed to the achievement of a Republican Congress. Even such pro-oil Oklahoma Democrats as Reps. James R. Jones, Mike Synar and Dave McCurdy are discovering that their opponents are getting substantial backing from individual oil producers and PACs.

Moreover, this is an industry with little public support. A Louis Harris survey conducted in April for *Business Week* magazine showed the public in favor of taking back oil tax breaks by a margin of 78 to 17.

In direct contrast, Senate Republicans, particularly those on the Senate Finance Committee, took on, with apparent impunity for the Republican party, a whole network of groups that are strong GOP supporters.

The Senate-passed tax bill includes, for example, restrictions on tax benefits that go to contractors who have multi-year contracts with the government. These restrictions were bitterly opposed by the Associated General Contractors. In its July 7 newsletter, the AGC listed the committee vote, which showed that the seven committee members "for AGC position" were all Democrats, while the the 13 "against AGC position" included 11 Republicans and two Democrats.

Two weeks later, AGC's July 21 newsletter listed 94 candidates who had received contributions ranging from $1,000 to $5,000 during the week of July 14–20. Of the 94 beneficiaries, 87 were Republicans.

On a broader scale, the tax bill put together by the Reagan administration and Senate Republicans takes back a set of investment tax breaks considered essential to a strong business economic recovery by the U.S. Chamber of Commerce.

On July 1, the day the Republicans on the Finance Committee completed the tax bill (which the Chamber's chief economist described as a victory for "the forces of darkness"), the Chamber gave out to its members a confidential list making recommendations in 84 Senate and House races. In 82 of those races, the recommended candidate is a Republican.

Even special interests who have been palpably hurt by Reaganomics seem determined to help Republicans defeat Democrats this November. For example, the realtors, whose members have been severely hurt by the recession and the administration-backed tight money policy at the Federal Reserve—not to mention the presidential veto of special housing aid—continue to remain loyal to the GOP and to "boll weevil" Democrats who backed the administration.

Through April of this year, the Realtors PAC gave $221,176 to Republicans and $112,758 to Democrats, an apparent 2-to-1 split. Of the money going to Democrats, however, $72,250 went in large chunks of $3,000 to $5,000 to conservative Southerners who had backed the Reagan administration's budget and tax legislation last year, while the remainder went in relatively small dollops of $200 to $500 to liberal and moderate Democrats.

This kind of loyalty to conservative politicians in general, and to Republicans in particular, has given the GOP exceptional political autonomy. The freedom allowed the Republican-controlled Senate under the direction of Finance Committee chairman Robert Dole (R-Kan.) to pass a tax cut benefiting business and the wealthy in 1981, when public opinion was very supportive of the administration program; and then in 1982 to raise taxes primarily on corporations and the rich at a time when public opinion had shifted because of the perception that Reaganomics favored the rich.

This isn't all bad for the Republicans' traditional friends; the Dole tax increase this year is about a quarter of the size of the Reagan tax cuts of last year. At the same time, Dole's bill is masterful public relations, and the Democrats have been utterly unable to counter it.

The Democrats' posture of inaction accelerates the process started by the 1980 election in which Democrats are being forced farther and farther from the center of the debate over national issues. For 50 years, gut questions of social and economic policy were fought out almost entirely within the Democratic party, as Republicans remained largely on the sidelines. In 1981, President Reagan took over center stage, crushing efforts within the Democratic party to regain its voice.

Enactment of Reagan's proposal to cut taxes by $749 billion through 1986 insured that subsequent deficits would dominate congressional debate. And the question of reducing deficits is inherently an issue that favors Republicans seeking to cut the size of the federal government, over Democrats who have strong ties to spending programs.

If, as it now appears, Republicans have partially defused the issue of tax equity, the GOP has further strengthened its control over the national economic debate.

# Business Tries Hand at Feeding GOP Early in Marginal Races

*First of two articles*

*The Washington Post,* September 12, 1982

In the congressional races that will determine the partisan and ideological makeup of the 98th Congress, a key segment of the business community has become a de facto arm of the Republican party, providing targeted money in key marginal contests for House and Senate seats.

Working in tandem with conservative political groups, this coalition of companies, wealthy oil producers and investors, and business organizations is leading a steady transformation of election financing, disclosed in campaign spending reports at the Federal Election Commission.

The money from this coalition is producing crucial early support and credibility for Republican challengers confronting potentially vulnerable Democratic office holders in the House and Senate.

It is also shoring up the defenses of Republican incumbents—particularly the GOP members of Congress elected in 1980 who likely would be most vulnerable to any voter backlash this fall against Republicans because of economic troubles. While this support is not the only factor in some 45 key House races and 6 to 8 pivotal Senate contests, it could determine outcomes in the closest of these targeted races.

Timing is one element of the transformation. The heavy flow of support in the earliest stages of campaigns for unknown challengers or junior House and Senate members is a sharp break with pre-1980 custom, when contributions generally favored veteran incumbents. The other is the one-sided concentration of support from this coalition for Republicans.

The business and special-interest groups providing this backing to the GOP fall into four categories: broad-based business organizations, including the U.S. Chamber of Commerce and the National Federation of Independent Business; such major trade associations as the National Association of Realtors and the Associated General Contractors; a relatively small number of corporate political action committees (PACs), many with headquarters in, or with major investments in Sunbelt states; and other political action committees financed largely by independent oilmen in Texas, Louisiana, Oklahoma, Colorado and Southern California, whose primary goal is to elect conservative candidates in the northern tier of states.

Business community support has shifted over the past four years toward Republican candidates, but these groups are distinctive in a number of respects:

they are willing to get into races early, often during primaries; many are willing to contribute large amounts, often up to the maximum of $5,000 per candidate; and, unlike many political action committees seeking to maintain access to incumbents, these organizations tend to target the marginal races, often financing challengers or those with neither seniority nor firm grips on their districts.

They share a common goal with major conservative groups such as the National Conservative Political Action Committee, the Fund for the Survival of a Free Congress, Citizens for the Republic and the National Congressional Committee: to shift Congress to the ideological right.

In the overwhelming majority of contests this fall, this has meant financing Republicans' campaigns.

To the extent that these organizations support Democrats, the backing is limited almost entirely to those who backed the administration's 1981 budget and tax cuts over the objections of the House Democratic Leadership. In addition, contributions to Democrats are limited almost entirely to conservative candidates in primary elections in solidly Democratic districts facing opponents who are more liberal.

The groups disavow any commitment to the Republican side. "We are nonpartisan," said Joseph J. Fanelli, president of the Business-Industry Political Action Committee (BIPAC), a comment echoed by spokesmen for the others. But an examination of contributions on file with the Federal Election Commission shows the following:

*The Business Organizations*    On August 20, the Chamber of Commerce issued a summary of 99 House and Senate races recommended for "business involvement." In only one case—the Senate candidacy of Rep. James D. Santini (D-Nev.)—is the endorsed candidate a Democrat, and that endorsement is limited to his challenge in the Democratic primary to Sen. Howard W. Cannon.

BIPAC, which puts what amounts to a business "Good Housekeeping Seal of Approval" on candidates that leads to contributions from other PACs and individuals, has given $112,010 to House and Senate candidates. Of that, $99,230 has gone to Republicans.

BIPAC endorsed nine Democratic candidates and gave them a total of $12,780, but the endorsement was made only in primary elections and was limited to conservative Democrats running against more liberal Democratic opponents. Every candidate endorsed by BIPAC in the general election is a Republican.

Similarly, by the end of June, the National Federation of Independent Business had given Republican candidates $79,650 and Democrats $12,100. All of the money going to Democrats went to "boll weevil" House members who had bucked the Democratic leadership to support the Reagan budget and tax bills of 1981, and to two of the most conservative Democratic senators, Lloyd M. Bentsen (Tex.) and Edward Zorinsky (Neb.)

*The Corporate Political Action Committees*    Campaign spending records show that some 20 major corporations are particularly active in making early contributions, heavily weighted toward Republicans. The leaders include the Fluor Corp., the Eaton Corp., Dart & Kraft Inc., Standard Oil Co. (Indiana), and Sears, Roebuck and Co.

The Sears PAC this year has given $42,850 to Republicans, most of it to GOP House members holding marginal seats. The list of GOP recipients reads, in many respects, like a list of key races put out by the Republican Congressional Campaign Committee.

The PAC has given $12,400 to Democrats, $7,950 of which was to Southern supporters of the Reagan program. Much of the remainder went to Democrats representing districts near Sears' Chicago headquarters.

With even stronger leanings to the GOP, the Eaton Corp. PAC has given $46,150 to Republicans out of a total of $51,650. Fluor Corp.'s PAC has given a total of $85,550 to GOP candidates and committees, and $13,650 to Democrats. In both cases, the Democrats who received money generally were Southern Conservative supporters of the Reagan program.

*The Trade Organizations*    Key supporters of marginal Republican candidates, often providing up to the $5,000 maximum, have been such groups as the Realtors PAC, the American Medical PAC, the Sheet Metal and Air Conditioning PAC, and the Associated General Contractors PAC. These groups have raised large sums for the 1982 election. Through June, the Realtors PAC has raised $2.2 million and the American Medical PAC $2.17 million.

Through April of this year, the Realtors PAC reported giving $221,176 to Republicans and $112,758 to Democrats. Though on the surface this is a two-to-one split, just over $72,000 of money earmarked for Democrats went to "boll weevils." This means that the organization gave well over three quarters of its money to participants in the Republican-conservative Democratic coalition that dominated much of the 97th Congress.

More important, the Realtors gave donations of $2,000 or more—amounts that can be significant to campaigns in their early stages—to Republicans, particularly those in close races, and to conservative Democrats. The $40,000 of Realtors' money going to moderate and liberal Democrats was almost entirely in amounts ranging from $200 to $500, contributions viewed less as expressions of support than as "courtesy" or "access" gifts.

The Sheet Metal and Air Conditioning Contractors have given $138,643 to Republicans and $27,051 to Democrats; of the money going to Democrats, $21,551 went to conservative supporters of the Reagan program. The Associated General Contractors reported giving $396,300 in direct contributions to Republicans and $86,900 to Democrats, although $50,000 of the money for Democrats went to Texas candidates for the House and Senate.

*The Conservative Organizations*    The conservative PAC community is split into two groups: One is the "old" right, represented by such organizations as the

American Conservative Union and the Fund for a Conservative Majority, which concentrate more on issues of conservative economic policy and defense spending than on "social" issues. The other is the "new" right, including such groups as the Committee for the Survival of a Free Congress, the National Conservative Political Action Committee and Sen. Jesse Helms' (R-N.C.) National Congressional Club, which focuses on such issues as abortion, school prayer and busing.

During the primary season, the old and new rights took slightly different paths. The old right remained firmly in the GOP camp; the American Conservative Union specialized in running Washington fund-raisers for incumbents, almost all Republicans.

The new right entered a number of primaries with different goals, with mixed results, at best. For example, it failed to defeat Rep. Jack Brooks (D-Tex.) and also challenged the Republican establishment and the business community in some open-seat Republican primaries, unsuccessfully running a House candidate against Cissy Baker, daughter of Sen. Howard H. Baker, Jr. (R-Tenn.), the majority leader, in Tennessee.

As the general election approaches, the old and new rights' inherent loyalty to the GOP is reasserting itself. The Fund for a Conservative Majority is targeting 13 Senate races and 72 House races; every candidate supported is a Republican.

The National Conservative Political Action Committee is preparing "negative" campaigns against six senators and eight House members; every target for defeat is a Democrat. The Fund for a Conservative Majority expects to be involved in about 55 general election races; a spokesman said that perhaps three of the candidates supported will be Democrats.

*The Independent Oil PACs*    Over the past four years, a network of political action committees financed primarily by independent oilmen has sprung up in Texas, Louisiana, Oklahoma, Colorado, and Southern California. A key strategy of these PACs is to funnel money into non-oil states with the specific goal of defeating liberal to moderate incumbents. In practice, this translates into the channeling of large sums into Republican campaigns.

These groups include the Dallas Energy PAC (DALENPAC); the Louisiana Energy National PAC (LENPAC); the West Central Texas PAC; the Houston PAC; the Intermountain PAC (IMPAC); the Petroleum Exploration PAC of California; and about six smaller PACs in oil producing states.

Among this fraternity, DALENPAC offers the best example of concentrated political firepower, giving out $88,500 through June. Not only has every contribution gone to Republicans, but also, with only one exception, each gift was at least $2,000, and 10 of the contributions were the maximum $5,000. LENPAC contributed through May of this year $48,500 to Republicans and $14,500 to Democrats. All the money going to Democrats went to conservatives running in primaries, almost all of which are in districts certain to elect Democrats. IMPAC has given out $42,700, of which $40,700 has gone to 36 Republicans, almost all in tight races.

# PACs Bankrolling GOP Challengers

*Second of two articles*

*The Washington Post,* September 14, 1982

Eight months ago, the Independent Petroleum Association of America put Bill Kennedy, a relatively obscure Republican candidate for Congress in the San Jose suburbs of San Francisco, on its list of "Wildcat Prospects."

The endorsement signaled a decision within the independent oil community that the Kennedy campaign has the potential of fulfilling a key goal: the defeat of a liberal member of Congress, in this case, Rep. Fortney H. (Peter) Stark (D-Calif.).

The decision represented a sizeable gamble, because Kennedy had lost to Stark in 1980 by a 12-percentage-point margin. But the gamble did not scare off the oil community's political contributors.

Just before the endorsement of Kennedy was announced, the Dallas Energy Political Action Committee (PAC) contributed $5,000—the maximum allowed—to Kennedy. In February, the Louisiana Energy National PAC contributed $5,000. W. C. Pickens and R. H. Pickens, partners in the Dallas firm of Pickens Oil and Gas, kicked in $500 each; Louis A. Beecherl, Jr., honorary chairman of Texas Oil and Gas, put up $1,000, and a number of other independent oilmen and PACs followed suit, providing Kennedy's campaign with a vital, early pump-priming of at least $20,250. Through July, Kennedy reported to the Federal Election Commission that he had raised a total of $141,108 from all sources, while Stark had raised a total of $170,235.

The ability of a challenger like Kennedy to run a financially viable campaign against an established incumbent is part of a major change in the financing of political campaigns that has taken place over the past four years.

Some of the major elements of this change include:

• Business and conservative groups viewed each other with suspicion as recently as 1978—business was regarded as willing to sacrifice principle for profit, while conservatives were often branded by business as being too rigid to compromise. Now the two have joined forces in most of the key, marginal races, usually behind Republican candidates.

"There is a coordinated passing around of polling information between Republican committees, candidates, groups like ours, and the corporate PACs," said Paul Dietrich, of the Fund for a Conservative Majority. "People talk about 2,000 or more PACs, but the truth is that there are only about 45 corporate PACs, 6 conservative PACs and 15 to 20 trade association PACs that really count . . . a group of less than 75 people."

• The 1974 election reforms enacted in the wake of Watergate have not only encouraged the massive growth of political action committees, but they also have encouraged the emergence of a new kind of political figure: men and women who specialize in directing the flow of political money to campaigns, in effect a new kind of political boss.

These people include Bernadette Budde, of the Business-Industry Political Action Committee; William C. Anderson, senior government relations representative for the Independent Petroleum Association; Richard Thaxton of the National Association of Realtors; Clyde A. Wheeler, Jr., vice president for government relations of Sun Co.; and Peter Lauer of the American Medical Association.

They not only have direct leverage over campaign funds, they also influence others making decisions on where to give money. The recommendations of Budde's BIPAC, for example, are followed by business groups across the country.

• There is an increasingly strong set of personal ties to the GOP within key elements of the campaign finance structure. Neil Newhouse, political director for the Chamber of Commerce, is former director of field operations for the Republican National Committee. Morton C. Blackwell, former head of the conservative Committee for Responsible Youth Politics and employee of conservative fund-raiser Richard Viguerie, organized regular luncheon meetings of conservative PACs before the 1980 election to determine election strategies; hired by President Reagan to work in the White House office of public liaison, he continues to run the luncheon strategy sessions for the conservative PACs.

Thaxton of the National Association of Realtors political committee is a former employee of the Republican National Committee and of the Republican Governors Conference. Lee Ann Elliott, former associate director of the American Medical Association's PAC, was appointed by Reagan to a six-year term on the Federal Election Commission.

• Sunbelt interests appear to have become the most aggressive private-sector forces in national politics. Although oil—particularly independent oil (as opposed to the major oil companies)—is the most prominent in this assertion of political muscle, it is also present in Sunbelt construction, banking and a host of other interests.

Early in the 1980 Idaho Senate contest, for example, Steve Symms raised $154,000 from Texas interests alone, mostly during a two-day swing through Houston and Midland in his successful bid to oust liberal Sen. Frank Church (D-Idaho). Symms's path is becoming well-worn. For the past two months, conservative congressional candidates from northern states have been flowing through Dallas, Houston, Tulsa, Oklahoma City and Denver at a rate of better than two a week. "Sometimes when it works right, and the guy makes the right kind of pitch, you get $30,000 to $35,000; sometimes you only get $20,000," said Arthur J. Wessely, a Dallas oilman who helps organize many of the events. "Sometimes they try to work it with a fund-raiser in Oklahoma City and Houston on the same wheel; they hit two places on the same day."

• Democratic incumbents have extensive financial resources, particularly from unions and a wide range of professional, trade association and business PACs seeking to retain access to members of Congress.

Republicans, however, have the overwhelming edge in resources that can be used to finance challengers and to shore up marginal junior members who have yet to gain a strong hold on their districts. The three basic Democratic party committees—the national committee, congressional committee and senatorial committee—have raised only $13 million from January 1981 through March 1982 compared with $120 million by the parallel GOP committees.

The result of these various changing spending patterns is that Republicans in marginal contests—including challengers with no automatic access to Washington-based political contributors—are able to raise enough money to ensure that they are competitive, while Democrats in comparable positions have no parallel resources.

For example, in the 37 contests where Republicans took over Democratic House seats in 1980, the candidates raised roughly equal amounts in two races, but Republicans raised more in 25 out of the remaining 35. The financial superiority existed although many of the Democrats were committee and sub-committee chairmen, equipped to draw contributions from a wide range of special interests. Republicans spent a total of $10.2 million in those 37 races, while the Democrats spent $7.3 million.

This pattern was recognized by the House GOP freshmen who, on October 30, 1981, sent a letter to all the business PACs declaring:

"We are writing you today as friends of the business community. . . . Many of us would not now be serving in the Congress were it not for your PAC's campaign contribution last year. . . . We all hope we can count on your PAC to make an ever-greater effort to provide pro-free-enterprise business Republican challengers and incumbents the financial assistance necessary to achieve our shared goal of a Republican-controlled House of Representatives."

With this network of support, the GOP is able not merely to protect marginal incumbents, but also to conduct forays into Democratic-held districts, prospecting to see if a major investment would be worthwhile.

In Oregon's first congressional district, for example, Democratic Rep. Les AuCoin (D-Ore.), a moderate-liberal, has all the earmarks of an incumbent with a safe seat. He won by 63 percent in 1978 and by 66 percent in 1980. The recession has thrown Republicans in the timber-dependent state on the defensive.

However, his Republican opponent, William J. Moshofsky, a former vice president for government relations for Georgia Pacific Corp., already has raised $299,105. Key sources of support for Moshofsky have been the business and conservative groups whose goal is not access to incumbents, but an ideological shift to the right of Congress.

In contrast, Bill McCollum, a freshman Republican representative from Florida's fifth district, may be vulnerable. His seat was altered radically by redistricting, and much of the new territory has been represented by his Democratic opponent, Dick J. Batchelor, who serves in the state legislature. The Republican Congressional Committee warns that Batchelor is a "proven vote getter," and the Chamber of Commerce describes him as a "strong Democratic challenger." McCollum, however, had a two-to-one fund-raising edge as of July, with $128,-158—$79,563 from PACs—to Batchelor's $64,629, of which $2,000 is from PACs.

# New Power Network
## Independent Oil Fuels the Right

*The Washington Post,* October 8, 1982

NORMAN, Oklahoma—In this congressional district, where lifelong Democrats are still stronger than a nascent Republican party in the growing suburbs, Rep. Dave McCurdy (D-Okla.) is learning the new rules of the politics of oil.

The freshman congressman has played by the old rules: any member of the Oklahoma congressional delegation who likes his job votes for oil. McCurdy, with a 100 percent rating from the Independent Petroleum Association of America, has toed the line.

On November 2, however, McCurdy faces an opponent financed almost entirely by independent oil. Howard Rutledge, 50, a former Vietnam prisoner of war and now the GOP nominee, boasts: "I've got most, no, all the major independent oil men backing my campaign."

The neighboring congressional district's Rep. Glenn English (D-Okla.) not only voted oil right down the line, but used his vote on a key budget issue as leverage to get a letter from President Reagan promising never to place a windfall-profits tax on natural gas.

But, like McCurdy, English has a Republican opponent, Ed Moore, whose campaign chest has been filled by independent oil men.

"This is a totally new network of power in the Southwest," an incredulous McCurdy commented. He said that, unlike such groups as the American Medical Association, the National Rifle Association and the Realtors, all contributors to his campaign, the oil men "see me as a liberal, which is just phenomenal."

Another member of the Oklahoma delegation, Rep. Mike Synar, a maverick Democrat, put it this way: "Oil men have the political loyalty of a copperhead."

To judge from the legislative results in the 97th Congress, the contributions have reaped significant benefits for the independent oil industry.

All 52 House freshmen Republicans, many of whom won with oil support, had 100 percent favorable voting records from the Independent Petroleum Association. The freshmen Republican senators had almost the same record, despite the fact that many were elected from Midwest and Northeast states where voting in support of oil can be a political liability.

The most important legislative victory was inclusion in the 1981 tax cut of $11 billion in oil tax reductions, much of it targeted to the independents. Of equal significance, these breaks endure despite repeated Democratic threats to take them back as Congress had to raise taxes by $99 billion over three years.

In fact, the funneling of oil money this year into the GOP campaigns of Rutledge and Moore, neither of whom appears likely to win, is part of a much broader development.

"The oil people are not disagreeing with Mr. McCurdy's position relative to oil," said Douglas R. Cummings, owner of Cummings Oil Co. in Oklahoma City and a $1,000 contributor to both Moore and Rutledge. "We just don't like the package. Not only are we oil people, but most of us are pretty conservative.

"I feel that as long as Tip O'Neill is speaker of the House, we are going to see leadership that is too liberal," Cummings said. "A Republican House would get rid of Tip O'Neill. I'd be pleased to see that done, as you can well imagine."

Oil, particularly independent oil, is in the forefront of an ideological drive to the right. This drive has resulted in a major source of GOP money, but it goes beyond that.

In a kind of political wildcatting spirit, a network of independent oil men and political action committees, or PACs, in Dallas, Houston, Midland, Tulsa, Oklahoma City, New Orleans, Denver and Southern California are willing to pour money into high-risk races.

Although a large proportion is being funneled into close contests, it is also flowing to GOP candidates who appear to have little chance of winning.

In this respect, the oil men and their PACs are showing a far higher willingness to put money on challengers than the business community as a whole. The Independent Petroleum Association, the key independent oil organization, has a policy of endorsing only conservative challengers to liberal incumbents.

The Chamber of Commerce, which is willing to target almost any race where a Republican has a chance of winning, is not touching the challengers to either McCurdy or English. Individuals with ties to the independent oil industry, however, already have kicked in a total of more than $115,000 to the two races.

Similarly, in the hard-core Democratic district of House Speaker Thomas P. (Tip) O'Neill, Jr., independent oil men and their relatives gave O'Neill's challenger, Frank L. McNamara, Jr., $24,500 early on. There is so little chance that O'Neill will be defeated that the financing of the challenger is a form of political harassment.

It is big-bucks harassment, however. The oil money has financed a very expensive fund-raising drive using conservative mailing lists that had raised $495,954 for McNamara as of August 25.

Political action committee contribution records reflect the surface but not depth of the influence of oil money in Senate and House races. The Citizen/Labor Energy Coalition's most recent examination of 196 oil- and gas-related

PACs, for example, shows that they had contributed $4.34 million to congressional candidates and had $2.76 million more to be distributed. About 75 percent of their contributions are to Republicans.

These figures, however, barely scratch the surface not only of money but also the role it plays in campaigns and in legislative decisions. Take, for example, the case of Arthur J. Wessely, who runs Wessely Energy Corp. in Dallas.

"Dallas and Houston and New Orleans have suddenly become much more politically aware," said Wessely, a key organizer of the Dallas Energy Political Action Committee (DALENPAC). "When a guy in Michigan votes, he affects the people in Texas."

Wessely has put his money where his mouth is. Federal Election Commission (FEC) reports covering 1981 and part of 1982 show that Wessely shelled out at least $31,000 to Republican political committees, energy PACs, GOP candidates and conservative PACs.

Among them are the National Republican Congressional Committee, $7,000; the National Republican Senatorial Committee, $4,000; the Conservative Victory Fund, $1,000; the National Conservative Political Action Committee (NCPAC), $5,000; DALENPAC, $10,000, and the Louisiana Energy National PAC, $1,000.

Among the candidates who have received the maximum allowable contribution of $1,000 from Wessely are McNamara, the GOP challenger to O'Neill; Moore in Oklahoma; Rep. Robin L. Beard (R-Tenn.), who is challenging Sen. Jim Sasser (D-Tenn.), and Bill Kennedy, a Republican challenging Rep. Fortney H. (Pete) Stark (D-Calif.).

In addition, Wessely's wife has given $1,000 to McNamara and a total of $10,000 to DALENPAC. Discussing oil contributions, Wessely said, "There has been a major shift, and I've seen it accelerate about four or five years ago. I know I was giving a lot more of my money to Democrats than I am today."

Wessely's contributions reflect more than just a shift to the GOP, however. They also indicate the flow of oil money to the Republican party committees and to conservative organizations such as NCPAC and the Conservative Victory Fund—and to conservative Republican challengers.

At the One Energy Square building, just four miles north of Wessely's downtown Dallas offices, is Roy Guffey, 80, who has risen from a $4-a-day roustabout in 1926 to owner of Guffey Oil Co.

Guffey has come to believe that "most of the time, a majority of the voters are a bunch of damn thieves," voting to continue receiving some form of federal benefit instead of recognizing the threat of a national debt that exceeds $1 trillion.

In a recent letter to Lyn Nofziger, Reagan's former aide, Guffey wrote: "I am completely convinced that this nation as a constitutional republic (it was never intended to be a democracy as the liberals so glibly called it) cannot continue with a debt of a trillion dollars and more—the dogs just won't hunt."

Guffey cannot, for example, comprehend the notion of paying a worker time-and-a-half for overtime: "It's impossible for a man to be worth more after the first 40 hours. If anything, they are worth less."

Like his friend Wessely, Guffey has backed his convictions with cash.

Over the past 18 months, according to the FEC, he has given the Republican National Committee $3,000; the National Republican Congressional Committee $3,150; the Republican National Senatorial Committee $1,500; the Conservative Victory Fund $2,000; NCPAC $9,800; Sen. Jesse Helms's (R-N.C.) National Congressional Club, $2,500; DALENPAC $1,000, and McNamara, O'Neill's opponent, $500. In addition, his wife has given NCPAC a total of $6,000.

There is a host of others, including H.E. (Eddie) Chiles, head of the Western Co. in Fort Worth whose "I'm mad" commercials are a part of the Sunbelt radio landscape, and his wife. The Chileses have given $10,000 to NCPAC, $2,000 to the National Republican Congressional Committee, $2,000 to Moore and $2,000 to Rutledge.

This kind of commitment has turned the Southwest into a political gold mine, particularly for conservative Republicans challenging liberal Democrats in Frostbelt races.

Since early 1980, after then-representative Steve Symms (R-Idaho) raised more than $150,000 for his successful challenge of then-senator Frank Church (D-Idaho) on a swing through Texas, candidates and their fund-raisers—as many as 10 in a single week—have been trooping through Houston, Dallas, Tulsa and Oklahoma City.

# Up from Watergate

## How the Republican Party Rose from Disgrace and Defeat to a Position of Wealth and Unity that the Democrats Can Only Envy

The Washington Post, August 16, 1984

When Watergate was as its height ten years ago, the short-term beneficiary of the scandal was the Democratic party. After losing the presidential contest in 1972 by 18 million votes, the Democrats in 1974 gained 49 seats in the House and five seats in the Senate and two years later took the presidency.

In the long run, however, the Democratic party has emerged as the major loser from Watergate. Before the party's fortunes were revived by the public disclosures of the criminality within Richard Nixon's Republican administration, the Democratic party was on the ropes. The fragile alliance of labor, blacks, party regulars, anti-war suburbanites, white southerners, liberals and reformers was showing signs of cracking, and the candidacies of George Wallace, Hubert Humphrey and George McGovern were showcases for Democratic conflict.

Just at a time when the party of the New Deal needed an extended period of retrenchment, the political accident of Watergate allowed the Democrats to regain majority control of the federal government. For a brief moment, from 1974 through 1976, the Democratic party could sweep all its problems under the rug and run to victory on the thin banner of reform.

At the same time it allowed the Democrats to avoid a major retrenchment, Watergate put the Republican party on the ropes. Faced with the sudden threat of extinction, the GOP did just what the Democrats might have been forced to do had Watergate never occurred: it quietly initiated the basic steps toward becoming a full-fledged political party, at least so far as that is possible in the anti-party tenor of politics in the United States.

This drive centered around party-based fund-raising; by the late 1970s, the GOP had become the most effective vehicle for raising cash in the history of political parties in the United States. Money permitted the Republican party to adjust to the basic change in American politics, the replacement of locally based organizations by television, a medium that had become increasingly critical not only in Senate elections, but also in growing numbers of House elections. At the same time, party-generated cash allowed the Republican party to take a giant step ahead of the Democrats in the use of new campaign technology, including targeted direct mail, computerized analysis of census data and political voting histories, tracking polls and specialized focus groups.

While traditional campaigning based on precinct lieutenants and ward captains—tactics favoring urban-based Democratic organizations—fell farther and farther into the past, the anti-Republican legacy of Watergate permitted Democrats to coast to victory in the elections of 1974 and 1976. The scandal allowed the Democratic party to remain blind to the importance of developing a party structure and a financial base designed to ensure that all viable candidates are equipped to conduct the kind of campaigns essential in the second half of the twentieth century.

At the same time, Watergate gave new impetus to the Democratic reform drive in Congress, encouraging junior members, who had ridden the wave of public outrage into office, to demand a massive decentralization of congressional power. This process gave nearly every member of the House and Senate at least one subcommittee chairmanship with original jurisdiction over specific legislative terrain.

In what are coming to be known as the "inadvertent consequences of reform," this diffusion of power, in turn, gave all the new subcommittee chairmen individual fiefdoms from which to raise money without party help, turning instead to the collection of special interests and political action committees falling under their committees' jurisdictions.

Armed with the power base of a subcommittee chairmanship (or two or three) to raise money, Democratic members of the House and Senate had no interest in pressuring the Democratic party to develop the fund-raising capabilities of the Democratic national, congressional and senatorial committees. For the three election cycles from 1977–78 to 1981–82, the Republican party's money advantage grew from just over 3 to 1 ($84.5 million to $25.4 million) to better than 5 to 1 ($214.9 million to $39 million), and the trend appears to be continuing.

As a result of these trends, the Democratic party, the supposed party of the underdog, has become the party of fat-cat incumbents who have shown great ability to raise money on their own, while Democratic challengers most often go hungry for cash. Republicans, in contrast, are able to channel their cash far more effectively to those who need it, particularly to marginal candidates in close races who do not have the leverage of incumbency to hit up potential donors.

It is only now—because of the defeats of 1980 and the failure to make significant gains in 1982—that the Democratic party is attempting to build up anything approaching the massive 1.6 million name direct-mail donor base of the GOP. In this competitive struggle with the GOP, the Democrats are eight years behind on the learning curve.

At a more subtle level, Watergate functioned to change the balance of power both within each of the two parties and among the groups seeking to influence the political process.

The Watergate-created victories of 1974 and 1976 resulted in the election of a major bloc of Democratic House members representing marginal districts, members extremely sensitive to organized "grass-roots" lobbying. After the election of 1976, the Democrats had a 292-to-144 advantage in the House, just four short of the 295-to-140 margin the party held after the 1964 election, when Lyndon Johnson was able to push through civil rights, anti-poverty and jobs legislation.

The 1976 majority, however, was not based on a popular affirmation of the Democratic party but on what might be called a negative consensus, a public rejection of the Watergate-tainted GOP. Many of the members of the suddenly strong Democratic contingents in the House and Senate had been elected from previously Republican districts and had no mandate to enact the Democratic party's legislative program—consumer protection, labor law reform, Election Day registration, tax reform. The Democratic majority was not a party prepared for action. Instead, many were anxious legislators extremely vulnerable to pressure.

Just as Watergate had been the driving force behind the revival of the GOP, it was the major impetus behind the restoration of the nation's business lobbying community. As a result of Watergate, "the danger had suddenly escalated," as Bryce Harlow, senior lobbyist for Procter & Gamble and a principal architect of restored corporate political strength, put it. "We had to prevent business from being rolled up and put in a trash can."

Business had been the source of most of the cash surrounding the collective Watergate scandals, including the "Townhouse Operation" and the secret funding of the 1972 presidential drive. As a result of public disclosures, public opinion surveys showed a massive decline in confidence in major corporations, dropping from 51 percent in the late 1960s to 20 percent in the mid-1970s.

Faced with the danger of being "put in the trash can," business, following the pattern of the GOP, took three major steps to regain power. The first was to take advantage of Watergate-induced reforms in federal election law to set up political action committees, a mechanism for the raising and distributing of campaign contributions specifically sanctioned by the new law. Originally designed to lessen the role of special interests in campaign finance, the law became the vehicle for creation of a huge expansion of corporate and trade association PACs (they grew from 407 to 2,095 between 1974 and 1982) and of corporate and trade association campaign contributions (which grew tenfold in the same period, from $8 million to $84.9 million).

Corporations, prompted by the anti-business public reaction to Watergate, adopted wholesale the "grass-roots" lobbying tactics of the environmental and consumer movements. Ideally structured for this kind of orchestrated application of political pressure, corporations mobilized management-level employees and stockholders into locally based pressure groups, writing letters to and demanding meetings with key members of Congress, particularly those elected from marginal districts who were (and are) extremely sensitive to expressions of "public opinion" from their constituents.

As the level most difficult to trace, the corporate and conservative communities initiated a strong drive to change the intellectual basis of the national legislative debate. From 1976 to 1982, the budget of the Heritage Foundation went from $1 million to $5.2 million, financed largely by contributions from Joseph Coors, president of Adolph Coors Company; the John M. Olin Fund, established by the chairman of the Olin Mathison Chemical Corporation, Mobil Oil Corp.; Dow Chemical; Fluor Corp; and Gulf Oil Corp. Similarly, the American Enterprise Institute went from a budget of less than $1 million in 1970 to $10.4 million in 1980, financed by many of the same sources.

This pattern was present across the country, as money from corporate treasuries and their foundations flowed to such conservative think tanks as the Center for the Study of American Business at Washington University in St. Louis and the Hoover Institution at Stanford University.

Together, the revival of the Republican party and the business community helped to set the stage not only for the election of Ronald Reagan, but also for the 1980 GOP takeover of the Senate, the enactment of the administration's 1981 tax and budget cuts and for a basic change in the substance of the national political and economic debate.

In this process, Watergate was one of many forces, but the political distortions it created were critically important in the entire sequence of developments leading to the current election. Walter Mondale, boosted by Geraldine Ferraro and a major voter mobilization drive, has an outside chance of winning the election, but the Democratic party continues to struggle to find its voice; the Republican party remains strong, without divisive internal conflict; and the Democrats face the danger of further erosion among such key groups as blue-collar workers, poor Southern whites and a wave of young voters who are showing a stronger tendency toward either the GOP or toward non-allegiance than their elders.

# CHAPTER FOUR

# MONEY AND CONNECTIONS IN WASHINGTON

**M**ONEY HAS PLAYED very different roles in the development of the Republican and Democratic parties, just as the enactment of campaign finance reform legislation has sharply contrasting consequences for each party.

For the GOP, there is little or no ideological conflict between the sources of campaign finance, the electoral base of the party, and the publicly declared goals of party leaders. The overwhelming majority of political contributors are those with incomes in excess of $50,000-a-year, and it is among this group that Republican partisan allegiance is strongest. The enactment in 1974 and 1976 of legislation restricting the size of contributions by individuals to federal campaigns effectively forced the Republican party to financially mobilize a segment of the affluent into a reliable direct-mail donor base, a base that at its height amounted to roughly two million people who contributed the lion's share—over 60 percent—of the $298 million raised by the three major GOP committees in 1983–84. A similar form of ideological-financial coherence emerges among Republican House and Senate candidates. Money effectively reinforces the GOP's loyalty to business over organized labor as political action committees tied to corporations and trade associations gave $47.8 million to Republican candidates in 1985–86, compared to just $2.3 million from labor, a ratio of 20 to 1.

For the Democrats, the opposite is true. The party's House and Senate candidates in 1985–86 received almost equal sums from labor, $28.7 million, and business-trade association PACs, $36 million—a split designed to encourage internal conflict over economic and ideological issues. Similarly, the Democratic party draws on a far smaller target population for direct-mail solicitations, limited almost entirely to affluent liberals concentrated in such communities as Manhattan, Beverly Hills, and Cambridge, Massachusetts. In order to remain solvent and to meet payrolls, the Democratic National Committee has become dependent on legally questionable sources of contributions, a form of donation known as "soft money": checks written directly from corporate and union treasuries, or from individuals giving in excess of the $20,000 limit. With the continuing decline of organized labor, businessmen tied to real estate and investment banking have increasingly become key sources of soft money, just as they have become principal fund-raisers in Democratic presidential campaigns. While technically soft money cannot be used to influence the outcome of federal elections, its receipt is justified on the grounds that it is used for the acquisition of buildings and equipment, or to pay the salaries of workers active in state campaigns unregulated by federal law. Aside from questions of the legality of some of its sources of money, the Democratic party faces the dilemma that almost none of its sources of financial support are from among those voters it claims to represent: men and women at or below the median family income. This tension has always been present within the Democratic party, but, as the role of political organizations has withered and the importance of political cash has risen, the conflict has become steadily more acute.

While money was a central factor in the rise of the Republican party, the affluence of the GOP has in itself now begun to create substantial problems. If there is a clear sign of political entropy, it is when men and women with the sharpest minds abandon ship to make a buck. This abandonment of the cause for the lure of cash has been endemic to the Democratic party; after years of controlling Congress, former Democratic elected officials, staffers, and committee aides now far outnumber their Republican counterparts in the Washington lobbying community. Since Reagan took office, however, trends within the lobbying universe have moved sharply in a Republican direction. This process began early on, as key GOP advisers from the 1980 campaign started as early as 1981 to open consulting and lobbying offices, and intensified after the 1984 election, when White House aides and staffers in the executive branch foresaw that their market value might drop precipitously with a Democratic takeover of the Senate in 1986 or of the White House in 1988.

The practice of capitalizing on political connections was raised to new heights by Franklyn "Lyn" Nofziger and Michael K. Deaver, former key Reagan aides whose public relations-lobbying operations grossed well in excess of $1 million annually, before Deaver was convicted in 1987 of perjury in connection with testimony about his lobbying activities, and Nofziger was convicted in 1988 of violating regulations governing the lobbying activities of former executive branch appointees.

At the same time, the Republican National, Senatorial and Congressional Committees increasingly became sources of easy patronage for well-connected GOP consultants, who routinely were hired for fees ranging from $3,000 to over $10,000-a-month. These practices became a major liability after the Republican party lost control of the Senate in 1986. Disclosures of the consulting contracts and bonuses to key staffers of up to $50,000 angered GOP donors, who sharply cut back contributions.

In addition to the role of money in the parties—the subject of a number of articles in this section—it is difficult to overestimate the extent to which money and fund-raising dominate the lives of members of the House and Senate. I have included an article about a special "breakfast club" with a $10,000-a-head entrance minimum set up by Sen. Lloyd Bentsen, the Texas Democrat who chairs

the Senate Finance Committee. In response to the story about him, Senator
Bentsen promptly declared that he had made a mistake, and returned the $92,500
he had raised. There are, however, very few effective ways to dam the flow of
campaign money; within six months, many of the same lobbyists whose breakfast
club donations had been returned, wrote out a total of $54,000 in new checks
to Bentsen's campaign fund. I have also included an article describing the growing practice among House and Senate members of accepting honoraria and free
trips from the same business and trade groups that lobby Congress. While the
amounts are smaller—as of 1987 the maximum that a Senator can accept in
honoraria is $30,040—the money goes directly to the member of Congress for
personal use, and consequently amounts to a practice far closer to legalized
bribery than campaign contributions.

# Fund-Raisers Are New Elite
# of Campaigns

*The Washington Post,* December 12, 1983

In late January, when Jackson T. Stephens, an Arkansas banker, investor, broker
and venture capitalist, joined Sen. John Glenn's presidential campaign, hardly
anyone noticed. It was, however, a decision that already has proved to be worth
more than a quarter of a million dollars to Glenn.

Stephens brought to the campaign an extraordinary network of financial
contacts growing out of a privately held investment banking firm ranked among
the top 10 in the nation, with $248 million in capital.

"We talk politics a lot," said Stephens, who declined to discuss the scope of
his own business interests. "I just call my friends from around the country."

Stephens is a part of a special campaign elite—men and women across the
nation, little known to the public, but expert in raising large sums of money.

In the campaign for the 1984 Democratic presidential nomination, the
competition for this donor elite is almost over.

These men and women are of critical importance in presidential campaigns.
With federal campaign laws setting a $1,000 limit on the amount a person can
give a candidate while the campaigns can cost in excess of $15 million, a fund-
raiser who can come up with $25,000 or more from 25 or more contributors is
golden.

With very few exceptions, the major Democratic fund-raisers have committed themselves, in most cases to one of the two front-runners, former vice
president Walter F. Mondale or Glenn.

"The last of the big fund-raisers to go," a Mondale aide noted with some
regret, "was Jess Hay," a Dallas-based mortgage banker who went with Glenn.

Glenn finance director Mark Emblidge said that Hay, who had computerized his personal fund-raising lists, is claiming that he will add as much as $1 million to Glenn coffers at a Dec. 14 gathering in Austin.

Mondale, however, has been no slouch in acquiring the backing of a host of experts at putting the touch on friends, clients, partners, associates, creditors, debtors, and any other potential donors.

In New York, for example, Robert Rubin, a senior trader for Goldman, Sachs & Co., an investment banking firm, and Roger Altman, a former assistant secretary of the Treasury and now head of corporate finance at Lehman Brothers Kuhn Loeb Inc., have put together a fund-raising structure that has produced about $1.1 million for the Mondale campaign. This week, they have organized a fund-raiser at the Tavern on the Green Restaurant in Manhattan, which Rubin said should produce another $250,000.

In the Washington area, Nathan Landow, a developer with extensive connections in the real estate industry and in the Jewish community, said that a dinner he organized produced $950,000 for Mondale.

Because federal law has restricted the role of major individual contributors—wealthy people able to write a check for $50,000—a new breed of money specialists has emerged in recent years.

Instead of corporate executives, the majority of major fund-raisers are in businesses involving extensive financial dealings with wealthy people: investment banking, movie production, real estate development, insurance, prestigious law firms, stocks and bonds, venture capital and lobbying. These businesses allow fund-raisers to develop lists of clients, partners, investors and others who are prime targets for $500- to $1,000-a-head political dinners.

Officials of the campaign of Sen. Gary Hart, for example, listed eight key fund-raisers, including two lawyers, two developers, one broker and one vice president at Orion Films. The other two are a Texas oilman and a Milwaukee businessman.

Although most of the major Democratic money men and women are committed to specific candidates, the finance directors in each of the campaigns, particularly the Glenn and Mondale campaigns, are keeping a careful eye on their opponents because, if any pulls out of the race, his fund-raisers will be up for grabs.

Two candidates—former governor Reubin Askew of Florida and Sen. Alan Cranston of California—come from prime money states and each has the loyalty of a number of major donors in his home territory.

Emblidge, of the Glenn campaign, has assigned full-time staff members to the two states—Florence Ochi in California and Laura Brenlaw in Florida—part of whose jobs are to prepare to pick up Askew and Cranston contributors in the event either candidate drops out.

Tim Finchem, Mondale's finance director, said he has not assigned anyone specifically to pick up the financial pieces of other campaigns if they fall apart, but he contended that in Southern California Mondale would gain half a million dollars or more if Cranston were to pull out.

In addition to the key role fund-raisers play in the pre-convention period, they are likely to emerge as major players in the general election in the event that the Democratic party attempts, as expected, to take advantage of a loophole in the federal general election public-financing law.

The loophole, enacted in 1979, allows state parties to support presidential candidates with private money, in effect supplementing the $40 million in public money grants that will go to the Republican and Democratic nominees.

Many states place no limits on the amounts individuals can give and, in many cases, permit contributions directly from corporate and union treasuries. Major fund-raisers would be essential to efforts to take advantage of the 1979 law.

Both parties are expected to take advantage of the law permitting the channeling of private money to state parties in the general election, a tactic Ronald Reagan's campaign organization used to raise from $10 million to $15 million in 1980.

# Partners in Political PR Firm Typify Republican New Breed

## Operatives in Demand by Candidates, Corporations, Governments

*The Washington Post,* April 7, 1985

On the day after President Reagan defeated Walter F. Mondale, H. Lee Atwater was a rich man.

The deputy campaign manager of the Reagan-Bush '84 Committee became a full partner in the political consulting arm of Black, Manafort and Stone, a firm that exemplifies a key element of the vitality of the Republican party: the potential for young tough, savvy political operatives to move into the political market and make big bucks.

In just five years, Black, Manafort and Stone—and now Atwater—has become a major new presence in the capital, specializing in connections, influence and hardball politics. It combines a political client list of influential elected officials with a lobbying clientele of corporations, foreign governments and trade associations.

Atwater and his colleagues represent the cream of Republican inside operatives. Charlie Black was a senior adviser to the Reagan '84 campaign and the campaign strategist for Sens. Jesse Helms (R-N.C.) and Phil Gramm (R-Tex.). Paul Manafort was the political director of the GOP convention in Dallas. Roger Stone was Northeast coordinator for Reagan-Bush.

Candidates are lining up to buy the firm's campaign services, and the list of lobbying clients is growing steadily.

The list includes: the investment banking firm of Salomon Brothers, which last year paid $135,000 to Black, Manafort and Stone; Kaman Aerospace, which laid out $255,000; the Dominican Republic, which signed on at $69,788 a quarter, and Rupert Murdoch's Australia-based The News Corp. Ltd., which is paying $180,000 a year for what the firm describes as an "activity limited to internal conferences and phone calls with client."

The cash flow to members of the firm started at a trickle when it was formed in 1980. By 1982, each partner's annual income reportedly had reached six figures, and they are aiming at incomes of $450,000 each for next year.

Atwater's first-year income reportedly will be at least $130,000, with the prospect of bonuses for new clients. His income will match his partners' next year. He said that, for his first year, he has an arrangement requiring that "I don't have to work but five or six days a month" while completing a thesis on negative campaigning for his Ph.D.

Even working part time, Atwater may have to work hard for his money. He reportedly has lined up at least three candidates running for governorships and the Senate in 1986, who will have to pay the firm in the neighborhood of $100,000 each in consulting fees and $250,000 to $450,000 in media placement charges.

At the same time, Atwater is on retainer to the firm's lobbying arm, on the verge of bringing in three or four new clients, each of whom will pay a retainer of $10,000 to $15,000 a month or more.

The lobbying branch of the intensely Republican firm is not ignoring Democrats, hiring Peter Kelly, finance chairman of the Democratic National Committee, and James Healey, Jr., former aide to Ways and Means Committee Chairman Daniel Rostenkowski (D-Ill.).

All between the ages of 32 and 36, Black, Manafort, Stone and Atwater were adolescents and college students in the 1960s and early 1970s, when the civil rights movement and opposition to the Vietnam War animated many of the nation's youth.

These young Turks of the Reagan revolution went in a different direction.

During Barry Goldwater's presidential campaign "in 1964, one of my neighbors [in suburban Lewisboro, N.Y.] was doing Republican precinct work," Stone said. "She gave me a copy of Goldwater's book *Conscience of a Conservative.* I was immediately transformed into a zealot. I was 12 or 13. . . . I was attracted to the anti-Communist position Goldwater took, I felt the government spent too much, too much on welfare. At 12 years old, I thought the world was going to hell."

That same Goldwater year, the year that politics came to life for a host of current GOP activists, Black, then a senior in a North Carolina high school, saw his conservative Democratic parents switch political parties.

"There was a general feeling of resistance or rebellion among white Southerners to Lyndon B. Johnson, to the things he was doing," Black said. "I wasn't conversant with the policies, or why the civil rights act was bad, but it caused me to focus on it."

In the years that followed, these young men threw themselves into the trench warfare of the College Republicans and Young Republicans. In 1977, at 25, Stone won the presidency of the Young Republicans in a campaign managed by Manafort.

Four years earlier, Atwater managed the successful campaign of Karl Rove to be president of the College Republicans, defeating John T. (Terry) Dolan, whose drive was run by Stone, Manafort and Black. Black and Stone were the founders of the National Conservative Political Action Committee in 1975, with Dolan.

At the same time they began to move up the ladder of political campaigns, working variously for Helms, Sen. Strom Thurmond (R-S.C.), James Buckley, who was then a senator from New York, Richard M. Nixon, the Republican National Committee and, ultimately, Ronald Reagan.

Black, Manafort, Stone and Atwater all come out of two current wellsprings of the Republican party: Northern, Roman Catholic suburbia and the middle-class, white South. Their colleges were not Ivy League: Newberry College in South Carolina for Atwater, the University of Florida for Black, Georgetown University for Stone, and George Washington University for Manafort.

Stone was born in Norwalk, Conn., and brought up in the Lewisboro section of Westchester County. He described his family as middle-class, blue-collar Catholics; his father owned his own well-drilling company. Black's father started out as a salesman and worked his way up to regional manager for Sealt-est Foods in Wilmington, N.C.

Atwater, unlike Stone and Black, did not get into politics until college.

"I was a rock-'n'-roll musician [guitar] and almost didn't go to college. I was with [singer] Percy Sledge. I was the only white guy there," he said. "My parents forced me to go to college; I was really in the southern soul movement."

Atwater's father, in Columbia, South Carolina, was an insurance adjustor and his mother was a schoolteacher.

"I decided I wanted to be a Republican simply because I was always an antiestablishment-type guy and all the establishment-type people on campus and in the state were Democrats," Atwater said. "The young Democrats in South Carolina were an elite group that went around in three-piece suits, Gant shirts and smoking cigars, acting like big shots."

Ten years later, serving as deputy political director at the White House from 1981 through the start of 1984, Atwater would bring such figures as singers James Brown and Wilson Pickett and cultural analysts John Nasbitt and Alvin Toffler to White House Friday luncheon sessions.

Atwater's antiestablishment views color his assessment of the current struggle between Republicans and Democrats.

"For 150 years, the establishment has always been business. [Franklin D.] Roosevelt came in and established another establishment, and it was government. So, for the first time, you have two establishments," Atwater said. "In 1980 we were able to define the establishment, insofar as it is bad, as government, not big business. Democrats tried [in 1984] and in 1982 to define the establishment as big business and corporations. . . .

"I read the *National Enquirer* every week. The *National Enquirer* readership is the exact key, swing voter I am talking about. If you read those *National Enquirer* stories, there'll be about four or five about wasteful government projects, spending $400,000 to study some flying tree lizard. But at the same time, there'll be some stories in there about some millionaire that has five Cadillacs and hasn't paid taxes since 1974, or so-and-so Republican congressman who never paid taxes. It's which one of those establishments that the public sees as the bad guy" that determines election outcomes.

For these young political operatives, Watergate, a disaster for the Republican party, was a blessing, clearing out of GOP ranks an entire generation of consultants, media specialists and tacticians, a generation just 10 to 20 years their elders.

The firm was formed out of political upheaval in the 1980 campaign. Immediately after the New Hampshire primary, Reagan fired his top staff, including Black, his field director. Black then founded the firm and Manafort and Stone joined, continuing work for the campaign as consultants.

One of the key talents they bring to a campaign is a killer instinct for what is known in the trade as "driving up the opposition's negatives."

"When I first got into this, I became a polling junkie," Atwater said. "I just stumbled across the fact that candidates who went into an election with negatives higher than 30 or 40 points just inevitably lost. One of the conclusions I've reached is that in a two-man race, if one of the candidates can't win, and the other one is yours, you are going to come out all right."

In 1978, this translated into the Atwater-designed destruction of Charles D. (Pug) Ravenel, the Democratic nominee challenging Thurmond.

"I got a call from Roger Stone, who had found a story in a little publication in New York called something like *The Village Thing,*" Atwater said. "Ravenel had gone to a Park Avenue fund-raiser without realizing that any press was there. The story said: 'Pug Ravenel, appearing at a plush penthouse party of limousine liberals and Porsche populists, said he was embarrassed to be from South Carolina and that he would make a good third senator from New York.' I felt like a guy standing on top of a 20-story building and seeing a $100 bill."

Atwater persuaded a dissident Democratic state senator to do a television commercial telling South Carolina voters: "This year we've got something more important than party. We need Strom Thurmond, instead of a third senator from New York."

Ravenel's negative rating went from 12 percent at the start of the campaign to 43 percent on Election Day.

Similarly Black, who served as campaign strategist for Gramm's successful fight for a Texas Senate seat against Democrat Lloyd Doggett in the recent election, recalled:

"Doggett got the endorsement of the big gay PAC in San Antonio. That wasn't unusual, but then we got onto the fact that the gays had a male strip show at some bar and Doggett takes that money. That became a matter of his judgment, so we rolled it out there."

Although the members of the firm have ties to various potential candidates, the odds are that their support will go to Rep. Jack Kemp (R-N.Y.), if there is a contest.

"I see these guys just relishing the chance to drive George Bush's negatives right off the map, starting out with his gun-control votes and his membership in the Trilateral Commission," said one close friend of the partners. Atwater, however, said that his own loyalties are toward Bush.

The firm is at a critical juncture. What began as a collection of conservative Republican insurgents whose theme has been a deeply rooted resentment of both the Republican and Democratic establishments, has become a multimillion-dollar operation in which partnerships bring with them memberships in their country club of choice, and Mercedes Benz automobiles.

Stone, now a GOP authority on winning the votes of working-class, ethnic Catholic voters, gives lawn parties catered by a French chef, with a special consultant to arrange flowers.

It is with a sense of irony that Atwater contrasts the affluence of his partnership with the economic problems facing the Republican party's key political target group, the baby-boom generation of voters born between 1946 and 1964.

"All of a sudden, these people who grew up thinking they'd get white-collar jobs get what, in fact, are blue-collar jobs," Atwater said. "Here I am, No. 2 in my home town Rexall Drugs, making 28 grand and I know if I stay here another 15 years I can be the No. 1 guy, making 36 grand."

Stone contended that the firm's affluence is a byproduct of struggle.

"We fought for a long time in this revolution in this party and in this country," he said. "The fact that it may also bring us individual economic prosperity comes as a little bit of a surprise. . . . I know what it was to be laughed at as an outcast. I remember when we couldn't get a framed picture of Ronald Reagan hung in the Republican National Committee."

# Good Connections
## Luring Clients: Ex-Aides Capitalize on White House Work

The Washington Post, October 27, 1985

As the White House began detailed preparations last winter for a presidential visit to Canada in March, a number of officials noticed that deputy chief of staff Michael K. Deaver had taken what they thought was an unusual interest in acid rain.

Deaver, who concentrated on skillfully packaging and enhancing President Reagan's image, had rarely delved into substantive issues. In this case, however, officials said, he stepped in and helped persuade Reagan to make a significant concession to the Canadian government: the appointment of a special envoy on acid rain.

Not only did the Canadians get a special envoy on an issue the White House had previously played down, but they got a heavy-hitter: Drew Lewis, a former secretary of transportation. Lewis later pleased the Canadians by calling for an acid rain cleanup program that far exceeds what the administration has proposed.

Less than two months after Reagan's trip to Canada, Deaver left the White House, as he had announced earlier he would, to form a lobbying firm. Three months later, he signed up one of his first clients—at an annual fee of $105,000— the government of Canada, which had a special interest in acid rain.

In an interview, Deaver said his activities at the White House before the U.S.-Canadian summit had nothing to do with the subsequent contract with Canada.

"Anything I did in the White House on that basis or any other basis was in the best interests of the president and it did not have anything to do with the Canadians," he said. Deaver has had notable success in attracting major clients who pay fees of $100,000 to $300,000. He is among what has become a wave of former White House officials moving into the private sector of Washington, selling influence, access and a claimed ability to manipulate public images and private deals.

When Reagan won the presidency in 1980 and the Republicans captured the Senate after a two-decade dry spell, there was a huge opening for the exercise of power and the reaping of profits that was just waiting to be filled.

"There are lots of companies that need representation, lots that don't have representation. There are not a lot of Republican firms out there," said Edward J. Rollins, who just left his White House job as chief political adviser to the president to form a political consulting-lobbying partnership.

Deaver acknowledges that in the case of Canada and other clients, he is providing help for a fee on issues he was involved in only months ago at the White House. But he sees no conflict and says he is following the law on such revolving-door issues.

On Canada, he said, "I would be involved in advising them on any issue. Acid rain happens to be the largest issue in Canada, so it is logical that I would advise them on that issue." Since taking on the job, he said he has talked to Lewis about the issue on behalf of Canada.

But, Deaver said, "I try to bend over backwards to be sure that I'm covered under the law."

The law governing the activities of high-ranking government employees after they leave office prohibits them from talking "to anybody that's in the executive office of the president for one year" on business matters, with no restrictions on social contacts, he said.

Donald E. Campbell, chief counsel in the Office of Government Ethics, said Deaver's interpretation of the law is accurate.

The one-year prohibition against business contacts applies in Deaver's case only to those working directly under Donald T. Regan, White House chief of staff. It does not apply to anyone else in government.

In addition, the prohibition does not preclude those who work for Deaver from calling executive office officials.

"I can't call Don Regan and say, 'Look, I've got a problem with sugar quotas,' " Deaver said. He added, "I can talk to anybody else in government that I want to on any subject. . . . I have people here in the firm who can deal with the White House."

Deaver remains a close friend of the Reagans and talks to them often, but he said he would never raise a business issue with them. "I would never talk to her [Nancy Reagan] about a client. The Reagans are friends of mine. I talk to them about other things all the time."

The Canadian contract is one small slice of business for Deaver, who estimates he has signed up eleven clients in less than six months. These clients produce annual billings in the neighborhood of $2 million. Deaver is known to have a goal of setting a minimum annual retainer for each of his clients at $300,000.

Deaver is hardly alone in using Reagan credentials to attract business after leaving the administration. Among the others who have moved from the White House into the world of consulting and lobbying are:

• Richard V. Allen, former assistant to the president for national security affairs. Clients of the Richard V. Allen Co. include the Panama Canal Study Group and the Republican National Committee.

• Joseph W. Canzeri, former deputy assistant to the president. The Joseph W. Canzeri Co. has represented Columbia Pictures; High Frontier, the lobby supporting the Strategic Defense Initiative (SDI); the White House Tennis Tournament, and Cable News Network's Ted Turner.

• Kenneth M. Duberstein, former chief White House lobbyist, now a partner in Timmons & Co., a lobbying firm whose clients include ABC, the American Petroleum Institute, Chrysler, Eastern Airlines and Standard Oil of Indiana.

• Wayne H. Valis, former special assistant to the president for contact with the business community, who now runs Valis Associates, which is associated with the public relations firm of Hill & Knowlton. Valis specializes in the representation of coalitions of business and trade associations on such issues as deficit reduction and banking deregulation. Among the various coalition participants are the Chamber of Commerce, the National Association of Manufacturers, the American Business Conference and the American Bankers Association.

• Lyn Nofziger, former presidential assistant for political affairs, whose firm, Nofziger-Bragg Communicators, has represented Conrail and the Long Island Lighting Co.

• Lee Atwater, former White House deputy political director and deputy campaign manager of the Reagan-Bush '84 campaign, is a partner in the firm of Black, Manafort and Stone, with clients ranging from the Dominican Republic to the Squibb Corp.

There are others who did not work in the White House, but whose earlier connections to President Reagan placed them in a position to capitalize on the partisan shift of power. Among them are Robert Gray of Gray & Co., and Peter Hannaford, a one-time partner of Deaver's who now heads his own firm, the Hannaford Co.

Deaver, however, stands out from the crowd. When he left his job as deputy chief of staff to join Washington's army of lobbyists and public relations specialists, he was the recipient of a special and symbolic gesture: the Reagans allowed him to keep his White House pass.

"The president has been very kind and allowed me to keep my pass," Deaver said in a recent interview. "The only time I've used the pass is if I go see the Reagans privately or to go play tennis" on the White House courts, he said.

The pass—the only one to be issued to a departing White House aide—symbolizes Deaver's exceptional, if tenuous, status in the intensely competitive world of Washington influence-peddling, where corporations and foreign governments are willing to pay as much as $300,000 a year or more for what appears to be power and access.

Deaver's client list includes CBS, TWA, the government of Canada, Phillip Morris, a coalition of Caribbean sugar-producing countries and Puerto Rico. He is expected to sign up soon an arm of the government of South Korea, and he is in negotiations with the government of China, according to sources.

"I just don't think I can talk about my clients," Deaver said, saying only that he has signed up eleven. "Like I don't talk about my clients, I don't talk about my fees. It's an annual retainer."

Deaver, according to reliable sources, is asking clients to commit to a minimum annual retainer of $300,000, although he is by no means getting that much from all eleven. Of four clients that could be identified through required public disclosures or other sources, only one, a group of Caribbean countries seeking to lower American sugar quotas, is paying the top dollar figure; the rest are paying from $105,000 to $250,000, according to public documents and background interviews.

While Deaver is reluctant to discuss most clients, he described strategies he has developed to help Puerto Rico defend a special federal tax break for corporations doing business on the island.

Deaver said he told his client he would not take on the issue unless "we never talked about it as a tax issue, only as a question of foreign policy." In return for retention of the favorable tax provision, 28 U.S. companies have agreed to build "twin plants" in other Caribbean countries, a step Deaver said would function to support the administration's Caribbean Basin Initiative, encourage capitalist development and increase employment.

"By doing that, we got the Department of State, AID [Agency for International Development] and the National Security Council to be strongly supportive. You can't go head-on with Treasury, because you'll go head-on until you're dead on the tax issue."

Just as Deaver's ties are key elements of his appeal to prospective clients, he has been the beneficiary of a growing belief in the corporate community that hostile takeover fights are not just marketplace struggles but contests subject to political influence.

"More and more companies are recognizing that Washington influence, and not just at the SEC [the Securities and Exchange Commission], can be vital," another well-connected lobbyist said. "If you can get someone at Treasury to raise questions about the economic implications, someone at Justice to mention anti-trust, even in an off-hand kind of way, or a congressman to call for hearings, you can slow the process down, or speed it up, depending. So these companies are looking more and more for help from political firms down here."

Deaver is not the only political lobbyist who has been hired by takeover candidates such as TWA and CBS. The firm of Black, Manafort and Stone has attracted similar business, as has National Strategies, a Democratic outfit.

One of Deaver's clients, who asked not be be identified, said: "When you're a company near the top of the Fortune 500 in the middle of a takeover battle, paying a couple of hundred thousand dollars to get someone who can call the secretary of the Treasury is just a drop in the bucket."

For the son of a Shell Oil distributor in Bakersfield, Calif., creation of Michael K. Deaver & Associates represents a gamble on shooting to the top in one of the nastiest, most competitive terrains in America.

Deaver, a political operative who rarely exibited interest in the mundane substance of legislation or policy, is now under pressure to perform in an arena of backroom negotiation over the minute details of tax legislation and administrative regulation.

This arena does not easily lend itself to his substantial talents—even some of his critics would say genius—as a driving force shaping the public essence of Ronald and Nancy Reagan, both in the presidency and on the campaign trail.

"You would never find Mike in the fight over the number of MX missiles or OSHA [Occupational Safety and Health Administration] regulation," said a friend and associate. Instead, Deaver excelled in the manipulation of public images, in the calculated use of individual heroes and historic backdrops to communicate a political message and in the use of the power of the presidency to change the terms of debate on a politically dangerous issue. (He did not succeed on every outing, however; the public relations fiasco known as Bitburg—Reagan's visit to a German cemetery containing the graves of Nazi storm troopers—was largely Deaver's responsibility.)

"He was very good at knowing the soul of Ronald Reagan," said a political operative who worked with Deaver. But, in an assessment shared by a number of persons interviewed, he added: "I don't know if that is a transferable skill. . . ."

But Lee Atwater, deputy manager of the Reagan-Bush '84 campaign, disagrees. "I think the guy has a true gift in public relations, and that certainly ought to be transferable anywhere," he said.

By his own description, Deaver's intention is to set up "a small organization that would take on a limited number of clients on an annual retainer that would not be involved in the putting out of fires, but rather involved in stategic planning. . . ." He added, "I hope people hire you for your general knowledge and ability and experience, and not just because of your access, although right now it's probably a mixture of both."

While access to power is central to Deaver's appeal, background interviews with clients show, one company has hired him for another reason.

The international arm of Phillip Morris has contracted with Deaver to represent the firm not in Washington, but in Taiwan, South Korea and Japan, each of which has an extremely lucrative cigarette market with high protective trade barriers preventing entry by American producers.

"Deaver has the Reagan imprimatur," a source at Phillip Morris said. When he goes to see officials of an Asian country, "they know that he worked at the White House and remains a deep, personal friend of the Reagans." The White House connection, he said, is expected to add a different dimension to the corporation's Asian negotiations for a larger market share.

Unlike many lobbying firms, Deaver's is owned totally by him. He has no partners. He has purposefully decided to maintain a very low overhead. He has a staff of eight, including three professionals—Doral Cooper, formerly with the office of the U.S. trade representative, William F. Sittman and Pamela G. Bailey, both former White House aides—on salary.

# Rollins's New Quest: Making a Fortune
## Working for "Love" Thing of the Past

*The Washington Post*, October 27, 1985

"I spent a lot of years doing things for love," Edward J. Rollins, the manager of the Reagan-Bush '84 campaign, said during his last day as chief political officer of the White House. "Now, I'm going to do things for money." At 42, Rollins has worked on campaigns or in government for all his adult life, never being paid more than $75,000 a year.

This month, he left his job at the White House to become a partner in the firm of Russo, Watts & Rollins, where he will serve as a consultant to campaigns and as a lobbyist.

In the process, his income will grow at least tenfold, by his estimate: "I think I can make between three-quarters and a million dollars. The bottom line is that they [Russo, Watts] had enough to guarantee about $700,000. Whatever I bring in as new clients will bring it up, and they will add some more."

As a lobbyist/consultant, Rollins joins the growing ranks of what are known in the trade as "double-dippers": specialists who get paid huge fees to help elect members of the House and Senate, and then get huge fees to lobby the members they helped elect on behalf of corporations and trade associations.

Rollins said such action raises "a legitimate ethical question," adding, "I don't know what the response is." But then, with a laugh, he said: "Actually, I guess I do: I'm going to continue lobbying anyone I can."

Rollins pointed out that lobbyists for years have increased their leverage with members of Congress by contributing money and holding fund-raisers, although he noted that a campaign consultant would have better access and clout than a contributor.

Rollins brings to his work golden credentials: he managed one of the most successful presidential campaigns in this century. At the same time, he is on the cutting edge of a surge in Republican strength, which can translate into huge sums of cash.

Lyn Nofziger, who left the same post as chief White House political operative after the 1982 elections to form the firm of Nofziger-Bragg Communicators, "had a goal when he left here to put away one or two million dollars in a couple of years. He told me he's ready to retire," Rollins said.

In his new role in the private sector, Rollins will function not only as a lobbyist and political consultant to campaigns, but also as the chief adviser to political action committees (PACs).

Rollins is negotiating to run political action committees for the Teamsters union and Marion (Pat) Robertson, the television evangelist. Robertson plans to set up his PAC to channel cash to conservative candidates in preparation for a possible bid for the Republican presidential nomination in 1988. Rollins said he will work for the Robertson PAC at no charge.

"There is no question that if I can get those two PACs, I would have control of a lot of money," Rollins said.

In the case of the prospective PAC for Robertson, who is the host of the "700 Club" on his own Christian Broadcast Network, Rollins claimed that a reasonable fund-raising target would be to get $5 from a significant percentage of the 2.5 million current donors to Robertson's organization, or $2 million to $3 million annually.

Teamsters president Jackie Presser, who heads one of the few unions to endorse President Reagan's reelection bid last year, has even more ambitious goals, Rollins said. Presser has set a target of raising $1 a week from a substantial percentage of the union's 2 million members. If half the membership reached the target level, it would produce $52 million, a sum unequaled by any PAC except those run by the Republican party.

As a PAC manager, Rollins said, "What they buy in me is [that] for five years now, I've watched 435 congressional seats, I've watched 100 Senate seats, together with the governors' races. I pretty much know who the players and candidates are, where you are wasting your money, where you've got some viable candidates."

Rollins declined to identify any of his corporate lobbying clients except Tenneco Inc. and Norfolk Southern Corp. railroad.

Describing his credentials, Rollins said: "I know all the Cabinet officers, and I know all the under secretaries, and I know all the assistant secretaries. What I think I'll do more of is provide assistance and guidance on how to deal with the administration, not much Capitol Hill stuff."

In his role as a political consultant, Rollins said he plans to handle three statewide races (governor or Senate) in 1986. His basic fee for campaigns is $10,000 a month, plus 15 percent of the media budget. Media budgets range from $1 million to $5 million, he said.

Among the candidates Rollins and his partners are expected to handle in 1986 are former Texas governor Bill Clements, who is seeking to regain his post; Reps. W. Henson Moore (R-La.), Ken Kramer (R-Colo.) and California Republican Chairman Mike Antonovich, all of whom are running for the Senate, and California Gov. George Deukmejian (R), who is seeking reelection.

"There is an awful lot of money out there," he said during an interview on his last day of work in the West Wing of the White House. "What I want to do is spend about two to three years doing this and then be financially independent and do whatever I want to do."

# Democrats for Profit

## Campaign Vets Make Smooth Transition

The Washington Post, October 28, 1985

In 1984, they were in separate camps, divided by one of the sharpest philosophical differences to emerge in a U.S. presidential contest since the Great Depression.

On one side, Robert Beckel and Timothy Finchem were, respectively, manager and finance director of the campaign of Walter F. Mondale. On the other, James Lake and Roger Stone were, respectively, chief spokesman and Northeastern coordinator for Ronald Reagan.

Today, however, the four have joined forces in the kind of political marriage that is solemnized when huge sums of money are riding on the votes of key members of a House committee.

They are conducting a $700,000 lobbying venture to defeat a key element of tax overhaul legislation now before Congress, a provision that would end deductibility of interest paid on bonds issued by states and municipalities to finance hospital, pollution control and other quasigovernment construction. This change would produce $5 billion to $16 billion for the U.S. Treasury over the next five years.

Beckel and Finchem are operating out of their new firm, National Strategies;

Lake is with the lobbying firm of Heron, Burchette, Ruckert and Rothwell, and Stone is a partner in Black, Manafort and Stone. And they have set up what amounts to a bipartisan political organization.

Using connections with mayors, governors, businessmen, labor and community officials, their goal is to apply pressure on 17 wavering members of the House Ways and Means Committee. "Between Stone and me, there is really not an area in the country we don't cover," Beckel said.

"It's patterned after a political operation for a campaign," Beckel said. "The concept going in is that you have targeted districts where you have potential votes if there's enough grass-roots support.

"Then you put organizers on the ground, you put a field organizer who's got responsibility for dealing with them every day, and you've got a campaign manager who worries about the funding and accounting."

The tab, which may run as high as $1.2 million, is being picked up by the Public Securities Association (PSA), an organization of investment banks that owes its existence to the tax deductibility of interest on government bonds.

The drive, however, is just one of a host of jobs that Beckel and Finchem have taken on in their new firm. Its office is on Pennsylvania Avenue, three blocks from the White House where both of them might now be working had Mondale won 270, instead of 13, electoral votes.

With David K. Aylward, former chief counsel for the Subcommittee on Telecommunications, Consumer Protection and Finance chaired by Rep. Timothy E. Wirth (D-Colo.), Beckel and Finchem have become quintessential entrepreneurs of the political marketplace.

They are now involved in corporate takeover fights, in real estate deals from Maryland to Texas, in the marketing of mortgage insurance and golf club memberships, the creation of new trade associations, airport development and in legislative contests between independent television stations and the networks.

In a confidential bid proposal to the homebuilding industry to lobby against restrictions on the importation of timber, the firm proclaimed, "Our organizing network is designed to identify and motivate on behalf of our clients the key state and local opinion-makers, influential political, business and community figures, campaign contributors. . . . This type of program adds real clout to state-of-the art, personalized constituent mail campaigns."

The firm told prospective clients that a four-month campaign would cost just over $350,000, including $60,000 for "grass-roots campaign management"; $72,000 for "district-based organizational expenses" in 18 districts at $4,000 per district, and $103,000 for "targeted mail contact" with "professional telephone followup."

Beckel, a liberal Democrat who worked for the Carter administration, numerous Democratic House and Senate candidates and the National Committee for an Effective Congress, pugnaciously defends his activities.

"If I go back through the Peace Corps and the time I've spent electing progressive people to office and the time I spent trying to keep Democratic presidents in the White House, or to elect them—all that time, I never made a dime. . . ."

"If I can live with myself, then it's perfectly all right. There are an awful lot of progressive Democrats in this town who have made an awful lot of money while I've been working in the vineyards, and I've never been one to criticize them."

National Strategies is taking on one of the most complex collections of clients in Washington, reflecting the different backgrounds of Beckel, Finchem and Aylward.

Beckel says he has participated in 160 campaigns and maintains what amounts to the skeleton of a national campaign staff around the country.

These contacts, he says, are available, for hire, to run local or federal "grass-roots" lobbying drives.

In addition to the PSA, clients include a toxic waste disposal company, Rollins Environmental Services, and, according to other sources, a group of insurance companies who want to limit their liabilities in toxic waste "Super-fund" legislation before Congress.

Corporations, trade associations and other groups using grass-roots lobbying are following a fundamental strategy that one of the best ways to persuade an elected official to take any action is to create, if not the genuine article, then at least the impression of a groundswell of local, popular opinion behind the hoped-for action.

In behalf of Rollins Environmental Services, for example, National Strategies set up paid phone bank operations in Brownsville, Tex., to build opposition to the plans of a competitor, Waste Management Inc., to burn toxic wastes at sea.

The callers identified themselves not as employees of Rollins but as representatives of "The Alliance to Save the Ocean."

Finchem, who in the 1984 campaign gained a reputation as an effective fund-raiser, is using his connections with major Democratic donors across the country to market mortgage insurance to savings and loans and other lending institutions, to sell corporate golf club memberships and to set up real-estate development deals.

"Over the years we have developed numerous friends," Finchem said.

"Through the people we know and have met over the years, instead of a marketing firm spending months trying to see the chief executive officer, we can get them in the door."

Finchem recently arranged a trip to Houston's Hobby Airport for 100 Chicago politicians, businessmen, airport board members and other key figures in an effort to build support for a proposal by Southwest Airlines to expand heavily into Chicago's Midway Airport, as it did 10 years ago into Hobby.

Because of his ties to rich contributors, "people are coming to us" looking for ways either to invest money or to obtain capital, Finchem said.

National Strategies now has an equity interest in a 1,500-acre development in Austin, Tex., he said, and is "about to close a deal" on a Montgomery County,

Md., upscale residential development where homes will sell for more than $400,000, according to Finchem.

Aylward, the subcommittee staff member, has sought clients whose interests coincide with positions he and Wirth took on Capitol Hill.

"I am known for substantive positions. For me to start representing positions contrary to where I stood for the past five years would shoot one of our strongest selling points," he said.

Among the clients Aylward has picked up are the Independent Television Association, made up of stations not affiliated with a major network, and many of the long-distance telephone competitors to AT&T and MCI.

In an aggressive move that would, in effect, create a client, Aylward is setting out to form a new trade association, the Alliance for Capital Access.

It is made up of corporations specializing in raising capital through high-yield bonds, known in the trade as junk bonds.

This high-risk technique of raising money is threatened by legislators seeking to end use of junk bonds to finance corporate takeovers.

"What we did is, we figured out what we wanted to do, and we figured out how to get someone to pay us for what we want to do," Aylward said.

Beckel said Aylward had worked on legislation changing competition among long-distance companies, adding that "we've got most of the long-distance" competitors as clients.

The idea of setting up a grass-roots organizing operation developed after the 1984 campaign, Beckel said, when he and Finchem realized that their experience in politics was a substantial resource.

"People who did precincts for us, people who did volunteer work for us . . . people who were paid organizers, people who were mayors, Democratic party people"—these political activists, Beckel said, provided an opportunity to set up a different kind of grass-roots service, compared with most Washington-based operations, which use direct-mail techniques to provoke constituents to write their senators or representatives.

Beckel described the rationale. "We thought we have a different slant which is that we would actually take people out and put them on the ground in a congressional district and say, 'These are professional organizers and here's what the issue is,' and begin to organize, so that you get quality grass-roots activity. . . .

"You find out it's like organizing for a candidate who's got a particular point of view, who's got a particular constituency. Tax exempt bonds have sources of constituent support, so do school loans, dormitories, waste-water treatment centers, stadiums, you can go down the line and you start to look at all the people who are affected by it, and it sort of becomes an organizer's dream."

Asked about the tactic of creating phony names, such as the Alliance to Save the Ocean, Beckel said criticism of the maneuver is "a lot of bull."

"I've been putting together alliances since the day I got out of the Peace Corps," he added.

"I don't care if it was the Committee to Impeach the President, which I started against Richard Nixon in 1973 and sold bumper stickers, or whether it was the Committee to Save the (C&O) Canal. . . .

"Why does Walter Mondale call his committee the Committee for the Future of America as opposed to the Walter Mondale Committee; why does [Rep.] Jack Kemp call his the Committee for America's Brighter Future? [Kemp's group is called the Campaign for Prosperity.]

"It's so . . . hypocritical to be attacking that, because that's what we do all the time. So we put together alliances of people and we come up with a name of an association or group and we do a campaign. We've done it for years. That's the answer. We got a hell of a good response."

None of the partners in National Strategies would detail how well the firm is doing, although each said it is, in its first year, producing much more money than he had anticipated.

Asked to compare their success with that of a major Republican firm, Black, Manafort and Stone, where partners this year say they may each make $400,000 or more, Finchem said current projections suggest that he, Beckel and Aylward will reach that level within a couple of years.

"This is Year Five for them [Black, Manafort and Stone]. I wouldn't be surprised if we weren't somewhere in their range by the end of Year Three."

# Corporate Chiefs Put Heart
# into Contributions to GOP

*The Washington Post*, August 29, 1986

In the world of high-dollar contributors, there are only so many ways to split $30,000 between the Democratic and Republican parties.

Lodwrick M. Cook and the corporation of which he is president and chief executive officer, the Atlantic Richfield Co., have done it in a way that sheds light on the financial underpinnings of both parties.

Cook's personal, publicly reported check for $10,000 went to the Republican National Committee (RNC). A loyal Republican, Cook not only gave the party enough money to qualify himself as a GOP "Eagle," the major contributor category, but also served as one of five co-chairmen of the party's 1986 inaugural anniversary dinner dance.

His company, however, split $20,000 down the middle, providing $10,000 corporate checks to the Democratic Congressional Campaign Committee (DCCC) and to the president's dinner, an event sponsored jointly by the National Republican Congressional (NRCC) and Senatorial (NRSC) committees.

The corporate money, known as "soft money," went into each party's special "building fund" to pay the costs of the headquarters facilities. Soft money is exempt from federal limitations and reporting requirements under a loophole in election law, although the DCCC voluntarily disclosed its receipts and a spokesman for Atlantic Richfield said the firm also gave an equivalent amount to the GOP.

The case of Cook and Atlantic Richfield reflects a strong pattern among elite contributors:

"The Republicans get both the CEO [chief executive officer] and his company," a conservative political activist observed. "The Democrats just get the corporate check."

The Republican party is benefiting from a national base of major donor support: leading corporate executives who have made a personal, financial commitment to give the GOP their own, after-tax dollars. Even with the collapse of world oil prices, the number of $10,000-a-year Republican donors has grown during the Reagan years from 800 to 900.

At the same time, however, money from sources more clearly defined as special interests—corporations and corporate and trade association political action committees (PACs)—is flowing to both parties.

The Republican party has compounded its financial advantage over the Democratic party by building up over the past decade a massive base of direct-mail donors. These donors have substantially contributed to the GOP's 5.8-to-1 advantage over the Democratic party ($146 million to $25 million) during the past 18 months, up from 3.7 to 1 ($246 million to $66 million) in 1983–84.

During the past six years, the Democratic party has begun to develop a base of direct-mail contributors of its own. Consequently, the GOP advantage among major individual donors is likely to become increasingly significant. At just one event, the RNC's inaugural anniversary dinner dance this year, at least 492 people gave a minimum of $10,000 in a commanding display of financial strength among the nation's corporate executives.

These contributions from an affluent donor base reflect a strong personal allegiance to the party that has advocated sharp tax cuts for those at the top of the income scale, eased federal regulation of business, and reduced social spending.

It is not yet clear how pending tax-overhaul legislation will alter the tax burden on the Republican donor base, and whether that alteration will change the allegiances of major donors.

In addition, the GOP is no slouch in collecting money from special-interest sources, including direct contributions from corporate treasuries and corporate PACs. On the program for the Republican senatorial and congressional dinner last May, 87 corporations, law firms and trade associations were listed as $10,000 contributors to the NRSC and NRCC's building fund, including Anheuser-Busch, Bechtel, Burger King, Citicorp, McDonnell Douglas, Mobil, Raytheon, and Shell Oil.

But, because the three major Republican committees collect so much more than their Democratic counterparts from individual donors ($229.1 million to $44.3 million in 1983–84), the GOP committees are far less dependent on these special interest sources of cash.

An examination of large individual contributors to the parties shows that among substantial contributors—those who give $500 or more a year—the GOP overwhelms the Democratic party. The three Republican committees received $42.4 million in amounts of $500 or more during 1983–84, nearly four times the $11.1 million their Democratic counterparts got in $500 or higher contributions. An analysis of donations to state and national political parties from members of the prestigious Business Council—an organization of the heads of major American corporations—shows a growing base of support for the GOP. From 1978 to 1986, the amount of money going to Republican committees from Business Council members and their families nearly doubled, from $314,000 to $621,800. In the same period the amount of money going from Business Council members to Democratic committees effectively stagnated, going from $40,300 in 1978 to $45,300 in 1985. Contributions from an affluent donor base reflect a strong personal allegiance to the party that has advocated sharp tax cuts for those at the top of the income scale.

The collapse of world oil prices and the booming stock market have substantially changed the base of contributors to the Republican party in ways that could have long-range ideological consequences.

In 1980, when Ronald Reagan won the presidency and the GOP took over the Senate, the most important sources of large contributions to the Republican party were oil men in Texas, Oklahoma and, to a lesser extent, Louisiana.

In 1981 and the first half of 1982, Texas and Oklahoma, with 7.8 percent of the population, produced far more large donations per capita to the RNC than any other state. Out of $7.1 million from contributors across the country, $1.74 million, or nearly 25 percent, came from Texas and Oklahoma.

In contrast, at that time, the entire state of New York, along with the Connecticut and New Jersey suburbs of New York City, and Massachusetts, produced only $963,000 in contributions, or 13.6 percent.

Since then, however, Texas and Oklahoma have been outpaced by the New York region and Massachusetts. During the first nine months of 1985, the most recent period for which data was available, the amount of money the two southwestern oil states provided to the RNC fell to 16.1 percent of the RNC's large contributions. The New York region, which is the financial center of the country and one of the major beneficiaries of the rise in stock prices, and Massachusetts, where the economy has been booming, increased their share to 19.2 percent of total large contributions to the RNC.

In Oklahoma, where natural gas prices fell with oil prices, the collapse of major campaign contributions has been most dramatic. Lew Ward, the state's GOP national committee man, said the number of Oklahoma "Eagles"—men and women willing to give at least $10,000 to the RNC—has dropped from 140 in 1980 to 15. The economic and political collapse of independent oil is likely to undermine the continuing strength of the conservative movement in the United States.

Independent oil men provided much of the "seed" money to the successful campaigns of such conservative Republican challengers to Democratic incumbents in 1980, as Sens. Steve Symms (Idaho), Charles E. Grassley (Iowa), the late John P. East (N.C.), and James Abdnor (S.D.).

"It's not good. It's pretty dismal," said Robert Pickens, head of the Dallas Energy PAC. "Our contributions will be down 40 percent."

The flow of money from the Louisiana Energy National PAC (LENPAC), a source of conservative GOP cash, has slowed to one-fourth of what it was in 1979–80. From 1979 through 1984, LENPAC gave a total of $658,000, or more than $100,000 a year, to Republican candidates; during the past 18 months, it has handed out $25,000.

The geographic shift from the Southwest to the Northeast has substantially changed the character of the GOP's major donor base. The number of men who achieved sudden and massive wealth in the oil boom of the late 1970s, and who saw political contributions as a kind of wildcatting investment in conservatism has been sharply reduced.

They have been replaced, in large part, by more establishment-type donors, the kind of financial supporters who have been associated with the old-guard, traditional wing of the Republican party dating to the days of Thomas E. Dewey and Dwight D. Eisenhower.

These are not entrepreneurs who gamble their fortunes on a geologist's report and a strong hunch, but Republicans who have capitalized on a stock market where the Dow Jones Industrial Average of 30 stocks has climbed from 970.99 the day President Reagan was first inaugurated to the 1900 level this week.

The key organizers of the RNC's 1986 dinner were not cowboy oil men but a group of men and women with strong ties to the Ivy League and who run or serve on the boards of corporate giants: James D. Robinson, III (American Express, Coca-Cola, Bristol Myers); Anne Armstrong (General Motors, General Foods, Boise Cascade); Howard M. Love (National Intergroup, Monsanto); George S. Pillsbury (the Pillsbury Co.); Andrew (Drew) Lewis (Warner Amex Cable Communications, Campbell Soups, Equitable Life Assurance).

To some extent, the now-troubled oil men have been replaced in GOP fund-raising circles by another kind of renegade, the corporate takeover specialists and some executives of the "high-tech" industry. But, in the main, the corporate takeover specialists are not ideologically committed to the conservative cause to the degree that many of the oil men were.

One exception is T. Boone Pickens, who straddles both the oil and the takeover industries. He and his firm, Mesa Petroleum, are major contributors to the Republican party and to conservative causes such as the Heritage Foundation and the National Conservative Political Action Committee.

However, other politically active participants in takeover fights tend, if they are Republicans, to support incumbents and party committees, while shying away from aggressively conservative groups and from gambles on relatively unknown nonincumbents.

Ivan Boesky, for example, has given $40,000 over the past 3½ years, most of it to the RNC and the NRSC in contributions earmarked for GOP Senate candidates.

However, Boesky gave $6,000 to Democratic candidates, including $1,000 to Walter F. Mondale's presidential bid in 1984. Others with similar patterns of campaign contributions were Nicholas and Theodore Forstmann, of Forstmann-Little Inc., a privately held firm specializing in leveraged buyouts, and Henry Kravis, of Kohlberg, Kravis, Roberts & Co., a similar firm.

# Firms, Lobbies Provide Much of Democrats' Funds

*The Washington Post,* August 12, 1986

The Democratic party, which has traditionally claimed to represent the working man and woman, depends substantially more than the Republican party on the contributions of special-interest groups, corporations and on the large donations of rich individuals.

Much of the money the Democrats raise from these sources is "soft money" —direct donations from corporations, lobbying firms and union treasuries, or from persons who have already given the maximum allowed under federal law.

Money from these sources would be illegal if used to promote the candidacy of anyone running for federal office. But the two parties have used a loophole in a 1979 law, designed to encourage the growth of state and local political parties, to raise millions in soft money from corporations, unions and big individual donors.

Raising soft money from corporations and unions, which are not permitted to make direct contributions to political campaigns for federal offices, has been attacked by such reform groups as Common Cause and the Center for Responsive Politics, and by some present and former staff and members of the Federal Election Commission. But the FEC has rejected suggestions that it issue new rules to govern the raising and spending of soft money.

Soft money contributions now account for 28 percent of the annual receipts of the Democratic National Committee (DNC). The Republican National Committee (RNC), by comparison, raises less than 5 percent of its considerably larger budget in soft money.

For the Democratic Senatorial Campaign Committee (DSCC) and the Democratic Congressional Campaign Committee (DCCC), money from political action committees (PACs)—most of which have been set up by trade associations, corporations and unions to influence legislation—now accounts for 27 and 22 percent of reported contributions respectively.

PAC contributions to the two Democratic campaign committees have grown from $271,000 in 1979–80 to $3.3 million in 1983–84, a twelvefold increase.

Today the Senate is scheduled to vote on legislation that would limit PAC contributions to House and Senate campaigns. One proposal to be considered in the Senate would prohibit PAC contributions to the Republican and Democratic parties and would mandate public disclosure of all soft money contributions.

The three major Democratic committees collect at least 35 percent of their funds from PACs and soft-money contributors; for their Republican counterparts, those sources provide less than 5 percent of total receipts.

All three Democratic party committees have been able to raise increasing amounts of money from direct-mail solicitations, but each receives a far higher percentage of support from PACs and large donors than their GOP counterparts, which raise much more in small contributions from individuals. And in the last 18 months, according to Frank O'Brien, director of direct mail for the DNC, the number of direct-mail contributors to the national committee has ceased to grow.

Democratic dependence on special-interest money has had an impact on the substantive positions adopted by the party and its candidates on controversial issues.

In the 1984 presidential campaign, for example, the adamant opposition of real estate developers, a major source of Democratic cash, to the depreciation provisions of tax reform proposals was a significant factor in the decision by officials of Walter F. Mondale's presidential campaign against endorsing tax reform legislation, according to reliable sources within the campaign.

That decision effectively allowed the Reagan administration to gain credit for what had been a Democratic legislative proposal, sponsored by Sen. Bill Bradley (D-N.J.) and Rep. Richard A. Gephardt (D-Mo.).

Real estate developers were among the most important fund-raisers and donors to the Mondale effort: Nathan Landow of Bethesda, William Batoff of Philadelphia, Thomas Rosenberg of Chicago, Jess Hay of Dallas, Robert H. Smith of Arlington, Va. "I would say half of the money from our list was from real estate," Landow, who emerged as one of the premier Democratic fund-raisers in 1984, said recently.

In addition, the fund-raising process has prompted key Democratic leaders to take on unusual roles for elected politicians.

The chairman of the DCCC, Rep. Tony Coelho (D-Calif.), for example, sometimes performs the same functions as a lobbyist, providing access to members of the House for campaign contributors, as an integral part of his drive to raise money for the DCCC. Coelho is now the leading candidate to become House Democratic whip after the 1986 elections.

Coelho, whose DCCC expects to raise $2 million to $3 million in soft money during this election cycle, and which has already raised $1.6 million from PACs, also takes pride in acting as a broker, joining contributors who want representation on Capitol Hill with favored lobbyists seeking additional clients.

Coelho argued that the services he provides for campaign contributors are the same as he would give anyone "important to the party, be it contributors or noncontributors." He argued that he has pushed hard to increase donations from PACs and from soft money contributors in order to build a television production facility, a headquarters building and to buy computers.

These expenditures have allowed the DCCC to expand its direct-mail operations significantly so that they now produce 48 percent of all funds raised, compared with 12 percent of receipts in 1980, according to a Coelho aide.

Along with its dependence on special interest groups, the Democratic party raises money from individual contributors who are significantly richer than Republican contributors, according to John C. Green, a political scientist at Furman University in Greenville, S.C., who has conducted extensive surveys of campaign contributors.

While givers to both parties are far richer than the national average, Green said his research showed that "more than half the Democratic donors earn more than $100,000 a year and it was only around 43 percent for Republicans. The Republicans reach down lower. The Democrats tend to draw pretty much from national-level big wigs, while the Republicans, in their direct-mail campaigns, reached right down into Main Street across the country."

Moreover, according to Green and James L. Guth, a colleague at Furman, their surveys reveal wide divisions among different groups of Democratic donors on basic issues. For example, contributors to trade union PACs are much more enthusiastic about national health insurance than the Democrats' big donors. Indeed, almost as many Democratic donors are hostile to labor unions as favorable to them, Green and Guth have found.

Terry Michael, spokesman for the DNC, contended that there is no way "to square what is our financial base with our political base."

He pointed out that political contributors—both major givers and those who respond to direct-mail appeals—tend overwhelmingly to be upper-middle class or affluent, and any substantial effort by the Democratic party to raise money from "keypunchers or steelworkers" would be futile.

Perhaps the most telling sign of Democratic dependence on special-interest money is reflected in the pattern of major—$500 and more—contributions from individuals reported to the FEC.

During the past year alone, the percentage of large contributions going to the DNC from donors in the Washington area has grown to 19.7 percent of the total, compared with 11 percent from California, 9.7 percent from New York and 6.4 percent from Texas.

This represents more than a doubling of the proportion of Washington-area major contributions, signaling a much stronger presence for the "inside the Beltway" lobbying community in Democratic party finances. In the 1983–84 election cycle, Washington-area contributors made up 9.1 percent of the major donations from individuals. In that period, California dominated with 20.4 percent, in part because the chairman, Charles Manatt, was from California, but New York was also much more important, providing 18.1 percent, along with Texas, which supplied 8.3 percent.

In contrast, Washington-area major donations to the Republican National Committee—though greater in dollar terms than the Washington-area donations to the Democrats—amounted to 7.3 percent of the GOP total in 1985, the most recent period for which figures are available from the FEC, and to 5.1 percent in 1981–82.

C. Victor Raiser, II, DNC finance chairman, said he and Paul G. Kirk, Jr., DNC chairman, are making a concerted effort "to develop new sources of support outside the Beltway." Raiser contended that this drive is beginning to pay off, particularly in the South.

Meanwhile, the party is doing well in raising soft money from special interests. For the first seven months of this year, a total of 28 percent of the DNC's budget, or $1.6 million out of $5.7 million, came from unreported donations of soft money. The DNC does not disclose the identity of contributors of soft money.

Soft money is illegal if it is spent on behalf of a party's nominees for federal office. How it can legally be spent is a matter of intense debate among the small group of lawyers who follow election law. It is accepted that corporate and union money can be used for building party headquarters, buying computers and similar capital expenditures not connected to a specific campaign.

Both the DNC and RNC also raise soft money for state and local candidates and for state parties where there are no restrictions on contributions. In 1984, Mondale backers used the DNC to raise $5.3 million in soft money for get-out-the-vote and voter registration programs, much of it channeled to state party organizations. If the cash had gone directly to the Mondale campaign, it would have violated the law.

The DCCC, under the leadership of Coelho, has aggressively sought out soft money support. In this election cycle, according to DCCC officials, the committee will raise $2 million to $3 million in soft money, out of a total budget of $15 million.

In contrast to the DNC, which gives general figures but refuses to identify soft-money donors, the DCCC does list soft money contributors who donate specifically for capital projects. The DCCC also gave a reporter copies of campaign expense reports filed in California, where the committee used soft money to fight Republican efforts to kill the state's redistricting plan.

The names of those DCCC donors provide a glimpse of who is giving the party this soft money. Major contributors include Merchant Sterling Corp., which was chaired by W. Averell Harriman, who died last month, $150,000; International Brotherhood of Painters and Allied Trades, $50,000; Phillips Petroleum, $15,000; Chevron Corp., $10,000; Atlantic Richfield, $20,000; the Tobacco Institute, $40,000; and the lobbying firm of Camp, Carmouche, Palmer,

Barsh and Hunter, whose clients include many major oil companies, $55,000. These contributions are, in most cases, made in addition to individual and PAC contributions reported publicly under federal election law.

Figures provided by the DNC showing general sources of soft money (committee officials declined to identify specific donors) show that over the past five years, corporate money has become far more important than union money.

In 1982, the DNC received a total of $2.92 million in soft money, of which $1.8 million, or 61 percent, came from unions; $909,370, or 31 percent, came from corporations; and $218,519, or 8 percent, came from rich individuals.

So far this year, union contributions to soft money accounts have dropped to just 34 percent of the total, or $542,381 out of $1.56 million; while corporate contributions have grown to 57 percent of the total, and individual contributions remain virtually the same at 9 percent.

Just under half of this money—$2.37 million, according to campaign documents obtained by the *Washington Post*—came from labor unions, particularly the Operating Engineers, $225,000; the International Ladies Garment Workers, $150,000; the Sheetmetal Workers, $250,000; the Steelworkers, $303,000; and the United Auto Workers, $372,800.

# Money (and Politics) in Both Parties

*Dissent*, Fall 1986

Underlying the continuing financial advantage of the Republican party over the Democratic party are changes in the sources of cash for each party that have significant consequences for both policy and candidates. For the Democratic party, the pressure to raise money from the restricted sources available to it are functioning to push the party to the right. For the GOP, the changing pattern of fund-raising is more ambivalent, although key sources of money for both the party's right wing and for the conservative movement as a whole are drying up.

The Democrats, after making some fund-raising gains in recent years, are now falling further behind the GOP. More important, however, money is to a considerable extent a reflection of the internal balance of power within each party. In this respect, the patterns of contributions to both parties signal significant changes in direction.

For the conservative movement, and particularly for the groups and individuals attempting to convert the Republican party into an arm of that movement, the collapse of the oil industry is a disaster. Independent oilmen in Texas, Oklahoma, and to a lesser extent in Louisiana and Colorado, have been the financial mainstay of the political right in this country. The right-wing ideological allegiance of the industry dates back to at least the early 1950s, when Sen. Joseph McCarthy was viewed by Texas oilmen as their third senator. The period from 1978 through the early years of the Reagan administration saw, however, a massive outpouring of financial commitment by independent oilmen suddenly made very rich by decontrol and OPEC-induced price increases. These oilmen poured their money into the campaigns of men and women challenging such liberal Democratic senators as Frank Church, John Culver and George McGovern; into such organizations as the National Conservative Political Action Committee; and into the Republican party.

For the Republican party, these oilmen wearing cowboy boots and diamond rings provided a kind of frontier toughness to a party traditionally dependent for large contributions on eastern bankers and Fortune 500 executives; they were, within the GOP universe, what might be described as populists of wealth, financing the Reagan revolution.

With the collapse of oil prices, dropping from $38 a barrel in 1981 to about $11 at this writing, the money and vitality of the oilmen have almost disappeared from the national political scene. In Oklahoma, the number of "Eagles"— individuals willing to give at least $10,000 a year to the Republican National Committee (RNC)—has dropped from 140 in 1981 to 15 in 1986.

At the same time, however, the doubling of stock market prices since Reagan took office has functioned to restore New York and the Northeast as a mainstay of financial support for the Republican party. As major contributors, the oilmen have been replaced in large part by the chairmen, presidents, and CEOs of large corporations. In fact, over the past six years, the northeast has eclipsed the Southwest, to become once more a major source of large campaign contributions to the RNC.

For the Republican party this may not be an unmixed blessing, because it suggests that the traditional view of the GOP as the party of the elite and of corporate America will gain additional legitimacy, at least in terms of the financial base of the party. In addition, it means that for the near future there is no financial base of support for the kind of conservative political challenge mounted in 1980; the kind of challenge that produced the election not only of a conservative president, but provided the troops to back him up in the House and Senate.

In 1980, in addition to President Reagan's victory, we saw the election of such conservative Republican senators as Steve Symms of Idaho, Charles Grassley of Iowa, Mack Mattingly of Georgia, Paula Hawkins of Florida, Alfonse D'Amato of New York, Jeremiah Denton of Alabama, John East of North Carolina, along with a cadre of new GOP House members who became known as Reagan's Robots. Most of these candidates not only got large amounts of support from oil, but received it very early in their campaigns, when the need is highest. There is no other source of committed money willing to gamble on seemingly marginal conservative candidates in the same way that the oilmen were willing to take financial-political risks in 1980.

Similarly, the changing balance of contributions to the RNC—which are an excellent indicator of the kind of money available to prospective presidential candidates—suggests that challengers to Vice President George Bush will have difficulty raising adequate funds. The growing importance of New York-based money signals a strong core of support for an establishment candidate along the lines of Bush, just as the erosion of oil money means that conservative challengers to Bush have lost a potential source of support. This is particularly true for Sen. Paul Laxalt of Nevada, a key Reagan backer since 1976, who is viewed as the most likely beneficiary of anti-Bush sentiments within the Southwest wing of the Republican party.

There are, however, two developments working against the partial restoration of Republican power to the traditional establishment wing—a restoration advantageous to Bush. The first is that the continued economic deterioration of the rust belt—the Midwest industrial states—has meant a decline in money flowing from such states as Michigan, Iowa, Illinois, and Ohio. These states have in the past supported moderate Republican candidates, including George Bush, who in 1980 beat Reagan in both Iowa and Michigan. The second is the rise of California—where defense spending and trade with the Far East have produced a booming economy—as a source of major contributions. California is, in political money terms, a wild card. Although the state has a strong conservative movement, its donors have also shown a strong willingness to support candidates who, within the GOP ideological boundaries, are moderates, including the current Senate nominee, Ed Zschau, who outraised his conservative opponents in the primary, and Bush, whose political action committee has done very well in the state.

For the Democratic party, money has increasingly become a force undermining coherence and commitment. The party desperately needs cash—its position relative to the GOP has worsened from a four-to-one disadvantage in 1983–84 to about six-to-one during the current election cycle—and party officials have responded to this pressure by turning to special interest groups.

The growing importance of money in elections works inherently to the advantage of Republicans: donors fall overwhelmingly in the top 20 percent of the income distribution, and it is there that allegiance to the Republican party is strongest. The GOP can make direct-mail appeals to selected groups within this affluent universe (subscribers to the *Wall Street Journal*, holders of American Express Gold Cards) and expand its donor base through partisan and ideological appeals. For the Democrats, the direct-mail donor base is far more restricted, limited effectively to affluent liberals in New York, Massachusetts, California, and academic communities scattered across the nation.

To compensate for this, the Democratic party has turned to two other sources of money: political action committees and a legally questionable form of contribution known as "soft money" (largely unreported donations made directly by corporations, unions, and by rich individuals who have already given the maximum amount allowed by federal law). Under strained interpretations of federal election law, "soft money" can be used for major capital expenses—new buildings or computers—and for local party development in states where there are no restrictions on campaign contributions.

The result is that the Democratic party, far more than the GOP, is dependent for survival on contributors who have little partisan or ideological interest in the party, but who do have a driving interest in gaining special legislative and administrative favors. The three major Democratic party committees—the national (DNC), congressional (DCCC) and senatorial (DSCC)—have so far in the current election cycle received a total of $4.5 million from political action committees, compared to the $993,000 in PAC money received by the parallel Republican committees. Not only does the Democratic party receive far more money from PACs, but, since the Democratic party raises far less money overall, the PAC contributions account for 18 percent of the party's budget, while for the GOP, PAC contributions amount to under 1 percent of receipts. (About 40 percent of the PAC contributions going to the Democratic party committees are from organized labor; the rest are from corporate and trade association PACs. If the labor contributions are discounted, on the premise that labor shares broad goals with the Democratic party and is not seeking only to advance a special interest—a possibly questionable assumption in the case of some unions—the remaining PAC contributions still far exceed those going to the Republican party committees.) Soft money contributions are generally unreported, but interviews with officials of both parties clearly point to much heavier Democratic than Republican dependence on this kind of contribution, roughly paralleling that on the PACs. A third indicator of the strength of the lobbying community in the Democratic party is reflected in the geographic pattern of contributions to the two parties. From January 1, 1985, through June 30, 1986, just under 20 percent of the large contributions from individuals going to the DNC were from people in the Washington, D.C., area, the overwhelming majority of whom were lobbyists, lawyers, and corporate representatives; for the Republican National Committee just 7 percent of the contributions were from the D.C. area.

The contribution patterns point to a series of vicious circles for the Democratic party that do not appear likely to find resolution in the near future. The Republican party appears, to a certain extent, to have been able to gain broad favor among campaign contributors, an affluent elite who have been the major beneficiaries of both Republican tax policy and the rise in the stock market. This has allowed the party to raise unprecedented amounts of money, but also to provide money and services to non-incumbent challengers. Challengers have the most difficulty raising money but they are critical to any party attempting both to replenish normal losses and to win in all marginal contests.

The Democrats, in contrast, have developed a base of donors primarily interested in wielding influence with the party's incumbents, and with little or no interest in the partisan goal of strengthening Democratic challengers. While the chairmen and chief executive officers of major corporations are writing personal checks for $10,000 to the RNC because they agree with the broad economic goals of the GOP, their corporate PACs are writing $10,000 checks to the DNC and the DCCC to gain access to key members of the Democratic-controlled Ways and Means Committee.

Not only does the GOP have an overall financial advantage that translates quickly to clout on the critical terrain of contests involving challengers to incumbents, but money within the GOP functions to affirm the party's ideological and economic goals. For the Democratic party, however, money is ideologically divisive. There are no political contributions made from the group most loyal to the Democratic party—the bottom third of the income distribution—except insofar as labor contributions function to represent these voters. Instead, the Democratic party must appeal to a universe of affluent liberals and special interest lobbyists, two groups with little or no stake in the adoption by the party of more aggressively populist strategies.

For the near future, then, money will continue to distort the ability of the Democratic party to represent its own constituency and to restrict the scope of elective strategies. The movement toward a kind of pro-business, centrist Democratic strategy, reflected currently by the Democratic Leadership Council, has gained strength in part from the pressures on major Democratic fund-raisers, seeking in many ways to develop a base within an essentially Republican constituency.

Conversely, while money does not produce for the Republican party internal conflicts with anywhere near the depth of those of the Democratic party, the shifts occurring within the GOP suggest that some of the vitality may be draining from the conservative-Republican alliance. One of the driving internal forces within the Republican party has been the angry repudiation of Wall Street, the Rockefellers, and the eastern bankers who dominated the party through 1960, a repudiation led by the new rich of the Sunbelt, particularly oilmen.

Insofar as old-guard, Eastern interests are regaining strength, the party will lose the momentum that comes from new money hungry to gain recognized status in a process uniquely possible within the American political system. In that light, while money may weaken the ability of the Democrats to put together a coherent challenge to the Republican party, the changing pattern of campaign contributions to the GOP is also undermining a source of strength within that party, which, for the moment, is likely to encourage a kind of ideological stasis between Democrats and Republicans—with neither one able to capitalize decisively on changes in the economy, in the nation's demographics, and in the fluid political allegiances of the 1980s, to achieve permanent majority status.

# GOP Committees a Bonanza for Ex-Aides and Relatives

*The Washington Post,* January 13, 1987

The three major Republican party committees have become consulting bonanzas for a network of former employees, White House aides and close relatives of major politicians. Participants in this network benefit from lucrative contracts ranging upward from $3,000 a month.

In the aftermath of the GOP loss of the Senate, public and private criticism of the party by Republican officials and strategists has increased. Much of this criticism has focused on the failure to develop a national party "message" or "theme" in the 1986 election, but an equally controversial target is the awarding of consulting contracts and bonuses.

Recipients of contracts paying $5,000 a month include President Reagan's daughter, Maureen Reagan, and Michelle Laxalt, daughter of retired senator Paul Laxalt (R-Nev.), the outgoing general chairman of the Republican National Committee. As general chairman, Laxalt received an estimated $50,000 a year; in addition, his son, John Paul, works for the RNC's finance division.

"It's a little kingdom with a big pot of gold," said David Keene, a Republican political strategist. Keene said that during a poker game at RNC headquarters he once mentioned that he has no consulting contracts with the RNC. "All these people, their mouths fell open, like 'How do you live?' "

Frank J. Fahrenkopf, Jr., RNC chairman, defended the party's operation, saying all consultants were earning their pay. Under his administration, Fahrenkopf contended, "consultants have to earn their money." Before he took office, Fahrenkopf said, the RNC "had been a warehouse [for consultants]. They didn't do anything and they were getting money."

Among former White House aides now holding consultant contracts:

• Joseph Canzeri, a former advance man for the Reagan administration. His public relations firm received $220,000 from GOP committees since January 1, 1985.

• Edward J. Rollins, former assistant to Reagan for political affairs. Rollins and the firm with which he is associated, Russo, Watts and Rollins, received $101,000 over the past two years. The firm's other clients include the National Corporation for Housing Partnerships, the McDonnell Douglas Corp. and Sears, Roebuck.

• Richard V. Allen, former national security adviser and now a lobbyist whose other clients include the Chinese National Association of Industry and Commerce and the Seoul Olympic Committee. He has a contract with the RNC providing him $3,500 a month.

• James Rosebush, former chief of staff to Nancy Reagan and now a private consultant. He received $3,000 a month from the RNC for nine months after he left the White House last year. Rosebush said the contract was to help with the RNC's "volunteerism" program, but he said, "I can't remember the name of the program."

Some of the most lucrative arrangements have been worked out by the finance directors of the National Republican Senatorial Committee and the National Republican Congressional Committee, Rodney Smith and Wyatt Stewart.

Instead of receiving a salary, both Smith and Stewart set up consulting companies. In Stewart's case, Wyatt Stewart and Associates was paid $473,900 from January 1, 1985, through last Nov. 24, the period covered by available Federal Election Commission reports.

Stewart received the fees despite a sharp drop in cash flow to the congressional committee, from $57.5 million in 1981–82 and 1983–84 to $33 million during the current reporting period. Stewart also held a fund-raising contract for the drive to renovate the Statue of Liberty, according to committee officials.

Smith's company, Fundraising and Financial Management, received $482,-900 from the GOP Senate committee. The company also got a bonus of $90,000 on November 5, the day after the election, to bring the total to $572,000.

The payment of the $90,000 bonus to Smith's firm was part of a package of $257,000 in bonuses distributed by the Republican Senate Committee, including $50,000 to Thomas C. Griscom, the outgoing executive director.

The spending practices of the GOP committees, combined with the Republican loss of the Senate in the November 4 elections, have resulted in harsh criticism within the Republican party.

A key staff member on the Republican congressional committee described the payment of bonuses by the Senate committee as "disgusting. I don't know any business that rewards failure."

In a television interview with columnists Rowland Evans and Robert Novak, Mitchell Daniels, chief of the White House political office, said he was "shocked" to learn of the bonus payments. "I think we have to question many of the ways in which money was spent" by the GOP Senate committee, he said.

The Griscom payment was defended by William Greener, former political director of the RNC, who said Griscom "did the best job of running the Senate committee I've ever seen."

In private, a number of present and former staff members of the Republican fund-raising committees said Griscom's problem was in the way he and Smith were paid large bonuses.

"Instead of getting a huge bonus that everybody's going to spot on a [Federal Election Commission] report, Tommy should have cut a deal like other staffers and gotten a consulting contract. That way, the money only shows up as a $5,000 or $6,000 payment every month, not a $50,000" amount, one former RNC employee said.

The Democratic party committees, which are routinely outspent by 4 to 1 or more, have far less discretionary money to pass out to consultants and other vendors. For example, the RNC spends well over $1 million annually on polls, while the Democratic National Committee often will go for two or more years without financing any polls. And unlike the GOP Senate committee, the Democratic counterpart did not receive big bonuses after the November election, officials there said.

A large number of former officials of the Republican party committees have consulting contracts. Among them:

• The political consulting firm Black, Manafort, Stone and Atwater has received at least $278,000 over the past two years. Charles Black is a former political director of the RNC. All the principals of the firm were active in Reagan's 1980 and 1984 campaigns.

• Eddie Mahe, Jr., a consultant who also was political director of the RNC, has received at least $130,000 from Republican committees.

• RSM, a consulting firm that includes Vincent Breglio, former director of the NRSC, Susan Bryant, former political director of the NRSC, and Jay Bryant, former public relations director for the NRCC, received $163,000 from all three GOP committees in the nine-month period from last March through November.

• Richard Bond, former deputy chairman and political director of the RNC, has consulting contacts providing $3,000 a month from the NRSC and $5,000 a month from the RNC. Bond, who recently joined the presidential campaign of Vice President Bush, received at least $167,000 over the past two years from Republican party committees.

• Nearly two years ago, Linda DiVall left her post as director of survey research and coalition development at the NRCC to form a polling firm, American Viewpoint. Largely on the basis of contracts from the NRCC, DiVall's firm received at least $1.2 million from GOP committees over the last two years.

In the process, she eclipsed such established polling firms as Arthur J. Finkelstein ($469,000) and Tarrance & Associates ($874,000), and has become a serious competitor to Richard B. Wirthlin's Decision/Making/Information, which got $2.64 million from Republican party committees, and Robert Teeter's Market Opinion Research, which got $1.7 million.

There is no sure way to judge the amount or quality of the work performed by political consultants, a group willing to criticize competitors in off-the-record conversations while claiming substantial victories for themselves in on-the-record interviews.

"Most of the consultants hired by the RNC do hardly anything to earn their fees and they get picked up because they know someone," said one consultant benefiting from one of the more advantageous arrangements with the RNC. But of his own efforts, he said, "We work hard for our money."

Griscom, of the NRSC, contended that the use of past executive directors of the Senate committee as consultants has proved useful. "I need to be able to draw on people [strategists] out there. Vince Breglio [of RSM] was an asset to me. When we were developing a whole strategic issue program for all our candidates, he helped design it and helped sell it [to the candidates]."

Greener, political director of the RNC during the election, said, for example, that he used Mahe, a former political director, to act as a combination overseer and auditor of projects who would "make sure the political things I wanted in our contract with DMI [the polling firm] got done." In addition, Greener said, Mahe "consulted with me on the particulars" of the RNC's $12 million get-out-the-vote drive last year, and performed general "trouble-shooting" duties.

Greener defended the RNC's extensive use of consultants: "The easiest thing to do is to be critical of the arrangement between the committee and consultants. My personal view is there are any number of projects that would never have been attempted, much less achieved, without the involvement of the consultants the RNC utilized."

Keene countered, however: "I have never felt that the RNC has performed up to its potential. It's become a big bureaucracy and it performs a lot of self-justifying activity. . . . It's an old-boy network."

# Breakfast with the Senate Finance Chairman for $10,000

*The Washington Post*, February 3, 1987

Sen. Lloyd Bentsen (D-Tex.), the new chairman of the Senate Finance Committee, last week offered 200 Washington lobbyists and political action committee (PAC) directors the opportunity to have breakfast with him once a month at a cost of $10,000 each.

Bentsen told the lobbyists that the $10,000, which would go into the senator's 1988 reelection campaign fund, would give them membership in his exclusive "Chairman's Council."

If too many people join to permit relatively small gatherings, Bentsen promised to hold multiple breakfasts.

"I will be relying on members of the Chairman's Council for advice, assistance and early financial support crucial to a successful campaign," Bentsen wrote in a letter inviting the lobbyists to an 8 A.M. breakfast briefing on the council at a Washington hotel last Thursday.

Bentsen, whose chairmanship gives him a major role in the writing of all tax and trade legislation in the new Congress, faces no known strong reelection opposition.

He told the lobbyists and PAC directors, however, that he expects the Texas Republican party to field a tough, well-financed challenger.

As of yesterday afternoon, about 40 of the lobbyists and PAC directors had signed up for the council, in a system that requires them to put up $5,000 now and another $5,000 by June 1.

Aides to Sen. Bob Packwood (R-Ore.), who served as chairman of both the

Commerce and Finance committees when the GOP controlled the Senate, said Packwood developed a similar breakfast program when he was chairman of Commerce, but the tab was lower: $5,000.

"It got to be very club-like," a Packwood aide said. "He began to look forward to the meetings. He got very attached to them."

Washington lawyer Patrick J. O'Connor said of the Bentsen offer, "A number of my partners will probably make a contribution and then I will go to some of my clients." His firm represents clients ranging from Armco to Westinghouse.

Bentsen told the group that "the purpose of the council is to talk about matters of trade and taxation and anything anyone wants to raise," according to O'Connor. "It was the strongest breakfast turnout I've ever seen," O'Connor said.

Lawrence F. O'Brien, III, a Washington lawyer and tax specialist, said when asked if he had attended the briefing, "Who didn't?"

"The amount of money that was being suggested was large enough that some people are going to pause over it," O'Brien said. "From a PAC, they are asking for a max-out," he added, referring to the fact that the most a PAC can give to a candidate is $5,000 for a primary and $5,000 for a general election.

After spending large amounts in the 1986 elections, "a lot of PACs have not recharged their batteries," he pointed out.

The money can be given directly by a PAC, or it must be collected from larger groups of individuals, who are permitted to give only $1,000 to a candidate in the primary and general elections.

Another lobbyist defended the event, saying, "I feel it's kosher."

"The fact that the digits went up, that's the coin of Washington. He's the chairman," the lobbyist said of Bentsen.

Jack R. DeVore, Jr., the senator's press secretary, said Bentsen promised to limit the number attending the breakfasts to 35 or 40.

In the event more than 40 join—a likely prospect—multiple breakfasts will be held each month. Bentsen will pick up the tab for the breakfast, DeVore said. The $10,000 commitment will cover council membership through the 1987–88 election cycle, he said.

"I suspect everyone of any consequence who was there will sign up," said Thomas Hale Boggs, Jr., whose firm's clients include ABC, Hitachi, the Scrap Iron and Steel Institute and Ford. "To raise $10,000 for the Senate Finance Committee chairman isn't very hard."

# Congress' Free Rides

## Many Lawmakers Supplementing Income with Trips, Speech Fees Paid by Lobbyists

*The Washington Post*, June 14, 1987

In 1984, Republican Mitch McConnell pulled off the upset of the year, using a "bloodhound" commercial to defeat Sen. Walter D. (Dee) Huddleston (D-Ky.). The ad showed a hunter with a pack of dogs unsuccessfully tracking Huddleston as he made speeches for fees of $1,000 and $2,000 in Puerto Rico and Los Angeles.

"We can't find Dee. Maybe we ought to let him make speeches and switch to Mitch for senator," the television commercial declared. The voters agreed.

Two years later, it would have taken more than a hunter with a bloodhound to keep track of McConnell; from January 10 through January 21, 1986 he went on an 11-day tour from Las Vegas through Southern California with all expenses paid by seven different special-interest groups.

To make the trip even more inviting, these groups paid McConnell a total of $10,500 for a series of speeches and "panel discussions."

Starting on January 10, the Electronics Industries Association flew McConnell from Washington to Las Vegas, paid him $1,000 for a panel discussion, and picked up the tab for two nights' food and lodging. On the 12th, the Tobacco Institute flew McConnell to Palm Springs, covered hotel and meals for three days and paid him $2,000 for a speech.

While in Palm Springs, McConnell flew to San Diego for a day at the expense of the National Association of Private Psychiatric Hospitals which gave him a $1,500 check for a talk.

The costs of the next three days, in Los Angeles, were carried by three defense contractors: McDonnell Douglas, Lockheed Corp. and Northrop Corp., which paid him $1,000, $1,000 and $2,000 for speeches. Finally, McConnell spent the last three days of his trip in San Diego, where expenses were covered by the Distilled Spirits Council, which also provided a $2,000 speech honorarium. In addition to McConnell's expenses, the groups paid expenses for a female friend, according to McConnell's administrative assistant, Neils Holch, who stressed that no rules were broken. McConnell is divorced.

McConnell avoided the trap of missing votes while making speeches—one of the charges he made against Huddleston. Congress did not reconvene until January 21, 1986, the day he returned.

"I have never done that [missed a vote while giving a speech]," McConnell said, adding that "many of us are not millionaires," and honoraria provide a "sanctioned way to earn money which is fully disclosed. It's nice to have some option."

McConnell's $10,500 sojourn, however, epitomizes the explosive growth for House and Senate members of honoraria and expense-paid trips to luxury resorts financed by corporations, associations and law firms that lobby Capitol Hill.

Public attention has focused on the growth of political action committees (PACs) established by the same interests to finance congressional campaign costs.

Simultaneously, however, members of the House and Senate have become increasingly dependent for personal income on organizations and individuals seeking their votes. These same groups are financing trips for members of Congress that have many of the earmarks of vacations.

In effect, such groups and companies as Pfizer Inc., General Electric, the American Medical Association, Amoco and a host of other interest groups are not only financing much of the cost of running for office, but are helping to pay the mortgages, food bills and college tuition costs of members of Congress.

Under Senate rules, members were allowed in 1986 to take speaking fees up to 40 percent of their $75,100 salaries, or $30,040. In the House, the limit is 30 percent, or $22,530. Money received in excess of these figures must be turned over to a charity. McConnell, for example, raised $46,600 and turned $16,660 over to charity, including $7,360 to his church, the Crescent Hill Baptist Church.

More than half the Senate receives at least a quarter of earned income—as opposed to investment income—from honoraria. Of 59 Senate disclosure statements made available right after the May 15 filing deadline, 36, or 61 percent, reported honoraria income in excess of $20,000, and 30 of those were at or just below the $30,040 maximum. (Many members of the Senate received extensions on the filing deadline). In the House, about a fifth of the members receive $20,000 or more of their earned income from honoraria.

"It's a form of institutionalized bribery," one member of the House said after returning from Las Vegas where he had been paid $1,500 to appear on a panel discussion. But he declined to say this on the record.

Among the findings from a survey of honoraria and trip payments for 1986 are: during debate on the 1986 tax reform bill, numerous corporations, associations and lobbyists provided honoraria and trips to members of the House Ways and Means Committee and the Senate Finance Committee. Many of these organizations benefited from special "transition" rules in the tax bill providing them with millions of dollars in tax relief.

Massachusetts Mutual Life Insurance Co., for example, paid a total of $16,000 in 1986 to eight members of the Ways and Means Committee, Reps. Guy Vander Jagt (R-Mich.), Sam M. Gibbons (D-Fla.), Ronnie G. Flippo (D-Ala.), Byron L. Dorgan (D-N.D.), Richard T. Schulze (R-Pa.), Brian J. Donnelly (D-Mass.), Philip M. Crane (R-Ill.) and Beryl Anthony, Jr. (D-Ark.).

The same year, the company received a break worth an estimated $11 million. The provision allowed Massachusetts Mutual and 14 other companies to pay capital gains tax rates on certain income from market discount bonds, even though the capital gains rate had been eliminated by the 1986 tax bill.

New England Life Insurance, which paid $10,000 in speech fees to members of the committee, received a $1 million tax break.

Joseph E. Seagram and Sons paid $9,000 in honoraria to House committee members and a total of $4,000 to Sens. Max Baucus (D-Mont.) and John H. Chafee (R-R.I.) of the Senate Finance Committee. Seagram's received a tax break estimated at $38 million, allowing it to retain capital gains rate on income received on installment payments. The Distilled Spirits Council, of which Seagram's is a dominant member, paid $18,000 more in honoraria to Ways and Means and Finance Committee members—along with at least five California trips—although council officials said they did not lobby in support of the Seagram's tax break.

The payment of honoraria does not guarantee success in Congress. Last year, for example, many heavy industries, their associations and such lobbyists as Charles Walker Associates paid honoraria, but lost some of their most treasured tax provisions, particularly the investment tax credit.

Perhaps the most effective method of winning tax breaks in recent years has been to hire lobbyists who have been key aides to prominent members of the tax-writing committees. These include James Healey and John Salmon, former assistants to Rep. Dan Rostenkowski (D-Ill.), chairman of the Ways and Means Committee; and Robert Lighthizer, former chief counsel to the Finance Committee when Sen. Robert J. Dole (R-Kan.) was chairman. These lobbyists won targeted tax breaks for such corporations as Drexel Burnham Lambert, Metropolitan Life, Bear Stearns and others worth at least $98 million, almost all of which allowed these firms to temporarily retain favored tax treatment after most other companies lost breaks as a result of the 1986 bill.

Companies and organizations mostly target members of committees with jurisdiction over legislation that affects them.

Sen. Jake Garn (R-Utah) was chairman of the Committee on Banking, Housing and Urban Affairs in 1986. Almost all the $30,040 Garn collected in honoraria that year was from groups vitally interested in committee decisions, including the Mortgage Bankers Association, the Association of Reserve City Bankers, the Association of Thrift Holding Companies, the Credit Union National Association, the U.S. League of Savings Institutions, the National Association of Federal Credit Unions and the California Bankers Association.

Washington-based industry associations have long paid honoraria. Now, registered lobbying firms have begun to pay members of Congress directly for speeches.

Among them are Williams and Jensen, whose clients include Texas Air Corp., First Boston Corp., the Pharmaceutical Manufacturers Association and Texaco; Dow, Lohnes and Albertson, representing at least 58 television stations, Presidential Airlines and Cox Broadcasting; R. Duffy Wall and Associates, representing Brinks Inc., Morgan Guaranty Trust and the N.Y. Bankers Association; and Preston, Thorgrimson, Ellis and Holman, whose clients include Aloha Airlines, Dravo Corp. and Martin Marietta.

Kenneth Kay and Lloyd Meeds of Preston, Thorgrimson, Ellis and Holman said the firm holds about ten "public policy luncheons" annually for partners, associates and clients at which members of the House and Senate are paid $1,000 to speak.

Meeds said such payment from lobbying firms "might be improper if it was a lot of money and it was meant to influence the member. We have limited our fee to $1,000 and we don't try to use it as an instrument to influence the member."

The firm was successful last year in preserving most of the research and development tax break for an alliance of corporations. While the tax bill eliminated such breaks as the investment tax credit and the capital gains rate, the R&D credit was reduced only from 25 percent of the cost of the investment to 20 percent.

In addition to speech fees, many members of Congress, and often their spouses, receive expense-paid trips to such luxury resorts as Palm Springs, Palm Beach and islands in the Caribbean.

Last year, for example, Rep. Bill Frenzel (R-Minn.) and his wife spent at least 17 nights in such places as Honolulu, Palm Springs, Palm Beach, Key Largo, and Naples, Fla., at the behest of such groups as the National Restaurant Association, Chase Manhattan and the American Electronics Association, while receiving more than $6,000 in speech payments. An aide to Frenzel said the trips did not seem strikingly different from those accepted by other members.

Similarly, Representative Schulze took at least nine expense-paid trips with his wife to such places as Miami, Palm Beach, Phoenix and St. Thomas on the tab of the Distilled Spirits Council, Pratt & Whitney, R. Duffy Wall and Associates and others. Asked about the propriety of accepting such trips and speech payments from groups seeking his vote, Schulze said, "you'll have to be the judge of that," and cut short the interview.

Schulze and Frenzel are members of the Ways and Means Committee. Their trips are a fraction of the 29 taken by Rostenkowski, including 12 with his wife. Rostenkowski's disclosure statement is one of the least informative of all House members, and there is no indication of where he went or how much time he spent on any of these trips. The House disclosure forms require far less detail than the Senate forms. Under the section where trip reimbursements are to be listed, the House asks only for a "brief description of reimbursements of $250 or more." Senate forms request specific information on location and date of a trip.

Rostenkowski did, however, attend the annual Bob Hope Classic golf tournament in January in Palm Springs, which has become known among lobbyists as "Washington West." One organizer called it "a giant group grope with lobbyists and members [of Congress], a feeding frenzy on honoraria." Among the companies and associations that have sponsored expense-paid trips to Palm Springs coinciding with the Bob Hope Classic are the Tobacco Institute, the Outdoor Advertising Association, the Distilled Spirits Association, Joseph E. Seagram and Sons, and the Air Travel Association, drawing as many as 50 members of Congress to the resort.

Officials of the organizations defend the practice, most often arguing that speeches by lawmakers provide insight and knowledge for executives and staff members.

Barry Gotterher, senior vice president for government relations at Massachusetts Mutual, said, "Back in 1983, we decided that it was really to be the beginning of the rewriting of the insurance tax law. . . . We concluded that at that time that we should try to bring in speakers from Washington. . . ." Members of Congress were invited to provide a "Washington overview: 'this is what's happening on taxes' . . . 'This is what's happening in your industry' . . . a snapshot of what's happening in Washington."

Geoffrey Peterson, director of federal government relations for the Distilled Spirits Council, said, "we have a small PAC. It [the giving of honoraria and trips] is a resource we do have." Peterson said members of Congress "appreciate your helping them. . . . It's a nice way to open up access to them."

Walker Merryman, a vice president of the Tobacco Institute, said the organization spent $91,000 on honoraria last year, but many members of Congress were also paid to attend institute meetings in Palm Springs and in Florida.

"Several members of Congress came and spoke at a number of seminars" at the Palm Springs gathering which, Merryman noted, was held "at the same time as the Bob Hope Classic." In Washington, he said, members of Congress are also paid $1,000 to $2,000 honoraria when they address members of the institute at breakfast sessions.

There is relatively little correlation between the politics of legislators and ideology and/or personal wealth. For example, while most senators accepted the maximum of $30,040, or close to that amount, neither liberal Sen. Carl Levin (D-Mich.) or conservative Sen. William L. Armstrong (R-Colo.) accepted honoraria as income, although Armstrong turned over a $2,000 speaking fee to charity.

Sen. David L. Boren (D-Okla.) is leading the fight for campaign finance reform and has always refused to accept PAC money. Last year, however, he accepted $29,413 in honorarium payments, almost all from interests actively seeking to influence his vote, including $2,000 apiece from such lobbying firms as Williams and Jensen and R. Duffy Wall, the American Bankers Association and the Tobacco Institute.

Among senators whose disclosure reports indicate they are worth $1 million or more, some—Sens. Dennis DeConcini (D-Ariz.) and Armstrong, for example—accepted no personal income from honoraria. The ones who did include John C. Danforth (R-Mo.), one of the wealthiest members of the Senate, who accepted $11,875; Frank H. Murkowski (R-Alaska), with $25,000 and Alan J. Dixon (D-Ill.), $28,040.

Over the past ten years, Congress has adopted conflicting positions on the honoraria issue.

The most severe restrictions were imposed in the post-Watergate period when, in 1977, honoraria were limited to 15 percent of congressional salaries, or

$8,625, as part of an arrangement under which congressional salaries were raised from $44,600 to $57,500.

Since then, however, pressure to raise honorarium ceilings have been intense, and the limit has grown to 30 percent in the House and 40 percent in the Senate. With salaries jumping to $89,500 this year, this translates to $26,850 in the House and $35,850 in the Senate.

CHAPTER FIVE

# PARTIES IN CRISIS:
# THE ELUSIVE MAJORITY

HE QUESTION of whether the country is in the midst of a realignment goes to the heart of American politics. The balance of power in the electorate effectively defines the range of options available to a newly elected and powerful president. For roughly 45 years, from the beginning of the Depression, a majority dominated by those in the bottom half of the income distribution was instrumental in helping to set the terms of the national debate, defining a significant part of the scope of legislative action and executive initiative. In 1952 and in 1968, for example, the country elected relatively conservative presidents, but neither Dwight D. Eisenhower nor Richard M. Nixon sought to press a conservative agenda—in large part, because the evolving New Deal coalition forming a majority of the electorate remained the central force in American politics, acting as a brake on any major shift to the right.

The collapse of the New Deal coalition in the 1970s effectively eliminated that brake, opening the floodgates to the right and allowing the Reagan administration to conduct a serious assault on the liberal establishment. The fundamental question now is whether a new majority is emerging—a realignment—that will define a new shape and a new set of goals for the national government. Ronald Reagan twice won election with majorities dominated by the affluent—an inversion of the New Deal coalition. As the Reagan era comes to an end, a number of Republican strategists contend that the GOP has the potential to shape a new majority. The tentative outlines of this coalition would include those who see the struggle between communism and capitalism as the dominant issue of international relations, and place the highest priority on increased military strength; those industries and those segments of the population that see themselves as having done well economically throughout this decade, and fear Democratic party fiscal and monetary policies; men and women who identify themselves as firmly religious, including, but by no means only, white, Christian fundamentalists; white voters, particularly in the South but also in the North, who no longer believe that the Democratic party represents their interests, and who see blacks displacing them, not only in the party, but, to some extent, in society at large; voters who believe government and the system of public education should reinforce the traditional family unit; those who cast their votes for the party most likely to press for harsh punishment of wrongdoers and to strictly enforce criminal statutes; and those who have come to see government as a collector of taxes rather than as a provider of services.

A majority alliance along these lines, should it materialize, would, over time, reshape the federal government, continuing the push to the right initiated in the late 1970s and early 1980s. While trends in poll data provide some support for this fundamental Republican strategy, the prospects for such a realignment are still very much uncertain.

Individual elections can often turn on other factors, but a realignment involving a sustained commitment to one party or the other by a majority of the electorate requires a level of consistent support based on the faith that the favored party can provide continued economic security. On this score, the outcome of the contest between the two parties will depend in part on the resolution of a number of unresolved domestic economic issues: 1) A determination as to whether the majority of new jobs created—as the country moves from manufacturing to services—provides opportunities for advancement and sufficiently good salaries, or whether these new jobs limit employees to low wages with few chances to move into the middle class; 2) the political consequences of the growing inequity in the distribution of income; 3) the strength and duration of the economic recovery that started in late 1982; 4) future changes in the rate of inflation and in interest rates; 5) the probability that the deficit will affect the economy in ways that are identifiable to the electorate.

At the moment, neither party has a lock on victory in the realignment contest. The Democratic congressional dominance has, to some degree, offset the Republican presidential victories, although the GOP continues to enjoy a marginal advantage. The articles in this section explore the issue of realignment during different stages of the Reagan presidency and reflect my own changing assessment of the partisan contest. As I noted in the Introduction, there is in these pieces a fair amount of repetition—since they originally appeared in different publications over an extended period of time. I suggest skipping over arguments or data the reader is familiar with, although I have generally tried to select articles which introduce at least some variation.

# Boom and Bust: Economic Ills Strain Alliance of Oilmen and the GOP

*First of two articles*

*The Washington Post,* April 25, 1983

On July 9, 1981, President Reagan, Vice President Bush and a number of aides met in the White House with a delegation of six oilmen organized by the

Independent Petroleum Association of America.

The petroleum association and the oilmen wanted billions of dollars of tax breaks to be included in the president's 1981 tax bill, then before Congress.

Their ultimate goal was an exemption from the "windfall" profits tax for the first 1,000 barrels of daily production, a step that would effectively have eliminated the tax for virtually all independents, at a cost to the Treasury of $25 billion over five years.

The president had already agreed to cut by half the windfall profits tax on newly discovered oil. This break, worth $3.2 billion over the next five years for the oil industry, would go primarily to the independents, the wildcatters and entrepreneurs whose business is the search for domestic oil and gas.

The president, however, was not yet prepared to make additional concessions. Instead, he declared in vague terms that he looked forward to a day when he and the oilmen could burn the profits tax "like a mortgage."

The oilmen, recalling Reagan's detailed campaign denunciations of the "windfall" profits tax, went away angry and dissatisfied, but fully prepared to move on other fronts.

Their anger was not based only on a campaign promise left unfulfilled. Five of the six oilmen—Cary M. Maguire of Dallas; Gene Miller of Allegan, Mich.; James E. Russell of Abilene, Tex.; Dalton J. Woods, of Shreveport, La.; and Lew Ward, of Enid, Okla.—had put their money behind their political convictions.

For the three and one-half years from 1979 through the first half of 1982, these five men and their close relatives were good for $305,300 in federal campaign contributions, almost all of it to Republican candidates and GOP committees.

Their largess provided the Republican National Committee with $113,000, the Republican senatorial, congressional and a network of federally registered state GOP committees with $65,750, and the Reagan campaign and committees supporting it a total of $29,750.

The five oilmen were part of a major transformation of the upper echelons of GOP fund-raising. Money for political parties and candidates comes from several basic sources: small donors, political action committees and large donors. In this last category of individuals willing to give $500 to $20,000 a year, independent oil has emerged as the single most important special interest in the financing of the Republican National Committee and the National Republican Congressional and Senatorial Campaign committees.

There is a long history of political giving by the oil industry, whose profits are influenced heavily by government tax breaks and price regulation. In the past, oil money flowed freely to both major parties.

But beginning in the late 1970s, oil contributions made a shift to the Republican camp, and the sharp rise in oil and gas prices seemed to cement a new alliance between the petroleum industry and the GOP.

Now, abruptly, that alliance is in trouble. Falling oil and gas prices are undercutting the wealth of the independents just as new political and economic pressures on Congress and the Reagan administration threaten their tax and regulatory goals.

In July 1981, however, the oil industry was still riding high. Undeterred by the presidential rebuff, the industry turned to powerful allies: a dozen oil-state congressmen whose votes would decide the outcome of the tax debate. Both the administration and House Democrats wound up bidding for the support of these "boll weevil" conservative congressmen, and the stakes of the bidding were tax breaks for independent oil.

After forcing the White House into this bidding process, the independents joined the administration in lobbying for the tax bill that passed a critical test on the House floor by 238 to 195 on July 29, and was signed into law August 13, 1981.

With only slight exaggeration, Lloyd N. Unsell, vice president of the Independent Petroleum Association of America, would write later: "Despite its divisiveness, the oil tax issue ironically became the glue that held together important elements of the coalition that produced the Reagan tax victory in the House."

The cost of that "glue" was $6.05 billion in tax breaks over five years directed primarily toward the independents—twice what they had before the July 9 session at the White House.

Passage of the tax bill represented the zenith of power for the independent oil industry, which had begun a nine-year, fast-track revival in 1973.

For the previous 20 years, from the early 1950s to the emergence of a powerful international oil cartel in 1973, the price of domestic crude oil was stagnant, moving from $2.68 a barrel in 1953 to only $3.39 in 1972, a drop in prices after accounting for inflation.

During this period, the independents watched in anger as Exxon, Mobil, Gulf and the rest of Big Oil imported relatively cheap foreign oil and profited all along the chain from production and refining to distribution and sale.

But the escalation of oil prices imposed by the Organization of Petroleum Exporting Countries in 1973 and 1979 gave the independents a piggyback ride up the profit ladder. From $3.89 in 1973, the price per barrel shot up to $8.84 in 1976, to $14.27 in 1979, to $23.26 in 1980 and was up to $33.76 in July 1981, when the oilmen met with Reagan.

As oil prices rose, the center of gravity in Republican fund-raising shifted from Wall Street and Chicago into the heart of the Sunbelt.

The Republican National Committee's big givers, who contributed at least $10,000 a year, are called "Eagles," and for years New York had more Eagles than any other city. Now, however, it has been eclipsed by Houston, the center of the oil industry. Moving up fast have been Oklahoma City, Tulsa, Dallas and Midland, Tex., a city with 84,200 residents but in the top 10 on the Eagle list, thanks to its location on the rim of the oil- and gas-rich Permian Basin.

In the heart of these longtime, bedrock Democratic states, the interests of the oil industry were protected from the 1930s into the 1960s by some of the most powerful figures in Congress. Sens. Robert Kerr (D-Okla.) and Lyndon B.

Johnson (D-Tex.) in the Senate and Rep. Sam Rayburn (D-Tex.), House speaker during a period of Democratic control from 1940 through 1961, determined the membership of the tax-writing committees and channeled oil money to help keep northern Democrats in line.

The last two decades, however, have seen a steady erosion of this relationship. The reign of Johnson and Rayburn ended in the House and Senate in the early 1960s; the rise of liberal influence in the House Ways and Means Committee led to the partial repeal in 1975 of the oil depletion allowance and the end of oil's control of the tax-writing panel.

Then in 1979, in the midst of a gasoline shortage, President Carter demanded that removal of government price controls on oil be accompanied by a "windfall" profits tax, a special levy on the industry's gains from decontrol of prices. The administration's campaign for the tax was punctuated with repeated complaints about oil industry profits.

"President Carter pushed all the oil people into the Republican party," said Chet Upham, an independent oilman and chairman of the Texas Republican Party. "There is no question about it: the principles of the Republican party are more akin to the things that oil and gas people are seeking."

The rightward bias of the oil community, however, has precedents dating to well before Johnson and Rayburn's departures from Congress.

It found expression at least as far back as 1948, when oil money lubricated then-Democrat Strom Thurmond's 1948 Dixiecrat presidential campaign, and in the 1950s, when such prominent independent oilmen as Hugh Roy Cullen, H.L. Hunt and Clint Murchison channeled support to the anti-communist campaigns of Sen. Joseph R. McCarthy (R-Wis.). On behalf of McCarthy, who was known as "Texas' third senator," they were hosts of only the second $100-a-plate dinner for a Republican in Texas history. Oilmen funneled $6.1 million in secret contributions to Richard M. Nixon in 1972.

The explosion in oil and gas prices during the second half of the 1970s coincided with the height of the conservative Republican movement, and the contributions of independent oilmen to this drive have been immense:

Of the $8.433 million in contributions of $500 or more to the Republican National Committee (RNC) for all of 1981 and the first half of 1982, $2.202 million came from only three major oil-producing states: Texas, Louisiana and Oklahoma. Although these states have only 9.4 percent of the nation's population, they supplied just over 26 percent of the major contributions to the RNC.

In contrast, the Democratic National Committee (DNC) raised a total of $2.633 million in contributions of $500 or more during all of 1981 and 1982. Of this, only $73,950, or 2.8 percent, came from Texas, Louisiana and Oklahoma.

Of the $5.71 million raised by the RNC from persons who would qualify as Eagles by giving $10,000 or more, $1.48 million, or 25.9 percent, was from persons with direct ties to the oil industry, and the overwhelming majority were independent oilmen, not officials of major oil companies.

Of all individual contributions of $500 or more to the DNC in 1981 and

1982, persons with identifiable ties to the oil industry gave $62,950, or 2.4 percent of the total of $2.6 million.

In a separate, murky fund-raising arena where the contributions are known as "soft" money and, for the most part, are not required by law to be publicly reported to the Federal Election Commission, independent oil in 1980 was to the Republican party much as organized labor is to the Democratic party: a major source of private cash for the presidential general election campaign over and above the $29.44 million given each candidate in public financing.

Herbert E. Alexander, head of the University of Southern California's Citizen Research Foundation, estimated in a study of the 1980 election that each party spent about $19 million in "soft" money. Under legislation passed in 1979, the money could be used for state "volunteer" and "get-out-the-vote" activities. For the Democrats, about $15 million of this came from organized labor.

No formal records were kept, but, in the case of Reagan's presidential campaign, sources estimate that at least a third of the soft money came from oil states. One September 1981, dinner in Houston raised $2.8 million for what was called the Texas Victory Committee.

Former RNC finance director Robert Perkins, who ran the soft-money drive for the Reagan campaign with Robert Mosbacher, a Houston independent oilman, and Ted Welsh, a Tennessee developer, said: "$20,000 was sort of the price of what we asked people to do. We basically raised it in $20,000 chunks." He said it is impossible in retrospect to determine how much was from oil states or from persons tied directly to the industry.

In addition to the role of oil in the presidential campaign and in financing national Republican committees, Houston, Dallas, Oklahoma City, Midland and Tulsa have become meccas for Republican congressional candidates, particularly conservative Republicans seeking to oust liberal incumbent Democrats.

Then-Rep. Steve Symms (R-Idaho) showed the way by going to Texas early in 1980 and returning with $150,000 to get his successful campaign against Sen. Frank Church (D-Idaho) off the ground. He was followed by a steady march of northern Republicans seeking oil money, and they were not disappointed.

At the same time, independent-oil political action committees with names like DALLENPAC and HOUPAC began to spring up throughout the Southwest, channelling money to conservatives and acting as forums for candidates to make their pitches to groups of oilmen flush with rising profits.

The oil communities stood out as bastions of Republican conservatism in the Texas-Oklahoma terrain of "Yellow Dog Democrats"—voters who, in the local vernacular, "back the Democrat even if he is a scraggy yellow dog and the Republican is Jesus Christ, incarnate."

Democrat Garry Mauro, for example, was elected Texas lands commissioner last year with over 60 percent of the statewide vote. "I carried all but six of the state's 254 counties," Mauro said, "but in Midland, I got 22 percent of the vote."

Rep. Kent R. Hance (D-Tex.) successfully engineered Midland out of his district when the lines were redrawn after the 1980 census. "For a Democrat to have Midland in his district is like trying to represent Munich in 1938," another member of the Texas congressional delegation commented.

In Oklahoma, Rep. Mike Synar, a pro-oil Democrat, noted that "Bartlesville, a town of 36,000 people is Phillips Petroleum. . . . I got 38 percent of the vote there compared with 54 percent district-wide in 1980. I was told I could campaign there day in, day out, and I might get 40 percent."

# Boom and Bust: The Hard Times of the Independent Gas Industry

Second of two articles

*The Washington Post,* April 26, 1983

After passage of the 1978 Natural Gas Policy Act, Bill Saxon, Robert A. Hefner, III and J.D. Allen rode a geyser of gas, oil and money out of Oklahoma's Anadarko Basin, gambling and winning on wells running three or more miles deep into the ground.

The 1978 act removed federal price ceilings on gas from such deep wells and, backed by bankers and investors with an unquenchable thirst for a piece of the action, the three independent oilmen made fortunes both immense and fragile. Their money flowed into the Republican party.

Saxon, according to Federal Election Commission reports, gave $87,000 from 1979 through 1982, including $30,000 to the Republican National Committee (RNC), $23,000 to the Republican Senate and House committees and $13,000 to committees backing President Reagan. Allen, former co-chairman of the Oklahoma Republican party's finance committee, handed out $73,750 in a similar pattern. Hefner and his close relatives, once Democratic party loyalists, gave $55,200 to Reagan and to Washington-based Republican committees.

Moving outside the political arena, Saxon stunned colleagues in the petroleum industry in October 1981, with the announcement of his pledge to Oklahoma University of $30 million toward the construction of an energy research and training institute.

Saxon said at the time that he knew he "couldn't spend it all . . . I don't mean to sound braggadocious, but it does not strap me or hurt me to do it."

At that moment, Saxon and his colleagues in the independent oil and gas industry, were on a winning streak that seemed to have no end. Their growing wealth was accompanied by growing political influence as their contributions to the Republican party escalated.

The end of that streak came suddenly with the collapse of oil and gas prices last year, with severe consequences for the industry and its alliance with the GOP.

The price of deep natural gas, the only kind that was fully decontrolled, began to dive late last year, in large part because of the recession. From a high of $9.77 a thousand cubic feet—the price equivalent of oil at $57 a barrel—the market price has now dropped to the $3 range, if there are any buyers at all, wreaking havoc in the Anadarko Basin.

Saxon's firm, the Saxon Oil Company in Dallas, has reported losses totaling $90.9 million for 1982, almost half of that, $41.1 million, in the fourth quarter. The firm is currently struggling to restructure $84 million in debts to InterFirst Bank of Dallas, and to win approval from a committee of drilling contractors, service companies and other suppliers for a special plan to pay off another $54 million in debts. Saxon, according to a company spokesman, is not responding to inquiries about the $30 million pledge to Oklahoma University.

J.D. Allen's company, Longhorn Oil and Gas, was one of the first to get caught in the undertow from the collapse of the Penn Square National Bank in Oklahoma in June 1982. Last February, Allen petitioned the U.S. Bankruptcy Court for a Chapter 11 reorganization, declaring that he owes $9.88 million in loans and personal guarantees to his companies, including Texas Oilfield Supply and Longhorn Oil & Gas.

More than 100 bankruptcies have been filed by oil drillers and producers over the past 12 months. "Producers who were overextended now have to pay off loans at the bank," said Julian C. Martin, executive vice president of the Texas Independent Producers and Royalty Owners (TIPRO). "They were betting on the come and now they are caught in the squeeze."

Already battered by the drop in oil and gas prices, the independents were jolted politically by President Reagan's proposal February 28 to remove price controls on gas. While some independents would benefit from decontrol, others, including those who specialized in deep gas, gas below 15,000 feet, would be hurt.

The result is a deep split in the industry. Hefner, whose Oklahoma City firm escaped the fates of Allen's and Saxon's companies, has become an aggressive critic of President Reagan's plan. Complaining that its main benefits will go to the major oil companies at the expense of most independents, he has formed the Independent Gas Producers Committee to defend the independent producers' interests.

A major element of the dispute is how deregulation will deal with the most important categories of natural gas. Gas discovered before 1977 is considered "old" gas under Section 104 of the 1978 natural gas legislation, while most gas discovered after that is termed "new" gas, under Section 102 of the act.

"The major oil companies are the ones that have most of the old gas and they are the ones that are going to get most of the benefit," said Lew Ward, an independent oilman from Oklahoma.

The Reagan decontrol plan is likely to provoke "a war between the 102 boys and the 104 boys," said Martin of TIPRO.

"For gas producers, proposed decontrol involves a redistribution of economic benefits on a grand scale," according to Deborah Warhoff, an industry analyst for Paine Webber Mitchell Hutchins Inc. The firm found the following:

If the price of oil is $30.30 a barrel in 1985, natural gas, a competing source of energy, could be expected to sell for an average wellhead price of $2.85 for each 1,000 cubic feet. Under existing regulation, old gas, which makes up 43 percent of the supply, would have to sell for $1.52, while new gas, which has a rapidly climbing ceiling price and makes up 57 percent of the supply, could rise to $3.84, to produce the $2.85 average.

With deregulation, however, old gas could rise immediately to the competitive price of $2.85 and new gas would be forced down to the same $2.85. The gain from deregulation to old gas producers for just one year would be $5.92 billion, while the loss to new gas producers would be $5.84 billion.

The change would impose a $2.78 billion loss in one year alone on the independent oilmen, who own an estimated 76 percent of the new gas and only 28 percent of old gas. For the majors, who have 24 percent of the new gas and 72 percent of the old, this would get a $2.86 billion bonus in one year.

In addition, those who would be hurt the most would be the deep well drillers of Oklahoma's Anadarko Basin, whose prices would fall the furthest.

The consequences for the Republican party are likely to be significant.

"Somebody's got to be able to explain those things, and right now a lot of people are just now beginning to say 'What in the world is wrong?' " said Lew Ward, a Republican National Committeeman who donated $38,500 from 1979 through mid-1982 to Washington-based Republican committees.

"Right now we don't have the answers," he said.

Just three years ago, Ward said, there were probably 140 contributors who gave at least $10,000 annually to the Republican National Committee—the "Eagles," as the GOP terms them. "I'd say the number has declined to probably 50. They are still supportive, but they are kind of sitting back and just kind of wondering a little bit, wondering if the members of the administration are ever going to listen," he said.

At the same time, a number of Republican fund-raisers said privately that while they expect continued support from the oil industry, they no longer see it as a growing base of support. Instead, they said, increased GOP attention is expected to focus on high-technology industries.

If a significant segment of the independent oil industry has a large stake in regulation, the same is true in spades in the tax arena. The independent oil industry has repeatedly fought for, and often won, amendments to tax legislation which give the industry an advantage over major oil companies, in contrast to the independents' customary appeals for deregulation and free-market policies.

When the cost of these tax breaks is calculated from the time of enactment, the lost Treasury revenues are about three quarters the size of the federal government's $8.2 billion contribution to the Aid to Families with Dependent Children, a basic welfare program:

• In 1975, Congress repealed the special minerals depletion allowance for major companies, but retained it, at declining levels, for independent oil companies. The value of this tax break is estimated at $1.7 billion in 1985, rising to $2.2 billion in 1988.

• Most independents are allowed to "expense" or write off in one year 100 percent of such "intangible" drilling costs as labor, hauling, ground clearing and site preparation, rather than having to spread the deductions over a number of years, as is required for most capital investment. (The majors are limited to 85 percent, according to the 1982 tax bill.) The revenue loss from expensing of intangible drilling costs is $4.2 billion.

• During the 1980 battle over the windfall profits tax, independent oilmen won a series of special tax rates that significantly shifted the burden of the tax. As initially reported by the House, the measure would have required independents to pay $57 billion over 11 years. After an intense lobbying effort of the House-Senate Conference Committee, however, liability falling on the independents was reduced to $22.5 billion out of a total of $227.3 billion, a $34.5 billion reduction.

• In the 1981 tax bill, the independents won further relief from the burden of the Windfall Profits Tax. The tax rate on newly discovered oil, which is much more important to the independents than the rate on old oil, was phased down from 30 to 15 percent at a cost to the federal Treasury of $113 million in 1982, rising to $1.8 billion in 1986. In addition, "stripper" wells (less than 10 barrels a day) owned by independent oilmen were exempted from the tax altogether, at a cost to the Treasury rising to $797 million by 1986.

Some Democrats, angered by the Republican bias of oil money, are looking carefully at these tax breaks as a way to both raise money and to penalize opposition. Rep. Daniel Rostenkowski (D-Ill.), chairman of the Ways and Means Committee, has asked the panel's oversight subcommittee to begin an inquiry into all the special tax breaks received by independent oil.

Another faction of Democrats, however, is struggling to bring oil back into the Democratic fold, at least partially. Two Texas Democrats, Reps. Charles Wilson and Kent Hance, have been seeking out oilmen, trying to persuade them to give either directly to Democratic candidates, or to the Democratic Congressional Campaign Committee (DCCC).

In a January 6, 1983, letter to "about 75 independents that I consider to be above average in political judgment," Wilson wrote: "It is perceived by the House leadership, as well as the vast majority of Democrats, that the oil and gas industry only supported Republicans in the last election, with the exception of a few oil-state Democrats.

"This comes at a bad time—not only because the House will be much more liberal this session, but also because we are threatened with all manner of violence concerning gas pricing, as well as our customary defense of depletion, intangibles and our concessions under the Windfall Profits Tax."

In a direct meeting, Wilson said "I've told them, you've got to stop trying to change the world or you are going to get hurt." Rep. Tony Coelho (D-Calif.), chairman of the DCCC, who represents oil interests in his district, has joined in this drive to pick up Democratic oil support, which has produced an estimated $250,000, a tiny sum in comparison to the amount of oil money flowing into GOP coffers.

There is now a reaction among some prominent oil producers against the sharp swing by the industry toward the Republican side in 1980 and 1982. L. Frank Pitts, one of the most influential oilmen in Texas, former president of TIPRO and now its chairman of the board, earlier this year withdrew from the board of the Dallas Energy Political Action Committee, one of the most aggressive oil PACs channeling money toward the defeat of vulnerable liberal Democrats.

In the 1982 elections, DALLENPAC and many of its supporters went beyond funneling money against marginal, anti-oil Democrats and helped finance the campaigns of Republican challengers to some firmly pro-oil incumbent Democrats, including Rep. Glenn English (D-Okla.), who had wrung a written promise from President Reagan to veto any legislation placing a windfall profits tax on natural gas.

"Some of the PACs, including DALLENPAC, may have gone overboard in the percentage of contributions to Republicans," Pitts said. "The industry is perceived as having tilted toward the Republicans. That's not good in the first place. Not just perceived, but rightly perceived."

It has been a long fall for the independents since 1980, when their political power was at a peak and their economic prospects looked limitless. There are signs now, however, that the fall may have reached bottom.

The decline of the industry over the past two years has also made it a less attractive target for tax increases.

"The guys who want to go after oil couldn't have picked a worse time," a congressional aide close to the prospective tax battle noted.

In addition, there is a strong possibility that the final outcome of the deregulation debate will be a continuation of controls on old gas, as Congressional Republicans from Kansas, Missouri and Illinois—where utility rates have risen sharply—have become increasingly worried about the impact of full decontrol on utility costs.

Under this scenario, which is subscribed to in many quarters, independent oil will emerge out of the first session of the 98th Congress largely untouched by Democratic retribution, and prepared, once the market revives, to resume its role as an elite participant in the congressional bargaining process and in the financing of American party politics.

# '84 Politics: "New Patriotism"
# vs. New Class Allegiances

The Washington Post, February 5, 1984

Three years of the Reagan presidency have reshaped the American electorate, changing it in ways that could determine the outcome of next November's voting. Forced to react to these changes, the two political parties are reassessing their approach to issues and campaign strategies to cope with a transformed political environment in 1984.

At this stage, unpredictable developments in the economy, in Lebanon, in Central America, in relations with the Russians, all have the potential to alter radically the political equation. But some elements of the road map to this election are already in place. Three of them seem particularly important, though they don't point in any one direction:

1) There has been a marked increase in divisions by economic class between Republicans and Democrats, a trend mainly helpful to the Democratic party, provided it can get and keep its many different acts together. The driving force behind sharpened class divisions has been an intensified perception of the Reagan administration and the Republican party as representatives of the rich, according to opinion polls. Democrats hope to exploit their large advantage among the poorest voters by registering large numbers of them before election day.

2) A factor that Democratic pollster Dotty Lynch has called the New Patriotism has come into play in ways that mitigate the impact of this intensification of class differences. Democrats from the lower end of the economic scale who would otherwise be inclined to vote against the Republicans have been drawn back to the GOP by patriotic feelings intensified by President Reagan's policies, particularly the invasion of Grenada, the polls show.

3) The electorate is extremely volatile. Those most inclined to change their political allegiance are from the middle and lower- middle classes—the largest bloc of voters. Many mind-changers seem to be Democrats and independents who abandoned traditional voting habits to vote for Reagan in 1980. At the depths of the 1982 recession, a great many of them had turned against Reagan; recently many have lined up behind him again.

Both parties see these facts; both are trying to adjust to them. The Democrats want to convince these lower-income voters that they do indeed have a class interest in replacing Reagan with a Democrat. They want to convince swing voters that Reagan's foreign policies are dangerous, and not deserving of patriotic support. At the same time—and this may be the Democrats' biggest challenge— they want to win more conservative middle-class support using the argument that Reagan's huge budget deficits are profligate and dangerous.

The Republicans want to convince middle-class voters that their policies are really good for everyone, not just the rich. They want to exploit the New Patriotism for all it is worth. ("America is back," President Reagan said in his State of the Union address.) The Republicans want to portray the Democrats as big-spending captives of special interest groups—as Reagan described them on his first campaign trip to Atlanta ten days ago.

The struggle to set the election agenda will also go on at a more subtle level. For example, the Republicans will be looking for ways to defuse their image as the party of the wealthy. So the Reagan-Bush '84 committee—which could easily raise the maximum legal amount of pre-convention campaign from major donors willing to pony up $500 to $1,000—will instead use the more expensive process of direct-mail fund-raising. This both spreads the political message to a larger group and lowers the average donation to a politically more acceptable $150 to $200.

Similarly, the Republican party will avoid discussion of the consequences for different economic classes of its budget and tax policies, which overwhelmingly benefit those in the upper brackets and penalize the poorest Americans. Instead, the GOP will emphasize the benefits to all income classes of reduced inflation and lower interest rates.

The Democrats' attempt to shape the '84 agenda will only succeed if they can put Reagan on the defensive. "The one thing we have to avoid is a debate over welfare cheats and soup kitchens," said a Democrat who worked on the response to Reagan's State of the Union address. "If we don't avoid that kind of debate, we'll end up spending the election defending our bottom ten percent and lose. We want Reagan to defend his ten percent, the rich."

For the 30 years before President Reagan won election in 1980, the relative strength of the Democratic and Republican parties remained the same, a constant ratio of about 5 to 3 favoring the Democrats.

During the same period, however, the two parties have slowly changed shape. Analysis of 1952 through 1980 survey data from the Center for Political Studies in Ann Arbor, Michigan, shows that the Democratic party has become, in terms of the income of its supporters, increasingly bottom-heavy, and the GOP has become increasingly top-heavy.

Dividing the Democratic party up into three income groups, those in the poorest third gained numerical strength within the party, while the proportion of Democrats in the highest-income top third declined. In the 1950s, for every 100 Democrats, 34 were in the bottom third, 34 in the middle and 32 in the top. By 1980, however, the division was no longer even: for every 100 Democrats, 38 were in the bottom third, 33 in the middle and 29 in the top.

The GOP began this three-decade period as a top-heavy party, and steadily became more so. The Republican party went from 29-33-38 distribution in the 1950s, to a 25-32-43 distribution in 1976–1980.

It isn't surprising that both the core financial supporters and the strongest electoral support for the Republican party come from the wealthiest Americans. (Those with income over $50,000 a year, 7 percent of the population, back the

Republicans by 55-37, according to the most recent polling data. This is the only economic group in the population that gives the GOP a majority of its support.)

Under Reagan, the Republicans have fulfilled a basic function of a political party, the rewarding of its most loyal supporters.

The net effect of changes in government policy and the inflation rate during these years has been major gains for the rich, significant cutbacks for the poor and working poor, and modest losses in government benefits for much of the middle class.

On the tax side, the Joint Committee on Taxation found that from 1980 through 1984, the combined effects of the 1981 and 1982 tax bills, changes in the Social Security payroll tax, and inflation (which pushes individuals into higher tax brackets) will mean higher tax burdens for all taxpayers making less than $75,000—increases averaging from $95 to $138. For those making above $75,-000, however, net gains will range from $403 to $17,403, with the largest amounts going to those making in excess of $200,000.

On the spending cut side, the Congressional Budget Office found that all income groups will take a beating, but the reductions will be far larger for the poorest groups, $1,340 over four years in lost government benefits for families making less than $10,000 a year. Households with incomes over $80,000 a year lost $490 in government benefits over the same four years.

A study of *Washington Post* polls over the three years of the Reagan administration suggests that voters responded very directly to these policies, whose effects were compounded by the recession. The partisan changes were most striking among the poorest of voters, those with incomes less $12,000 a year (22 percent of the population). The Democratic majority among these voters grew steadily, from 55-31 in 1981 to 64-27 during the first nine months of 1983, a 13 percentage point gain. Slightly smaller Democratic gains of 8 to 9 percentage points were made among those in the working and middle classes, who earn from $12,000 to $30,000.

These trends, combined with the recession, sent a wave of anxiety through the stomachs of Republican strategists. "For income to all of a sudden produce the differences that it did represented a real departure from American norms," a GOP specialist in poll analysis noted. Not only were the Democrats gaining support through much of 1983, but their gains appeared to be holding, despite the start of a steady improvement both in the economy and in President Reagan's voter approval ratings.

But this landscape was transformed by late-1983 economic improvements and the invasion of Grenada. During the two months after the invasion, not only did Reagan's approval ratings shoot up, but significant changes showed up in the percentages of people describing themselves as Republicans or Democrats. In November and December, *Washington Post* polls showed, the GOP made significant gains among middle-income voters, picking up about 13 percentage points. Only among the very poor did the Democratic gains hold.

As the memory of Grenada fades, however, *Post* polling data gathered two weeks ago suggest that the Democratic party has regained some of the November-December losses, winning back the loyalty of most of the defectors in the $12,000 to $30,000 range. The upper-middle class, $30,000 to $50,000, remained evenly split, and the GOP majority remained firm within the highest income group. President Reagan's approval rating, however, dropped only slightly from the November-December highs, remaining far above the mid-recession levels.

The power, first, of the improved economy to weaken Democratic gains, and then, in one major swoop, of the invasion of Grenada to produce a significant shift in public opinion lasting for at least two months, has intensified concerns among Democratic strategists and brought new optimism to the GOP.

Entering the '84 campaign, the Democrats remain a majority party, but are caught in a network of internal conflicts; the Republicans have the disadvantage of minority status, but can adopt—and finance—coherent election strategies based on party unity.

The Democratic party's internal conflicts are reflected in the difference between its strongest base of voter support and its sources of financial backing. Poorer voters provide the most support in the polls, but the party's financial backers, including the growing base of contributors acquired through direct mail, are very affluent. Their average incomes are among the top ten percent in the country.

This apparent schizophrenia is echoed in Democratic strategies. On one side there is an attempt to mobilize and register not only the largely poor, black and Hispanic non-voters angered by President Reagan's budget cuts, but many members of the middle class, particularly the elderly, who place a high value on such programs as Medicare and Social Security, which provide benefits to all income classes.

At the same time, the Democrats want to capitalize on deficits now approaching $200 billion under a Republican administration, and to replace the GOP as the party cultivating an image of fiscal responsibility, drawing in conservative middle-class support.

How can the Democrats effectively pursue both these goals? Peter Hart, the pollster, in a widely shared view, is recommending that the Democratic party avoid association with "the policies of the past," and instead focus on the future by emphasizing, for example, the threat to economic recovery created by the deficit. Dotty Lynch, another Democratic pollster, argues that "in a depressed economy . . . traditional Democratic solutions may have been the panacea voters were looking for," but the current improved economy requires Democrats to wage campaigns "on the future rather than the past or the present."

Conversely, Victor Fingerhut, a Democratic consultant and pollster with strong ties to organized labor, contends that "the strength of the Democratic party stands in the past. . . . [Republicans] would love to obliterate the past." Fingerhut, who argues that the sustaining base of the Democratic party is "the widespread belief that the Democrats stand for ordinary working people and the Republicans stand for big business and the rich," asks (and answers) this question:

"If you walked into a bar and told three guys the Democrats have a super plan to balance the budget, what kind of response do you think you would have? If we have a future plan to balance the budget, the American people will sit back and roar with laughter."

The Democratic conversion to fiscal responsibility has prompted a number of Republicans to contend that the GOP has, in fact, regained control of the political dialogue. "In domestic debate, roles reversed," Frank J. Fahrenkopf, chairman of the Republican National Committee recently wrote. "There was a time when Republicans said yes, we agree with Democrats that new federal programs are needed, only we want them smaller and we want to pay less for them. . . . Now it is the Democrats who say yes, we agree that government got too big, we agree about tax and spending cuts, only we want to cut less and not so fast. . . . The refrain is a familiar 'me too, but not so much,' but that refrain is being sung in a new key by a new choir."

Reagan has exploited Republican money, party unity and the most extensive and detailed polling data available to any president in history to adjust the content and tenor of his administration to an ever-changing political terrain. Political agility has helped, too.

For example, after the emergence of public opposition to the large business tax cuts of 1981, Reagan endorsed 1982 legislation rolling back some of them. When poll data show that administration cuts in education provoked sharp voter criticism, Reagan shifted the debate from education spending to merit pay for teachers and safety in the classroom. From November 1981, to August 1983, the Democratic advantage on the education issue fell by 15 percentage points, according to Democratic-sponsored polls.

Faced now with growing voter concern over the prospect of nuclear war, Reagan recently abandoned his characteristic, highly aggressive anti-Soviet rhetoric and adopted a conciliatory tone.

These are attempts to dominate the election-year agenda. Whoever does it best will win in 1984.

# Exploiting the New Affluence: The GOP's Road to Dominance

*The Washington Post,* August 19, 1984

Over the past three decades, Americans on the whole have become more educated and more affluent, a fact that has fundamentally changed the composition of the Republican party. As millions of Americans moved up the economic ladder between 1950 and 1984, the GOP tended to gain their allegiance, while the Democrats kept the loyalty of those who stayed on the bottom rungs.

As the nation's demography has changed, the GOP has defied the conventional wisdom. At a time when political parties are said to be increasingly irrelevant, the Republican party has become the most sophisticated and potent national political organization in this century, and probably in the history of the United States.

The rise of the New Republican party has been facilitated by cash, but the transformation grows out of basic changes in American society since World War II. The GOP has gained strength among the economic winners at the same time that the economic status of people who call themselves Democrats has remained unchanged compared with the 1950s. The Democratic growth has come from the ranks of the less fortunate, especially blacks and Hispanics.

At the same time, television and the computerized technology of polling and direct mail have replaced precinct lieutenants and ward captains in American elections. As campaigning depends increasingly on services that can be bought, the GOP's cash advantage has turned into a major political advantage. It permits the party to field and finance candidates in any district or state where an incumbent Democrat shows signs of vulnerability.

Thus, as the Republican party gathers in Dallas this week to affirm the nomination of Ronald Reagan for a second term, the status of the party mirrors economic and social changes in America over the last 30 years. The 1984 election promises to be the most polarized in recent history—by race, income, gender and ideology. It will provide a test of whether a party that represents the more economically successful, a party that has almost no support in the nation's black community and only token backing in the Hispanic community, a party that advocates tax cuts benefiting the rich more than the poor and middle class, can retain control of the federal government. The class divisions between the two parties are growing. People who identify themselves as Democrats are increasingly in the nation's poorest third, a sharp contrast to the 1950s when Democrats were spread almost equally among income groups.

The GOP, in turn, has moved from a party whose membership in the 1950s was only slightly skewed to the top third of the population by income, to one in which nearly half of those calling themselves Republicans were in that top third in the 1970s.

In addition to the growing enfranchisement of blacks and their commitment to the Democratic party, a major reason for the widening income divergence between the two parties is the growing concentration of poverty among women.

Women, much more than men, have retained their self-identification as Democrats, and the party has responded by nominating Geraldine Ferraro for the vice presidency.

Republican gains, by contrast, have been among increasingly affluent Northern Catholics, Southern whites, and whites moving into the Sunbelt. Where the GOP has lost allegiance from less affluent voters, it is because traditional Republicans—such as lower-middle-class Vermont Yankee farmers, and once-Republican clerks and postal workers in the rural and suburban Northeast and Midwest—are no longer guaranteed to vote for the GOP.

The Democrats have retained their greatest asset—their 50-year-old position as the party that the majority of Americans say they belong to. Just over five of every 10 voters identify themselves as Democrats, even if they do not always vote that way. Thus, it is important that for the first time in 20 years the Democrats are concentrating on their strongest card: voter registration and turnout. Mobilization of voters for the Democrats is essential. In heavily black and Democratic Watts and southwest Los Angeles, for example, the turnout rate was 35 percent in 1980, 22 percentage points below the turnout rates in the Republican districts surrounding San Diego and Santa Ana.

But what the Democratic party considers to be the major liabilities of the Republican party—the GOP's ties to the economic and corporate elite, its homogeneity and its policies favoring the well-off—have proven in some respects to be political assets. Republican affluence is a strong plus at a time when the history of economic stagnation and inflation under Jimmy Carter continues to undermine Democratic claims to be the party of growth. One clear benefit for a party with strong ties to the affluent is money. The Republican National, Senatorial and Congressional Committees have, over the past decade, emerged as the central force in the revival of Republican fortunes. Together, these three committees raised $190.4 million in 1982, and will raise well over $200 million for the 1984 elections. This is at least five times the amount raised by their Democratic counterparts.

For any Republican candidate with the slightest chance of winning (or losing) a seat, the Republican committees are prepared to provide a solid one-third of the cost of running a strong campaign. This cash, however, is only the start. The GOP committees finance polling, both long-range and daily, tracking movement in voters' opinions; the production of television, radio and newspaper ads; computerized analysis of precinct and neighborhood voting histories; targeted direct mail; demographic analysis of each media outlet; and candidate and campaign-manager training.

The GOP has historically had a financial edge, raising twice as much money as the Democrats from 1948 through 1956. The current difference is that both the total amount of money the GOP can raise and the margin of electoral advantage over the Democrats that this cash can buy have grown by leaps and bounds.

The Republican fund-raising behind the GOP cash advantage depends upon a highly sophisticated direct-mail program created in the mid-1970s at the party's lowest moment—after Watergate. That was when GOP strategists realized that election-law reforms restricting most individual contributions to candidates to $1,000 required the development of an army of small donors.

Their success with small donors notwithstanding, the GOP has been no slouch at attracting major contributors who can legally donate to political parties—as opposed to individual candidates—up to $20,000 a year.

At his July 24 press conference, President Reagan correctly accused the Democratic party of receiving a higher proportion of its cash from big contributors than the Republican party: about one-third of Democratic party money comes from political action committees and donors of $500 or more, while about 15 percent of GOP support is from similar groups.

These percentages take on different significance, however, when actual dollars are counted: the GOP, with its massive fund-raising advantage, took in $27.1 million from major donors giving $500 or more during 1981–82, just under the total raised from all donors, large and small, by the Democratic National, Senatorial and Congressional Committees combined—$28.5 million. The GOP has increasingly become a party of affluent whites. Democrats see this concentration or homogeneity as a vulnerability. But it has reduced conflict within the Republican party. In political terms, this has two major advantages.

The first is that a relative lack of internal conflict makes it far easier to govern.

On appointments as controversial as those of James Watt and Anne Gorsuch Burford or issues as divisive as the Marines in Lebanon, arms-control negotiations and tax policy, various Republicans—and at times, a majority of Republicans—have challenged President Reagan on specifics. But they have never posed a broad, serious challenge to his legitimacy as president. This kind of loyalty—even in the depths of the 1982 recession, when Republicans foresaw a substantial loss of House seats—does not exist in the Democratic party.

Similarly, Republican voters, while a statistical minority, are a far more dependable bloc, in terms of both partisan loyalty and voter turnout, than are Democratic voters, among whom significant groups either sit out elections—as liberals did after the 1968 nomination of Hubert Humphrey—or vote Republican—as disproportionately high percentages of blue-collar and white Southerners did in 1980.

The advantage of Republican homogeneity is that television tends to focus on and magnify the kind of internal conflict characteristic of the Democrats.

If Democrats' diversity is the core of the party's strength, over the airwaves this diversity often comes across as discordant, producing conflicting images of races, regions and accents unsettling to viewers of a medium that demands a brief and coherent message.

Throughout the congressional struggle over Reagan's budget and tax proposals of 1981, the GOP was able to pick any one of a host of spokesmen, from the president to Treasury Secretary Donald Regan to Senate Majority Leader Howard Baker of Tennessee, and the message was the same—and basically telegenic. For the Democrats, in contrast, on the issue of tax and budget cuts, party voices were mixed and ambivalent: blacks were angry, neoliberals undecided, "boll weevils" (Southerners) under strong pressure from the right and party regulars worried more about the erosion of their powers in Congress than the merit of the issues. The basic loyalty shown to the party and its leaders by elected Republican leaders has also been present among Republican supporters.

A leading conservative, John (Terry) Dolan, has told such GOP moderates as Sens. Lowell Weicker (Conn.) and Robert Stafford (Vt.) that the best thing they can do for the party is to get out.

But Dolan's organization, the National Conservative Political Action Committee (NCPAC), is preparing to spend anywhere from $5 million to $10 million on the reelection of President Reagan, and to continue its overwhelming support for GOP House and Senate candidates. On the moderate side of the coin, Susan Bryant, a Republican activist and consultant who supports passage of the ERA and is firmly pro-choice on the abortion issue, is more than willing to submerge these concerns in favor of reelecting President Reagan. "We are all technicians," she contends, referring to the activist party structure.

Besides electing people, the GOP has become adept at performing a basic function of any political party: rewarding the loyal and punishing the opposition.

The core Republican constituency, according to every public-opinion survey, is the affluent. The only income group in which a majority consistently identifies with the Republican party is the 8 to 9 percent of the population making in excess of $50,000 a year. An analysis of the income and educational levels of voters in the 1950s and 1970s who described themselves as Republicans shows a marked increase in the percentage of those considered "upper status." Conversely, Democratic support grows increasingly strong as one moves down the income ladder, reaching margins of 65-20 for those making less than $12,000 a year.

Budget, tax and spending policies under the Republican administration of Ronald Reagan have, in turn, been far more favorable to just those affluent income groups in which Republican loyalty is strongest, and have inflicted the heaviest burdens on the most Democratic groups at the bottom of the income ladder.

When the combined effects of the budget and tax bills enacted in 1981 and 1982 are examined by income group in terms of the winners and losers, on the basis of analyses by the Congressional Budget Office and the Joint Committee on Taxation, all the big winners are in Republican terrain, and the biggest losers are those who give the Democratic party its largest margin. While the political demography of the United States is highly fluid, a Republican party flush with cash and the voting affluent could well be the dominant party for the decade—reversing recent history. For the GOP to maintain control of the national agenda will depend on the ability of a minority party armed with a very effective politician at the top of the ticket, more money than it knows what to do with and strong party loyalty to win in a political system in which a majority of the population still call themselves Democrats.

This is not to say there is no opposition to four more years of Republican hegemony. Another Republican victory is threatened by the prospect of sharply increased turnout by blacks and women, whose alienation from the GOP appears to be growing. At the same time, there is what the Republicans acknowledge to be the Democrats' natural advantage: polls suggest that of the 110 million registered voters, about 57 million would describe themselves as Democrats, about 40 million call themselves Republicans and the remainder are independents.

Fully aware of its vulnerability, the Republican party has begun a counter-registration drive: a computer-run program designed to track down, register and get to the polls every unregistered Reagan sympathizer. This will cost well over $15 million and require virtuoso technology.

If successful, it will be instructive. For it will be a demonstration of the GOP's ability to take the Democrats on in the terrain of supposed Democratic strength—voter mobilization.

# More Bad News for Mondale

## Party Bosses and Feuding Factions Sabotage the Drive for New Voters

*The Washington Post,* October 21, 1984

Could the liberal-left coalition be revived with a massive voter registration campaign? Could newly enfranchised poor people, blacks and Hispanics halt the Reagan revolution? That dream attracted millions of dollars and mobilized thousands of people during the past year, but by all indications, it is a dream that will not come true.

In some of the worst slums in the nation, where the pool of unregistered voters is massive and the probability of anti-Ronald Reagan sentiments highest, local Democratic organizations are actually opposing voter registration. They are intent on maintaining a small, controlled electorate, guaranteed to cast majorities for endorsed candidates in Democratic primaries. They bitterly oppose letting outside groups add unknown voters to their rolls.

Individuals and organizations drawn into voter registration by the prospect of millions of new dollars have often spent more of their energy competing for foundation grants than actually signing up the disenfranchised.

And, perhaps most deflating for the original dreamers, the Republican party succeeded in putting together an $11 million registration program which, backed up by a drive to mobilize fundamentalist white Christians, produced more new GOP voters than Democrats in such states as Florida and California, and matched liberal/Democratic efforts in many other states.

The dream of creating a 1980s version of the New Deal coalition through massive voter registration grew out of decisive Democratic victories two years ago in such states as Texas and New Mexico where there were massive and unexpected increases in voter turnout on Election Day.

Within the liberal community, the belief that registration is the key to a fundamental change in government policy reached a high point at a September 1983 meeting in New York sponsored by the New World Foundation, a liberal philanthropic organization.

One hundred fifty men and women representing the extremes of wealth and poverty—from the offices of the Rockefeller Foundation to the back roads of Quitman County in the Mississippi Delta—reached the conclusion that they just might be able to change the balance of political power in America.

That diverse group determined "that political participation is a central staging ground" to alter "the conditions of life and work for people who do not have a fair share in the power, wealth and income of this country."

That meeting was a critical step in a process that turned voter registration into a multimillion-dollar proposition, a source of cash, patronage, prestige and power. Money for voter registration from foundations alone increased by an estimated 500 percent, from about $1.2 million in earlier years to $6 million this year.

At the same time, the prospect of a revived Democratic coalition prompted a number of wealthy donors to pull out their wallets and checkbooks.

At a breakfast meeting during the Democratic National Convention, a newly formed group called the Committee to Register and Vote the Missing Half claims to have received $1 million in pledges, half of its total for the year. Richard Dennis, a wealthy Chicago commodities dealer and strong backer of Walter F. Mondale, put up $500,000, according to one credible account.

For organizations working with the poor, the money was a godsend. Beleaguered by Reagan administration budget cuts and defeat at the polls, the cash offered the possibility of restored political muscle, and the chance of winning sympathetic representation in Washington and in state houses across the country.

As the deadline for voter registration is now passing, there is no question that the cash resulted in a sharp increase in the number of people registered to vote. In New York state, for example, election officials were swamped with registration applications before the October 13 deadline, and around the country there has been an unprecedented surge of blacks and Hispanics signing up to vote on November 6.

Throughout the South, however, the surge of new black voters has been countered by a mobilization of conservative whites unprecedented in recent memory. And throughout the country, polls suggest that the newly registered are not a driving force for a revival of liberalism; instead, they are as pro-Reagan as traditional voters.

Dispirited by Republican success and the inability to achieve its original goals, the massive effort to revive the liberal-left coalition through the mobilization of minorities and the poor has left deep scars and, in some quarters, a pervasive sense of failure.

"It's been a year and a half of disappointment," Hulbert James, director of the Human Serve Fund, which sought to register voters in welfare centers, unemployment lines and food stamp offices. "In spite of all the efforts of everybody, we still are going to be standing still."

Norman Adler, political director of New York's District 37 of the American Federation of State, County and Municipal Employees, who set up a computer-based Network for Voter Registration, said:

"I'm discouraged. Einstein once said at the end of his life that he felt like a small boy playing with pebbles on the beach and a whole ocean lay out before him. We have been sitting here playing with a lot of pebbles and there is still an ocean out there."

In New York State, Adler said, "we had a potential audience of one and a half million of which we estimated we would register half a million. We have actually registered—between us and other groups—maybe 350,000. Maybe."

Both James and Adler can provide a litany of what James calls "bitter organizational feuds" and what Adler calls "turf wars, people wanting to take credit, a lot of ego, a lot of internecine battling between groups. It's not healthy competition. It's like a roller derby, everybody trying to kick everybody else over the rails, edging people out."

And the voter mobilization drives have, in some cases, deepened racial conflicts. "Liberal organizations that have been out saving the whale and the redwood forests and the snail darter are now coming into the black community talking about they want to save, you know, me," said Joe Madison, director of voter registration for the NAACP.

Madison, whose organization received relatively little foundation money because it lacked a special tax designation for nonprofit organizations specializing in voting registration, complained: "Most of the money went basically to white liberal organizations."

Gracia Hillman, of Operation Big Vote, a black registration organization, saw her group's budget grow from nickels and dimes before 1984 to $650,000 this year, and is far less bitter than Madison. She complained, however, of a "delay (resulting from) some miscommunication between what I will generally describe as the black community and the foundations. . . . On the face of it, I'd have to say, yes, there was the appearance of some racial overtones, or undertones, however you want to describe it."

All these groups are nonpartisan, but the Democratic party was depending on them to produce a wave of pro-Democratic new voters for the 1984 election. An extensive *Washington Post*–ABC News poll late last month of 2,092 voters who said they registered after the 1980 election, including those who signed up to vote this year, showed President Reagan running ahead of Mondale among the new voters by a 54-40 margin.

If this pattern holds through Election Day, it will raise a number of basic issues in the strategy of voter registration as a political tool. The most important issues involve financing, centralized coordination and the choice between partisan and nonpartisan registration drives.

The cash-poor Democratic party depended on a decentralized collection of liberal and left-wing, technically "nonpartisan" organizations to do its work mobilizing the electorate. (The Democratic National Committee did distribute less than $3 million to state parties in September, but this came very late in the process, leaving no time for effective planning.)

The Republican party, in contrast, ran a highly centralized, party-financed program putting at least $10 million into voter registration in 28 key states. The high-tech GOP program began in 1983, well over a year before the election. The partisan GOP effort was supplemented by a major drive to enroll white, conservative fundamentalist Christians.

Despite the fact that the pool of 30 million or more unregistered people should offer a bonanza for Democrats—it is disproportionately black, Hispanic and poor, groups that are traditionally Democratic—preliminary evidence suggests that the GOP succeeded in taking the edge off Democratic voter registration, if not equalling it.

The final results will not be known until the polls close on November 6, and even then it will be very difficult to accurately evaluate the success or failure of competing registration drives.

Developments in New York, however, and interviews with organizers and backers of national drives, make a strong case that the lack of a powerful central organization severely weakened the effort to mobilize blacks, the poor and Hispanics.

In one of the ironies of pro-Democratic, but nonpartisan, voter registration, some of the strongest opposition to voter registration emerged in the poorest, most solidly Democratic, urban sections of the country.

In New York, Adler, the political director of AFSCME, set up a system in which all voter registration groups could funnel names into a centralized computer. Participants could get their own names back coded by election district, zip code, phone number, councilmanic district and assembly district; any participant providing at least 3,000 names could have access to the entire list of names.

In a city where the key election is the Democratic primary, not the general election, many local political groups, public housing tenant organizations and ethnic political leaders had no interest in participating in a drive that would result in sharing the names of the newly registered.

"Everything in poor neighborhoods is political and has got money behind it," Adler said. "Our people go in and register and it goes into our computers. Any affiliate can have that list. If you are a housing project tenant leader, you register them (the residents) and only you know who's on that list, nobody else. You control the information.

"Everything is locked into this control. Who the district leader is, who the assemblyman is, who the city council member is, what kind of multiservice grant money comes in, what kind of money comes in for tenant patrols, what money comes in for CB radios, what money comes in for part-time jobs."

In this terrain—where, for a local leader, control over a small list of registered Democrats is more important than an unknown, expanded electorate—the Network for Voter Registration was barred from working in a number of major housing projects and much of the Lower East Side. In addition, a key Brooklyn assemblyman, Albert Vann, who had been conducting a registration drive among blacks, refused to work with the network, seeking instead to protect the confidentiality of his names.

"The worst voter registration was among the Hispanics," Adler said. "A lot of the Puerto Rican leaders don't want anybody else to vote because there is a very small turnout in Puerto Rican neighborhoods and they want to keep it that way."

Another disabling force was the competition for cash and for power.

Margaret McEntire, of Women USA, a New York-based organization set up by Bella Abzug, said that for many groups, "looking for money" often superseded voter registration. The question became, she said, "Are you out in the streets registering voters, or are you in your office rewriting grant proposals?"

The competition for "names"—lists of people who had been registered that were used to persuade foundations and individuals to give more money—created a host of problems.

As an example, she said one group, Physicians for Social Responsibility, registered about 1,000 people. The group then wanted to make sure that the newly registered would be contacted for get-out-the-vote purposes, and separately told both Women USA and Human Serve that they could have the list.

In the confusion of events, however, Human Serve organizers "thought I was making a raid" on the names, preventing Human Serve from taking credit for accumulating these new names. "It seems very nitpicking, but it blew up in our faces," she said, briefly creating a conflict when in fact she said there was no reason not to share the names.

Cate Bowman, who works with Adler at the Network for Voter Registration, said registration among women's groups was slowed "by a terrible war between the New York Women's Political Caucus and NOW (the National Organization of Women). There was a chairmanship fight, and voter registration became one of the rocks they were flinging at each other."

On a much larger scale, the sudden influx of cash grants for voter registration from liberal, but financially cautious, foundations produced a racial split within the liberal-left community no one had initially anticipated. It grew out of what some of the participants call the "4945(f) problem," referring to a section of the tax code.

Under the law, foundations can make "general support" grants to any non-profit organization with the required tax status (technically 501 [c] [3]). But if a foundation wants to make a grant specifically for voter registration, the recipient must have special 4945(f) status, which stipulates that the primary purpose of the receiving organization must be voter registration; that it must be active in at least five states, and that its activities must extend beyond one election.

Before this year, when voter registration was not a central concern within the foundation community, these classifications were of little importance. Many civil rights groups did not seek to get 4945(f) status, because they were active in many more areas than voter registration and foundations were giving general support grants instead of grants specifically for registration.

When, however, voter registration jumped from a $1.2 million proposition within the foundation community to a $6 million-a-year source of cash, 4945(f) suddenly became critical, as many of the foundations getting into registration for the first time wanted to be sure they complied with the letter of the law.

Caught behind the eight ball without the protection of 4945(f) status were such groups as the NAACP, the National Urban League, Operation Big Vote and the Southern Christian Leadership Conference—all black.

At the same time, such new groups as Project Vote and Human Serve, which are integrated but are seen by some of the black groups as heavily influenced by whites, had received 4945(f) status and, as the foundation cash began to flow, were fully "qualified" to receive it.

Most of the black groups sought and received 4945(f) status, but nonetheless there was a substantial delay in getting money—"by the time it was straightened out, it was May of this year," Hillman of Operation Big Vote said—and the NAACP is still awaiting final approval.

Madison of the NAACP said: "Nuclear freeze groups called my office consistently and said, 'Will you give us the names of your NAACP branches so we can get them involved in voter registration, because we've gotten a grant from a foundation and we need your branches to help us implement it?' Well, goddam. We were being, for lack of a better word, pimped."

The racial tensions within voter registration efforts were not limited to New York, but involved a nationwide competition for cash from California to New England.

And the conflicts between local political organizations and voter registration groups, while intense in New York, emerged in a host of Democratic enclaves across the country, from Boston and Bridgeport, Connecticut, to rural communities in Arkansas and predominantly Hispanic sections of South Texas.

"We got a lot of stuff," Adler of AFSCME concluded, "but the opportunities were so much greater and we never succeeded in getting them. What went wrong? All the things that divide human beings, both institutionally and individually—jealousy, ego, the search for financial reward."

# An Extremely Fluid Electorate, without Partisan Roots

The Washington Post, November 4, 1984

As Ronald Reagan marches toward a decisive victory Tuesday, a central question emerges: Is a realignment of the electorate taking place? This question, however, may miss the point altogether. Instead of a realignment of the partisan allegiance of the voters, the central change may be in the economic contours of the "natural" majority. If so, the present alteration of the electorate is fundamentally nonpartisan, although it clearly benefits the Republican party.

From the 1930s at least until the 1960s, the Democratic party established a "natural" majority, which became known as the New Deal Coalition. This majority was unquestionably partisan—its adherents identified with the Democratic party—and, in economic terms, it was bottom-heavy. The strongest Democratic margins were to be found at the bottom of the distribution of income and wealth. This majority was shaped, in effect, like a pyramid, narrowest at the top, among those who make the most money and among those with the most extensive holdings.

The "economic shape" of the Democratic majority gave direction and vitality to the content of government for 40 years. The core of political power within the Democratic voting majority was the bottom third of the income distribution, and the result was the enactment of tax policies and social programs modestly redistributive in a downward direction, providing money, food, job training and medical care to those in the middle and bottom of the income distribution.

Since 1952, Democrats have been defeated in five out of eight presidential elections. But the continuing strength of the "natural" Democratic majority was demonstrated by the fact that, until 1980, no Republican president seriously sought to reverse the direction of the "Democratic" content of government. The inability of Republican presidents to reverse Democratic policy reflected the fact that they were elected either on the basis of personal attributes—such as Eisenhower's reputation as a war hero—or on the basis of conflict within the Democratic majority—such as the divisive intraparty struggles over the Vietnam War in 1968 and over the nomination of George McGovern in 1972.

Developments over the past four years suggest, however, that there has been a fundamental change in the political/economic equation. Ronald Reagan was elected in 1980 with a bloc of votes bearing a shape directly inverse to that of the traditional Democratic majority. In effect, Reagan's majority four years ago represented the turning upside-down of the Democratic pyramid, with the broadest part of the pyramid—that is, the new majority—now at the top of the income distribution, and the tip at the bottom. Reagan's margin of victory increased in direct proportion to the income of the voting bloc, and his tax and budget cuts succeeded in distributing the benefits of government in an upward direction—to the same group providing his strongest voting margins—while penalizing those at the bottom, whose votes remained firmly Democratic.

The same, top-heavy pattern of support for Reagan is recurring in the current election. This was strikingly apparent in a September *Washington Post*–ABC poll. Reagan led Mondale by 15 points overall, but among the poorest voters—those with incomes below $12,000—Mondale ran ahead of Reagan by a 26-point margin. Among the most affluent—those with incomes above $50,000—Reagan had a 40-point margin over Mondale, 69-29.

The income pattern of the Reagan vote is parallel to the income patterns of voters who identify themselves as Republicans, although the Reagan vote is much larger in every income group. If, then, Reagan is in the forefront of a partisan realignment of the voters in favor of the GOP, it is a realignment in which the affluent will be the dominant force. In economic terms, such a partisan realignment would suggest that the upward distribution of government benefits in the first Reagan term has set a precedent for future government policy making. The rich will get richer, and the poor will get less.

There are, however, a number of factors suggesting that the political changes taking place today do not involve a full-scale realignment, particularly a partisan realignment with the strength and vitality of the Democrats' New Deal Coalition.

For one, the decline of the "natural" Democratic majority resulted less from a Republican challenge than from a host of other changes in the society at large. From 1960 to 1980, the percentage of the work force holding white-collar jobs rose from 43.4 to 52.2, while the blue-collar percentage fell from 36.6 to 31.7. Over the same period, per-capita income rose in real dollars from $3,069 to $5,322, a 73 percent increase. Union strength, as a percentage of the work force, has been about halved. In the South, race has become the critically important factor in partisan divisions, with the result that in presidential elections, the Democrats are a poor, heavily black party, while the Republicans have emerged as the party of the white middle and upper class.

Perhaps the most damaging development for the Democratic party was a self-inflicted wound. From 1960 to 1980, Democratic Congresses allowed bracket creep and sharply increasing marginal tax rates (in 1960 a consideration only of the top 10 percent) to become a fact of life for many blue-and white-collar working men and women. A carpenter promoted to foreman with a 50 percent pay hike in 1960 would see no increase in his tax rate, while the same carpenter in 1980 would see his marginal rates go up by at least 6 percent.

All of these forces have worked to undermine the traditional Democratic majority, but there is no evidence that they have produced a significant revival of public identification with the Republican party; in fact, the evidence is to the contrary. From 1972 to 1984, according to the Committee for the Study of the American Electorate, Democratic registration in states with partisan registration has declined from 43.8 to 35.2 percent, while Republican affiliation has fallen from 24.4 percent to 22.8 percent.

Perhaps more significant, Martin P. Wattenberg, in his book *The Decline of American Political Parties*, shows that parties have generally lost meaning to the American electorate. From 1952 to 1980, the percentage of the public with positive views of one party and negative views of the other—i.e. strong partisans—has declined from 50.1 percent to 27.3 percent. At the same time, the percentage of the public with neutral or flat feelings about both parties has nearly tripled, from 13 to 36.5 percent.

What these figures suggest is not a Republican realignment but, instead, an extremely fluid electorate, without partisan roots. In a development which may at first seem contradictory, these figures point toward the growing importance of political party structures. In a fluid electorate without strong ties to either the Republicans or Democrats, the ability of the parties to finance, develop and use effectively the mechanical and technological elements of politics—television, polling, direct mail, the computerization of electoral data—become critically important to the ability to influence the voters, not just in political campaigns but also in building support for legislative agendas.

On this score, the Republican party has flourished. Money is the most obvious area of GOP success, but it is by no means the only area. In the political arena, the GOP has capitalized on its financial advantages to produce waves of generic television advertising encouraging the public to vote Republican; to pay for daily tracking polls in marginal House and Senate races in order to catch minute changes in public opinion; to computerize the demographics and voting histories of precincts across the country; to turn direct mail into a highly targeted system of campaigning. On this front, the GOP has been able to walk all over the Democratic party. The most recent evidence of this has been in the drive to register voters. On what should have been ideal Democratic terrain, the GOP has held its own, as the Democrats failed to put together a well-organized campaign to mobilize the nonvoting electorate.

The Republican party and its allies have demonstrated the same savvy in both mobilizing sympathetic constituencies and in building intellectual support for legislative agendas. Such groups as the American Coalition for Traditional Values, which registered white, fundamentalist Christians, and the American Defense Foundation, which has been registering members of the Armed Forces, have been financed in large part by Republican fund-raisers and the Republican party. Similarly, growing GOP muscle has been intellectually nurtured by the explosive growth of conservative think tanks—Heritage, American Enterprise Institute, Hoover, and a host of others—in what amounts to the creation of a new intellectual "establishment" countering the traditional liberal establishment.

The 1984 election may not be a realigning election, but, given the effectiveness of the Republican party structure and of its allied organizations, and given the parallel weakness of the Democratic party structure, the short-term results may be identical to those of a national realignment.

In 1985 the federal government is likely to address both the deficit and proposals to alter the tax system, two related issues, each of which has the potential for radically altering the distribution of government benefits and tax burdens. President Reagan appears headed toward victory with an economically top-heavy majority larger than that producing his 1980 mandate. If this majority extends down the ticket into a Republican gain of 20 or more seats in the House and continued GOP control of the Senate, the political pressure will be to reduce the deficit and alter the tax system in ways that do the least harm to the group providing the strongest support—the affluent—and to place the strongest burdens on those least likely to vote Republican—those at the bottom of the income distribution.

# Politics and the Power of Money

*Dissent,* Spring 1985

For the future of the Democratic party, the 18-percentage-point defeat of Walter F. Mondale in the last election was far less important than the decisive failure of the party's basic strategy: voter mobilization. Both the Mondale campaign and the Democratic National Committee calculated that in 1984 the party had the potential to register and turn out sharply increased numbers of blacks, Hispanics, and women to reverse a 20-year decline in the rate of voter participation in presidential elections, and to produce a record-setting 100 million voters.

The strategy proved to be a dismal failure. Turnout grew from 86.5 million in 1980 to 92.7 million last year, just a 0.7 percent increase when population growth is accounted for. More important, most of this modest growth appears, from all the evidence available, to have been among individuals who voted for Republican candidates. Participation by blacks and women actually fell by a percentage point each, according to ABC exit polls, for blacks from 9 to 8 percent, and for women from 50 to 49 percent of the electorate. Hispanic voting grew, from 5 to 7 percent of the electorate but, at the same time, Democratic strength in presidential voting among Hispanics declined, from an 18-percentage-point advantage in 1980 to a 12-point advantage in 1984, more than canceling out for the Democratic party the gain in turnout.

Instead of bringing to the polls more blacks and women, major increases in voter participation did emerge among two very different groups: white, fundamentalist Christians and military personnel. The importance of the growing strength of the "Bible-believing" vote extended far beyond the presidential election.

In House contests, Republicans have gained 16 seats, and eight of these seats are in two states, North Carolina and Texas, both of which have been key targets of the religious-political movement coordinated by an umbrella organization called the American Coalition for Traditional Values (ACTV).

These trends clearly point to the continuing difficulty of the Democratic party in finding new sources of electoral strength to replenish the decaying New Deal coalition. The last major movement of voters to the party occurred ten years ago, based on the ultimately ephemeral public reaction to Watergate. In contrast, the Republican party appears to have made solid gains among conservative, white Christian voters, although this expansion of the GOP voting base carries with it significant liabilities, reflected in part by the resurgence of Democratic voting among Jews, and the potential threat of alienating from the GOP younger voters who do not share conservative Christian social values.

The intraparty conflict inherent in the expansion of the GOP voting base points to what is likely to become the most important source of tension for the Republican party in the near future. While GOP strength is growing, the party faces a delicate balancing process similar to that within the old Democratic coalition between Northern liberals and Southern conservatives, as the party attempts to keep a firm grasp on the conservative Christian vote as well as to capitalize on significant new shifts toward the GOP among the young and Hispanics. At a different level, a deeper source of tension within the Republican party will develop between the small minority holding large amounts of wealth, and the far larger groups targeted by Republican strategists: blue-collar workers, Southerners, and students.

Voting patterns in 1984 point toward a highly significant change in the relationship between political parties, the partisan allegiance of the electorate, and voter manipulation. While there is considerable evidence right now of a partisan shift to the GOP among the electorate, a similar shift emerged in polls taken in late 1980 through much of 1981, only to quickly disappear in the recession of 1982. Instead, the far more sustained trend has been a consistent move away from partisan allegiance among voters on both sides of the aisle. In one of the most interesting analyses of polling data, Martin P. Wattenberg, professor of political science at the University of California, Irvine, finds in *The Decline of American Political Parties* that the percentage of the electorate that can be defined as unquestionably partisan—having positive feelings toward one party and negative feelings toward the other—has nearly halved from 1952 to 1980, falling from 50.1 percent to 27.3 percent. At the same time, the percentage of voters who perceive both parties in basically bland, neutral (nonpartisan) terms has nearly tripled, from 13 percent in 1952 to 36.5 percent in 1980.

On the surface, these figures suggest that parties are becoming increasingly irrelevant; in fact, the opposite is true. In an increasingly de-aligned electorate, candidates of both parties have lost the ability to depend on binding partisan loyalty for a substantial core of support going into elections. Facing a much more malleable electorate, the critical factors in politics become a party's ability to raise money in order to use the media to set the terms of political debate and to finance complex, computer-organized voter mobilization strategies.

In fact, the importance of the techniques of voter manipulation, primarily through television, intensifies in an electorate without commitment to political party. And it is in the application of such techniques that the Republican party has in recent years moved far ahead of the Democratic party, not only at the presidential level but increasingly in contests for every partisan office. The steady diminution of the core of guaranteed Democratic and Republican voters—the emergence of a fluid electorate—places increased stress on campaign technology. Fund-raising, polling, computerization of both demographic information and precinct voting histories, direct mail, the precise application of all relevant information to television commercials, issue selection, and more targeted mailings have become the terrain on which campaigns can be won or lost.

Money and technology do not predetermine the outcome of elections, but they are major forces in determining a candidate's or a party's ability to fully capitalize on advantages and to defuse liabilities. In the last election, the Reagan–

Bush '84 Committee and the Republican National Committee (RNC) together put at least $10 million into a highly sophisticated voter-registration campaign. First, computerized lists of all registered voters in 28 "battleground" states were purchased and, in localities where lists were not computerized, GOP personnel keypunched the names. These lists were then run against commercial lists of all residents with telephones and, when registered voters were "purged," the remaining names (and phone numbers and addresses) provided a basic list of unregistered voters. Using varying strategies, these names were then run against precinct lists showing areas of high GOP support, or against lists showing the value of homes and income levels by census tract. In the case of registration targeted toward Hispanics, these lists were run first against Hispanic surname files available from the census, and then against lists of households with two cars, or those subscribing to the *Wall Street Journal*, in an effort to find affluent unregistered Hispanics.

What had begun as a defensive strategy designed by the GOP to take the edge off an expected massive Democratic registration drive became, in effect, an offensive strategy, matching, if not exceeding, Democratic efforts. The Democrats, in the meantime, depended almost entirely on supposedly "nonpartisan," third-party voter registration drives by civil rights, peace, and community organizations. These efforts were severely hampered by (1) requirements of nonpartisanship, (2) intense competition for grants from foundations, leading to inflated claims of success, (3) the inability to follow through on registration to make sure that the newly eligible actually got to the polls, and (4) racial conflicts growing out of the fact that such black groups as the NAACP did not obtain until late in the game an obscure tax status many of the grant-giving foundations considered essential before handing out cash. In effect, while the GOP ran a centrally directed program in which each state effort was ultimately held responsible to the RNC and to the Reagan–Bush campaign, the Democratic effort involved a disparate collection of organizations, none of which had any structural fealty to the Democratic party.

The success of the GOP in voter registration reflects only one element of a substantial Republican advantage in the technology of politics. This advantage is, ultimately, based on money. The Republican party apparatus has, over the past ten years, demonstrated an extraordinary ability to develop a base of contributors, large and small, adequate to produce in excess of $200 million for the RNC, the Republican Senatorial and Republican Congressional Campaign committees, money that is separate and apart from the money raised by the candidates themselves.

The Democrats, whose *candidates* have been able to raise as much as their Republican opponents, have not, as a *party*, been able to approach the GOP success. In the last election, the Democratic party made modest gains in terms of fund-raising, enough to finance a new headquarters and purchase a media production facility, but its receipts remain one-fourth of those taken in by the GOP. More significantly, the centrifugal forces within the Democratic party are much stronger than those within the Republican party. While Democrats like to complain that the GOP raises more money because it is the party of the fat cats, the complaint is not entirely justified. In fact, the Republican party has, for many conservative donors, become the vehicle for ideological and political expression. In contrast, much of the Democratic donor base remains more loyal to such issue and reform groups as Common Cause, the Sierra Club, and the National Organization of Women than to the party.

For the moment, it is difficult to see how, in the immediate future, the Democratic party can gain centrality among all the organizations from labor to environmentalist that now form its core of support. The Republican party achieved this kind of leverage over its constituent organizations at a moment of crisis for the GOP in the mid-1970s, when Watergate threatened the party's survival.

For the Democrats, there is no such action-provoking threat; instead, the Democratic party is suffering from the kind of slow erosion of which the 1984 voter-turnout statistics are only one symptom. This erosion is particularly difficult for the party to stem when most of its incumbent members, particularly those in the House of Representatives, are confronting neither the threat of defeat nor the loss of majority control in the near future, permitting key leaders to retain a sense of false comfort in the face of a postponed danger.

# Onward, GOP Christians, Marching to '88

## Are Evangelicals Amassing as Much Clout with Republicans as the AFL-CIO Has with Democrats?

*The Washington Post,* June 30, 1985

In the suburbs of Minneapolis, Sharon Mueller, a woman once shunned by the GOP establishment, has emerged as a driving force in a conservative-evangelical Christian takeover of the state Republican party.

Just seven years ago, when Mueller went to her first Republican precinct caucus, almost no one would talk to her.

"I tried to volunteer for things, but I was never called," Mueller said. "What I didn't know was that there was kind of a shut-out policy which isn't quoted, it's just there. There was liberal and moderate control. They had their people involved, they had their people doing the work."

Today, Mueller is a leading grass-roots organizer in a Christian vanguard that is changing the way the Republican party conducts politics in states as diverse as Texas, North Carolina, Alaska, Georgia, Virginia and Oklahoma.

On a national scale, this movement is emerging as a force to be reckoned with in Republican presidential politics. Viewed in terms of power within a political party, and disregarding ideology, the muscle of the Christian right in the GOP is roughly parallel to the power of the AFL-CIO or the National Education Association within the Democratic party.

In 1984, just over 20 percent of the delegates to the Democratic convention were members of the AFL-CIO and about 12 percent were NEA members. Republican officials privately estimate that from 15 to 20 percent of the GOP delegates in 1988 will come out of the Christian movement.

The glue holding the Christian right together is its members' intense opposition to abortion, although other common goals include school prayer, the mandated teaching of "scientific creationism" and the elimination of both moral "relativism" and "man-centered secular humanism" from the political and educational processes.

In Minnesota, Republican political gatherings are now being held in places like The Jesus People Church in Minneapolis as well as at golf clubs; at the Temple Baptist Church in St. Paul instead of at a union hall. The arcane procedures of precinct caucuses are taught after the lessons of the scripture. This brand of conservativism took on and crushed Rep. Bill Frenzel (R-Minn.), the senior member of the state's congressional delegation, in a battle for control of the Third District's Republican party machinery. In the March 1984 Minnesota precinct caucuses, says Mueller, "we just won everything, including the state central committee in the Third (Congressional District), the Fifth, we're good in the Sixth and not quite solid in the Fourth."

Across the country, the strength of the Christian-Republican movement varies widely from state to state. In many southern and Rocky Mountain states, it is a significant force, lacking majority control but in a position to flex strong muscles through alliances with right to life, anti-ERA and other conservative factions.

In Virginia, for example, the Christian right now dominates the Republican party in the area surrounding Norfolk and Virginia Beach, but remains a minority statewide, unable to determine the nomination of favored candidates for governor or lieutenant governor. In the Texas GOP, officials estimate that a sixth of the state executive committee is made up of persons clearly identified as part of the Christian evangelical movement, as were a fourth to a third of the 5,000 delegates to the state convention last year.

Warren Tompkins, executive director of the South Carolina Republican party, said, "Christians are a very integral part of our party. At a state convention, it's about 25 percent of the delegates. We've got two or three groups. We've got a group that's got leadership out of the Bob Jones University, and then the Pat Robertson group and somewhere along the line the (Moral Majority's Jerry) Falwell group is meshed in."

In Oregon, there is a continuing struggle for control of the state GOP between party regulars and Christian conservatives that dates back to 1964, when the nomination of Sen. Barry Goldwater (R-Ariz.) mobilized the Republican right throughout the West and South.

In Alaska, the Moral Majority, run locally by the Rev. Jerry Prevo, took over the GOP in 1980. Since then, party regulars have regained at least partial control, although the Moral Majority remains a major force. Republican sources there said that both the regulars and the Moral Majority have agreed to downplay the organization's role in the GOP because the Moral Majority has a highly negative image among many Alaska voters.

The emergence of the Christian movement in Minnesota is not a chance event resulting from a weak local Republican party ripe for takeover by any group prepared to mobilize a few troops. This is a state with a long history of a strong state Republican party, and the gains made by the Christian movement have been in battles with a sophisticated GOP establishment. The Christian-conservative coalition has not yet taken over the statewide GOP leadership, but its power includes enough votes to run over the opposition at the state party convention on specific issues.

Allen Quist, a freshman Republican elected last year to the Minnesota House as part of a cresting wave of Christian political activity, said: "I don't know how to gauge it, but I can say this: At the last convention, the Christian right was able to do virtually anything it wanted to."

In recognition of the importance of the movement to the GOP—not just in Minnesota but across the country—the Republican National Committee has appointed a liaison officer, Doug Shaddix, specifically assigned to work with evangelicals, along with the right-to-life and conservative ideological movements. Similarly, in the last election, Joe Rodgers, finance chairman of the Reagan–Bush '84 Committee, organized a separate, private fund-raising program designed to channel over $1 million into the Christian movement, primarily for voter registration.

The movement has stunned Minnesota GOP stalwarts such as Frenzel and Sen. David F. Durenberger.

"In Minnesota and other parts of the country, we seem to be narrowing the structural base of the party," Durenberger said. "That is, the party organization itself is gradually being taken over by those who have strongly held views and little tolerance for people in political life who hold different views."

Durenberger says the Christian evangelical movement is becoming so strong nationally that he believes its members will determine the 1988 Republican presidential nominee.

"It means that the range of the 1988 convention will be narrow," he said. "And it means that you can almost predict that whoever gets their blessing is going to be the Republican candidate for president. It's not going to be (Vice President) George (Bush), (Senate Majority Leader) Bob (Dole) or (former Senate Majority Leader) Howard (Baker), some of those kind of centrist types. It's going to be somebody who can accommodate to their views on most of the issues."

Asked if Rep. Jack Kemp (R-N.Y.) fit this bill, Durenberger said: "Oh yes, you bet."

Senator Dole, asked how strong he expects the Christian right to be at the

1988 GOP presidential convention, said cautiously: "It will be a factor." He said he "will know better after next year," referring to the fact that he faces reelection next year and has yet to decide whether to organize a serious drive for the presidency.

Two key GOP presidential strategists, who spoke off the record out of reluctance to challenge the movement, both argued that the Christian right movement will be a strong minority faction at the 1988 Republican presidential convention, but both contended that there are a number of forces working against the movement becoming the determining force in 1988.

They pointed out that Jerry Falwell of the Moral Majority has already endorsed the candidacy of George Bush, despite the belief held by a number of Republicans that Kemp has a stronger appeal than Bush among evangelicals. Both strategists were critical of the claims of power made by a number of leaders of the Christian movement, although both talked only on a background basis, choosing not to publicly challenge it.

A number of the Christian leaders are far more assertive in their assessments of their own power:

"The Republican party cannot elect a presidential candidate without the evangelicals," said Ray Allen, a rural Granberry, Tex., pastor and president of Christian Voice, which issues moral "report cards" on members of Congress. "We are everywhere."

Perhaps most assertive is Gary Jarmin, executive director of the Christian Voice Moral Government Fund and chief lobbyist for Christian Voice, a hybrid political organization.

"There is a realignment occurring," he said. "There are very few states in the country where we can't make it happen. The way I look at it, no state is safe."

A backer of Kemp for president in 1988, Jarmin predicted the following scenario in the next competition for the GOP nomination:

"We swamp the caucuses in Iowa in 1988. You heard it here. We are going to swamp the caucuses in Iowa. Jack Kemp is going to get it. He is going to go to New Hampshire and win it, and by that time, it's all over."

Christian Voice, which played a central role in mobilizing over 1,000 Christian fundamentalists—all political neophytes—as delegates to the 1984 Texas State GOP convention, is making a conscious effort to expand the "Texas plan" to other states:

"What we want to do is take the Texas thing as our prototype, we want to take this nationwide," Jarmin said. "Where the Republican party is weakest, in the South, we are strongest."

In a separate drive, Dr. M. G. "Pat" Robertson, founder and president of the Christian Broadcast Network (CBN), is setting up a national network of "Freedom Councils," which CBN officials describe as "nonpartisan." Robertson is also considering a run for president, according to CBN spokesman Earl Weirich. "He said a number of people had come to him and proposed this, that he consider it. And he said 'The best I can say right now is, "I'll consider it." ' "

Many politicians, both Republican and Democratic, have suggested that the growing involvement of evangelical, born-again Christians will become a liability to a Republican party seeking to build strength among young people who are fiscal conservatives but more liberal on social issues.

In this view, the Christian right's opposition to abortion, to increased sexual freedom and to "secular humanism," along with its support of school prayer, will alienate many young voters who supported Reagan in 1984, but who do not want their own life styles suddenly regulated.

To date, however, the GOP's Christian mobilization has been a political gold mine.

Of the 15-seat Republican gain in the House in 1984, eight were in districts where conservative Christian activity was clearly an important part of the election, particularly in Texas, North Carolina and Georgia. The Christian mobilization was critical to the reelection of Sen. Jesse Helms (R-N.C.) and contributed substantially to the decisive victory of Sen. Phil Gramm (R-Tex.).

Most important of all, however, is the fact that the Christian mobilization is an expansion of the Reagan constituency that has translated directly into straight party-line voting for Republican candidates right down the ticket to lower-level offices.

In the once firmly Democratic terrain along the Route I-85 corridor from Greensboro to Winston-Salem in North Carolina, Republicans last year more than doubled their numbers in the state legislature from 18 to 37. In Texas, GOP state House strength grew from 37 to 53.

Another force behind the movement is the populist challenge by the lower-middle-class and middle-class whites to an elitist, affluent and privileged Republican establishment. "Traditionally, the Minnesota Republican Party has been a closed, small group of people who were primarily interested in fiscal conservativsm," said Frank Grace, the Minnesota GOP national committeeman. "It got to be very exclusive. The Reagan movement inspired these people who thought the country was going bad to come in."

Republicans in Minnesota made decisive gains at the bottom of the ticket, despite the fact that it is the one state in the union Reagan failed to carry. The Republican captured the Minnesota House as a 77-57 Democratic majority shifted to a 70-64 Republican majority, and a Republican party once considered among the most liberal in the nation pushed through conservative legislation that included sharp welfare cuts, shifts in education aid from the cities to the suburbs and reductions in summer jobs.

In the process in Minnesota, Sharon Mueller has become what amounts to a Christian political boss, although she prefers to call herself a "motivator."

Knowing the 1984 precinct caucuses—the grass-roots base of the Minnesota Republican party—would be held in late March, Mueller, working with the Greater Minneapolis Association of Evangelicals, "started in January. I did three months of caucus workshops, in schools, churches, homes."

Frenzel, recognizing that he was in danger of losing his own district party structure to conservative forces adamantly opposed to his pro-choice abortion stance, pulled out the stops to get his allies to the precinct caucuses. It was futile.

"At our convention," said Maybeth Christensen, Frenzel's district director, "there was a young man who stood in one of the aisles and had on one of those straw bowler hats.

"When he had his hat on, everybody would vote yes, when he took his hat off, everybody would vote no. It was an amazing thing to watch. The votes went exactly the way his hat went. We had less than 100 votes out of more than 300. They were in total control."

In this atmosphere, Frenzel did not attempt to become a delegate to the Republican National Convention in Dallas. "He said he had been twice and did not need to go again," Christensen said, with a laugh. But the Christian right knows it would lose if it challenged Frenzel in an open primary. This reflects its strengths and weaknesses elsewhere in the country.

The movement has been strongest in party battles where power comes from producing blocks of voters at precinct caucuses. Caucuses have little appeal to most voters, making them ideal targets for groups such as churches that can produce ready-made constituencies.

In a process very similar to that in Minnesota, the Christian right in Oregon has periodically taken over the state GOP but has been unable to oust such adversaries as Sen. Bob Packwood (R-Ore.). "They don't do all that well at the ballot box, but they do a hell of a job in the party organization," Jack Faust, a moderate Oregon Republican, said.

The growing strength of the Christian right within state Republican parties is, however, likely to translate into relatively strong delegate strength at the 1988 presidential convention since just under half of the convention delegates are slated to be selected through caucus systems, as opposed to open primaries.

The influx of Christians to the party has produced a different breed of politician. Take the case of Minnesota's John M. Hartinger, pastor of the Victory Baptist Church and a follower of the Moral Majority's Jerry Falwell. He first ran for the legislature in 1982 and lost.

After much agonizing—"I had people coming to me after the election and saying, 'Johnny, your prayers don't mean a thing' "—Hartinger ran again in 1984.

"At 4 A.M., there were three precincts left, I was 124 votes behind. I said 'Lord, it's in Your hands. You've got to make up 124 votes.' There was a lot of boldness in my prayers. I went to sleep. At 6 A.M., my wife rapped me on the shoulder and said, 'You're ahead by 54 votes.' "

# New Politics of Rich Man, Poor Man

*The Washington Post*, December 22, 1985

American politics—dominated for fifty years by a Democratic coalition built around urban workers, minorities and the rural poor—has been turned on its head in the last two presidential elections and is now dominated by a Republican coalition built around the rich and the upper-middle class.

If this Reagan revolution can be converted into an enduring partisan realignment, the ascendancy in the 1930s of those dispossessed by the Great Depression will have been replaced in the 1980s by the ascendancy of the affluent.

The energies of such a coalition would be spent overwhelmingly on continuing the pattern of tax, spending and regulatory decisions of the Reagan years in which it is the affluent who benefit most, whose taxes are reduced most, whose incomes rise fastest during economic recovery and whose acquisition of wealth is facilitated by actions of the federal government.

The growing strength of the Republicans—now nearly equal to that of the Democrats in terms of how voters identify themselves—has significance beyond realignment of the parties. Just as the Democrats' once-solid partisan advantage acted as a brake on conservative policies under such presidents as Eisenhower and Nixon, so today's revived GOP not only supports the current administration's policies redistributing income upwards but will act as a firm brake on traditional Democratic initiatives if that party regains control of the Senate and the White House. In the current session of Congress, the struggle to shape legislation overhauling the nation's tax system will be a major test of the balance of power in the electorate.

In strictly political terms, the most striking element of the Reagan coalition is its restoration of political divisions along class and income lines reminiscent of those of the Great Depression. From the early 1950s through the mid-1970s, class divisions between the two parties were muted. But recent years have again seen a strong correlation between income on one side and voting and partisan commitment on the other.

The extraordinary intensification of class voting is clear when the landslide victories of two Republican presidents running for reelection are compared: Eisenhower in 1956, when he won with 58 percent of the vote, and Ronald Reagan in 1984, when he won with an almost identical 59 percent. But despite their similar overall results, the two mandates had strikingly different compositions.

This point is illustrated in the following chart based on data compiled by Martin P. Wattenberg of the University of California at Irvine from National Election Studies (NES). The voting population is divided into five income groups: the poor (lowest 10 percent), lower-middle class (11th–30th percentile), middle class (31st–60th percentile), upper-middle class (61st–90th) percentile, and rich (top 10 percent). (Chart I.)

## I · VOTING BY INCOME GROUP

### Percent for Eisenhower in 1956, Reagan in 1980

| Class | Eisenhower | Reagan |
|-------|-----------|--------|
| Poor | 59 | 32 |
| Lower middle | 56 | 43 |
| Middle | 58 | 57 |
| Upper middle | 57 | 64 |
| Affluent | 75 | 75 |

Eisenhower won in every income group, and all groups except the rich gave him almost the same degree of support—56 to 59 percent of their vote. In statistical terms, there was no difference between his support by the poor and his support by the upper-middle class.

Reagan, in contrast, was carried to victory by the nation's haves and was decisively rejected by the have-nots. In the 1984 election, the difference between Reagan's support by the poor and by the upper-middle class was 32 points. The poor and lower-middle class, which had given Ike 59 and 56 percent respectively, gave Reagan 32 and 43 percent.

The re-emergence of class voting patterns has been paralleled by growing class divisions in partisan allegiance. This can be seen in the following NES-Watteberg chart showing, by income group, Democratic allegiance as measured by the number of voters per 100 who call themselves Democrats minus the percentage who call themselves Republican. (Chart II.)

## II · DEMOCRATIC ALLEGIANCE

### Percentage identified as Democrats minus percentage identified as GOP

| Class | 1956 | 1984 |
|-------|------|------|
| Poor | +18 | +36 |
| Lower middle | +22 | +29 |
| Middle | +17 | +6 |
| Upper middle | +13 | 0 |
| Affluent | −22 | −33 |

In 1956, Democratic strength varied only slightly according to income group—except for the rich, who then and now were firmly in the hands of the GOP. Though the Democrats were somewhat stronger toward the lower end of the scale, the poorest voters were only five points more Democratic than the upper-middle class.

The same pattern held true in 1960. But by 1984, the pattern of partisan commitment was following clear income/class lines: the poorer the voter, the more likely he or she would be a Democrat. The five-point spread between the poor and upper-middle class had grown by 1984 to a 36-point difference, and the 40 point spread between riches and poorest had grown to 69 points.

Reagan, then, was elected by a constituency of the affluent, and his political revolution has helped shape a new majority of the economically privileged.

This same period, according to Census Bureau data, has seen a shift in the distribution of income. From 1980 through 1984, the median income for all families dropped slightly, from $26,500 to $26,433 (in constant 1984 dollars). But when median family income is calculated by income group—the bottom 40 percent, the top 40 percent and the top 10 percent—a clear pattern of redistribution emerges. (Chart III).

### III · DISTRIBUTION OF WEALTH

*Shift in median family income toward affluent*

| Year | Bottom 40% | Top 40% | Top 10% |
|------|-----------|---------|---------|
| 1980 | $12,966 | $43,531 | $68,145 |
| 1981 | 12,469 | 42,799 | 66,873 |
| 1982 | 12,069 | 43,035 | 68,870 |
| 1983 | 12,124 | 43,604 | 70,191 |
| 1984 | 12,489 | 45,300 | 73,230 |
| Net shift | −$477 | +$1,769 | +$5,085 |

Changes in the pattern of income distribution result from a host of forces, including recession, recovery and government decisions on taxes and spending. In 1984, the Congressional Budget Office estimated that tax and spending legislation enacted since Reagan took office—particularly in 1981—would have the following net effects for 1983 through 1985 for different income groups (Chart IV).

### IV · REAGAN PROGRAM EFFECTS

*Gains and losses by income group*

| Income | Taxes | Benefits | Gain/Loss |
|--------|-------|----------|-----------|
| $ 10,000 or less | +$70 | −$1,170 | −$1,100 |
| 10,000–20,000 | +1,000 | −840 | +160 |
| 20,000–40,000 | +3,560 | −470 | +3,090 |
| 40,000–80,000 | +9,060 | −430 | +8,630 |
| 80,000 or more | +24,600 | −340 | +24,260 |

In the classic American political tradition of "dancing with the guy who brung you," the Reagan administration has rewarded its new, affluent constituency of Republicans. Just as the Democratic majority of the 1930s was rewarded by a Democratic administration with Social Security, the National Labor Relations Board, unemployment compensation and tax policies designed to redistribute income downwards, the Reagan administration has won enactment of tax and spending legislation redistributing income upwards, has weakened the federal regulatory aparatus governing the relationship between corporations, workers and consumers, and has lessened the tax burden on wealth through reductions of the capital gains and estate taxes.

While Reagan's success has been widely credited to his popularity and broad array of telegenic skills, he could not have achieved this substantial alteration of the federal government without a major change in the electorate itself. In this context, the most important changes have been not only the revival of class cleavage between the parties but the simultaneous growth in the Republican party's competitive strength.

Market Opinion Research (MOR), a Detroit-based polling firm, has found that from 1952 to 1978 the Democrats enjoyed a consistent and overwhelming advantage over the GOP in terms of the way voters described themselves. During those years (and probably as far back as 1932 if data were available), the percentage of persons identifying themselves as Democrats was 14 to 30 points higher than those calling themselves Republican.

Despite the Democratic dominance in those years, Republican presidential candidates Eisenhower and Nixon won decisive victories and Eisenhower even carried both branches of Congress in 1952. But unlike the Reagan victories of the 1980s, the triumphs of the 1950s, 1960s and 1970s saw no conservative revolution in public policy accompanying Republican control of the White House. One central force preventing such a revolution was the overwhelmingly strong Democratic majority in the electorate, which acted as a shield against major initiatives from the economic and ideological right. A substantial proportion of voters remained committed to the principles—if not the presidential candidates—of a party supporting a strong, active federal government willing to intervene in behalf of those out of work and those organizing the workplace.

This Democratic restraint on a conservative political agenda began to erode between 1978 and 1980 when the Democratic advantage reflected in how voters described themselves fell from 23 points (53 Democratic, 30 Republican) to 13 points (53–40), according to MOR figures. The shift has had consequences far more important than the momentary status of a political party.

By 1984, a Republican party increasingly dominated by the upper-middle class and the rich had achieved near parity with the Democratic party, running just three to five points behind in most opinion polls of party identification. Even this slight disparity disappears when turnout rates, which are much higher for the well-to-do than for the poor and lower-middle class, are taken into account.

The strengthened GOP's partisan gains mean that the electorate has applied a conservative template to legislative policy. Just as the Democratic majority in the electorate limited the scope of policies permitted to GOP administrations in the 1950s, 1960s and early 1970s, the GOP's current parity has created a conservative veto on liberal, Democratic initiatives in the 1980s. This conservative template has severely undermined the Democratic party's groping efforts to redefine its goals after the defeats of 1980 and 1984. A Democratic party that set the national agenda for nearly 50 years has been consistently on the defensive since Reagan took office.

The Democrats' inability to take the initiative was reflected most recently and perhaps most graphically in the passage by Congress of the Gramm-Rudman-Hollings proposal to mandate severe budget cuts in order to achieve a balanced budget by 1991. House Democrats voted 130 to 118 against the measure. Senate Democrats split 22–22, and among the supporters was Sen. Edward M. Kennedy (D-Mass.), for years the Democrats' liberal standard bearer. Kennedy epitomizes the quandary Democrats now face, given the changed electorate: "In order for (Kennedy) to establish credibility as a liberal Democrat with the general public, he first has to gain fiscal credibility," a key Kennedy adviser said.

In a development even more threatening to the Democratic party, a series of focus groups financed by the Democratic National Committee has found that the issue considered most advantageous to the party—"fairness"—appears to have turned into a potential liability among major portions of an increasingly conservative and self-interested electorate. "Fairness," according to those who conducted the studies, has come increasingly to be seen as a code word for "giveaways" to the poor.

What all this suggests is that even if the Democratic party regains control of the Senate and White House, the scope of its legislative program will be severely restricted by conservative forces in the electorate. In this light, it is quite possible that the Republican party and its conservative base could lose political control of the federal government in 1988 but retain de facto control over the national debate and the legislative agenda.

# An Enduring Republican Majority?

*Dissent,* Winter 1986

The Republican party under Ronald Reagan has shaped a fragile majority in presidential elections whose strength and vitality will be tested in 1988. In terms of partisan allegiance, the GOP has made striking gains over the past five years, reaching near-parity with the Democratic party for the first time since the late 1940s. None of the prospective candidates—Vice President George Bush, New York Representative Jack Kemp, Kansas Senator Robert Dole, Nevada Senator Paul Laxalt—has demonstrated the political appeal of Ronald Reagan; for any one of these politicians to win against a credible Democratic candidate will require the conversion of what has been the *Reagan* coalition into a *Republican* coalition. The success or failure of the 1988 Republican nominee is likely to be, in effect, a gauge of realignment.

In many respects, the Reagan–Republican coalition has the kind of coherence suggesting durability, if not growing muscle. In terms of presidential voting, the major strength of this coalition is geographic: in the past five elections, a bloc of Southern and Western states has voted Republican by significantly stronger margins than the country as a whole. These states provide 202 of the 270 electoral votes required for election. In terms of ideology, there are divisions within the Republican universe—ranging from the fiscal conservatism of Senator Dole to the tax-cutting strategies of Jack Kemp—but these are not fissures. Neither camp is in any way likely to bolt to the Democratic party in a fashion paralleling, for example, the shift of once Democratic Southern whites to the GOP.

Demographically, the coalition of voters who identify with the Republican party is not only white, but it is coming to increasingly represent the emergence of a new majority of the affluent. The Administration of Ronald Reagan has intensified a strong return to class divisions between those who identify with the Republican party and those who identify with the Democratic party. The shift of upscale Southern whites to the GOP and the increasingly strong ties of blacks to the Democratic party have produced a restoration of economic divisions between the two parties very similar to those of the 1930's. The difference now, however, is that this time the party of the poor and the working class is no longer the majority party.

The partisan makeup of the electorate has substantial consequences for the internal strength of each party. Financially, Republican ideological and economic homogeneity makes party activists an ideal donor base, perfectly suited to the direct-mail fund-raising tactics required by the campaign finance reforms of 1972 and '74. At the same time the GOP has been the beneficiary of the steady erosion of participatory politics, through the decline of the precinct and ward organization. This decline has produced a parallel rise in the importance of a national fund-raising apparatus to finance the acquisitions of political high technology: computerized poll and census data, telemarketing, demographic targeting of mail, television (cable, UHF, and VHF), and radio appeals. The extraordinary disparity between the financing of the two parties is reflected in part by the fact that this past fall the Democratic National Committee financed its first poll since 1981, at a cost of $125,000; during 1984, the Republican National Committee paid Richard Wirthlin's Decision-Making Information $168,000 for poll data *every month.* Overall, the three major Democratic committees—the Democratic National, Congressional, and Senatorial—were outspent by the parallel Republican committees in the 1983–84 election cycle by a margin of four to one.

These strengths, combined with the presence of a highly popular incumbent president, economic recovery, and a Democratic party in shambles, raise a basic question: With all these advantages, why hasn't the Republican party already gained clear majority status? Why has a realignment failed to fully materialize?

Perhaps the central liability of the Republican party is the continuing public identification of the GOP as the party of the rich and of corporate America. This perception was reinforced in spades by the enactment of the budget and tax cuts of 1981—when the GOP became, in effect, the party of regressive redistribution—and by the subsequent recession of 1981–82. Over the past generation, however, the identification of the GOP with the rich has become less and less a liability as the population as a whole has become more affluent. In 1958, for example, when a recession severely undercut the Republican party under the leadership of Dwight Eisenhower, just 14.3 percent of all families had incomes in excess of $25,000 (in 1980 dollars). By the start of the Reagan administration, however, this percentage had grown to 39.3. The Republican party has gained strength in large part because the nation itself has become more affluent.

But the nation does not yet appear ready to grant a full-fledged majority commitment to a party of the elite. Republican strategists are aware of this liability, and a central political rationale behind the Reagan administration's sponsorship this year of tax reform was to create a "populist" appeal to the middle and lower-middle classes by attacking loopholes used by corporations and the rich. This turned out, however, to be a demonstration of the continued strength of the affluent in the Republican party. As proposed by President Reagan, the "populist" tax-reform bill gave by far the largest tax breaks, in dollar and percentage terms, to those making more than $200,000 annually, in effect making a mockery of populist goals. In addition, whatever political momentum has developed behind the legislation has come from one segment of the business community—such "high-tax" corporations as IBM and Procter and Gamble, which would benefit from the proposed lowering of the top corporate rate from 46 to 33 percent—while there has been no public outpouring of support. Clearly, the Republican party is not equipped to tap into either popular suspicion of corporate power or into the belief that the nation's tax policies are designed for the benefit of the rich.

The second major Republican vulnerability is its deep dependence for support on the mobilization of the fundamentalist religious community. By conservative estimate, the rise of the Christian right, and its firm alignment with the Republican party, resulted in the switch, from 1976 to 1984, of about 8.25 million to 9 million voters from the Democratic party to the Republican party. These voters, in turn, are demonstrating a commitment to the GOP far deeper than voting for Ronald Reagan: over half of the GOP's 1984 gains in the House of Representatives, and a substantial proportion of the Republican pickup of 300 state legislative seats, particularly in North Carolina and Texas, came in areas where fundamentalists were most active.

In a reflection of Reagan's political genius, the religious right has, to date, been drawn into the Republican fold without making significant headway at the federal level on its own agenda of banning abortion, restoring prayer, teaching creationism in public schools, and regulating the content of school textbooks, the publication of pornography, and sexual relations generally. To the extent that these issues become central to either the legislative agenda or the political debate in the contest for the Republican presidential nomination, the Republican party will be in a no-win situation, threatened by losses from the social-issue right insofar as its agenda is rejected, and by losses among the broad spectrum of voters who do not support the notion of government regulation of personal behavior.

In addition to the fundamentalist vote, new Republican support comes in large part from those voters who initially describe themselves as political independents, and who voice a leaning toward the GOP only when pressed. Among many of these independent voters the religious right agenda is unacceptable.

In this context, the most advantageous scenario for the Republicans between now and the 1988 convention would be to avoid an intense nomination fight. A bitterly fought struggle for the nomination is the only way for the discordant factions within the GOP to force consideration of their own objectives, in a process that could replicate the degeneration of the Democratic party from the collective expression of a majority consensus to a network of conflicts between isolated interest groups.

While it is far too early to predict anything concerning the outcome of the 1988 Republican primary fight, current signs are that Vice President George Bush is moving toward an early lock on the nomination. If Bush is to be successfully challenged, it will have to be from the ideological and Christian right of the party; but at the moment the right remains divided, while Bush is proceeding to expand his base significantly among party moderates, his 1980 supporters, and Reagan loyalists. Jack Kemp, at the moment, has emerged as the main challenger to Bush, but Kemp is already experiencing difficulty holding his base together.

Leaders of the hard ideological right—direct-mail specialist Richard Viguerie, Conservative Caucus chairman Howard Phillips, and Paul Weyrich, leader of the Committee for the Survival of a Free Congress—have all begun to criticize Kemp for failing to adequately stress abortion and other social issues. Kemp, an opponent of abortion, has attempted to maintain his conservative credentials by emphasizing the "pro-family" elements of his economic policy, including the proposed raising of the personal deduction to $2,000, instead of promoting his stands on more divisive social issues. At the same time, Marion G. (Pat) Robertson, the television evangelist and host of the Christian Broadcasting Network's 700 Club, has set in motion the start of his own bid for the GOP nomination, which, if he follows through, will further divide the GOP's conservative wing. Kemp, in addition, damaged his own credentials among conservatives and other supporters by the vacillating stand he took on sanctions against South Africa: first voting against them, then voting for them and, after his second vote, saying President Reagan would be "wise" to veto the legislation. His way of dealing with the issue did not boost support on the right and, more generally, damaged his credentials as a candidate equipped to make the kind of decisions required of a president.

Bush, in the meantime, has quietly set up an organization that is expanding his support into the Republican right, largely by capitalizing on his loyalty to the president in order to win the support of conservatives who backed Reagan in 1976 and 1980, including many who were bitterly opposed to Bush when he ran against Reagan in 1980. Bush set up a political action committee to channel money to 1986 House and Senate candidates, and in just six weeks the PAC raised far more money than any of his competitors were able to raise over six months. His supporters include the two top strategists of the Reagan–Bush '84 Committee— Edward Rollins, the campaign manager, and Lee Atwater, the deputy campaign manager—along with Republican pollster Robert Teeter, who has the best data base of any survey specialist of either party.

Bush also brings to a campaign for the Republican nomination a set of substantial liabilities. Most important, his public persona lacks Reagan's appeal: he claims Texas roots while appearing most relaxed sailing off Kennebunkport, Maine. As a candidate claiming the Reagan mantle, he looks, walks and talks like a quintessential Eastern, Wall Street Republican, the enemy of the conservative wing of the GOP from Taft through Goldwater to Reagan.

In this highly delicate process not only of determining the Republican nominee but of determining whether the Republican surge will continue after Reagan, perhaps the central question will be the timing of Administration efforts to control the economy. If the Administration and the Federal Reserve determine that a recession is inevitable between now and the 1988 election, the key questions will be, first, should an attempt be made to time the emergence of the recession and, if the answer is affirmative, then when—before the 1986 election or before the 1988 election?

For the Reagan administration, this is a tough choice to make. Timing a recession to occur after the 1986 election would significantly increase the likelihood of the GOP holding onto the Senate. Continued GOP control would sharply increase Reagan's ability to determine the nation's legislative agenda through his entire eight years in office. Timing a recession to occur before the 1986 election would, in turn, ensure Republican loss of the Senate. It would also, however, create the possibilities of a replay of Reagan's first term to the benefit of whoever is the Republican nominee in 1988. In Reagan's first term, a recession forced significant losses in the 1982 election, but then set the stage for an economic resurgence for the 1984 election, making Reagan invulnerable, and leading to a GOP landslide. This latter alternative represents the kind of gamble no politician is likely to take, particularly when there is any expectation at all that a recession could be avoided altogether.

If George Bush is to be the Republican party's nominee, his liabilities and strengths will, in many ways, make him an ideal test of the degree of realignment that has taken place in the United States. George Bush, unlike Ronald Reagan, would have severe difficulties making a quasi-populist appeal. For Bush to win the presidency would, then, suggest that a majority of the electorate has made a commitment to a party demographically dominated by the affluent, and that there has been an economic inversion of the New Deal coalition into a new Republican majority.

# Jockeying for Position: Only 1,000 Days to Go

## *Bush Plans to Conquer the Right by Dividing It*

*The Washington Post,* February 9, 1986

Vice President George Bush, sharply criticized in recent weeks for pandering to the conservative movement, is in fact out to split and neutralize right-wing opposition to his unannounced bid for the presidency. Although Bush has been taking the heat, the right may suffer as well from the division and disorientation caused by Bush's tactics.

At a time when conservatives can claim to dominate the agenda and the ideology of Republican presidential politics, Bush's goal is to divide the right early in the campaign to prevent Rep. Jack Kemp of New York—or any other candidate—from getting the support of a united conservative wing.

Bush's performance at a series of conservative events over the past two months has provoked a firestorm of criticism from conservative and liberal columnists—a storm far more intense than anticipated by his strategists:

• "Smarmiest"—Lars-Erik Nelson, *New York Daily News.*

• "Raises the question whether or not he ever had any principles"—Tom Wicker, *New York Times.*

• "The unpleasant sound Bush is emitting as he traipses from one conservative gathering to another is a thin, tinny 'aft'—the sound of a lapdog"—George F. Will, *Washington Post.*

A Bush supporter countered: "When you go hunting in a swamp, you get your boots dirty. But now we've got time for a shoe shine before the primaries begin."

"It's been nasty, but we are getting it over with three years before the election," another Bush aide contended. He noted that waiting until 1988 to address the concerns of the right would not only permit potential opposition to build, but would also subject Bush to charges of special-interest politicking in the heat of the campaign, when it could prove much more dangerous.

"If Gerald Ford had done what Bush is doing now, he never would have been challenged by Reagan," a Bush strategist said, arguing that early accommodation of the right wing is a critical step for a leading "progressive" GOP candidate.

Kemp is the main target of Bush's strategy. Bush succeeded on January 23 in converting what was billed as a Kemp–Bush confrontation before the New

York State Conservative Party into a confrontation between Bush and Mario Cuomo, New York's Democratic governor. Kemp dropped to the tail end of the news coverage and a backer of the vice president commented: "His (Kemp's) oxygen is being cut off. It's iron-lung time for Jack Kemp."

Now Kemp and Bush have completed the first round of major appearances before conservative groups, and Kemp aides concede that Bush has made inroads into what they had seen as their terrain. David Hoppe, Kemp's administrative assistant, acknowledged: "There is a group of people on the conservative side of the Republican party who look favorably on the vice president."

On the surface, all this kow-towing to the right wing would seem to prove that it is increasing its power and independence. In fact, the reverse may be true: Bush has succeeded in splitting the right, for the moment at least, and there is growing evidence of conflict and deterioration within the middle-aged new right and within the religious right.

The religious right, the most important source of new voters for the GOP in 1984, has already divided into factions. Jerry Falwell, who has endorsed Bush, has been forced by adverse public sentiments to change the name of his organization from Moral Majority to the Liberty Federation. Marion G. (Pat) Robertson, host of the 700 Club and president of the Christian Broadcast Network, is exploring the possibility of making his own run for the nomination. The leadership of Christian Voice, a source of support for Kemp, has split into factions, and the flow of cash to the Christian Voice Moral Government Fund has slowed to a trickle.

Similarly, the American Coalition for Traditional Values, which organized the unprecedented voter registration of white, born-again Christians in 1984, has faded into the minor-leagues now that the 1984 election is over and Republican fund-raisers are no longer bringing in large amounts of money.

The National Conservative Political Action Committee (NCPAC), a significant factor in the Republican takeover of the Senate in 1980, was a paper tiger in the last two elections. Dependent on publicity, positive or negative, to boost its direct-mail fund-raising, NCPAC now has a hard time attracting any media coverage of its battle against the left.

These divisions on the right are unlikely to create an opening for a more liberal Republican candidate to break into serious competition for the nomination, according to most strategists. Rather, the consensus behind the conservatism of the Reagan revolution, among a broad spectrum of Republican party activists, is strong enough, barring unforeseen events, to lock out anyone making a challenge from the Republican left. Both Senate Majority Leader Robert Dole (Kan.) and former majority leader Howard H. Baker, Jr., (Tenn.) are portraying themselves as conservatives, and both face steep uphill fights to gain competitive stature.

Meanwhile, the conservative right, despite its weaknesses, has already forced both Bush and Kemp to adjust their strategies to its demands.

In 1985, Kemp initially ran a nonideological campaign. Working, in the words of one conservative activist, on the assumption that he is the Republican party's "fourth man"—heir of a conservative lineage running from Ohio senator Robert Taft through Sen. Barry Goldwater (Ariz.) to Ronald Reagan—Kemp portrayed himself as the candidate who could complete a Republican realignment. He stressed his antiestablishment credentials as a populist tax-reformer who could win the votes of Democratic blue-collar workers and reach out for black support.

Kemp's de-emphasis of his strong anti-abortion position provoked continued complaints from such new-right leaders as Free Congress Foundation president Paul Weyrich and direct-mail specialist Richard Viguerie. These men not only sniped at Kemp but encouraged Robertson to get in the race, undermining Kemp's backing within the religious right.

Faced with the threat of crumbling conservative support, Kemp restored abortion to a central place in both his speeches and his legislative activities. After watching Kemp give an anti-abortion address last fall, Weyrich declared with a smile of satisfaction: "The market system works."

Meanwhile, Kemp's strategists are banking on the theory that press criticism of Bush will pay off once the 1986 elections are over and public attention begins to focus on the differences between the two candidates in position, character and style.

"When you get to the presidency, it's more than left-right," one of the engineers of the Kemp drive said. "It's who has the consistency and the guts to be president. Kemp will be able to say things like: 'If elected, I would fire Secretary of State George Schultz. How about you, Mr. Vice President? I'd replace him with former U.N. Ambassador Jeane Kirkpatrick. How about you, Mr. Vice President?' How's Bush going to handle that?"

Like Kemp, Bush has been forced to humble himself. At a dinner honoring the memory of William Loeb, late right-wing publisher of the Manchester, N.H., *Union Leader,* Bush first read aloud from past Loeb editorials denouncing him and then sought to affirm his credentials as a political leader equipped to stand up to communism, outlining his own record in World War II as a pilot shot down in the Pacific.

In appealing to the members of the New York Conservative Party, Bush veiled his privileged, moneyed roots to speak in the vernacular of the streets, using phrases like "cop killers" and saying "Maybe it's the old Navy pilot in me, but I believe you don't cut and run on your friends."

Bush's Eastern, upper-class background and roots—he is the son of a Brahmin Connecticut Senator, was born in an elite Boston suburb, and was educated at Andover and Yale—are as much impediments to his attempts to soften up the conservative wing of the GOP as his past moderate views.

Over the past 45 years, a central conflict within the Republican party has been the warfare between the Eastern-Wall Street-New England wing, which dominated presidential nominations until 1964, and an antiestablishment, intensely conservative wing, which took root in the rest of the country and gained and has held party power since 1964.

Even in his adopted home state of Texas, where Bush bolsters his conservative credentials by citing his selection as a Goldwater delegate in 1964, he has been identified with the establishment wing of the party.

When he ran as a moderate against Reagan in the 1980 Texas primary, according to a Bush operative, it was "Bush who won the establishment areas in Dallas and Houston, while Reagan won the rest. Bush won the silks and the linens, and Reagan won the polyesters and double knits." Reagan won the primary.

Sensitive to this history, Bush's supporters are attempting to undercut its threat to his nomination. Falwell attempted at the recent Conservative Political Action Conference to address this complex issue: "In our experience (political) conversion is usually from the left to the right. . . . I hear conversations about where the vice president was or is or whatever, but I am so glad he is where he is."

# Shifts in the Political Alignments

*Dissent,* Spring 1986

The balance of political and economic power in the nation's capital is in flux. By the end of the 1985 session of the 99th Congress, the House had passed a tax reform bill shifting—over the next five years—$140 billion of the nation's tax burden from individuals to corporations, and eliminating entirely the tax liabilities of six million workers at or below the poverty level. At the same time, Congress enacted the Gramm-Rudman balanced budget amendment sharply reducing federal spending through 1991, a proposal that potentially forces a major withdrawal of the federal government from domestic economic activity, thereby achieving one of the central goals of the conservative movement.

These conflicting developments reflect an increasingly complex set of forces at work in the determination of national policy—complex in comparison with the relatively simple days at the outset of the Reagan administration. In 1981, when Ronald Reagan first took office, the battle lines were visibly drawn, and power was clearly on the side of the political right. Perhaps most important, the business community was at that time united behind tax and spending cuts, providing the strongest base of support in at least a generation for a set of policies redistributing income upwards. This leverage was reinforced by the sudden ascendancy of the political right—the National Conservative Political Action Committee contributed significantly to the 1981 Republican takeover of the Senate; the Christian right was emerging as a national force with the capacity to produce votes; and such issues as the Panama Canal, abortion, and SALT II had produced a steadily rising flow of cash for both the Republican party committees and the conservative organizations capitalizing on the high-tech fund-raising techniques pioneered by such men as Richard Viguerie, Steven Winchell, and Bruce Eberle. The entire right-wing movement was given at least the veneer of intellectual and economic legitimacy by the growth of such conservative think tanks as the Heritage Foundation, the American Enterprise Institute, and the Hoover Institution.

Over the past five years, the conservative movement and the Republican party have continued to demonstrate muscle, and both the Democratic party and the political left have yet to regain the coherence necessary to compete effectively. The political map has, however, changed substantially. What follows is an outline of some of the developments that will, in part, define the political outcomes of the 1986 and 1988 elections, and the shape of national economic policy.

Perhaps the single most important political development in recent years has been the reemergence of class- or income-based commitments to the two major political parties. In a process sharply accelerated by the Reagan administration, the central difference between the Republican and Democratic parties has come to be the income of their supporters, reviving the kind of partisan division characteristic of the 1930s and 1940s. These income-based commitments to the two parties declined sharply in the 1950s and 1960s, only to begin to resurface in the 1970s, probably as a result of a stagnating national economy, and then to return in force in the 1980s, almost assuredly because the policies of the Reagan administration produced a regressive redistribution of tax burdens and spending benefits. In 1956, for example, the nation's poor and lower-middle class—the bottom 30 percent—were only 8 percentage points more Democratic than the upper-middle class, and 43 percentage points more Democratic than the nation's affluent, those falling in the top 10 percent of the income distribution. By 1984, these differences had grown respectively to 31 and 64 percentage points.

The changing structure of partisan allegiance to the two parties has been paralleled by voting patterns. Eisenhower in 1956 received majority support from all income groups; Reagan in 1984, while winning almost the same overall percentage as Eisenhower, decisively lost among the very poor, 32-68, and only slightly less so among the lower-middle class, 43-57, while overwhelmingly carrying the upper-middle class, 64-36, and the most affluent, 75-25.

While the emergence of class- and income-based commitments worked to the advantage of the Democrats in the realignment of the 1930s, in the 1980s it has worked, so far, to the advantage of the Republicans. After 50 years as a minority, the GOP has now gained effective parity with the Democratic party, particularly when voter turnout patterns favoring the affluent are taken into account. The GOP gains in part grow out of the fact that from the postwar period through the mid-1970s, median family income, in real, constant dollars, grew significantly. From 1950 to 1973, the median family income went from $12,341 to $24,663 (in 1981 dollars) and the percentage of families with income in excess of $25,000 (in effect, gaining some degree of economic security) grew from 8 to 42 percent.

Over the past decade, however, growth in the median family income has come to a dead halt. More important, economic pressures on working adults, particularly young adults entering the marketplace during the past 10 years, have sharply intensified. From 1973 to 1984, average gross weekly earnings fell from $198.35 to $173.48 (in 1977 dollars). The cost of financing the mortgage on a median-priced home has gone from 14 to 44 percent of a 37-year-old median wage-earner's income.

All these trends—both the rising median income from 1950 through 1974, and the stagnation since—have worked to the advantage of the GOP. Rising incomes increased the pool of likely Republican voters, particularly as the correlation between Republicanism and high income grew. Stagnation gave credibility to the GOP charge that liberalism had failed, and encouraged a zero-sum view in which government transfers to the poor were increasingly seen as reducing the income of moderate-income workers.

One of the core strengths of the Republican party has been its ability to place the Democratic party in the position of defending a liberal establishment. The GOP has portrayed the Democratic party as dominated by a bureaucratic and special interest elite, more concerned with protecting those dependent on the state than in promoting economic growth.

The debate over tax reform has, however, demonstrated that the GOP is in no way prepared to take its "populist" stands on social issues—opposition to abortion, support of school prayer—into the arena of economic policy. As originally proposed and sent to Congress by President Reagan, the tax legislation billed by the White House staff as the means to convert the working and lower-middle classes to the Republican party was, in fact, another attempt to lessen the tax burden of the richest Americans. When the Democratic House by the end of last year modified the legislation to restore a progressive distribution, the strongest opponents were House Republicans.

Similarly, on the political front, the Republican drive to press for a realignment among voters has not worked as well as party officials had expected. A $500,000 program last summer to persuade 100,000 Democrats to re-register as Republicans in four states fell far short of the goal. More important, the four most prominent converts to the GOP among Democratic politicians, who together provide a sampler of what was once the Roosevelt–Truman coalition, all now appear unlikely to win governorships: Kent Hance, a Texas redneck by his own description; Edward King, the conservative Massachusetts pol of Irish descent; Robert Martinez, the Hispanic mayor of Tampa; and William Lucas, black Wayne County executive in Detroit and surrounding suburbs.

In one respect the situation of the Democratic party parallels that of the GOP. The withdrawal of Senator Edward M. Kennedy (D-Mass.) from the presidential race will lead to intensified competition for the support of the left in the Democratic primaries, just as the absence of Ronald Reagan leaves the constituencies of the Republican right up for grabs in the GOP.

Democrats are, however, under severely conflicting pressures. One significant wing of the elected leadership—the ad hoc Democratic Leadership Council run by Rep. Richard Gephardt of Missouri, Arizona Gov. Bruce Babbitt, former Virginia Gov. Charles Robb, and Georgia Sen. Sam Nunn—is attempting to create a moderate-to-right power center in the presidential nomination process. What this generally translates into is a drive to reduce the leverage of blacks, women, and labor. To further this effort, many Democrats are pressing for a Southern regional primary to be held early in 1988, during the week of March 8. This strategy has the strong potential, however, of accomplishing just what the Democrats are attempting to avoid: if, early in the contest, there are still, say, seven or eight serious contenders for the nomination, the one most likely to win the largest number of delegates in a Southern regional primary is Jesse Jackson.

In addition, the emergence of a strong correlation between income and partisan commitment—i.e., the poorer the prospective voter, the more likely he/she is to be a Democrat—has significant consequences for a Democratic party in ideological turmoil. It means that candidates and power centers seeking to push the party toward the right have a strong tendency to disregard, if not repudiate, the strongest Democratic voters: the poor and the black. The Democratic party loses presidential elections for a number of reasons, but two simple ones are that the party fails to persuade the poor and lower-middle classes to turn out, and it fails to win adequate votes among the middle class. Insofar as the Democratic party splits into centrist and Kennedy–Jesse Jackson wings, the two goals of getting more votes from the poor and the middle class become mutually exclusive, and party prospects decline. This kind of conflict exacerbates the Democrats' substantial losses, starting with the independent candidacy of George C. Wallace in 1968, of conservative working and lower-middle-class white voters, alienated from the party by its liberal social agenda, and by a belief that they are the losers under public policies promoting affirmative action, busing, and, in some cases, abortion and equal rights for women.

In this respect, just as both parties are experiencing similar vacuums created by the absence of Reagan and Kennedy as candidates, 1988 is likely to force both parties to address their most severe fissures. For the Democrats, these conflicts are between the middle class and poor, and between the party's liberal elite and white, working-class social conservatives whose economic and cultural identification with the party has been frayed, if not broken. For the Republicans, these divisions are very roughly between the Eastern establishment wing (currently represented by Bush), the traditional Midwestern wing (Sen. Robert Dole), and the new guard seeking to institutionalize a version of the "Reagan Revolution" (Jack Kemp, who claims to represent both cultural and supply-side conservatism).

The business community, which, when united in 1981, was the single most important force supplying political backing to the Reagan administration's budget and tax cut program, is now severely split. Tax reform legislation has divided American corporations between firms and industries (wholesalers, IBM, high-tech) paying high effective rates of taxation, and companies (Chrysler, steel, heavy manufacturers, defense) paying low effective rates or no federal taxes at all. A similar, but not identical split within corporate America has been created by the debate over junk bonds, and the attempts of both the FEC and Congress to regulate the issuing of these financing mechanisms, often used to provide the capital for takeover bids.

In this split, the Reagan administration has generally sided with the high-tax corporations in the debate on tax reform (these companies would sacrifice the investment tax credit and accelerated depreciation in order to lower the top corporate rate), and with the corporate users of junk bonds (many of whom are part of the GOP's affluent base of support in the Sunbelt). These divisions split House and Senate Republicans according to the special interests of their states and districts. The same divisions are true in the case of Democrats, although the party, with its strongest base in the Northeast and Midwest, is more inclined to support low-tax corporate interests from areas with heavy industry.

The persistence of divisive issues within the corporate community suggests that for the time being there will not be a recurrence of the political glory days of business when, in 1981, a unified lobby, through campaign contributions, grass-roots lobbying, and the financing of think tanks, effectively defined tax policy for both parties.

The New Right, particularly the network of organizations financed by direct-mail specialist Richard Viguerie and those trained by him, has run into hard times. The National Conservative Political Action Committee and the Conservative Caucus have been unable to raise the kind of money they have in the past through direct-mail solicitation, and Viguerie spent much of 1985 struggling to stay afloat. A combination of business practices premised on the notion of a continually growing marketplace and, more important, of complacence growing from the landslide victory of Ronald Reagan, has helped dry up the conservative fund-raising pool of small donors.

Despite financial setbacks, Viguerie, Howard Phillips of the Conservative Caucus, and Paul Weyrich, head of the Free Congress Foundation, have all demonstrated an ability to exercise political muscle, capitalizing on the anxieties of George Bush and Jack Kemp that the conservative movement will somehow repudiate their candidacies.

The religious right in 1984 showed tremendous strength, adding somewhere between two and three million new GOP voters to the rolls. The religious right has not yet, however, shown anywhere near the capacity for permanent political organization of the economic right, which now has such institutions as the Heritage Foundation and the Center for the Study of Public Choice, and which exercises significant power in the Republican party. The Moral Majority has run into hard times, as a low cash flow and negative public perceptions have forced Jerry Falwell to change the organization's name to the more neutral Liberty Federation. The possible entry of Christian Broadcast Network president Marion (Pat) Robertson into the GOP presidential primary contest could split the religious community.

While still conducting what amounts to a rear-guard, defensive action, the "issue-based" moderate left-liberal community has experienced a resurgence of financial support. Such organizations as Common Cause, Planned Parenthood, abortion rights groups, and the anti-Moral Majority group, People for the American Way, have all had banner fund-raising years. Just as the presence of Reagan in the White House has quieted the enthusiasm of conservative donors, it has inspired liberals. Liberal donors have not, however, been inspired to give to the Democratic party, which experienced an extremely sharp decline in direct-mail support after the 1984 election.

The ability of House Democrats to convert Reagan's tax reform proposal into a traditional Democratic bill suggests that there is more political vitality on the economic left than many thought after 1984. Such groups as liberal unions, the Children's Defense Fund, the Center for Budget Priorities, and the labor-financed Citizens for Tax Justice demonstrated an ability to significantly influence the tax debate in a fashion that has not been seen in Washington for over a decade.

In this context, the two key tests of strength for left and right throughout the remainder of this year will be the tax bill, which faces lengthy Senate consideration, and the Gramm-Rudman mandated budget cuts, depending on the outcome of court decisions. Gramm-Rudman has an inherent conservative bias—its function is to reduce the size of the federal government. At the same time, however, it is a wild card with as yet undetermined consequences not only for domestic spending, but also for the defense buildup; for the network of education, mass transit, road, and public works programs benefiting all groups, particularly the middle class; and for the nation's economic stability, contributing to what has become an extremely fluid political and economic situation.

# Slicing the Pie

*The New Republic,* March 3, 1986

The strength of the Republican coalition, and of its current leader Ronald Reagan, has forced a fundamental change in the American debate over equality, placing the issue at the center of political competition between the two parties. The intensified struggle for dominance between the Republican and Democratic parties has become the forum for the continuing attempt to define in policy the public meaning of equality. The growing ideological coherence of the GOP, particularly at the level of presidential nomination politics, and continuing Democratic party strains between left and center have combined with the emergence of sustained partisan parity for the first time in over 50 years to end what had been a largely consensual agreement on egalitarian goals. For the present and immediate future, the battle between proponents of equality of opportunity and equality of result is being forced into the partisan arena.

The debate over equality is the subject of these two books.* Their strength is that both, from different vantage points, set the stage for understanding the nation's politics in the decade before the Reagan revolution began. This strength, however, is also their central weakness; each depends almost entirely on poll data from pre-Reagan years, even before the onset of stagflation under a Democratic administration. Neither book explores the critical changes within the American electorate since 1980, six years marked by a resurgence of class-based politics, as well as by an exacerbation of the conflict between Democratic elites and Democratic voters.

Both books focus on a complex set of attitudes toward equality, examining the opinions of national elites and of the population at large in the 1970s. That decade marked a key turning point in the history of the last half-century—50 years of bitter and often violently polarized struggles over the egalitarian American vision. In *Equality in America,* Sidney Verba and Gary Orren explore the views of leaders of ten groups—business, farm, organized labor, intellectuals, Republicans, Democrats, blacks, feminists, media, and youth. Herbert McClosky and John Zaller's *The American Ethos* is a comparative study of the views of three groups—community "influentials," opinion leaders, and the general public. Although the core of each book is opinion poll data, both also include analytical essays that discuss the fundamental division in America between those who advocate the importance of equality of access (that is, legal prohibitions against discrimination) and those who press for equality of outcome (in income, employment, housing, and so on). In many respects, these differences parallel the disagreement between those who advocate political equality but oppose economic equality, and those who advocate both.

Verba and Orren demonstrate that in America there is a stronger commitment to political equality than in any other developed nation. At the same time, Americans hold views and adopt policies that produce one of the lowest levels of economic equality. Opposition to progressively redistributionist policies is strong not only among corporate leaders and Republicans, but also among Democrats who describe themselves as "very liberal" or "far left." "Even the least egalitarian leaders of Sweden, those of big business, are considerably more egalitarian not only than their business counterparts in the United States but also than the most radical American groups," Verba and Orren write. Very liberal or far-left Democratic and union leaders in the United States each supported income ratios of 12 to 1, or income gaps 250 percent larger than the 4.7 to 1 ratio favored by Swedish big businessmen.

Verba and Orren explore in detail the finding that throughout the 1970s the growing liberalism of Democratic leaders increasingly alienated the party from its supporters, who were more conservative. Still, when issues of equality are

---

*Sidney Verba and Gary R. Orren, *Equality in America: The View from the Top* (Cambridge, Mass.: Harvard University Press, 1986) and Herbert McClosky and John Zaller, *The American Ethos: Public Attitudes Toward Democracy* (Cambridge, Mass.: Harvard University Press, 1986).

broken down into subcategories of economic, gender, and racial equality, a very different picture emerges. Democratic leaders and Democratic voters were equally firm in their support for New Deal social welfare issues, including a strong commitment to government intervention in the economy. By contrast, on race and gender equality issues (quotas, the ERA), a liberal Democratic leadership was severely split from its supporters. On those same issues, Republican leaders were closer to the general electorate than their Democratic counterparts. Further analysis of the views not just of party leaders but of Democratic-leaning elites (blacks, feminists, labor leaders) and Republican elites (businessmen and farmers) points to some of the reasons the Democratic party has recently had such difficulty in defining the national debate, in contrast to the GOP.

On six different measures of attitudes toward equality—gender, income redistribution, quotas, race, the causes of inequality, and social and economic programs enacted during the New Deal—Republican party and business leaders hold almost identically conservative views. Farm leaders were also consistently conservative in their views, although not in perfect harmony with GOP and business leaders. (The survey was taken at a time when the emergence of an ideologically conservative elite was not yet taken seriously; thus the data does not include the views of right-wing leaders, ideological or Christian. If the votes of many of the New Right members of Congress on budget and tax issues are any reflection, however, there probably is little disparity between this group and current GOP and corporate leaders.)

In contrast, Democratic elites are spread out from left to center of the ideological map on questions of economic, racial, and gender equality. The most divisive issue is quotas, with blacks far to the left, feminist leaders just slightly less so, Democratic leaders closer to the center, and labor leaders just to the right of center. And where Democrats ten years ago rallied behind New Deal issues, they may no longer do so; the survey was taken in 1976, before the emergence of double-digit inflation undermined a common willingness among party members to place stronger emphasis on jobs than on controlling prices.


*The American Ethos* approaches many of the same issues, but from a different angle. McClosky and Zaller attempt to explore the subtleties of ideological differences between liberals and conservatives, and perhaps more important, between those holding strong, pro-capitalist views and those firmly committed to democratic principles. They argue that a central theme of the period running roughly from the rapid industrialization before the turn of the century to the 1950s and 1960s was the growing divergence between the values of capitalism and those of democracy. From the nation's founding through the post-Civil War period, capitalism and

free enterprise provided the foundations for a democratic and largely egalitarian social order. Economic competition, for example, implied almost literally the elimination of special privileges . . . the people who took strong stands in favor of free competition and unfettered enterprise were, by and large, the same people who championed popular sovereignty, equality of rights, and individual freedom.

The emergence of large corporations and the growing concentration of wealth at the turn of the century functioned to erode the shared goals of capitalism and democracy:

The traditional faith in minimal government, originally associated with the desire to prevent the powerful from subjugating the weak, was now invoked to strengthen the economic power of the wealthy few. Thus capitalism and democracy, once allies against the inequities of the old European order, increasingly diverged.

This split became a central theme in American politics from Bryan to Teddy Roosevelt to Truman, as antagonism toward trusts and corporate America became a mobilizing tool.

Both of these books, then, describe the last moment of Democratic party hegemony, but neither examines in any detail contemporary alterations of public attitudes and of partisan allegiance, and the massive infusion of money from conservative foundations and corporations to move the political and intellectual climate to the right. Perhaps more important, however, is the substantial effort by Ronald Reagan, by much of the conservative movement, and by a substantial wing of the Republican party to alter what we may call the American ethic. If there is a central theme to the work of the current administration, it is an attempt to restore the unity between capitalism and democracy, to revive corporate endeavor as an emancipating force, and to portray government as an adversary to widespread productive activity. Announcing his 1985 tax-reform bill, Reagan declared:

My goal is an America bursting with opportunity, an America that celebrates freedom every day. . . . For starters, lowering personal tax rates will give a hefty boost to the nearly 15 million small businesses which are individual proprietorships or partnerships. To further promote business formation, we propose to reduce the maximum corporate rate—now 46 percent—to 33 percent.

Reagan's success in altering the basic terms of the national debate on issues of equality cannot be overemphasized. It is partly the product of major economic and demographic changes influencing the nation's politics. In the 1960s Americans crossed a political divide, and the Democratic party lost its ability to piece together a coalition of the deprived and those who remembered deprivation. Median family income in the 20 years from 1950 to 1970 nearly doubled in constant, 1981 dollars, from $12,539 to $23,111, while the size of families was declining. More important, not only did the poverty rate fall from 22.2 percent in 1960 to 12.6 percent in 1970, but the percentage of families with incomes above $25,000 (in constant, 1980 dollars) grew geometrically, from just 8 percent in 1952 to 19 percent in 1960 and 38 percent in 1970.

At the same time, whites began to leave the Democratic party when its national agenda shifted toward blacks. In the South, in particular, the Republican revolution began as an insurgency of affluent whites; they provided, in the early 1960s, the volunteers, the structure, the financial resources, and the initial voting strength for the nascent GOP. Southern Republican party allegiance then slowly seeped downward, first to the middle class and now to the white working class.

Partisan political changes reflecting these demographic shifts were distorted by Watergate, which propped up a Democratic party in serious trouble, postponing the need to address the intensifying problem of a party elite increasingly distant from its constituents. Watergate glorified a Democratic reform vanguard that had little relationship to major voting blocks. For the Republican party, the scandal merely postponed the achievement of competitive status.

In other words, the decade that belonged to the GOP, the 1970s, was ceded to the Democrats because of a political fluke that disrupted the relationship between economic demographics and partisan politics. The Democratic party gained ascendancy at a time when the sustained growth of the middle and upper-middle classes suggested, if not a realignment, then a period of Republican strength, as the partisan commitment of the electorate adjusted to relative affluence and to the end of the New Deal coalition. The Watergate-induced distortion of the political process was a political disaster for the Democratic party—and for proponents of government intervention in general—when 1974 to 1981 unfolded as a period of high-order economic stagnation.

The segment of the Republican party that best survived the devastation of Watergate was the intensely conservative wing, nourished by its own ideological commitment and by the fact that the ability of conservatives to raise money grew with the election of strong Democratic congressional majorities in 1974 and 1976, and with the election of Jimmy Carter in 1976. Finally the election of 1980 produced a majority Republican electorate that was, in many respects, a top-heavy inversion of the Roosevelt majority. By overwhelming margins, Ronald Reagan's strongest support was among the very rich, steadily declining as one moved down the income ladder. In this same period, income became an increasingly accurate predictor of partisan allegiance—better than region, education, and social status.

The immediate legislative aftermath of the 1980 election—the enactment of the 1981 Gramm-Latta budget cuts and the $750 billion tax reduction—reflected the exercise of power by an elective majority dominated by the rich. It marked an alliance between an affluent elite and an intellectually vigorous conservative movement with an anti-egalitarian agenda—two wings of a new establishment often linked by grants from the former to the latter. In the process, the electorate itself has become increasingly polarized by income. In the 1950s and 1960s, there was relatively little correlation between income and partisan allegiance, except among those at the very top—the richest ten percent, who were overwhelmingly Republican. The 1970s and the first half of the 1980s have produced, however, a restoration of Depression-era, income-based voting and partisan commitment, with one major difference: this time it is the Republicans who have demonstrated an ability to win decisive victories.

Reagan's 1984 majority was heavily skewed by income class, according to data compiled by Martin P. Wattenberg of the University of California. Like Eisenhower, Reagan got 75 percent of the vote of the richest 10 percent, but among the bottom 10 percent, who gave Ike 59 percent of their votes, Reagan received only 32 percent. Among the working and lower-middle class, Reagan's 43 percent was 13 points behind Ike's 56 percent; among the upper-middle class, however, Reagan ran seven points ahead of Ike, 64 to 57. The same pattern follows for partisan allegiance. The poor and lower-middle class, who were only 7 points more Democratic than the upper-middle class in 1956, by 1984 had become 31 points more Democratic.

Despite Reagan's overwhelming reelection in 1984, the persistent absence of a firm political realignment makes Republican attempts to fashion a permanent majority extremely difficult. In the summer of 1985 the administration proposed a "populist" tax-reform bill in a calculated effort to win support among the middle and lower-middle classes—in effect, to cement a realignment. As originally sponsored by Reagan, however, the legislation granted disproportionate benefits to the wealthy, rewarding the most loyal Republican voters, but defying populist tradition. In subsequent House consideration, it was Democratic members of the House Ways and Means Committee who gave the legislation a populist edge, redirecting tax cuts toward the poor and middle class, while raising additional taxes from corporations and reducing the benefits for the most affluent. On final House passage, Republican members offered the strongest opposition, reflecting the contradictions between populist political goals and the strength of business and affluent constituencies within the GOP electorate.

For the Republican party, the central roles played by the affluent and by the ideological and Christian right have proved to be both an asset and a liability. The intense concentration of Republican allegiance among the wealthiest voters has provided an enormous source of campaign contributions, a source generally in ideological harmony with the economic conservatism of the party. At the same time, Republican economic elitism and the party's history of demonstrated indifference to egalitarian undertakings continue to be a political weakness that, with candidates less personable than Reagan, can easily, in a country where the median family income has stagnated for the past decade at $24,500, become grounds for defeat. (By contrast, the Democratic party has been forced to depend heavily on special-interest large contributors, including developers, lobbyists, and PAC directors.)

The ideological and Christian right have been key to Republican party victories. The ideological right has been a source of sustained moral commitment, not only helping to carry the party through the difficult years of the mid-1970s, but also providing a small cadre of workers to push conservative candidates to victory. Charles Black, a strategist for the Reagan–Bush Committee, the RNC, and for such Senate candidates as Jesse Helms and Phil Gramm, was a founder of the National Conservative Political Action Committee. Such Republican fund-raisers as Wyatt Stewart, of the Republican Congressional Committee, Ann Stone, a GOP consultant, and direct-mail specialist Stephen H. Winchell all learned their trades as executives of the Viguerie Company.

Similarly, the Christian right in 1980 and 1984 provided the GOP with its single most important source of votes. The shift of white fundamentalists to the GOP from 1976 to 1984 was twice as large as that of the young between 18 and 24. Equally important, the realignment of conservative white Protestants was critical to at least half of the 14 Republican House seat gains in 1984 and to Jesse Helms's reelection in North Carolina.

Still, the Christian and ideological right have severely constricted the ability of Republicans, particularly of ambitious Republicans, to adopt flexible positions on a number of issues—the most salient among them being abortion and a host of family and church-state issues. And the restrictive forces of the religious and ideological right have hampered the members of such groups as the Conservative Opportunity Society, led by Representatives Vin Webber, Newt Gingrich, and Jack Kemp, in moving to the left on the more obviously egalitarian question of South Africa.

On a broader scale, key leaders of the New Right and the Religious Right— Richard Viguerie, Howard Phillips, Marion G. (Pat) Robertson, Jerry Falwell— have supported such concepts as a ten percent flat tax, a highly regressive proposal, and have been ardent proponents of the sustained goal of both the Reagan administration and the business community of sharply reducing the top tax rate, which would lessen the progressivity of the tax system. The commitment of many in the leadership of the Christian right to economic policies benefiting the affluent may, in the long run, undermine the ability of this leadership to produce GOP votes among working- and lower-middle-class constituents. If these voters perceive their own economic interests subordinated to the interests of the rich, their newfound allegiance to the Republican party is going to be tested.

Within the Republican party, pressure to choose between competing distributional strategies will depend in part on the solidity and permanence of the surge of GOP partisan allegiance during 1984. If this commitment extends beyond Reagan, and if it proves reliable for a much less charismatic candidate along the lines of Vice President George Bush, the Republican party will not need to expand its base significantly into the lower-middle class. If GOP gains prove ephemeral, however, then the Republican party will be under intense pressure to decrease the share of government benefits aimed at the rich, particularly in its tax policies, and to address in a more overtly political context issues of both economic and social equality.

The adoption of an egalitarian political strategy would not only require the GOP to challenge strong constituencies within the party, but would be impossible to initiate under the provisions of the Gramm-Rudman balanced-budget amendment. Gramm-Rudman, if ruled constitutional, has the potential to force the Republican party to become the party of austerity, returning to its traditional role of fiscal conservatism, abandoning the newfound advocacy of largess and growth through supply-side economics that has given the GOP its current political vitality.

For the immediate future, however, the national debate over equality is very likely to take a new turn in which the partisan contest for majority status between the two political parties will play the key role. The growing movement toward middle-class electoral competition has already produced a style of politics capitalizing not only on the pursuit of affluence and individual prosperity, but also on resentment and distrust. "In the 1980 campaign, we were able to make the establishment, insofar as it is bad, the government. In other words, big government was the enemy, not big business," Lee Atwater, deputy campaign manager of the Reagan–Bush '84 Committee, said. "If the people think the problem is that taxes are too high, and government interferes too much, then we are doing our job. But, if they get to the point where they say that the real problem is that rich people aren't paying taxes . . . then the Democrats are going to be in good shape. Traditionally, the Republican party has been elitist, but one of the things that has happened is that the ;Democratic party has become a party of elites. . . . Now you have for the first time two establishments."

With each party carrying the baggage of a distrusted establishment, campaigning will increasingly become a struggle to define the agenda in ways that emphasize the points of dissonance between opposition-party elites and the general electorate. For the Republican party, this has become a relatively easy task. The GOP has two advantages: the first is that key Democratic constituencies—blacks, women, and organized labor—are seen by significant portions of the electorate, including each other, as elite-dominated special-interest groups, forcing Democratic candidates on the defensive. More important, Republican candidates are far better able than Democrats to capitalize on a central target of middle-class resentment: high tax burdens and government spending. Attacks on taxes and spending coincide with the interests of the strongest Republican constituency, the affluent.

For the Democrats, there are strong indications that the leadership of the Democratic party—the nation's liberal elite—is dangerously out of touch with its own constituency, which prevents the party's strategists and elected officials from transforming the political debate in such a way as to focus on the Republican party's central liability: its ties to the rich and to business.

This conflict within the party is reflected in a series of survey questions reported on in *The American Ethos* that effectively tested the depth of populist perceptions—how powerful is wealth and business?—among segments of the general public and among opinion leaders. Consistently, the general public was more likely than opinion leaders, including liberal elites, to see corporations and the rich as excessively powerful. The general public holds significantly more populist positions on such statements as: "Corporations and people with money really run the country," "When it comes to taxes, corporations and wealthy people don't pay their fair share," and "Working people in the country do not get a fair share of what they produce."

As the partisan struggle increasingly tackles the issue of equality in public policy, Democratic leaders enter into the fray ill-equipped to initiate a populist attack on the Republican establishment. These leaders are inhibited not only by their own allegiance to an elite liberal establishment, but by the moderation of their own worldview at a time when politics requires a willingness to go after the opposition's jugular vein.

# Republican America

*The New York Review of Books*, April 24, 1986

In the 1984 presidential election, the Republican party played its trump card— the power to combine, throughout the country, the votes of the well-to-do with solid blocks of middle-class and working-class whites. For the first time in fifty-four years, this alliance extended beyond a presidential voting majority and produced a sustained surge in the numbers of voters who identified themselves as favoring the GOP, ending two generations of Democratic domination of the electorate. The current ascendancy of the Republican party has become the vehicle for a double-edged revolution in American politics: a shift in the balance of national power from the Northeast to the South and West, and a shift in strength from a diverse collection of voters who knew or remembered depriva-tion—the remnants of the New Deal coalition—to an alliance of voters domi-nated by the nation's economic elite. The United States is in the midst of a political upheaval as significant as those of the 1890s and the 1930s.

During the past ten years, the two major political parties have become more important than at any other time since the New Deal. They are adapting new technologies to transform politics—through fund-raising, direct mail, computer-ized registration drives, public opinion surveys, and television. Mastery of the political process at the technical level has led in turn to the preeminence of the political parties in deciding which issues get national attention and in determin-ing how ideological and economic interests and classes are represented in all branches of government.

Xandra Kayden, a Democrat and a member of the Campaign Finance Study Group at Harvard's Institute of Politics, and Eddie Mahe, Jr., former deputy chairman of the Republican National Committee, have written a pro-vocative book documenting the resurgence of American political parties.* Kay-

---

*Xandra Kayden and Eddie Mahe, Jr., *The Party Goes On: The Persistence of the Two-Party System in the United States* (New York: Basic Books, 1986).

den and Mahe challenge a generation of academics and journalists who have argued that the Democratic and Republican parties are no longer equipped to perform such basic functions as building coalitions, raising funds, or mobilizing voters, and that the parties have lost the allegiance of an increasingly independent electorate. Such arguments were put forth fourteen years ago by David Broder in *The Party's Over* (1972) and more recently in Martin P. Wattenberg's *The Decline of American Political Parties* (1984), Bryon E. Shafer's *The Quiet Revolution* (1983), and Nelson W. Polsby's *The Consequences of Party Reform* (1983).

Concentrating almost entirely on the mechanics of politics, such as money raising and campaigning, Kayden and Mahe demonstrate that the Republican party has become during the past twelve years a powerful, centralized, and highly disciplined national force, raising more money than any other political group or interest in the country. As city, county, and state political machines have declined, the Washington-based Republican National Committee has turned itself into a major electoral power, providing cash, services, and advice for campaigns throughout the country. Mahe and Kayden undermine the significance of their own work, however, when they argue that Democrats are rapidly catching up in power and sophistication with their Republican competitors, and that the strengthening of the political parties is a bipartisan phenomenon. Kayden and Mahe contend that "a two-party system has always balanced itself out. If the organization is strong in one party, it will be strong in the other." This conclusion, as I shall argue, misrepresents the most significant aspects of partisan political change taking place in the country today.

Republican strategists in recent years have been more sophisticated than Democratic strategists in recognizing how the political landscape has been transformed. This has been demonstrated repeatedly in campaign after campaign and in campaign memo after campaign memo. Consider, for example a memo written in 1983 by Lee Atwater, then deputy campaign manager of the Reagan–Bush committee and now chairman of George Bush's political action committee. "We have," he wrote,

as the three main voting groups in Southern politics country clubbers, populists and blacks. The first group—the former Bourbon Democrats who controlled the South by excluding [white populists and blacks]—are today reliably Republican. The third group—blacks—are reliably Democratic. In no state does either group have the numbers to assure a statewide victory. Both groups must contend for the votes of the second group—the populists. Actually, the populists are uneasy about alliances with either group. Their resentment of the wealth and status of the country clubbers offsets their historic antipathy for blacks. The class struggle in the South continues, with the populists serving as the trump card in the game of politics.*

The South has been the driving force in the growing polarization of American politics according to income and race, although the pattern is national in

---

*Lee Atwater, memo to the Reagan–Bush Campaign Committee, *The South in 1984* (April 1983).

scope. The changing geographic and economic contours of the two political parties can be seen in the following tables.

## I · SOCIAL GROUP PROFILES OF THE
## PARTY COALITIONS, 1952–1984*

*Democratic party identifiers*
*(percentage of the Democratic party from each group)*

|  | 1952–60 | 1962–72 | 1976 | 1980 | 1984 |
|---|---|---|---|---|---|
| Northern WASPs | 19 | 20 | 17 | 17 | 19 |
| Catholics | 13 | 16 | 19 | 16 | 23 |
| White Northern union members | 22 | 19 | 18 | 18 | 13 |
| White South | 31 | 25 | 23 | 23 | 20 |
| Jews | 5 | 3 | 4 | 6 | 5 |
| Blacks | 10 | 16 | 18 | 21 | 20 |
| Total | 100% | 100% | 100% | 100% | 100% |

*Republican party identifiers*
*(percentage of the Republican party from each group)*

|  | 1952–60 | 1962–72 | 1976 | 1980 | 1984 |
|---|---|---|---|---|---|
| Northern WASPs | 56 | 51 | 51 | 43 | 34 |
| Catholics | 10 | 10 | 14 | 16 | 16 |
| White Northern union members | 18 | 13 | 11 | 14 | 10 |
| White South | 11 | 23 | 21 | 24 | 34 |
| Jews | 1 | 1 | 1 | — | 2 |
| Blacks | 5 | 2 | 2 | 3 | 2 |
| Total | 100% | 100% | 100% | 100% | 100% |

*Both charts replicate data supplied by Market Opinion Research, Detroit, Michigan. (Because of rounding of figures, some columns do not add up to 100 percent.)

## II · GROWING PARTY ALLEGIANCE BY INCOME*

*The figures show the percentage advantage (+) or disadvantage (−) of the*
*Democratic party among different income groups in 1956 and 1984*

|  | 1956 | 1984 |
|---|---|---|
| The Poor (bottom 10%) | +18 | +36 |
| Lower Middle Class (11%–30%) | +22 | +29 |
| Middle Class (31%–60%) | +17 | +6 |
| Upper Middle Class (61%–90%) | +13 | 0 |
| The Affluent (91%–100%) | −22 | −33 |

*From Martin P. Wattenberg, "The Hollow Realignment: Partisan Change in a Candidate-centered Era," paper delivered at the 1985 annual meeting of the American Political Science Association, based on data from National Election Studies surveys in 1956 and 1984.

The first—based on data compiled by Market Opinion Research, the Republican polling firm of Robert Teeter—traces the demographic characteristics of those who identify themselves as pro-Democrat and those who identify themselves as pro-Republican. The second, based on data compiled in 1985 by Martin P. Wattenberg of the University of California at Irvine, shows how, over the past thirty years, partisan identification within the two parties has increasingly become determined by income. Wattenberg's table shows that during the last thirty years the Republican party has become even more decisively the party of those whose income is above the national median, and the Democratic party has similarly become even more strongly the party of those whose income is below it.

These tables suggest that the Republican party has been moving in two seemingly contradictory directions. Geographically and ethnically, the party has become more diverse. Northern white Anglo-Saxons, an absolute majority of the GOP through 1976, now make up just one-third of the party. The dominance of northern WASPs has been eclipsed by the surge of identification with the Republican party among white southerners. Their share of the GOP has more than tripled over the past thirty years. At the same time, the Republican party has become almost entirely white. The Democrats, by contrast, have gained from blacks what they have lost from white southerners. For both parties the power of the trade union vote has declined as the proportion of union members among American workers has been cut roughly by half between the 1950s and the present.

However, as the GOP becomes more diverse, it has also become, by the measure of personal income, more exclusive. In 1956, there was very little difference in Republican strength among different income groups, except for the most prosperous, among whom the GOP had a clear majority. By 1984, after four years of the Reagan administration, the two parties had split to a much greater extent along economic lines reminiscent of the national division during the Depression. Robert Teeter of Market Opinion Research plausibly concludes that "income has become the clearest determinant of party allegiance."

One of the main forces behind the economic division between the two parties is race. The 1964 contest between Lyndon Johnson and Barry Goldwater eliminated the remnants of black support for the Republican party of Abraham Lincoln; the Voting Rights Act of 1965 enfranchised millions of blacks who were pro-Democrat, most of them poor. At the same time, the large surge in southern white support for the Republican party that began during the Goldwater campaign was sustained with the active help of the region's economic elites. The southern Republican party is, in many respects, a vehicle for the assertion of power by relatively prosperous whites. The party's highest margins over the Democrats were registered in such well-to-do communities as Houston's River Oaks, the Lexington County suburbs of Columbia, South Carolina, and Mississippi's coastal strip running from Gulfport to Pascagoula.

The racial division between the parties has been compounded by the large-scale conversion to the Republican party of white, evangelical, and born-again Christians between 1976 and 1984. Among such fundamentalists there has been

a nearly complete realignment. In 1976 white born-again Christians voted Democratic by a majority of 56 to 44 percent; in 1984 they voted Republican by a
majority of 81 to 19 percent. This shift has meant the addition of eight million
white voters to the Republican constituency. In surveys of the southern Baptist
clergy in 1981 and 1984 James L. Guth of Furman University found that during
this period the religious leaders went from being 41 percent Democratic, 29
percent Republican, and 30 percent independent, to being 66 percent Republican, 26 percent Democratic, and 8 percent independent.*

The growing divisions between the two parties based on income and race
have major repercussions both for national policy and for control over the machinery of electoral politics. During the two previous, post-World War II Republican administrations—Eisenhower's between 1953 and 1960, and Nixon's and
Ford's between 1969 and 1976—the Democrats at no time lost their decisive
advantage—ranging from 14 to 30 percent—in voter identification. Unlike the
Reagan presidency, the presidencies of Eisenhower, Nixon, and Ford did not
produce a sharp turn toward conservative economic and social policy. The presence of a strong majority of the electorate that identified itself as Democratic
acted as a brake on economic initiatives from the right. A majority of voters
remained committed to the principles, if not to the candidates, of a Democratic
party supporting the intervention of government on behalf of those in need and
out of work.

This liberal brake on conservative officeholders began to weaken between
1978 and 1980, when a 23-point Democratic partisan advantage in voter identification (53–30) fell to 13 points (53-40). By 1984, the restraint that the
relatively liberal tendency of the Democratic majority was able to exercise had,
for all purposes, disappeared, as the GOP pulled to within 2 points of the
Democratic party. Such virtual parity masked what was in fact a slight Republican advantage because of the higher rates of turnout among upper-income voters.
The electorate has now produced what amounts to a conservative brake on
legislative policy. The current parity of the GOP has created a roadblock, ob-
structing liberal Democratic initiatives during the 1980s.

The achievement of Republican parity—a parity based on a new, right-of-
center coalition sharply tilted toward the affluent—first provided the Reagan
administration with the public support essential for its successful promotion of
a national conservative program. In the long run, the development of a numeri-
cally strong Republican party means that within the electorate there is now a
body of voters who can stop public policies from being steered in a liberal
direction, just as an earlier, more liberal coalition of voters could stop public policy
from being steered in a conservative direction. For a Democratic party seeking

---

*James L. Guth, "Political Converts: Partisan Realignment Among Southern Baptist Ministers," in
*Election Politics* (Winter 1985–86), published by the Institute for Government and Politics, Washington, DC.

to develop legislative and political strategy, the presence of an entrenched conservative force within the electorate severely inhibits the scope of available choices, restricting, if not eliminating, many liberal policies. Excluded from current national debate are spending programs that would progressively redistribute income, including national health insurance, a guaranteed annual income, sustained federal financing for low-cost housing, and federal legislation to ensure bargaining rights for unions and to create jobs for the unemployed.

At the same time, the sharp economic division between the two parties has been a critical factor in the revival of the GOP's traditional party functions: providing cash, tactical assistance, research, manpower, and technical expertise to its candidates. Campaign reforms enacted during and after Watergate revolutionized methods of election finance, eliminating contributors of $100,000 or more, replacing them with three different sources of cash: major donors willing to give between $500 and $10,000; a large "universe," or potential group, of small donors willing to respond to direct-mail appeals; and political action committees (PACs).

Of these three sources, PACs are the least important to the financing of the two parties, because PACs make their donations directly to candidates, not to the Republican and Democratic national committees. Rich donors who make large contributions are still significant sources of cash, but the most important source for the political parties is now direct mail, which, when shrewdly planned, provides a sustained, renewable base of financial support. And in raising funds by direct mail and from major contributors, the Republican party enters the competition for dollars with an enormous advantage: campaign contributors are overwhelmingly upper-middle class or rich, the very constituencies that provide the highest margin of GOP voting support. The Democrats, in contrast, with their far poorer constituency, have been stuck with only two major sources of direct-mail support: well-to-do liberals from such sophisticated enclaves as Manhattan; Madison, Wisconsin; Montgomery County, Maryland; Cambridge, Massachusetts; and Beverly Hills; and the relatively well-off elderly, who are prompted to contribute by Republican threats to Social Security.

For support from major donors, Democrats have been far more dependent than the GOP on contributors who are seeking special-interest advantages. Prominent among these are real estate developers benefiting from urban spending programs, contractors still tied to Democratic-controlled state and city governments, and an army of corporate and trade association lobbyists—including many who were once either Democratic members of Congress or members of their staffs. The GOP, by contrast, has a far broader base of financial support from those who are in ideological agreement with the Republican party's promises to lower taxes for the well-to-do and cut domestic spending for the poor.

The result has been a huge rightward flow of money during the twelve years following the enactment of the 1974 campaign reforms—money that has financed the explosive growth of a powerful Republican party organization. So far as the traditional functions of a political party are concerned, the Republican

National Committee and its two sister organizations, the national Republican congressional and senatorial campaign committees, have emerged as formidable high-tech political machines. Replacing the functions of earlier party bosses with expanding party bureaucracies, the GOP organizations now raise $125 million annually. They conduct polls regularly in every state to anticipate the weaknesses and strengths of enemies and allies. They pull together statistics on census trends, voting behavior, and political attitudes in computer data banks. They provide a source of lucrative off-year consulting contracts for the party's out-of-work functionaries. They conduct carefully organized voter registration drives calculated to increase the number of Republicans. They finance campaigns not just to promote candidates, but to promote allegiance to the GOP itself.

Mastery of these essentially mechanical techniques has been central to the growth of a Republican party sharing a remarkably cohesive economic vision. More than any other major party in this century, the Republican party has formed, or is coming close to forming, a conscious ideology. While the GOP has become geographically and ethnically more diverse, its relative homogeneity of income, race, and class has produced a political party equipped to reward its most loyal constituents—the well-to-do—through favorable tax and regulatory policies, and to penalize its strongest adversaries, the poor, blacks, and organized labor, through domestic spending reductions, the judicial selection process, and weak or non-enforcement of civil rights initiatives, workplace safety regulations, and collective bargaining protections.

Both the rewards and penalties have been substantial ones. The recession of 1981–1982 and the sustained economic recovery since then, combined with the enactment of regressive tax and spending legislation, have produced in the Reagan years a strikingly partisan pattern in the distribution of income and government benefits. According to the Bureau of the Census, the median income of those in the bottom 40 percent—a largely Democratic constituency—has fallen by $477, from $12,966 to $12,489, between 1980 and 1984, in constant 1984 dollars, while the income of those in the top 10 percent—a largely Republican constituency—has risen by $5,085, from $68,145 in 1980, to $73,230 in 1984. Similarly, the Congressional Budget Office has found that the net effect of spending and tax cuts has resulted in a loss of $1,100 between 1983 and 1985 for those making less than $10,000 a year, while those making more than $80,000 annually have gained $24,260 as a result of government policy.*

The most recent addition to the Republican coalition—white, born-again Christians—has not yet been rewarded with legislative enactment of the bills and constitutional changes they seek; but conservative policies and programs have been honored in the selection of judges to the federal bench, in numerous appointments to executive positions, and in the virtually countless legal and

---

*See Bureau of the Census, *Money, Income and Poverty Status of Families and Persons in the United States: 1984* (August 1985), and Congressional Budget Office, Staff Memorandum: "The Combined Effects of Major Changes in Federal Taxes and Spending Programs Since 1981" (April 1984).

administrative decisions emanating from those appointments.

Republicans have, in effect, found that they can perform the traditional functions of a political party—rewarding the loyal and penalizing the opposition—not only through tax and spending policies but also through broad enforcement of administrative policy in all branches of government. The Democratic party, in contrast, has found that much of its own elite—composed of an affluent base of liberal donors, party activists, and a significant portion of its elected leadership—is increasingly distant from the party's largest constituencies, those who are at or below the median income. For the GOP, there is little or no conflict between the interest of its party elite and the party's most consistent voters on issues of tax and spending policy. For Democrats, the situation is far more ambiguous, particularly in the case of tax policy. While a substantial number of low-income Democratic constituents have seen their tax burdens increase under the Reagan administration, and many others at the lower end of the middle class have received proportionately the smallest tax reductions, the generally upper-middle-class elite that leads the party, works for it, and contributes to it, has largely benefitted from these same Republican policies.

The result is that, for the moment, competing with the Republican party will, for the Democrats, mainly take the form of a holding action; some Democrats hope to invade Republican constituencies by emphasizing such issues as environmental protection and the improvement of the "quality of life" aimed at attracting young, upwardly mobile professionals. For Republicans, the problems of partisan competition are more subtle, growing out of success. Victory has drained two major sources of energy from the Republican party. The first of these sources was the popular revolt against high tax burdens, leading to the campaigns that resulted in the enactment of such tax-cutting initiatives as Proposition 13 in California and Proposition 2½ in Massachusetts. With the decline in the rate of inflation and the recent trend toward reducing federal, state, and local taxes, public anger over taxation, which translated quickly into a deep hostility toward government, has significantly quieted.

Richard Wirthlin, the President's pollster and head of Decision Making Information, has used a series of surveys to document a sharp decline in antigovernment feelings during the past five years. While public suspicion of government remains high, Wirthlin found that the percentage of people agreeing with such statements as "Government is run by a few big interests" and "Government cannot be trusted to be right" fell by 13 to 14 percentage points between 1978 and 1986, dropping from an average of 75 percent of respondents to 61 percent. A real test of the ability of the Republican party to hold on to its current parity with the Democratic party will be its ability to transform itself from an antigovernment party into a party controlling government, when government is no longer seen as a tax-guzzling adversary.

The second source of Republican energy is more subtle: the resentment of party officials in the South, West, and Midwest toward the eastern, Wall Street wing of the GOP that just twenty-five years ago controlled the party. This internal party battle, which sustained Reagan's bids for the presidency from 1968 to victory in 1980, has in effect been won with the defeat of the Wall Street and Rockefeller factions of the GOP. It is not clear at all whether the growing momentum behind the 1988 presidential candidacy of George Bush will provoke a revival of this bitter division within the GOP. The question raised by party strategists is whether Bush, educated at Andover and Yale, the son of a Wall Street investment banker and Connecticut senator, can capitalize on his reloca- tion in the 1950s to a job in the Texas oil business, on his long political career in the burgeoning Republican party of the Sunbelt, and on his eight years as Reagan's vice president in order to mend the split that continues within the party. In some ways Bush symbolizes the internal conflict within the Republican party. If he is nominated, he will be defying the successful postwar Republican tradi- tion—reflected in the family origins of Eisenhower, Nixon, and Reagan—of selecting as presidential candidates men born to hardship, acutely aware of the resentments, hopes, and concerns for status of the lower-middle class.

A Bush candidacy would test the ability of the GOP to continue to carry out its most successful strategy—combining the votes of both middle-class and work- ing-class whites in a durable political realignment and thus ending fifty years of minority status. A sense of the political power of that realignment is what is missing in Kayden's and Mahe's account of the renewed importance of both parties. It is not so much that they overestimate the ways in which the Demo- cratic party has become more modern in its techniques, as that they fail to appreciate the full extent of the GOP's achievement—not only in the flexibility and effectiveness of the Republican party apparatus but in its ability to exploit the economic, demographic, and cultural trends that underpin the success of the party as a whole.

Even if the Democratic party were to capture the presidency, the Senate, or both, in the two upcoming elections, Democrats will continue to be severely constrained in any attempt to turn public policy back to the advantage of those whose incomes are below the national median. They will be blocked in no small measure by the strength of the Republican party itself in transforming both the balance of political power in America and the climate of public opinion.

# Money Paves Way for GOP
## *Fund-Raising Woes Shifting to Democrats*

*The Washington Post*, May 22, 1986

BATON ROUGE, La.—A quiet realignment is taking place in this state among the movers and shakers who not only write the checks but pull the corporate and political strings.

The Louisiana monied elite is defying a 6-to-1 Democratic voter registration edge over Republicans, and pouring cash like bourbon at Mardi Gras into the campaign of W. Henson Moore, the Republican candidate for Senate.

Moore has raised a total campaign war chest of $2.9 million and is sitting on a cash balance of $1.6 million going into the last five months of the campaign. Here in Louisiana, as in other parts of the South, money is no longer a problem for viable GOP candidates; instead, there are signs that for Democrats, fundraising may get tougher and tougher.

Since the 1964 nomination of Sen. Barry Goldwater (R-Ariz.), the South has been a gold mine of contributions for Republican presidential candidates, but the money mostly flowed in the other partisan direction, to the Democrats, below that level. Now, the pattern is beginning to change. GOP statewide candidates and local GOP party structures are beginning to tap into the money lines.

Southern campaign money, however, is just one part of the mix of politics, class and income in the region. The growing emergence of a competitive Republican party has changed the economic face of politics in the South in many ways:

• Well-to-do conservatives, including Democrats who controlled politics in many sections of the South, have moved in droves into the Republican party.

• As primarily poor blacks, enfranchised in the 1960s, have moved into the Democratic party, the division between the Republican and Democratic parties has become increasingly a division based on both race and income. The only substantial blocs of white voters to retain strong Democratic loyalties in the region are the poor and near-poor.

• While the southern Republican party has become the home of the elite, the Democratic party in most states has been unable to maintain its role as the populist voice of the South, representing the "have-nots" in the struggle against the "haves." Instead, in this poorest region of the country, conflicts over race and social issues have fractured potential populist alliances between poor and middle-class blacks and whites. At the same time, growing Democratic dependence on the local business establishment for campaign contributions has made it difficult for Democrats to adopt strong antibusiness populist stances.

Lee Atwater, a South Carolina native who helped map out President Reagan's campaign strategy in the South, argues that today there are three major voter groups in the South—the business elite or so-called country-clubbers, the populists and the blacks. In this political equation, the country-clubbers, he says, are reliably Republican and blacks are reliably Democratic.

The result, according to Atwater's thesis, is that "the class war in the South continues, with the populists serving as the trump card."

Merle Black, a political scientist at the University of North Carolina who recently completed a major book on the politics of the South, said: "The educated conservatives have realigned, and they are the ones who always ran things." Democratic by a 3-to-2 margin 18 years ago, this elite had become Republican by a 5-to-1 margin in 1984, according to Black.

Growing partisan competition in the South has resulted in strong class disparities between those who call themselves Democrats and Republicans as poor blacks and affluent whites move in opposite political directions.

In the South, the difference between the median income of whites and blacks is larger than in any other region of the country. More than half of the 2.16 million black families living below the poverty line in the United States are in the South.

In some areas, this has produced a form of political near-feudalism, reaching the most extreme levels in the Mississippi Delta. In many Delta counties, the vote in presidential and congressional races splits between Democratic blacks, whose main source of income is welfare, and Republican whites, whose largest source of income is rent from their land.

Among whites across the South, the rise of Republican party allegiance has been closely tied to income. In 1956, southern whites from rich to poor were overwhelmingly Democratic, by margins of 2-to-1 or better.

By 1986, however, Democratic majorities remained only among poor and lower-middle class whites. Among middle-class whites, Republicans held a slight edge, while rich whites went from a 69-31 Democratic margin in 1956 to an 11-point GOP majority in 1984, according to surveys by National Election Studies. The rise of Republican partisan commitment in the South has been a revolution dominated by the affluent.

Here in Louisiana, Republican State Representative James Donelon says: "Polarization is taking place. We could now as easily call ourselves labor and conservatives as we do Democrats and Republicans . . . not talking race, I'm talking economic lines."

This growing split between the two parties in the South has major consequences for locally generated campaign contributions, almost all of which come from the affluent. Twenty years ago, a Republican Senate candidate would be considered a long shot at best, making it difficult for the campaign to raise funds. Today, in every contested race, the Republican Senate candidate has raised more cash than the Democrat.

In Louisiana, Moore has raised $1.8 million more than Rep. John B. Breaux, a conservative Democrat who just five years ago would have had no trouble raising money. In Florida, Sen. Paula Hawkins (R) has raised $3 million, according to Federal Election Commission records, $737,000 more than Democratic Gov. Robert Graham. In the North Carolina Senate fight, both the winner of the Republican primary, Rep. James T. Broyhill ($1.22 million), and the loser, David Funderburk ($1.1 million), raised more than twice the amount raised by the Democratic nominee, former governor Terry Sanford ($350,130). In Georgia, Sen. Mack Mattingly (R) raised $1.96 million, almost twice the $1 million raised by Rep. Wyche Fowler, Jr., (D). In Alabama, Sen. Jeremiah Denton (R) raised $1.47 million, $462,000 more than Rep. Richard C. Shelby (D).

Republican trends in the flow of money are showing up not only in statewide and presidential contests, but also down at the grass-roots level of politics.

For nearly a generation, the South Carolina Democratic party has depended on a committee of 100 made up of corporate leaders willing to kick in $500 or more annually. "You'd go to those meetings [15 years ago] and it damn near was South Carolina's finest. Every major bank was represented by either the chairman of the board or the president, all the major textiles. . . . Now, it's not the state's frontline business community. You just get a different crowd, the second and third level."

In direct contrast, South Carolina Republicans this year held a fund-raiser with Treasury Secretary James A. Baker, III, as the guest speaker. Selling tables of eight for $5,000, the state GOP raised $150,000. Warren Tompkins, the South Carolina GOP executive director, said, "In all the years, we'd never gotten a $5,000 contribution from any but one man," textile executive Roger Milliken.

Growing Republican financial muscle has major, and in many ways unanticipated, consequences for the substance of politics in the only region of the nation with a strong populist history, where the struggle of haves versus have-nots once characterized the Democratic South.

That populist tradition is nowhere stronger than in Louisiana, where in the 1930s Gov. Huey Long established a broader welfare state than that of the New Deal, and forced the political debate into a contest between the little guy and the corporations.

The recent rise of the Republican party here is tied to sustained efforts to counter that Democratic populist tradition. One of the GOP's major weapons here, considered the single most important recent development in Louisiana politics, has been the emergence of a powerful business lobby, the Louisiana Association of Business and Industry.

LABI superseded the AFL-CIO as the dominant force when it elected a majority of antilabor, probusiness members to the legislature during the 1970s, setting the stage for many of the striking Republican gains in the 1980s.

The new legislators provided fertile terrain for the GOP, which doubled its strength in the legislature from 12 to 25 over the past two years by persuading conservative Democrats to switch parties.

During the same time that the Republican party in Louisiana and other southern states was strengthening its ties with business, it was linking itself with political reform movements.

Reform here in Louisiana, where Democratic Gov. Edwin Edwards was recently found innocent of federal corruption charges, has taken on a strong Republican edge. The GOP, working in alliance with conservative Democrats, has linked reform with an attack on the welfare state. Reform has come to mean not only an attack on corruption, but also reform of such unique—and expensive—Louisiana state programs as a state charity hospital system and high state contributions to school lunches.

John J. Hainkel, Jr., a former Democratic speaker of the Louisiana House, who recently switched to the GOP, said, "The southern populists in the '30s and '40s, that philosophy, you know, soak the rich—the state gives everybody everything—that was sort of a phenomenon that became intertwined with integration and segregation" and took on a new character.

The rise of the GOP in Louisiana "is a natural realignment," he said. "I don't think they have never not been class parties. With some exceptions, the Republicans have been the middle-income and upper-income voters. And the blue collar and poor have generally been more Democratic oriented."

This kind of polarization causes significant anxieties among Democrats who are dependent on the business community for the money to finance campaigns.

"We are in a holding action," Bill Hamilton, a Democratic pollster who specializes in southern states, particularly Florida, acknowledged. He said the only factor keeping money in the Democratic column is the fact that Democrats still have a hammerlock on most state and local offices in the South, except some governorships. "Power is still Democratic," he said. "If it ever breaks and goes the other way, I won't be in business."

"If we ever lose a significant part of the [southern] economic elite, financially we are in bad trouble, we have no party structure to fall back on," he said. "One of the things Republicans have to understand, they've got to crack one of the legislatures. . . . They've got to be able to block things somewhere. The big mules in Alabama, they don't give a damn who is governor. They want the lieutenant governor; he's the one who runs the Senate and appoints the Senate committees. That determines policy. Once Republicans are in control of that, it makes the economic elite move [to the GOP] even faster because it goes to their normal fiscally conservative philosophy."

In Louisiana and other states, however, some key players in the Democratic power structure—just the people Hamilton is counting on to keep the money people in line—are playing both sides of the street.

Lawrence Chehardy, a Democrat like his father, controls the politics of Jefferson Parish through the assessor's office. But unlike his father, who proudly claimed the populist mantle of Huey Long, Chehardy, a nominal Democrat, is political director of the Moore Republican Senate campaign:

"I think you would find I am as responsible, if not more responsible, for Republicans being elected in the parish than anybody. In all honesty, many of the people I am close to politically, as well as socially, most of them are Republicans."

Similarly, in Mississippi's Rankin County, Irl Dean Rhodes, Democratic courthouse boss of the county, routinely backs Republicans: "In my situation, I think I've got the blacks and the Republicans too."

In Tennessee, the economic elite has, in the main, become firmly Republican, producing three of the most successful national finance chairmen for the Republican National Committee—Joe Rodgers, Ted Welch and David Wilson. But Democratic control of the state has forced GOP-leaning donors to give to Democrats. "To win [in Tennessee], a Republican needs Democratic votes, and a Democrat needs Republican money," said Frank Gorrell, former speaker of the state Senate.

The growing importance of money in elections is one reason why the emergence of two-party politics in the South has not meant the revival of a new class-based version of the old populist politics.

Don Fowler, Democratic National Committeeman from South Carolina, said that southern politics for generations was "characterized by continuing competition between the populists—the rednecks—and an elitist class of planters, doctors, lawyers and bankers."

The pool of poor and lower-middle-class voters has grown in recent years, as more of them have registered to vote, but this phenomenon has not produced a surge in populist politics—and thus has not been a boon to the Democrats. "It [the growing enfranchisement of blacks and poor whites] didn't take control of government out of the hands of the elitists, the establishment," Fowler said.

In part, the reason is successful Democrats need the money of "haves" to get elected. One example is South Carolina Democratic Governor Richard W. Riley. He has, according to Fowler, a distinctly liberal-moderate cut, but he has been very careful to make sure he retains links to some of the political, elite establishment, the economic and social elite."

One way to keep establishment support, according to Fowler, is to be against organized labor: "The modern-day version of civil rights is you can't be for labor unions. Riley has been steadfastly opposed to repeal of right to work laws and things like that."

The continued struggle between Republicans and Democrats for support, political and financial, from the establishment defies a 1949 prediction of V.O. Key, perhaps the greatest political analyst of the pre-civil rights South.

In the landmark book *Southern Politics,* Key wrote: "Southern liberalism is not to be underestimated. . . . If the Negro is gradually assimilated into political life, the underlying Southern liberalism will undoubtedly be mightily strengthened."

In fact, southern liberalism—like southern populism—has not flourished, a development attributable in part to Democratic dependence on the monied establishment, but, perhaps more important, to the fact that blacks were not gradually assimilated into the political system, but brought in suddenly in great numbers. The racial turmoil of the '60s and '70s prevented the formation of an integrated alliance of have-nots. Observed Black: "It was an abrupt, bitter fight," setting the stage for the modern transformation of southern politics.

# Stockman as the Judge
# and the Judged

*The Boston Sunday Globe,* May 25, 1986

David Stockman's autobiographical account of Ronald Reagan's first term is one of the best descriptions in political literature of the petty, haphazard and reckless manner in which most important government policies are conceived and carried out. Stockman has made a serious contribution to the study of the highest levels of government decision making, documenting in detail key presidential actions executed on the basis of a dual distortion of reality: Cabinet members playing on Reagan's affability and ignorance to reach policy decisions antithetical to administration goals, and the creation of false economic assumptions to achieve political ends. Despite the sharp eye for detail Stockman brings to this recounting of his four years as director of the Office of Management and Budget, however, he ultimately distorts the much larger truth of the Reagan administration's first term. The basic conclusion of *The Triumph of Politics**\* is that the Reagan Revolution failed. As a free market ideologue, Stockman is blind to the subtle, substantive revolution that has produced the most far-reaching change in the politics and policies of the country in fifty years.

Stockman reveals the operation of government as it is: incoherent, random, ruled by cliché and driven by bureaucratic self-interest, a portrayal of the operations of the executive branch characteristic of both Democratic and Republican administrations—openly revealed in the discordancy of the Carter years, carefully suppressed in the highly orchestrated Reagan White House.

The central flaw in *The Triumph of Politics*, however, is its failure to appreciate the overriding achievements of the Reagan administration. Stockman's perspective, clouded by his own intensely moralistic commitment to the dismantling of the welfare state, misses the three cornerstones of change set in place by the administration: 1) There has been a complete transformation in the terms of public policy debate, as President Reagan has driven home an antitax ideology, with a multibillion-dollar deficit, decried by Stockman, functioning to undermine the revival of all liberal Democratic initiatives; 2) The tax and budget cuts adopted in 1981 have amounted to a significant redistribution of income and wealth from the bottom to the top by an administration that has repeatedly denounced the redistributionist policies of the Democratic party; 3) The power of government has been used to accelerate the declining influence of institutional and cultural forces on the political left, particularly of organized labor.

The result has been a substantial, although highly fragile, change in the balance of power in American politics. The Reagan revolution has produced, for the first time since the 1920s, a sustained majority coalition dominated by conservative interests: the affluent, the growing fundamentalist Christian community, the old and new right, right-wing think tanks, most of the corporate elite, foes of abortion, neoconservative policy theorists and right-of center members of the academic establishment.

This is a coalition that depends for survival on maintaining a delicate balance of cultural and economic policies to win the votes not only of the board of

---

*David A. Stockman, *The Triumph of Politics: Why the Reagan Revolution Failed* (New York: Harper & Row, 1986).

directors of the Heritage Foundation, but, more important, the votes of redneck southerners, Italians who have moved out to Long Island, and farmers in the Wheat Belt. These are not voters who share Stockman's vision that "much of the vast enterprise of American government was invalid, suspect, malodorous. Its projects and ministrations were not spawned from higher principles, broad idealism or even humanitarian sentimentality; they were simply the flotsam and jetsam of a flagrantly promiscuous politics, the booty and spoils of the organized thievery conducted within the desecrated halls of government."

Stockman contends that the Reagan administration has failed because "a drastic shrinking of the welfare state was not [Reagan's] conception of the Reagan Revolution. It was mine. The president had a half-revolution in mind." In fact, however, insofar as the Reagan Revolution is a success, it will be a triumph of politics. The ability of the Republican party to fashion an alliance between subscribers to Phyllis Schlafly's newsletter and subscribers to *Esquire*, between the CEOs of the Fortune 500 and the red-clay farmers of Georgia, will determine whether the GOP achieves majority party status in the only kind of revolution that takes place within the pluralism of American politics.

In power for only six years, the leaders of this new Republican coalition have yet to face the kind of testing that results when two central members of the coalition go toe to toe on an issue that cannot be shunted aside, the kind of conflict characterizing the Democratic party during the struggles over civil rights and the Vietnam War. For an embryonic political alliance to adopt the search-and-destroy, antigovernment policies suggested by Stockman would have been to invite defeat. The genius of the Reagan administration has been to push close to the political edge, but to back off before going over—that is, whenever serious cracks in the coalition appeared. Judged in terms of changes in the balance of economic and political power, the Reagan administration strategy has been an extraordinary success. Moving from recession to recovery, there has been a significant alteration in the distribution of income as those in the top ten percent, one of the strongest Republican constituencies, have experienced solid gains, while those on the bottom, a Democratic constituency, have lost income. Unions, a mainstay of the Democratic party, are in the worst shape they have been in since before World War II. Democratic party officials, particularly those in the South, are now in the position of having to worry that blacks, the most loyal of Democratic voters, will gain disproportionate influence in the party.

It may be, as Stockman warns, that "at some point global investors will lose confidence in our easy dollars and debt-financed prosperity, and then the chickens will come home to roost"; that without major new taxes the "orgy of debt creation on the balance sheets of American consumers and corporations" will become a dead weight on the economy. This theory of deficit apocalypse has yet to materialize, however, and, in the interim, the Reagan administration has laid the political groundwork for the achievement of the only kind of shift in power possible in America without war, economic disaster or global cataclysm: a reshaping of the contours of government. New social and domestic initiatives from the left have been at least temporarily ruled out, while the military has gained wide latitude to experiment with such massive and expensive innovations as the Strategic Defense Initiative (Star Wars) and the Stealth Bomber. The pending debate over tax reform suggests that the Reagan administration will achieve its basic economic goal of cutting in half the top rate of taxation for the richest people in the nation.

The alteration of American politics and economics over the past decade has been less than revolutionary, but more than incremental. The driving momentum behind the alliance of ideological conservatives and the business community—an alliance providing the muscle for radical budget and tax bills in 1981—was cut short by the recession of 1982–83. At the same time, however, the Democratic party has been dealt a series of body blows in the elections of 1980 and 1984 from which it has yet to show signs of recovery; and the Republican party has made significant gains toward ending its longstanding status as minority party, prevented from achieving a full-fledged realignment in large part because of the GOP's continued vulnerability to charges that it is the party of the rich. Within this complex universe, all three of these books over-magnify the role of David Stockman. Stockman contributed mightily to the Reagan administration, although his major achievement—the Gramm-Latta budget bill, legislation primarily cutting benefits for the working poor—would, in the climate of 1981, probably have been enacted without his personal attention. At that time, a host of forces were at work, including a unified and politically mobilized business community; a newborn, flourishing collection of conservative think tanks; a sustained national tax rebellion in regions as diverse as California, Michigan and Massachusetts; an enclave of well-positioned and prolific "supply-side" economic theorists; and the emergence in the 1970s of persistent stagflation discrediting traditional Democratic economic responses.

None of the books under review treats Stockman as part and parcel of these much larger political and economic changes.

Owen Ullmann has produced the most balanced and insightful account, exploring the importance in Stockman's thinking both of growing up in a Michigan where there were two downtowns, white St. Joseph's and black Benton Harbor; and the significance of Stockman's maternal grandfather, William Bartz, the Berrien Country treasurer, a Goldwater conservative and a graduate of Moody Bible Institute.*

*The Real David Stockman*, by John Greenya and Anne Urban, is a scattershot indictment of the man they call "America's most controversial power broker."‡ The book is a good reflection of the scope of antagonism toward Stockman, as willing critics emerge from left and right. The book is one of a series of reports by Ralph Nader's Presidential Accountability Group, but, as an attempt to

---

*Owen Ullmann, *Stockman: The Man, the Myth, the Future* (New York: Donald I. Fine, 1986).

‡John Greenya and Anne Urban, *The Real David Stockman: The True Story of America's Most Controversial Power Broker* (New York: St. Martin's Press, 1986).

provide a record and accounting of Stockman's role in the Reagan administration, it would have been much improved by a detailed footnoting of sources. The index to Stockman's own book is a delightful resource for those interested in how policy is made. Under "Reagan, Ronald W.," for example, you can look up "balanced budget promise of" on pages 123 and 273 and "balanced budget plan abandoned by," on pages 349–50. Other presidential entries include "contradictory remarks on deficit spending," "kind and sympathetic nature of," "his knowledge and thinking based on anecdotes," "limited grasp of economics," "one year-at-a-time frame of reference of."

It is Stockman who provides the best, and most honest, description not only of the chaos of behind-closed-doors policy making, but also of the brutality of power in Washington, as Stockman's own stock begins to fall, even before publication of William Greider's *Atlantic Monthly* article: At a November 1981 meeting, Stockman recounts how Senate Majority Leader Howard Baker rejected a Stockman proposal to cut appropriation bills by 12 percent. When Stockman protested, Baker "whirled around in his chair and glared directly at me. 'Don't you ever, ever lecture me on how to run the United States Senate.' . . . At my last session with Greider I'd said that [Baker] would outclass Lyndon Johnson hands-down as the greatest Senate Majority Leader of modern times. 'He's good,' I'd remarked, 'one of the greatest legislators in decades. That guy is better than anybody else who's ever been on the track.' Until that Sunday morning, I had thought Howard Baker took me seriously, considered me a force to be reckoned with. Now, I realized that was an illusion, too."

*The Triumph of Politics* is dominated by Stockman's mistaken belief that the underlying, and unrealized, goal of the Reagan Revolution has been the surgical removal of the vast federal spending and regulatory apparatus. It is, in fact, this massive federal armada of cash, patronage and regulatory power that has provided the Reagan administration with the tools to attempt to hammer out a political and economic realignment. Throughout the Reagan administration, the strategy, as distinct from the theory, of political practice has been to restructure the federal government to the benefit of its most loyal supporters, with the objective of building a new constituency in what may prove to be the most significant political development of the last half century.

# New Right Finally Gains
# Control of Huge Southern
# Baptist Convention

*Largest Protestant Denomination
Likely to Move Toward GOP*

*The Washington Post,* June 14, 1986

ATLANTA—An eight-year power struggle within the Southern Baptist Convention (SBC) has given the key figures in the new Christian right control over the nation's largest Protestant denomination and is likely to result in stronger ties between the religious body and the Republican party.

The election last week of the Rev. Adrian Rogers to the presidency of the SBC brings to near completion a religious and political transformation of the denomination that has major consequences for the GOP and its potential candidates for president.

The SBC has become a fertile hunting ground for prospective candidates for the GOP presidential nomination. SBC supporters of Vice President Bush conducted private meetings with the group's current leaders and with pastors likely to win office in the near future. Television evangelist Marion G. (Pat) Robertson made a personal appearance here two days before the start of the convention and reappeared on the final night.

Supporters of Rep. Jack Kemp (R-N.Y.) did not send any emissaries, in what aides consider a significant mistake. Kemp's inaction, combined with strong efforts by Bush and Robertson, threatens to erode a potential base of Kemp support among Christian evangelicals, according to sources here both for and against his prospective candidacy.

In addition to wooing such present and former SBC presidents as Rogers, Charles Stanley and Jimmy Drapper, campaign workers for many of prospective GOP candidates are targeting the next generation of Southern Baptist leaders including Ed Young of Houston, O.S. Hawkins of Florida, Dwight Reighart of Georgia and Jay Stack of Florida.

The victory Tuesday of Rogers, a Memphis pastor, in a heated contest for the SBC presidency not only affirmed conservative domination of the elective offices, but it guaranteed success for the long-range goal of the denomination's right wing to take over the massive publishing and academic empire serving 14.5 million members.

At the moment, much of the SBC professional staff and academic community does not support the growing politicization of church leaders. The professional staff now faces a tough fight holding jobs as the conservative leaders gain power this year over key boards of trustees empowered to govern the bureaucracy.

"We are not trying to tell any [seminary] professor what he must believe, or any denominational employee, that is between him and God," Rogers said. "But we are saying that those who work for us and those who have their salaries paid by us ought to reflect what we want taught."

Affirming a belief in the separation of church and state, Rogers said at a news conference that he believes "none of us who are Christians are disenfranchised because of religion. . . ." Referring to his own advocacy of legislation to allow prayer in schools and to his opposition to abortion, he said, "Some of the things we do may seem overtly political, but to us, they are moral and spiritual issues."

Since 1979, the conservatives led by Houston Judge Paul Pressler and W.A. Criswell, pastor of the First Baptist Church in Dallas, have successfully promoted the SBC presidential candidacies of Rogers, Stanley, Drapper and Bailey Smith.

These men have been closely tied to Republican-Christian Right politics, serving of the board of the American Coalition for Traditional Values (ACTV), the organization that coordinated the registration of an estimated 1.5 million to 2 million evangelical voters in 1984, the vast majority of whom voted for Republicans.

Joe Rodgers, former finance chairman for the Republican National Committee and the Reagan–Bush '84 committee, raised more than $1 million for ACTV.

In addition, almost all these conservative leaders were active supporters of President Reagan's reelection.

The steady movement to the right among Southern Baptists has been a key element in Republican elective gains in the South. The almost all-white denomination has provided large numbers of votes to Republicans, and it is a critical element of the long-range GOP goal of gaining majority status.

But while the Southern Baptists are a source of numerous votes, their growing alignment with the GOP is not entirely an unmixed blessing, some Republicans said, because of their religious views, "I wouldn't give you half a hallelujah for your chances in heaven if you don't believe in the virgin birth," Rogers said in a sermon last week.

The Baptist Convention has been going through a process "very much like what the Republican party went through" during the period Sen. Barry Goldwater (R-Ariz.) won the presidential nomination in 1964, a Republican strategist said. "It is a conservative conversion of a major American institution," he added, pointing out that this year conservatives are expected to gain majorities on at least half the governing boards of the SBC, and on three quarters of the boards next year.

"The leadership is basically with the new religious right and the right-wing political movement," Wilmer C. Fields, SBC news representative who is to retire later this year, said.

"With the changes going on the in SBC, you are going to see the steady departure of staff members who do not support the growing conservative political activism of the denomination," a well-placed SBC staff member added.

The Exeter and Princeton educated Pressler, who over the years has acquired a well-deserved reputation as the preeminent backroom boss and strategist of

Baptist politics, contends that his goals are religious, not political. He said his purpose is to "create an atmosphere, to create a direction" in the SBC so that "the people whose salaries we pay will be responsible to their constituents."

While Pressler's goals may not be political, a consequence of his success has been a "quantum jump" in political activity within the already highly politicized SBC, Republican strategists agreed.

# Why the GOP Is Still Waiting on Realignment

*The Washington Post*, September 14, 1986

Just two years ago, euphoric Republican strategists thought that their main goal—political realignment granting the GOP majority status for the first time in over 50 years—was close at hand. Now, as the Reagan administration approaches its final two years in office, that goal is proving to be elusive.

After November 1984, not only had the GOP won a landslide election with the first president in nearly a generation able to sustain high favorability ratings, but the Republican party had emerged triumphant in two areas traditionally dominated by the Democratic opposition: voter registration, and support among the young.

Since then, however, the momentum behind this drive to gain political ascendancy has faltered.

Polls exploring voter allegiance show that the GOP gained parity with, if not a slight advantage over, the Democratic party right after the 1984 election. Since then, the Democrats have regained a slight edge, running ahead of the GOP by a fairly consistent 49-46 ratio.

More important to the realignment issue, however, is a series of damaging questions that are being raised about the economic recovery that provided muscle to the Republican victory of 1984.

The central achievement of the Reagan administration has been the restoration of stability through a sharp reduction in the rate of inflation and lowered interest rates, combined with an economic recovery that has produced a record 11.6 million new jobs.

The Reagan recovery has not, however, solved core economic problems that undermined the administrations of both Gerald Ford and Jimmy Carter. There has been no return to the growth in family income and wages that America became used to from 1945 through the mid-1970s. In addition, most indicators point to a widening gap between the rich and the poor, an erosion of the middle class, and diminished prospects for young working men and women, precisely those on whom a Republican realignment depends.

Perhaps the most important economic fact of life for production and non-supervisory workers—their average weekly wage—has remained stagnant since Reagan took office, going from $172.74 in 1980 to $171.60 in 1985 (in constant 1977 dollars).

From 1980 to 1984, median family income fell from $26,500 to $26,433, and the decline would have been far sharper without growing legions of women in the workforce creating two-income families.

Sheldon Danziger and Peter Gottschalk, of the Institute for Research on Poverty at the University of Wisconsin, found that from 1979 to 1984, the mean income of families with children actually fell for all groups except the most affluent 20 percent.

An essential ingredient of a political realignment—an economy providing new workers a strong chance of doing better than their parents—has not been restored under the Reagan administration.

Analysis of income patterns by Frank S. Levy of the University of Maryland and Richard C. Michel of the Urban Institute shows that before 1973, a young man could expect his earnings to grow by 118 percent between the ages of 25 and 35, and by another 30 percent between the ages of 40 and 50. Since 1973, however, the younger man going from 25 to 35 could expect only a 16 percent increase in earnings, and the older man, going from 40 to 50, experienced an actual loss of 14 percent of his income. Compounding this economic frustration is the fact that the cost of financing a median-priced home has grown from 21 percent of the average gross earnings of a 30-year-old in 1973 to 44 percent by 1983, effectively pushing home ownership out of the realm of possibility for growing numbers of people.

In these circumstances, the robust Republican drive to achieve a realignment of the electorate during the early 1980s shows some signs of lagging in 1986. The substantial debate over tax and spending policy, on which much GOP success was based, has been subordinated, in part, to a form of political trench warfare in which the GOP is attempting to achieve victory as much by capitalizing on its advantages in campaign contributions and high technology as on its policies and programs.

This kind of political contest amounts to a war of attrition, as the Republican party takes advantage of its far superior sources of information, its ability to target resources and its cash reserves to chip away at a still-wounded Democratic party.

This strategy may result in continued GOP control of the Senate, minimized losses in the House and near certain gains in the state houses across the country. But it is taking place amidst a host of other signs that the Republican party is not equipped to win the kind of long-term, deep allegiance within the American electorate characteristic of a realignment in which one political party becomes unquestionably dominant. Among these signs are:

The army of hungry political operatives and activists who were the lieutenants and captains of the Reagan revolution has all too readily become a part of the Washington establishment, capitalizing on connections and influence peddling to achieve incomes often well into the six-figure range where they have become accustomed to the pursuit of a life of chauffeur-driven Mercedes and lavish expense-account lunches.

At closed meetings of party strategists, one of the growing concerns is the lack of fresh blood to replace the phalanx of grass-roots workers in the states who, once the GOP won the presidency and the Senate, latched onto patronage jobs.

"It is very tough to find anyone with real political savvy willing to work for $20,000 to $30,000 as organizers in states, or as campaign managers, press aides and finance directors of House races," said one party strategist, who has himself risen from running marginal House races to Washington insider status.

Those who have made it from the grass-roots to jobs within the federal government or national party committee structures are far less likely to go back to the vineyards than to seek high-dollar, "inside the beltway" jobs as lobbying or political consultanting in an attempt to make the $400,000-plus incomes of such well established GOP operatives as Ed Rollins, Lee Atwater, Roger Stone, Charles Black and Michael Deaver.

The difficulties the GOP is having in finding first-rate political talent to staff the trenches reflect a Republican party which has become rich before its time. In just six years of control in Washington, the driving hunger for power and status, an essential ingredient of a party seeking to turn political gains into a lasting realignment, has already been at least partially satisfied, undermining the vitality of what had been a deeply committed political movement.

The ability of the Republican party this year to hold onto the Senate will be determined as much by money as by policy. The one area in which the Republican party has achieved an unquestioned realignment is among political contributors, a universe of the affluent, who have profited most from both the rise in the stock market and from the administration's tax policies.

The result is a Republican party that has in many ways cut out much potential opposition by raising overwhelming amounts of cash.

In states as diverse as Oregon, Kansas, New York and Iowa, where it is impossible to tell what the voters' mood will be on November 4, legitimate Democratic challengers chose not to run against Republican incumbent senators whose cash balances in many cases exceeded $1 million by the end of 1985.

In effect, to the extent that there has been a realignment of the electorate, it is as much a conversion based on cash and technology—and the advertising time and public opinion data they buy—as it is a diffuse and spontaneous grass-roots–originated upheaval of American voters producing the kind of transformed allegiances characteristic of the political revolutions of 1932, 1896, 1860, and 1828.

Among GOP donors, however, there are signs that the deep commitment to expanding Republican victories—beyond the presidency and Senate to the House of Representatives—is faltering.

The once-vibrant fund-raising of the National Republican Congressional Committee—the key vehicle to provide early support to non-incumbent GOP House candidates—has badly deteriorated, falling from $45 million during the first 18 months of 1981–82, to just $25 million in the parallel period in this election cycle.

What this suggests is that the Republican contributors' hopes of taking over the House are waning. More important, it suggests that Republican donors are no longer convinced of the importance of restoring in the House a "Reagan majority" of Republicans and conservative Democrats, a far more achievable goal.

Instead, the contributors have been concentrating donations on the more highly publicized, sexier Senate contests—a pattern far more characteristic of Democratic donors during the 1970s and early 1980s than Republicans.

The rise of the Republican party has been singularly dependent on negative campaigning. Sustained attacks on the divisions within the Democratic coalition—between whites and blacks, between culturally conservative working-class voters and liberal elites, between doves and hawks, between union and non-union workers—have been as important to GOP gains as positive claims about the achievements of the Republican party.

The shared talent of the three premier GOP campaign strategists—Lee Atwater, Charlie Black and Roger Stone—is the calculated ability to seize on the weaknesses of opponents and "drive up their negatives." For Atwater and Black, key training has been in southern political fights, where the central goal is to drive wedges in what had been a deeply rooted Democratic dominance.

"Republicans in the South could not win elections simply by showing various issues and talking about various issues. You had to make the case that the other guy, the other candidate, is a bad guy," Atwater said, describing his approach to elections. "You simply could not get out in a universe where 60 percent of the people were Democrats and 28 percent Republicans, and win by talking about your issues."

Detailed analysis of what is perhaps the most central and important claim of a revived Republican party—the growing allegiance to the GOP among young voters—suggests that the partisan switch is far more fragile than previously thought.

The 1984 elections produced an unprecedented swing to the GOP among the youngest voters.

However, Warren Miller, a political scientist at Arizona State University and director of the biennial National Election Survey, found that careful study of young voters showed far more complex developments have taken place. Among those young voters who are active in the political process and knowledgeable about the subtleties of elections, there was, in fact, an intensification of Democratic support.

In contrast, among younger voters (and non-voters) who care little about the workings and details of politics and government policies, Republicans made substantial gains, far outweighing the Democratic advances among the more knowledgeable. It is among these voters that Reagan and the GOP flexed real muscle in 1984.

The partisan commitment of these relatively apathetic voters was not based on a new-found allegiance to the Republican party or to conservative principles.

Instead, it was based on a belief that Reagan would protect pocketbook interests better than Mondale, a fragile base on which to build a Republican majority in light of the continuing stagnation of key elements of the economy, and on an equally fragile personal loyalty to Reagan.

In political terms, this kind of partisan movement is not the stuff of realignment. Instead, it is a vacillating political commitment, and subject to possible Democratic approaches from candidates who make calculated appeals to young voters, such as Sens. Gary Hart (D-Colo.) or Joseph Biden (D-Del.), and from Democrats equipped to make a strong appeal to the economic interests of the young electorate.

On a different tack, the collapse of the oil industry has, in many ways, taken the wind out of the sails of the GOP-conservative movement. Oil money was a driving force behind the conservative revolution that took over Washington in 1980, through the election of Reagan and, equally important, through the election of Reagan's shock troops in the House and Senate—arch conservatives willing to back his budget and tax cuts down the line.

The sharp decline in oil contributions—most of the oilmen's political action committees have seen revenue drops of 40 to 90 percent—resulting from the recent nosedive in oil prices, has meant a precipitous reduction in donations not only to relatively unknown conservative Republicans challenging Democratic incumbents, but has meant also a major loss of money to the network of conservative political action committees that played a key role in changing the political landscape in 1980.

In contrast to the last Republican realignment at the turn of the century, there is no one currently on the political horizon to fulfill the critical role played by Theodore Roosevelt in solidifying the realignment initiated with the election of William McKinley in 1896.

Teddy Roosevelt expanded McKinley's business-based politics to incorporate within the GOP much of the progressive movement and many of the voters distrustful of growing monopoly power, in the process providing the GOP an entrenched base within the nation's middle class.

At the moment, the only current prospective Republican presidential candidate whose goal is to seek ways to expand the GOP base is Rep. Jack Kemp (R-N.Y.), whose campaign to date has failed to gain momentum. The Kemp effort has been unable to achieve its basic goal of uniting Republican conservatives, and an attempt to use the 1986 Michigan primary—the first test of 1988 strength—to wound the campaign of Vice President George Bush failed, as observers questioned the organizational strength and expertise of the Kemp organization.

The most likely Republican presidential nominee, Bush, is privately described by his own aides not as a force to bring new vitality to a reborn Republican party, but as a "maintaining" president, a politician who bridges the gap between Republican traditionalists (his own base) and the newer, more intensely conservative activists, whose loyalty Bush has earned by his own loyalty to Reagan.

The establishment wing, in contrast to many of the conservative activists drawn to Republican politics through the candidacies of Ronald Reagan, has been far less interested in the dynamics of achieving realignment than in a return to a less venturesome, more businesslike, form of government and administration, with more attention paid to deficits and to achieving a balanced fiscal policy. If this wing is on the way back to power in the Republican party, the chances of realignment are all the less likely.

# Massachusetts: A Model for Democrats?
## Dukakis Is Trading Blue Collars for Brie and Chablis

*The Washington Post*, October 5, 1986

BOSTON—Here at the Bayside Club, state Senate president William M. (Billy) Bulger maintains one of the vital traditions of Massachusetts politics: Yankee baiting.

At Bulger's annual St. Patrick's day luncheon two years ago, Republican Brahmin Elliot Richardson was foolhardy enough to stop by. For an appreciative crowd, Bulger produced a phony edition of the Boston Globe with a headline reading: "Vote Richardson—He's Better Than You."

Bulger's wit is a reflection of a richly productive political structure where class and ethnic conflict have traditionally defined the struggle between Democrats and Republicans.

This political class system is, however, crumbling. In an economic reversal of the traditional New Deal coalition, the Massachusetts Democratic party has, over the past decade, increasingly become the party of affluent, liberal, middle-class suburbanites. This realignment, reflecting what MIT political scientist Walter Dean Burnham calls the "yuppification" of the Democratic party, is emerging in similar fashion in neighboring Maine and Vermont, where Protestant farmers used to produce unwavering Republican majorities. Today, an affluent Democratic party has achieved parity if not majority status, controlling both houses of the Maine legislature and the state Senate in Vermont.

Blue-collar white Catholics, once the mainstay of the Massachusetts Democratic coalition, have in large part been dealt out of the system. They vote in far fewer numbers than in the past, and their votes are no longer reliably Democratic, particularly in presidential contests. However, they have not formed a new base for the Massachusetts GOP, which is floundering as patrician Yankees have lost their grip on the party structure.

In economic terms, the change in the Massachusetts Democratic electorate clashes head-on with a realignment that has taken place in the American South.

There, affluent suburbs that were once the hard core of a one-party Democratic system are now the precincts most firmly in the hands of the GOP, with margins as high as 80-20 for Republican candidates. This southern trend has been the most powerful force altering the shape of national politics. It has produced a sharp intensification of class disparities between the two parties, as Democrats in the South increasingly gain the loyalties of the poor and working class, while Republicans expand their margins among the more affluent.

The diametrically opposed trends in the Democratic party in the Northeast and South are likely to come into increasing conflict during the next several years. The opposing trends are central to the continuing dilemma of the national Democratic party. In the South, an often-repeated fear of white Democrats is that the party is becoming a party of the poor and the black. "Blacks understandably are restless in the Democratic party," said South Carolina Democratic National Committeeman Donald Fowler. "But on the other side of it is that if we gave them everything they wanted, it'd be a black party."

The regional differences exacerbate conflicts over strategy. Advocates of generally conservative strategies and policies want to appeal to middle- and upper-middle-class whites, who in the country as a whole have become increasingly Republican in recent years. Supporters of more liberal approaches are trying to pull in poor and working-class constituents, many of whom do not at present vote.

The leader of the newly upscale Democratic party in Massachusetts is Gov. Michael Dukakis, who has developed a strategy for victory in primary and general elections that provides a model of a fundamentally center-right coalition—winning with the votes of the upper-middle class—to a national party struggling to regain majority status after the presidential defeats of 1980 and 1984.

Defeated for reelection to the governorship in 1978 by conservative Democrat Ed King, Dukakis returned to office in 1982 when he allied himself with the state's vibrant business community and adjusted his campaign strategy to attract an increasingly powerful body of "independent" Democrats from such well-to-do suburbs as Brookline and Newton.

"The realignment here can be read as the 'yuppification' or perhaps 'Dukakization' of the Democratic party," said MIT's Dean Burnham. "The retirement of [House Speaker Thomas P.] Tip O'Neill represents the end of an era in Massachusetts politics."

"This is the only state where you can buy brie and chablis in gas stations," says Democratic political consultant Ralph Whitehead. "Class consciousness has been muted and Dukakis has muted it. Dukakis has played a conciliatory role [between blue-collar urban Democrats and the new, affluent suburban Democrats], but the suburban side has the upper hand. The suburban side is the growth side."

According to pollster Irwin (Tubby) Harrison, "What you have in Massachusetts is that many of your upscale voters are liberal, and many of your blue-collar voters are more conservative. The core of the liberal party is not the blue collars, it's more the people who earn a good income, the core of your liberal party is in the suburbs, even with the beautiful people. The lunchpail Democrats, their registration is still Democratic, but they come and go."

In the 1980 and 1984 presidential election, many of these working-class Massachusetts Democrats went, and the state was carried both years by Reagan, even though no Republican has won statewide office since 1972.

The economic trends in voting are reflected in Lowell, a city where the median income is well below the state's average, which went from casting a 12,596 plurality, or 70-30, for Dukakis when he first ran in 1974, to voting Republican by a 1,792-vote margin in the 1984 presidential race. Conversely Newton, where the median family income is nearly $10,000 higher than the state average, went from voting 54-46 Republican in the 1974 gubernatorial contest to giving Walter Mondale a 63-37 victory in the 1984 presidential race.

While working-class whites are, in many cases, voting for Republican presidential candidates, in state elections they have not joined the GOP, which has conspicuously failed to take advantage of altered voting patterns.

"To the question 'Whatever happened to the Massachusetts Republicans?' the best answer is, simply, Dukakis. He has ruined them partly by resembling them so," wrote Christopher Lydon, anchorman of WGBH News, in *The Boston Phoenix.* "Cheap, clean, smart, un-Irish, Dukakis seems built to deliver rational services. . . . The old Republican party, as a vehicle of any mass will, [is] history."

Burnham contends that in addition to rising Democratic strength among the affluent, an equally profound development is a growing lack of interest in voting among working-class Catholics.

Non-voting in predominantly Catholic areas shot up from 25.8 percent in 1960, the year John Kennedy ran for president, to 59.6 percent in 1984, and in working-class communities, the rate of non-voting during the same period grew from 27.1 percent to 66.5 percent, according to Burnham.

"It is not too much to say that the modern, increasingly yuppified and technocratic Democratic party simply doesn't offer such lower-class potential voters any particular incentive to participate," he argues.

In the most recent primary, the only major contest in which class-correlated voting emerged in traditional patterns was in the Eighth Congressional District, where Joseph Kennedy beat State Sen. George Bachrach largely with the backing of the "have-not" communities in the district against the affluent sections. It was, however, a race in which the Kennedy name, combined with over $1 million and the backing of both fellow politicians and the *Boston Globe,* produced a reaffirmation of traditional voting patterns and voting turnout.

"If Kennedy falls short," warned Globe columnist David Nyhan before the election, "it's the demise of the Irish political tradition here."

With Kennedy's victory, that tradition has momentarily survived, although it leaves unresolved for the national Democratic party fundamental policy choices in the selection of issues and tactics to expand popular support among often conflicting constituencies.

# A Grass-Roots Battle
# to Control Redistricting

*Republicans Struggle to Extend Their National*
*Success into State Legislatures on Election Day*

*The Washington Post,* November 2, 1986

DEARBORN, Mich.—In this city, where Democratic loyalty has nose-dived almost as fast as jobs at the Ford Motor Co. plant, Bill Runco, a young lawyer backed with nearly $200,000 from the Republican party, has been slicing like a knife through a wounded Democratic organization.

Runco is part of an army of Republican candidates for seemingly minor state legislative offices. They are, however, shock troops in a struggle to carry Republican success—the presidency in four of the last five elections and control of the U.S. Senate since 1980—down to the grass roots.

For the state-by-state winners of the grass-roots battle, the prize is power to control redistricting after the 1990 census. Redistricting is a key factor determining which party will control the bastion of national Democratic power, the U.S. House of Representatives, now 253-to-180 Democratic.

From Washington, the Republican and Democratic parties are each investing $1 million in local statehouse contests in a spending war sure to escalate in the elections of 1988 and 1990. Local candidates and the state party caucuses across the country are also raising and spending uncounted sums as the cost of winning a contested state Senate seat has reached $250,000 in some states, and as much as $1 million in California.

Across the country, the Democratic party goes into this fight with a strong advantage: Democrats outnumber Republicans 1,188 to 753 in state senates, controlling 31 of 49; and by 3,136 to 2,317 in state houses, controlling 31 of 49. (Nebraska has a nonpartisan, unicameral legislature.)

The GOP, however, is going after local districts where the Democratic party is in trouble, particularly in conservative, white areas, where a combination of issues—race, crime, abortion, defense spending and a distaste for Jimmy Carter and Walter F. Mondale—have worked to build Republican support. Often the premier issue is an economy that voters saw sour in the 1970s while the Democrats held the White House and both houses of Congress.

Here in Dearborn, the number of men and women walking daily through the Rouge plant gates has dropped from 80,000 to 14,500 in a generation. A pervasive fear of crime and deep anger at Detroit Mayor Coleman Young have become central political issues for voters who were once mainstays of the New Deal coalition.

"The traditional soft Democratic support—it's gone," said Jack O'Reilly, campaign manager for Democrat George Hart, who is running against Runco for the open state Senate seat here. Runco is doing everything he can to keep it that way:

"Have you been to downtown Detroit lately?" the headline of one of Runco's direct-mail pieces asks, "Your tax dollars have!" In this overwhelmingly white district bordering majority black Detroit, Runco hammers home themes linking his Democratic opponent to a steady flow of taxpayer dollars "from our pockets . . . to downtown Detroit."

Seemingly obscure, this contest is a key test for the Republican and Democratic parties. The white precincts of gritty cities like Dearborn, Allentown, Pa., and Akron, Ohio, have emerged as the quintessential partisan battlegrounds of the North, turf where the GOP's challenge to the Democrats' 50-year hold on majority status will be won or lost.

Each of those communities is the terrain of a guerrilla war fought far below the surface of highly publicized fights for U.S. Senate and gubernatorial seats. These struggles, however, will determine party control in as many as 21 state senates and houses in every region of the nation, except the South where Democrats remain dominant. Most of the statehouse battles are in midwestern and northeastern states, including Illinois, Ohio, New York, Connecticut, Pennsylvania and Iowa.

"Right now, Democrats control both chambers in 26 states representing 262 House districts. The Republicans control both in 11 states representing 42 districts," Will Robinson, a Democratic strategist said, pointing to the power now in the hands of the Democratic party.

This kind of power is often won by razor-thin margins. Democrats currently control the Pennsylvania House by one seat, 101 to 100. In Oregon, just 812 votes spread across four districts gave the Democrats their 34-to-26 majority in the state House.

While both parties are investing $1 million in state legislative battles—the Democrats through Project 500, a coalition of party, labor and liberal groups; the Republicans through The 1991 Plan, run by the Republican National Committee (RNC)—the seeming parity distorts what is a major GOP financial advantage.

The Republicans' 1991 Plan meshes with two other programs. One is a $10 million to $12 million voter mobilization drive that finances computerized voter lists, telephone banks expected to make 12 million calls, direct-mail operations sending as many as 12 million letters, and the distribution of absentee ballots to voters favorable to the GOP. The other is GOPAC, an ongoing fund-raising program channeling as much as $3 million to state and local Republican candidates nationwide.

This financial cushion has permitted the Republican party to spread its largess across a far broader spectrum of candidates than the Democrats. Ed Brookover, of the RNC, said that in addition to backing candidates in tight contests in states where the partisan balance is close, the GOP is pumping cash into states where it has little chance to get control, but where the GOP has made substantial gains.

Many of these states are in the South—Florida, North Carolina, Texas,

Tennessee, along with Missouri—where the minority Republican party has gained in state legislatures on the coattails of Ronald Reagan. The RNC is seeking to protect the gains in an off-year election.

In addition, in states like Oklahoma, the GOP has invested in Republican legislative candidates as part of a drive to control at least one-third of the legislature in order to sustain vetoes by Republican governors.

The Democrats, in contrast, are putting their cash and staff into a far smaller universe of key states where partisan control is at stake.

"We are in a kind of triage situation," said Robinson, of the Democratic Project 500. "There are chambers where we don't have a chance and there are chambers [particularly in the South] where we can hold off for a while. We are concentrating on the ones in the middle." He estimated that out of 6,270 state Senate and House seats up for grabs on November 4, the number of decisive contests will boil down to just 35 by Election Day.

In Michigan and in both parties' national headquarters, there is no question that the Runco–Hart state Senate contest will turn out to be one of those key races.

The state stands to lose three congressional seats after the 1990 census, as many as any state in the union, in a process sure to leave Democratic or Republican blood on the floor of the legislature. States gaining or losing seats are forced to make the most significant changes in district boundary lines, and every shift can mean political life or death for incumbents and challengers.

In this struggle to control redistricting, "our No. 1 priority is Dearborn," said John Long, chief of staff for the Republican State Senate Caucus, which has pulled out the stops to keep its fragile GOP 20-to-18 majority in the state Senate, a majority that has shifted between parties in recent years. A victory in the district this year would sharply increase prospects for holding the seat in the critical election of 1990.

Twenty-seven state political action committees (PACs) closely tied to the Michigan Republican leadership have channeled "the overwhelming majority" of cash to finance Runco's $210,000 budget, Runco said. And the GOP has independently spent at least $50,000 more for five direct mailings to the district.

In Runco, the GOP has fielded a savvy, ambitious campaigner who in 1980, at the age of 23, won a county commissioner seat when his Democratic opponent died before the general election.

Two years later he beat state Democratic Rep. Lucille McCullogh, who had been serving in the legislature for three more years than Runco had been alive.

The collapse of Democratic hegemony in the area prompted Michigan Democrats to finance a major study of defectors in white, working-class neighborhoods. The findings presented by Stanley Greenberg of The Analysis Group of New Haven were not optimistic:

"These white Democratic defectors express a profound distaste for blacks, a sentiment that pervades almost everything they think about government and politics. . . . These Democratic defectors believe the government has personally intervened to block their opportunities. Appeals to fairness, opportunity, etcetera, are now defined in racial terms that have been stripped of progressive content."

In these circumstances, the contest early on looked like a walkaway victory for Runco.

His opponent, Hart, is a genial man whose political campaigning was in a past of billboards, weddings, wakes and campaign buttons—he first ran for Dearborn constable in 1949—not the targeted direct mail and specialized radio ads of the 1980s. He is known in the district as the Singing Senator, ready with a serenade at any occasion, armed with his own record, "Songs From The Hart." In a harsh editorial endorsing Runco, *The Detroit News*, a Republican newspaper, said Hart "appears close to brain dead."

O'Reilly, Hart's manager, said the campaign will spend about $85,000, although Hart has the added benefit of running with the Democratic team of popular U.S. Rep. John D. Dingell in his sixteenth District campaign.

It is, however, the central irony of this contest that in a district where racial issues have been crucial to the emergence of the Republican party, it is a black Republican, gubernatorial nominee William Lucas, who represents the biggest threat to a Runco victory.

Running at least 30 points behind Democratic Governor James J. Blanchard, Lucas has become a lead anchor at the top of the GOP ticket in Dearborn. Nowhere in his literature or in his campaign speeches does Runco mention Lucas. Instead, Runco's brochures prominently feature photographs of him with Blanchard. Hart has countered with radio commercials of Blanchard endorsing his candidacy.

Racial antagonism toward Lucas is widely credited for the fact that Runco, far ahead in polls at the start of the contest, is now dead even with Hart, according to local newspapers.

*In this election, Hart, the Democrat, beat Runko, the Republican, in what was a national pattern of Democratic gains in 1986 state legislative contests. In Michigan, Hart and a number of other Democratic candidates benefitted from the strong popularity of Democratic Governor James Blanchard at the top of the ticket and racial antagonism to William Lucas, the GOP's black gubernatorial candidate.*

# Why the Democrats Are Still Losers

*The Washington Post,* January 11, 1987

The apparent ascendancy of the Democratic party masks complex changes in the political balance of power. A substantial erosion of Democratic support lies just beneath the party's takeover of the U.S. Senate, its gain of 179 state legislative seats and the major damage to the Republican party resulting from the Iran-contra scandal.

Over the past six years, traditional Democratic dominance in voter identification has been replaced by a fragile parity between the two parties in which neither has majority status.

Two Reagan administrations have produced a sharp decline in allegiance to the Democratic party among white working- and lower-middle-class voters according to *Washington Post*-ABC News poll data. This fall-off has emerged despite the fact that voters whose incomes lie below the median income, white and black, have done relatively poorly under the Reagan administration. The failure of low-income whites to return to the Democratic fold suggests that Democratic solidarity is not surviving as well as it traditionally has during periods either of economic adversity in the 1930s or prosperity in the 1960s.

The Democrats won the Senate in 1986 in an election unusual in some key respects. In contrast to the contests of 1980, 1982 and 1984, there was a sharp decline in the economic polarization of the electorate: a lessening of the pattern of the poor voting heavily Democratic and the affluent heavily Republican.

Comparison of *Washington Post*-ABC poll data in 1981 and 1986—the six years of the Reagan presidency—show a sharp decline in support for the Democratic party. Voter allegiance has shifted from a 53-37 Democratic advantage in 1981, on the basis of three separate polls and interviews with 3,418 voters, to just a 49-45 Democratic advantage in 1986, using cumulative data from seven polls of 8,688 voters.

Most damaging to the Democratic party is the shift among the white lower-middle class and poor. From 1981 to 1986, the poorest white voters, those making less than $20,000, have remained Democratic, but the Democratic margin has fallen from a strong 55-36 percentage point edge in 1981 to a far more tenuous 51-43 margin in 1986.

White voters in the lower-middle class—those with family incomes between $20,000 and $30,000—have shifted from a 46-42 Democratic edge in 1981 to a 50-45 Republican margin in 1986, a devastating blow to a Democratic party claiming to represent the interests of the less powerful in society.

Blacks, in the meantime, have remained firmly Democratic: among all income groups, Democratic loyalty ranges from 82 to 87 percent.

The decline in white Democratic support has occurred despite the fact that poor and moderate-income white families have fared badly during the Reagan years.

Sheldon Danziger, of the University of Wisconsin, and Peter Gottschalk, of Bowdoin College, have found that for white families with children, median family income for those in the poorest 20 percent fell from $9,651 to $7,433 from 1979 to 1984; that for those families in the second poorest quintile, income fell from $21,222 to $18,748 and for those in the middle, income fell from $30,299 to $28,112. All these figures are in 1984 dollars.

It may be that the two trends toward increasingly unequal distribution of income and income reduction or stagnation for those in the working and lower middle classes are functioning to increase the political polarization between moderate-income whites and blacks. If so, the Democratic party faces a major task as it attempts to maintain a biracial coalition.

Among all voters, black and white, below the median family income of $30,000, the Democrats retained in 1986 a substantial 53-40 edge, but this advantage has fallen from a 56-35 advantage in 1981.

As a result, Democrats are not only losing support among the economic group traditionally most loyal, but class-skewed voter turnout declines have further weakened Democratic vote-getting ability as the poor and lower-middle classes go to the polls in fewer numbers.

In California, for example, this trend was most apparent: voter turnout dropped "through the floor in 1986," according to Mark DiCamillo, managing director of the California Poll. By almost every measure, DiCamillo pointed out, those who voted in California's election were a far more elite group than the entire population of the state:

"Sixty-nine percent of the adults in California are white, non-Hispanics, but 84 percent of the voters are white, non-Hispanics. . . . Twenty-nine percent of the public are college graduates, but on Election Day, 38 percent of the voters were college graduates. In terms of family income, 20 percent [of the people] make $50,000 or more, but on Election Day, 29 percent of the voters made that much."

The decline in polarized class-based voting was critically important to the Democrats. Voter turnout in the 1986 election fell to the lowest level since World War II, and voter drop-off has been sharpest among Democratic-leaning poor voters.

If economically polarized voting had not declined and the upper-middle class had remained as Republican as it had been in the prior three elections, the Democratic party would have been decisively defeated; voters with incomes of $50,000-a-year or more shifted from a 63-37 GOP percentage point edge in 1982 to 53-47 in 1986, a 20 point Democratic gain, according to CBS-*New York Times* exit polls. These 20 percentage points more than made up for the losses among low-income voters.

The extreme fragility of the Democratic Senate victory in 1986 is reflected by the fact that Republican Senate candidates got a higher total percentage of the vote in 1986, when the GOP lost eight seats—49 percent—than they did in 1980, when the Republicans won 12 seats—47.2 percent. Taking the first three states in alphabetical order—Alabama, Alaska and Arizona—shows how this is possible: in 1980, the GOP swept all three states winning a combined total of 51 percent of the vote; in 1986, the GOP lost the Alabama seat, but its average vote in the three states went up to 54 percent, because of a decisive victory in Arizona.

In many respects, what seems to have taken place is that the Democratic party is currently equipped to perform fairly well as long as the electorate is not markedly polarized, not only in terms of voting, but also in terms of major interest-group support.

Democratic victory last November came at a time when not only was there a significant lessening in class-based voting, but also when another major group—the business-lobbying community—was severely split, particularly by tax and trade issues.

In the election of 1980 and during the legislative session of 1981, a generally united business community was central to the success of the Republican party and the Reagan administration. In the subsequent years, however, the continuing debate over trade legislation has split those firms seeking protection from those seeking to import foreign goods. Along very similar lines, the 1986 tax bill split companies paying high rates of taxation from those paying low rates.

Another polarizing issue that has quieted in recent years is the explosive anger against high tax burdens that severely undermined the Democratic coalition in the late 1970s and early 1980s.

The reemergence of polarizing issues remains a substantial threat to the Democratic party.

In relatively quiet periods such as the present, the pluralism of the Democratic party works to its advantage, as it can claim to at least partially represent a wide range of interests, even if those interests sometimes conflict.

At times when, however, there are sharp issues dividing the country—as taxation and spending policies did in the 1978–1981 period—the Democratic party's pluralism makes it very difficult to produce a coherent response.

Despite the expansion of the Republican constituency, the Democratic party remains far more pluralistic. This is partially reflected in the money Democratic candidates receive and in the votes key members cast.

In the 1984 election, Democratic candidates had far more diverse support from political action committees than Republicans. Democratic House and Senate candidates received a total of $24.4 million from labor PACs and $28.2 million from business and trade association PACs, almost equal amounts. In contrast, Republican candidates received only $1.5 million from labor while getting $38.3 from business and trade association PACs, a ratio of 25 to 1.

Similarly, among the new Democratic Senate Committee chairmanships, *Congressional Quarterly* recently noted that half have records of supporting President Reagan while the other half have been strong opponents of the administration.

For the more homogeneous Republican party, adopting consistent responses to polarizing issues is far easier, since there are fewer internal conflicts to resolve. In the long run, a political party's ability to respond successfully to sharply divisive issues is of critical importance, because it is the divisive issues around which new partisan realignments are formed.

Despite Democratic erosion, the party has survived an extremely difficult decade, and the Republican party has been unable to consummate a realignment

in American politics. Stalled before the November elections, Republican momentum is now likely to be further slowed as a result of the Iran-contra scandal, a
severe blow to a party in the midst of an attempt to piece together a heterogenous
coalition including country clubbers, supply-siders, ideological conservatives and
fundamentalist Christians.

The 1986 election results suggested for the first time that the infusion of
voter support to the GOP from the white Christian community carries with it
some major liabilities. In states as diverse as Minnesota, South Carolina, Oregon
and Texas, struggles for control of local Republican parties between old-guard
regulars and newly active Christians, and parallel contests for party nominations,
have created open wounds resulting in the general election defeat of a number
of Republican candidates.

While it is not clear how the Republican party will react to the current
Iran-contra crisis, it is unmistakable that after 12 years of developing the most
sophisticated, high-tech political organization in the history of the nation, the
Republican party has grown fat and needs a substantial reorganization.

In the last election, the Republican party structure had become dominated
by a tiny universe of pollsters, consultants and vendors who had a lock on much
of the party's huge cash flow, encouraging the kind of entropy that produced a
$12 million computerized get-out-the-vote campaign without any appreciable
content to motivate voters.

In many respects the Republican party structure has begun to act more like
the management of an overweight Fortune 500 company than a lean and hungry
political party. Corporate self-dealing was reflected in the payment of $250,000
in bonuses to the staff of the National Republican Senatorial Committee the day
after the election; in the payment over two years of $473,000 to Wyatt Stewart,
finance director of the Republican Congressional Committee, despite a 40 percent decline in revenues; and in the appointment of President Reagan's daughter,
Maureen, as co-chairman of the Republican National Committee.

If nothing else, the Iran-contra scandal will animate as well as disrupt the
struggle for the Republican presidential nomination, a process in which Vice
President George Bush appears intent on taking the route of money and endorsements in the tradition of Walter F. Mondale, while providing little rationale for
a revitalization of the Republican coalition. The competition to determine who
will have the chance to become the heir to Ronald Reagan is now an open battle
in which all the candidates will be under pressure to debate, vigorously and
publicly, substantive issues and policies in a contest likely to test the public will.

At the same time, Democratic candidates and officials of the Democratic
National Committee are reflecting a growing awareness of the party's minority
status. As a result, the DNC has already sharply reduced the power of special
interest caucuses, and the party appears to be preparing for a potentially construc-
tive debate on the basic economic issues of productivity, international trade and
the structure of the federal budget.

# Political Changes
# in the South

## Black Majorities, White Minorities,
## and the Fundamentalists

*Dissent*, Winter 1987

In Louisiana this past year, two seemingly disparate political events took place: the election of Sidney Barthelemy, a black Democrat, as mayor of New Orleans; and the endorsement of the Reverend Marion G. (Pat) Robertson's bid for the Republican presidential nomination by televangelist Jimmy Swaggart. In fact, both developments represent embryonic trends within the Democratic and Republican parties that are likely to intensify conflict within the GOP coalition and to ameliorate some of the tensions within the Democratic coalition.

The election of Barthelemy in New Orleans was significant because it reflects the revival of the importance of white voters in majority black communities. In first a primary and then a run-off, Barthelemy defeated credible white and black opponents. White voters supported Barthelemy by large margins, after deciding against throwing their votes away on a white candidate sure to lose a run-off against a black.

In the final election between two blacks, Barthelemy and William Jefferson, Barthelemy lost in the black community but overwhelmingly carried the white community. "When blacks were in the minority, they could decide who would be the white candidate," Barthelemy said. "Basically, what has happened is the white community is now in the position that the black community was in before."

In one respect, the voting patterns suggest the undermining of black voting strength by a white minority in a process the local paper, the *Times Picayune*, called "the white veto." From another vantage point, however, the outcome of the New Orleans election—which was replicated in the Atlanta September congressional fight, when whites effectively elected John Lewis over Julian Bond—suggests a potential lessening of political conflict between blacks and whites, the most divisive force in the Democratic party.

Even in Memphis, a city where blacks are about to become a majority and where race has been the single most important factor in politics for the past two decades, blacks and whites have been quietly discussing the possibility of joining forces to beat the conservative white mayor, Richard Hackett.

These developments in New Orleans, Atlanta, Memphis, and in scattered legislative districts in Alabama and Virginia put whites back in the political equation in majority—or near majority—black communities. This is a phenomenon which in the long run can only help a beleaguered southern Democratic party. Until now, the political process in many of these communities has functioned in many ways to convert the two-party system into a means of dividing the races. In Memphis, there has been an extraordinary correlation between the racial makeup of a precinct and its Democratic and Republican margins. This division by race was partially repaired only recently when moderate whites, including many Republicans, backed a black woman over a white man—both Democrats running in a nonpartisan election—to elect the first black to a city-wide post. The victory of the black woman resulted from a unique set of alliances in the byzantine politics of Memphis, but it set in process a quiet examination of a biracial alliance to back a moderate black for mayor in 1987, including such prospective candidates as Dr. Willie Herenton, the respected superintendent of schools.

Black politics in many communities has entered a new stage in which the struggle for black control has been achieved, and the battle is now between various black factions. Jim Duffy, a political consultant who has worked on campaigns throughout the South, recently noted: "Once the fight is between black factions, the white vote becomes a central factor, and in this kind of contest, the code words for a successful candidate are: 'I am going to be fair, I'm going to be the elected official of everyone.'"

While trends in these cities are encouraging coalition politics, just the opposite is taking place within a key constituent group of the Republican party: fundamentalist and evangelical Christians. Within this community, the presidential campaign of television evangelist Marion G. (Pat) Robertson is serving to lessen prospects for a successful alliance between traditional country-club Republicans and politically converted fundamentalist Christians.

In Michigan's August 1986 primary, Robertson's Freedom Council demonstrated the power of the Christian movement to influence a complex, low-turnout political event by winning a substantial number of "precinct delegates" while coming in second to Vice-President George Bush in the first test of prospective candidates for the 1988 GOP nomination.

From another vantage point, however, exit polls of the voters in the Michigan primary revealed strong suspicion and hostility toward his candidacy among Republican primary voters, as even born-again Christians were more supportive of Bush than Robertson. These findings were a severe blow to a man who had considered that his background—as old-line Virginia gentry, son of a U.S. senator, graduate of Yale Law School, and the successful entrepreneurial developer of a spectacularly successful religious-commercial television broadcasting empire grossing over $200 million annually—would provide broader credibility and legitimacy to his presidential bid.

In the months after the Michigan primary, Robertson has focused his activities on firming up his own base within the conservative fundamentalist and evangelical communities. The success of this drive has surprised both religious and more pragmatic Republican strategists, as many Christian leaders who were openly or privately scornful of Robertson have been forced by pressures within the fundamentalist Christian community to join the Robertson bandwagon. Among those who have endorsed Robertson or are leaning his way are Swaggart, who had earlier described the Robertson bid as a mistake; Robert Grant, head of Christian Voice, a lobby that issues moral "report cards" on elected officials; two former presidents of the Southern Baptist Convention, Charles Stanley and Jimmy Drapper; the Reverend Tim LaHaye, founder of the American Coalition for Traditional Values and perhaps the leading critic of "secular humanism"; and Ed McAteer, president of the Religious Roundtable.

The coalescing of Christian support behind Robertson has two consequences. First, Christian leaders already committed to a candidate are taken out of the bargaining process normal in the early phases of selecting a presidential nominee. This process is critical for any group seeking to gain political influence and leverage. The placement of a substantial bloc of the leadership in what is sure to be a losing campaign almost guarantees deep resentment and anger within the Christian community when the GOP rejects Robertson. Instead of negotiating for influence in the campaigns of the mainstream competitors, and in the next administration if one of the competitors wins the presidency in 1988, the Robertson campaign is forcing much of the conservative Christian community to place all its chips on a campaign sure to lose the nomination.

The second, and related, consequence is that the Robertson campaign has become a magnet coalescing much of the religious right. Just as it is reducing the ability of such other prospective candidates as George Bush, Jack Kemp, and Paul Laxalt to bargain with the religious right, Robertson's drive is functioning to meld together those forces seeking to force action on the most divisive political matters: abortion, school prayer, tuition tax credits, and other "value laden" issues. All this adds up to a high probability of conflict within the GOP, undermining the Republican party's ability to maintain the highly fragile coalition that worked so well for President Reagan. The emergence of Swaggart as an important force in presidential politics epitomizes the prospective difficulties for the GOP. Swaggart is a sharp critic of other religions, particularly Catholicism which he has denounced as a "false cult" and a "doctrine of devils." Working and middle-class Catholics, however, have been an essential ingredient of recent Republican success, and Swaggart provides the Democratic party with material almost perfectly designed to push Catholics back into the Democratic fold.

One of the major successes of the GOP over the past two decades has been the driving of wedges between important elements of the Democratic coalition, as the forces and mechanisms for compromise and negotiation within the Democratic party weakened during the Vietnam and civil rights conflicts. In this context, another strong supporter of Robertson, Jamie Buckingham, founding pastor of the Tabernacle Church in Melbourne, Florida and publisher of the religious newsletter the *Buckingham Report*, reflected the potential for divisiveness when conservative Christians are pulled together within one campaign. In an interview with *Christianity Today*, Buckingham said: "Now we need a man to call us back to righteousness. There is a growing feeling among many Christians—myself included—that Robertson may be ordained by God for this task. . . . This ability to hear from God should be the number one qualification for the U.S. Presidency. If Christians believe God has a plan for this nation, shouldn't we want a man in the White House who listens to God, rather than a man who acts on the basis of political expediency?"

It is, however, expediency that gives strength to successful political alliances, both in the case of the biracial drives for elective office in the South, and in the case of the alliance between martini-drinking Republicans and Bible-thumping fundamentalists as they line up at the polls.

# Dole's Transformations
## *Ideological Blur Characterizes Career*

*The Washington Post,* March 9, 1987

On election night, November 2, 1976, Sen. Robert J. Dole (R-Kan.) angrily lashed out at his staff as he saw his chance to become vice president disappear. "He was like a snake," said a friend who was with him.

The defeat was particularly bitter for Dole, whose harsh attacks on the Democratic ticket of Jimmy Carter and Walter F. Mondale—"If we added all the killed and wounded in all Democrat wars in this century, it would be about 1.6 million Americans, enough to fill the city of Detroit"—were often cited as a key factor in the outcome.

After emerging from a black depression, Dole began to perform what amounted to political surgery on himself.

As part of this process, he went to Dorothy Sarnoff, a New York specialist whose firm, Speech Dynamics, attempts to restructure the presence, image and style of politicians, corporate executives and other public figures.

"He was a wonderful student," Sarnoff said. "We discussed his sense of humor. We changed that. We took the snideness away from him. We changed the way he dressed to more of a classy look."

The program, which costs $3,500 and involves extensive work before cameras and lengthy discussions, was highly successful. "We change behavior very, very fast," Sarnoff said. "My father was a surgeon and I like to think of the camera like a surgeon's knife."

It was a process that Dole had experienced in physical terms after World War II when he spent 39 months in the hospital and submitted to seven operations to rebuild his battle-wounded body. In many respects, his political career represents a series of self-performed transformations of his public persona in a process friends call growing and critics call a cynical manipulation of his public image.

"If you get a guy who is 50 years old or more, you've got what you've got," one of Dole's backers pointed out. "But Dole, when he sees he's got a problem, he tries to change it. Take the hatchet-man issue. When he decided 'I've got to fix that,' he was able to change it. He can overcome those things. Dole is perceived very differently today because of conscious acts. That's something most politicians just cannot do."

For Dole, who is 63, some of the most influential factors in the development of his legislative career have been his close elections, a near defeat while running for a second Senate term in 1974, and real defeat in his two previous bids for national office, the vice presidency in 1976 and the presidency in 1980.

Over the years, he has assumed a series of different and often contradictory postures.

As majority leader in 1985–86, and as minority leader this year, he has put on a full-court press to shore up support from the conservative wing of the Republican party. He adopted positions on foreign policy often more conservative than President Reagan's, brought the New Right's agenda on abortion, gun control and school prayer to the Senate floor, and engineered Senate approval of the controversial judicial appointment of conservative Daniel A. Manion with tactics that left a bitter taste among moderate GOP colleagues.

During the past two weeks, controversies have emerged over his willingness to publicly join forces with the National Right to Work Committee to oppose a labor legislative initiative, and over his vote switch last year, in which he first voted in favor of sanctions against South Africa, then voted to support Reagan's veto of the measure.

Dole's sharp rightward turn beginning in 1985 struck those on the right, because in the previous three years he had won the respect and admiration of an entirely different political universe: tax reformers, much of the moderate-to-liberal media elite and even a number of Democrats.

As Senate Finance Committee chairman, Dole became, in 1982, a populist of the prairies, singlehandedly persuading Congress and the administration to raise corporate taxes by $280 billion over five years, far more than Sen. Edward M. Kennedy (D-Mass.) ever contemplated.

In that same period, he led the floor fight to make the Rev. Martin Luther King, Jr.'s, birthday into a federal holiday, and backed the Reagan administration into accepting the landmark 1982 Voting Rights Act, which permits the Justice Department to bring suit even when it cannot prove that local authorities consciously intended to deny political power to minorities.

This ideological blur has characterized most of the 26 years Dole has served in the House (1961–68) and Senate (1969–present). He is a politician who could vote against the creation of Medicare and consistently earn conservative ratings from most interest groups, while at the same time emerging as a key congressional proponent of food stamps and other nutritional programs.

"There is a deep ambiguity about Senator Dole. It's almost a Jekyll and Hyde," said civil rights lobbyist Joseph Rauh, Jr. At the same time, conservative

Paul M. Weyrich declared that the change in Dole over the past three years is "overwhelming, almost impossible to describe."

Even by the standards of presidential candidates, Dole's ambition and all-consuming interest in the process of politics, to the near exclusion of family life and extracurricular activities, are exceptional.

One of his most revealing statements about himself came last year in the heat of a bitter Senate floor fight. Then-Senate Minority Leader Robert C. Byrd (D-W.Va.) accused him of abusing his powers as majority leader. Dole replied: "I didn't become majority leader to lose."

Dole devotes almost every waking hour to the legislative and political process. He and his second wife, Elizabeth Hanford Dole, the secretary of transportation, do not even have breakfast together, in order to get to the office as early as possible. After ten years of marriage, they have yet to take time to buy a house, living instead in what was Dole's bachelor apartment in The Watergate. When they are in Washington at night, supper is most often at a restaurant or delivered from a restaurant, if not taken from the freezer.

Dole regularly works and campaigns six or seven days a week, and most working days are at least 12 hours long. He does not tolerate mistakes and errors by aides and campaign workers. "I've seen him blow up if someone is late getting the car. Afterwards, when he is still angry because someone screwed up, he won't talk to the guilty party for days or weeks. It can be pretty tough if you are thin-skinned," an associate commented.

For those who share his immediate goals and his willingness to work, however, there is often a deep allegiance, even among Democratic staffers who, for example, backed his 1982 tax bill.

"Dole is fantastic to work with," a liberal House Democratic aide said. "He loves the fight. He is constantly thinking of the angles. You can feel the electricity. He is in the battle all the time and, unlike a lot of senators, he knows some or all of the details. He is not emotional, not the kind of guy who puts his arm around you. He's always thinking."

Asked to describe the most revealing incident they knew about Dole, friends and adversaries often cited a bitter fight involving the 1982 tax bill, which included a Dole-backed $2.8 billion provision requiring restaurants to deduct taxes against waiters' and waitresses' income from tips.

The provision was adamantly opposed by the National Restaurant Association. The fight over the provision finally came to a vote at 2 A.M. and, in an outcome that threatened to undermine support for the entire bill, Dole was beaten.

When the restaurant lobbyists went home to bed, dreaming of their victory, Dole remained on the Senate floor, where he quietly won Senate approval for a "three-martini luncheon" amendment, a body blow to the restaurant industry that would have eliminated half of the deductibility of business meals.

Sheepishly, restaurant industry representatives returned to the Senate begging to replace the business-meal amendment with the original waiters' tips proposal. "We gave it back to them and they ended up thanking us," said Robert Lighthizer, who was chief counsel to the Finance Committee and is now a private lobbyist.

"When Dole sees there is something wrong, or gets beaten on something like the tip amendment, he will work on it until he finds a way to resolve the problem and then he will not waste anyone's time, especially his own, waiting around to get done what has to get done," another close associate commented.

This single-minded, no-nonsense approach can sometimes be brutal. The late Huck Boyd, a Kansas newspaper publisher, Republican national committeeman and Dole mentor, said in an interview last year that once Dole decided his first marriage was no longer working, he wasted no time dissolving it. "He saw that it was over so he ended it."

Phyllis Buzick, his first wife, said what she remembers most about the divorce was "the suddenness of it. . . . He came in and told me he wanted out. He came back a month later and asked how do we divide the property. I told him to talk to my lawyer. I'm not a person who begs, I'm not a woman who begs."

Dole then arranged to have the proceedings held under a special emergency divorce law in Kansas that resulted in the dissolution of the marriage in three months, she said. "I went to the hearing, and it was over."

Despite this experience, Buzick said, "I think he's the best man to be president. He doesn't know how to do a job halfway. . . . I'm glad I'm not there. I don't want to be first lady."

The same kind of ambivalent feelings toward Dole are voiced in private by some civil rights advocates, who describe Dole as one of the most important senators to have on your side. But when he is an adversary, they say, his will to win outweighs his willingness to remain within some of the traditional rules of legislative conflict.

They cite both the Manion nomination and a 1983 battle over appointments to the U.S. Civil Rights Commission. In the Manion fight, the Republican Senate leadership was able to avoid defeat by using a complicated series of maneuvers in which some absent senators were incorrectly described as Manion supporters. In the Civil Rights Commission debate, Dole was accused of failing to live up to the terms of a compromise.

"These are the kind of gray events that take place in the heat of battle and you never know who is really lying, and who is telling the truth about what went on on the Senate floor. It is, however, the kind of thing that makes you worry," one key negotiator in both contests said while discussing Dole's role.

"I never felt it was intentional," Sen. Nancy Landon Kassebaum (R-Kan.) said about the misportrayal of her voting intentions and those of other senators. "It would have left a better taste in everybody's mouth if it had been done correctly." Then she added: "Bob Dole, when he wants something, he is some- body who works all the angles."

While he took on the civil rights community in backing the Manion nomina- tion, Dole has been a key ally of that community on other issues, including the key 1982 Voting Rights Act.

During that debate, Dole demonstrated one of his key leadership talents: his ability to manipulate the Reagan administration into supporting legislation it had originally opposed.

In the case of the Voting Rights Act, Dole unilaterally declared that a version strongly opposed by conservatives in the Justice Department and White House was "the compromise." The move effectively forced the administration to acquiesce in a bill that significantly expanded the powers of the federal government to initiate voting rights cases. "He pulled off a shotgun marriage between the administration and the bill, all because he knew the administration was scared to look anti-civil rights," a Dole ally said. "The White House had to swallow and take it."

At the moment, Dole is engaged in a similar tactic through the creation of his Republican Task Force on Farm and Rural America, an organization of 30 GOP members of Congress and governors designed to further his presidential bid in such key states as Iowa and South Dakota.

In terms of substance, the group appears headed toward endorsement of a program directly at odds with many of the basic free-market tenets of the Reagan administration. But by defining the group as the "Republican Task Force," Dole has taken the edge off likely criticism from within the party.

Rep. Pat Roberts (R-Kan.), a leading task force member and Dole ally, said a central goal will be to remedy a Reagan administration farm policy of "benign neglect" that has now "turned malignant."

Policies of deregulation mean that "everything we have to have [in rural America] to stay alive is under threat," said Roberts, noting that 69 Kansas communities face loss of bus services. In a basic disagreement with Reagan market-based policies, Roberts said that in regulatory decisions, "revenue cannot be the sole" criterion.

Perhaps Dole's crowning achievement in the co-opting of the Reagan administration was the 1982 tax bill.

That year, Dole forced a deeply anti-tax administration to accept, over the bitter complaints of conservative hardliners, what was the largest tax hike in the history of the nation.

Not only did the bill raise taxes, but it gutted many of the breaks won by business in the administration's 1981 tax cut. In terms of business taxes, the 1982 bill represented a 180-degree reversal of policy for an administration that the year before had won sharp cuts in effective corporate rates, along with cuts that benefitted wealthy taxpayers far more than the middle class.

After persuading a reluctant administration to join forces behind the bill, Dole declared with some irony that Democratic charges that the Reagan administration was "unfair" had been "erased since the president's strong support of the tax bill."

The 1982 tax bill was also a showcase for Dole's Kansas populism.

Delighting in disclosures of profitable Fortune 500 businesses paying no taxes, Dole persuaded a Republican-controlled Senate Finance Committee (and later the entire Congress) to eliminate or cut back special provisions allowing corporations to buy and sell tax breaks, permitting defense contractors to continually postpone paying taxes and giving corporations enlarged depreciation allowances.

While a populist in the 1982 tax debate, Dole has achieved considerable affluence. His most recent financial disclosure report shows total 1985 income for himself and his wife of about $350,000, including salaries, honoraria and other sources. Their stock and property holdings appeared to be worth just over $1.2 million that year, with liabilities of about $150,000.

Populism on the tax issue and support of nutritional programs and aid to the handicapped are, however, just part of a record that overall is deeply conservative. Over the years, Dole has built a record of high ratings from such conservative groups as the American Conservative Union and the American Security Council (76 percent and 96 percent, respectively), while such liberal organizations as Americans for Democratic Action and the AFL-CIO (6 percent and 16 percent, respectively) have regularly given him low ratings.

The core of Dole's philosophy remains closely tied to a midwestern conservatism, a traditional Republicanism that predated supply-side theory, where hard work and balanced books are the key to success.

The one issue that brings forth a passionate, animated reaction from Dole is the deficit. The deficit "is going to engulf this country one of these days. That may be gloom and doom, but it's a fact," Dole said.

At a New Jersey Republican gathering two days ago, Dole concluded his speech with: "The most exciting vote I've ever cast in the Senate was on May 10, 1985. . . . The vote was 50 to 49, and in that vote we terminated 14 federal programs, we froze every COLA [cost-of-living adjustment]. . . . In the U.S. Senate that morning, we demonstrated to the American people there was a majority willing to take on everyone in America for the sake of America, to put on the brakes and tell the American people that someone was willing to vote no. . . . The deficit is not going to grow away or go away. We are going to have to address it head-on, without taxes, and we are going to have to do it the hard way."

This posture has turned him into an ideological adversary of one outspoken wing of the Republican party: supply-side proponents of the theory that tax cuts will pay for themselves through new growth.

The centrality of the deficit to Dole's approach has led him to be one of the leading advocates of tax increases—a position he has backed away from as the contest for the GOP nomination gets closer—and a supporter of budget cuts, including controversial freezes on Social Security benefit levels.

The decision by Dole and other members of the Senate leadership to force a vote on Social Security freeze proposals as part of an overall budget package in 1985 was widely seen as a significant contributing factor to the difficulties faced by many Republican senators who encountered repeated Democratic attacks on the issue in the 1986 campaign.

After the election, Dole acknowledged the importance of the issue, commenting: "I think we lost [Republican control of the Senate] frankly because of a lot of negative, distorted advertising on Social Security by the Democrats."

A second theme consistently underlying Dole's career has been a fundamental partisanship. Early in his Senate career, he emerged as the leading defender of the Nixon administration, lashing out at critics during the Watergate investigation. "This newspaper," he said about the *Washington Post,* "which makes a comfortable living off publishing stolen government documents and memoranda, which happily ran in its news columns the purloined top secret documents of the U.S., is today howling for the blood of anyone who may conceivably have seen the purloined documents of Mr. Larry O'Brien, chairman of the Democratic National Committee."

After barely surviving a 1974 reelection fight, in which he gained an even stronger reputation for slashing attacks, Dole began to moderate his tactics.

"In 1974, he almost lost because he was almost too conservative," William Taggert, a former Dole aide, told the Kansas City *Times.* "The electorate thought that he had no concern for the needy, that he was too capitalist oriented. . . . We got the drift real quick that it [support for food stamps] would be a new thrust."

Bill Roy, an obstetrician who lost the 1974 race to Dole by less than one percent, still remembers hearing reports of Dole telling high school students to ask their parents if they knew "how many abortions Bill Roy has performed." Since then, Roy said he has spoken to Dole, who said, "If I continued to be doing what I was doing in 1974 and 1976 [his vice presidential bid], I wasn't going anywhere."

In the years since then, Dole has taken the harsh edge off attacks on adversaries, but he has remained deeply partisan. In the Finance Committee, Dole successfully used the strategy of producing legislation first by reaching agreement in closed sessions of the Republican majority, and then presenting to the full committee what amounted to an accomplished fact, with enough votes to win approval.

On the Senate floor, where there has been a tradition of openness since the majority leadership of Sen. Mike Mansfield (D-Mont.) starting in 1961, Dole established a degree of tough control unseen in a generation.

He carefully orchestrated the amendment process, and the rules under which senators get recognition, to effectively prevent Democrats from forcing issues that could be embarrassing to the administration or to the GOP.

His leadership tactics produced a brief explosion of anger last August 5, when then-minority leader Byrd declared: "I have had enough of this business of having the majority leader stand here and act as traffic cop on this floor. . . . He determines who will call up an amendment, when they will call up an amendment and what will be in the amendment." The conflict was never resolved, except by the Republicans' loss of the Senate.

Since then, Dole has indicated that he relishes the opportunity to go to battle with the Democrats as the leader of the Senate minority. Anticipating a drive by the Democrats to force compliance with the terms of the SALT II nuclear arms treaty, Dole recently warned:

"One thing I can guarantee above all, they are going to get a battle royal on the floor of the U.S. Senate. . . . We are ready to do battle. We conservatives enter the fray with a few less soldiers on our side. We're not going to win them all, but we're not going to duck any. We're not going to concede any."

As Dole now attempts to capitalize on the damage of the Iran-contra scandal to the presidential chances of Vice President Bush, his advisers are pressing him to attempt to complete one more transformation of his approach to politics.

"It's what some are calling his 'vision' problem," one adviser said, "but it really involves doing something he is not comfortable with, talking about values and views in a generic sense. He's got to break through the legislative mind-set. He has to extrapolate into the future."

At various appearances, he has been clearly uncomfortable with questions asking him to describe his larger goals for the country.

"I've always found that it's great to make speeches about what you are going to do when you take over. But you've got to have the votes. It's the bottom line in this town," Dole said on John McLaughlin's "One on One" television show on November 14.

Asked two days ago what sets him apart from the other presidential candidates, Dole said: "I'm a producer. . . . I've been tested in my lifetime, both personally and legislatively. I'm a survivor. I keep coming back."

# The Political Impasse

*The New York Review of Books,* March 26, 1987

Two years ago, after President Reagan's 1984 landslide, Republican strategists saw the 1988 presidential election as an opportunity to solidify the GOP's substantial gains in their long campaign to make the country Republican. The 1986 election and the Iran-contra scandal have not only severely damaged those expectations; they have revealed weaknesses in both political parties and in their leadership, leaving a tangled prospect for the next few years.

The takeover of the Senate by the Democrats last November was less a mandate for the party—a shift of just 26,000 votes would have left the Senate in Republican hands—than the result of a string of lucky breaks. The Democratic party has only begun the painful process of accepting that it is no longer the permanent majority party in the country. For Democrats who still don't understand this, the Iran-contra scandal may prove a dangerous diversion, just as Watergate in the 1970s allowed the Democrats to gloss over the deep divisions between the party's centrists, who supported Hubert Humphrey for president over George McGovern and now look to such politicians as Sam Nunn or Gray Hart, and its leftists, who were drawn to McGovern, and then to Ted Kennedy, and are now left without a clear choice after the withdrawal of Mario Cuomo.

In recent elections many working-class and lower-middle-class whites have chosen either not to vote or to vote for Republican presidential candidates. Cuomo's decision not to seek the nomination means that there is likely to be no Democratic competitor whose basic strategy is to mobilize such people. Instead, with the exception of Jesse Jackson, who has no chance of being nominated, the Democratic field is made up of candidates whose chief political aim has been to strengthen the party's appeal to the middle classes, although some of the candidates are now trying to appeal to Cuomo's former supporters.

A prominent Democratic poll taker, Paul Maslin, recently said:

From 1976 through 1984, the biggest single decline in Democratic voting has been among the lower- and middle-class white voters below forty—the Springsteen vote. If 1988 becomes a battle of elites and neither party can generate enthusiasm from the majority of Americans, the Democrats may get lucky and win, but the party will not have done much to advance a real foundation of public support. If on the other hand the Democrats start to inspire these people, at least increase voting levels, bring some back into the system, it will provide a real chance to govern successfully and for a long time.

The Democratic party will have a hard time achieving the goals outlined by Maslin, no matter who is selected from a prospective field that now includes, in addition to Hart and Nunn, Sen. Joseph Biden, Rep. Richard Gephardt, Massachusetts governor Michael Dukakis, and former Arizona governor Bruce Babbitt. The difficulty the Democratic nominee will have to overcome is reflected in *Washington Post*- ABC polls in 1981 and 1986 showing a sharp decline in support for the Democratic party on the part of white voters. Among such voters from families with incomes between $20,000 and $30,000, the percentage calling themselves Democrats compared to those calling themselves Republicans has shifted from a 46-42 Democratic advantage in 1981 to a 50-45 Republican advantage in 1986. This was a devastating blow to a Democratic party claiming to represent the interests of the less powerful in society, and a reflection of continuing racial conflict within the party. Among the poorest white voters, those making less than $20,000, the Democratic margin has fallen from a strong 55-36 in 1981 to 51-43 in 1986.

At the same time, conflicts within the Democratic party itself work against the kind of cohesion essential to a presidential candidate seeking a strong mandate. As Democrats take over the Senate, for example, seven of the fourteen new Democratic committee chairmen have records of providing strong support to the Reagan administration, while the other seven have records of intense opposition. Foreign policy remains extremely divisive. This winter's bitter fight among House Democrats over Rep. Les Aspin's chairmanship of the Armed Services Committee reveals the extent to which such issues as contra aid and the MX missile—

both formerly favored by Aspin—remain unresolved. The party has yet to formulate a military policy it can sell to the public.

The Democrats' sources of campaign money also reveal their internal divisions. In the 1984 election, for example, Democratic candidates for House and Senate received roughly the same amounts of money from union PACs, $24.4 million, as from business and trade association PACs, $28.2 million—that is, money representing opposing political interests. This pattern of contributions helps to encourage paralysis in legislation. It gives no clear sense of direction to party leaders facing difficult choices on military and domestic spending. With the national debt exceeding $2 trillion, the legislator must often make a decision favorable to business at the expense of labor, or vice versa.

The schisms facing the Republicans in the post-Reagan years appear likely to be at least as serious. The conservative wing of the GOP is full of discontent with Reagan but it has been unable to coalesce around a candidate, and it has wavered at various times between Rep. Jack Kemp, Patrick J. Buchanan, and the television evangelist Pat Robertson. Vice President George Bush is running into increasing difficulty as he attempts to become an ecumenical nominee supported by both Reagan conservatives and by the GOP's moderate, East Coast faction. Sen. Robert Dole, in turn, is trying to revive the Taft wing of the Republican party, for which the principal issue is the danger of the federal deficit, the same deficit that has made the Reagan economic and military program possible. Dole seeks, moreover, to expand his constituency with support for such liberal programs as food stamps and aid to the handicapped, as well as for such right-of-center causes as opposition to abortion and to gun control, and conservative appointments to the federal bench.

Campaign money has also created problems for the Republicans, but, unlike the Democrats' difficulties, these spring from the party's prosperity. The three major Republican party committees—the national, senatorial, and congressional—raise roughly four times the amount of cash that their Democratic counterparts do. During the late 1970s and early 1980s, this huge financial advantage was used very effectively to identify vulnerable Democratic office holders, and to finance challengers to run against them. Recently, however, Democratic politicians have become increasingly sophisticated in both raising money and building up local support in anticipation of well-financed Republican challengers. The Democratic committees have begun to channel what funds they have into elections where Republicans are particularly vulnerable. One might even say that in 1986 the accumulation of campaign funds reached a point of diminishing return. In a number of races including the Senate contests in Georgia, North Dakota, and Alabama, huge amounts were raised and spent but made no discernible difference in the outcome of the election.

The Republican party, during the last four years, has used its financial leverage to invest in expensive, national computerized drives to get out the vote, but these failed to increase turnout. Instead these drives, using commercial TV marketing companies and programmed telephoned messages, suggest that the Republican party faces the danger of becoming overdependent on promotional technology. At the same time, the three Republican party committees have gotten in the habit of handing out $3,000- to $7,500-a-month consulting contracts to former White House aides and former party officials, and to the relatives of the powerful—including President Reagan's daughter, Maureen, and Senator Paul Laxalt's daughter, Michelle.

But the pattern of contributions to Republican House and Senate candidates does not encourage paralyzing conflicts over legislation as it does for Democrats. For Republican candidates, there is a 25-to-1 ratio in favor of business and trade association PACs ($38.3 million, to $1.5 million for labor). This decisively probusiness bias worked to the advantage of the GOP in the late 1970s and early 1980s, when the electorate was sharply divided on issues of taxes, military spending, and programs subsidizing the poor and unemployed.

Since then, however, the continuing dependence on business money has damaged Republican efforts to promote a more populist image. Pressures from business supporters and donors were a major factor behind the extreme reluctance of House Republicans to support the 1986 tax reform bill, which transferred $120 billion in taxes from people to corporations over five years. The Democrats were thus able to take much of the credit for the legislation. Similarly, opposition to appropriations to clean up toxic waste sites has been more intense among Republicans than among Democrats—and such opposition does not help to convert the Republican party into a majority party.

For the Democrats, the effect of unemployment and inflation during the Carter years has been that fewer voters trust the party to deal with economic issues. The current issue of *Public Opinion* magazine, in an analysis of 1986 poll data from the major networks and newspapers and from both the Harris and Gallup polls, finds that voters have strikingly different evaluations of each party. Voters said that the GOP was more likely to produce prosperity (by 10 to 18 percentage points), to cut inflation (14 to 22 points), and, by a 5-point margin, to deal with the "most important problems facing the country." For the Democrats, the most damaging finding is that the party has lost its status in the minds of voters as the party of prosperity and of high levels of employment. According to the polls the major strength of the Democratic party is that it is now seen as caring about and protecting individuals and groups. So were the Democrats favored when voters were asked which party would better handle the problems of farmers (by 18 to 29 points, depending on the poll), the elderly (by 27 points), the unemployed (by 17 points), women (17 to 23 points), and minorities (23 points).

Population trends favor the Republicans. In presidential elections, the GOP has carefully constructed a southern and western base that will be difficult for the Democrats to break up in 1988. The 1986 victories for Republican candidates for governor in Florida, Texas, South Carolina, and Alabama demonstrate that this core of support remains strong. In the House of Representatives, the 81-seat Democratic majority depends in large part on the continuing success of congressmen who won traditionally Republican seats in the Watergate elections of 1974 and 1976, and on victories during the recession year of 1982.

The metropolitan regions with the highest growth rates, many of them in the suburbs of the South and Southwest, are likely to vote Republican (particularly when new districts are created after the 1990 census). "When you travel through the old South and see a McDonald's or a Pizza Hut going up, you know the Republicans are coming," John Morgan, a GOP consultant, said recently. At the same time, Democratic strongholds in Chicago, Cleveland, Detroit, and Boston will have to have their election districts more and more ingeniously rearranged to produce Democratic victories.

These trends—particularly the growth of Republican-leaning suburbs in the South and Southwest—have been at work for the past two decades, however, and the Republican party has yet to translate such advantages into gains that give them a decisive advantage. After the Reagan victories of 1980 and 1984, Democrats control 259 seats in the House of Representatives, slightly more than the party's average for the entire period from 1950 to 1986, the period when the Sunbelt was growing in population and wealth.

The two political parties have thus achieved an equilibrium that is remarkable in American history: neither the Democrats nor the Republicans are a majority or plurality party. At the start of the 1980s, the two parties had seemed poised for a sharp confrontation on three central policy issues: income distribution, race, and the place of religion in public life. This confrontation was reinforced by the growing divergence of partisan voters according to income, race, and religious affiliation. Low-income voters, blacks, and relatively secularized Protestants, Catholics, and Jews largely voted for Democrats. In a country where only half the citizens are willing to vote, these divisions were working to the advantage of the Republican party, whose more affluent, white, and religious-minded constituents turned out in greater numbers than the Democrats' most loyal supporters.

However, the recession of 1982, the recent weaker performance of the economy (after three strong years), and the current Iran-contra arms scandal have all given the Democrats opportunities to slow, if not halt, the momentum behind the resurgence of the Republican party. Blacks and white fundamentalist Christians remain among the two most partisan groups in America; on the whole, blacks vote Democratic, white fundamentalists vote Republican. But the last election suggests that partisanship based on income has diminished. In 1982, those making less than $12,500 voted Democratic by a margin of 73 to 27, and those making more than $50,000 voted Republican by a margin of 63 to 37. In 1986, according to the *New York Times*–CBS exit polls, those with incomes below $12,500 voted Democratic by a margin of 56 to 44, a Democratic loss of 17 percentage points. Those making more than $50,000 voted Republican by a margin of 53 to 47, a Republican loss of 10 points among the well to do. At the same time, polls asking voters which party they prefer found that both parties have the allegiance of between 44 and 46 percent of those questioned. The result is a country with two minority parties.

They are minority parties partly because, as national organizations, they are amorphous. One conventional view has been that the national political parties reflect the capacity of the nation's disparate social and economic groups and interests to form sustained alliances. A political party with the allegiance of a majority of the voters has the power to govern—to carry out a coherent set of policies—but the use of this power has been evident only twice during the past generation: after Lyndon Johnson won in 1964 and went on to enact the pro-grams of the Great Society, and in 1981 when Ronald Reagan's victory, accom-panied by a GOP takeover of the Senate, enabled the Republican administration to enact regressive tax cuts, sharply increase military spending, and substantially reduce social welfare programs.

The more closely one looks, the more complex and elusive the shape of our political parties becomes. Parties can be seen as loosely aligned blocs of voters; as bureaucracies in Washington raising funds and making the rules for national conventions; as groups organizing Congress; or as representatives of competing interests, whether national or local.

Leon Epstein, of the University of Wisconsin, has produced in *Political Parties in the American Mold* the most comprehensive textbook I have read on American political parties.* Written before the current partisan impasse, the book does much to clarify the extremely fluid and often fragile structure of our two major parties—parties that, in comparison with their European counterparts, have relatively weak ties to social classes and religious groups.

Both the Democratic and Republican parties, Epstein points out, are really confederations of state and local organizations connected more or less firmly to the Democratic National Committee and the Republican National Committee. The national committees have become increasingly powerful in both parties, but for very different reasons. In the case of the Democrats, the national interest groups—women's organizations, homosexuals, blacks, antiwar activists—have pressed the national committee to impose rules on state parties that will give them more power in the national convention. The Republican National Commit-tee has used money as a lever to force local party organizations to hire its own approved staff members and to back the programs of the Reagan administration.

Unlike many other scholarly texts, Epstein's has much to say about money in politics, whether in the form of private contributions or of partly public financing. Most public attention has concentrated on political action commit-tees, largely because of the often aggressive conservatism of the Republican PACs

---

*Leon D. Epstein, *Political Parties in the American Mold* (Wisconsin: University of Wisconsin Press, 1987).

and because they are an example of a reform that turned sour for the reformers. But Epstein correctly notes that political parties spend far more money than PACs, particularly the Republican party. In 1981 and 1982, party committees spent a total of $254 million, $215 million of which was spent by GOP committees, while all PACs, including business, labor, trade associations, conservative groups, spent $190 million.

Epstein himself has few recommendations for improving the system; his book is a sophisticated primer on political parties. W. Russell Neuman's *The Paradox of Mass Politics* is far more ambitious.* The central argument of what he calls a "theory of political sophistication" is that American democracy works and has worked for two centuries because the population is divided into "three publics." At the bottom are "the roughly 20 percent of the population who do not monitor the political realm at all" and "at the top of the continuum is a group of active and attentive individuals, who represent approximately 5 percent of the population." Most people fall somewhere between these extremes. While generally only "half-attentive" to public issues, they "can be alerted if fellow citizens sound the political alarm"; they may then insist that their interests and opinions be taken into account in the decisions of the top 5 percent who have an active part in politics.

Neuman's idea of "three publics" is useful for describing the deterioration of the Democratic party during the 1970s. The reformist movement that arose after the 1968 Democratic convention—and was given impetus by the Watergate scandals—resulted in a party dominated by upper-middle-class liberals who had little sense of the economic and social pressures on the Democratic party's traditional working- and lower-middle-class constituents. This gap between the party's elite and its major voting blocs became most damaging during the Carter years when Democratic leaders failed to recognize that inflation was forcing working-class voters into higher and higher tax brackets, steadily eating away a larger and larger proportion of their take-home pay. Through California's Proposition 13 and other antitax movements, the "half-attentive" mass of voters began to "sound the political alarm," to use Neuman's imagery; but it was Reagan and the Republican party that were able to respond to their anxieties in 1980.

Neuman's model of a periodically aroused middle tier of voters is also useful for understanding public response to the current Iran-contra aid scandal. Public reaction is mixed. Support for Reagan has dropped significantly, according to polls by the *Los Angeles Times,* but hostility to the press and television is growing. Like Watergate this scandal could severely undermine the short-range prospects of the Republican party. The administration's policy can be seen as a calculated attempt to interpose a barrier between the top and the middle of the "three publics": to insulate, that is, a White House elite centered in the National

---

*W. Russell Neuman, *The Paradox of Mass Politics: Knowledge and Opinion in the American Electorate* (Cambridge, Mass: Harvard University Press, 1987).

Security Council both from congressional oversight and from a general public wary of involvement in Central America, and opposed to the sale of weapons to such a regime as Khomeini's. Until now, the Reagan administration has been remarkably adept at controlling public perception of events as diverse as the invasion of Grenada and the collapse of the Reykjavik summit; but the current crisis has been much more difficult for the administration to manage, especially since the president's cabinet and staff have been openly fighting among themselves over who is responsible for illegal activities and for covering them up.

While the Iran-contra controversy will work to the immediate disadvantage of the Republicans, it is not likely to alter permanently what is most characteristic about contemporary politics: the near equality of the two political parties, an equality that works to prevent either the Democrats or the Republicans from formulating a coherent program for government. The chief reason for the impasse between the two parties is the presence of conflicting pressures within each partisan coalition, conflicts that have plagued the Democrats since the mid-Sixties, and that, for the Republican party, are currently reflected in the inability of the Reagan administration to propose a federal budget that seems plausible even to members of its own party on Capitol Hill.

During the last ten years, the number of voters who say they are Republican has grown enormously, from 25 percent of the population to over 40 percent; and as a result of this growth, the GOP has changed shape, becoming far more heterogeneous. In 1976, northern, white, Anglo-Saxon Protestants made up a majority of the men and women willing to identify themselves as Republicans in public opinion surveys by pollster Robert Teeter. By 1986, northern WASPs made up just under a third of the Republican constituency. Such WASPs had not abandoned the GOP; they had simply become a minority, joined by millions of white southerners and, to a lesser extent, by middle- and upper-middle-class Catholics.

In 1980 and 1981 the ideological and economic conflicts within the Republican coalition had not yet emerged. Instead, the main forces behind that coalition—a unified business community, a nascent Christian right, a well-financed conservative movement that has been gathering political and intellectual momentum for a decade, and a growing number of white voters who no longer supported Democratic welfare policies—provided Reagan with a strong base of support. His administration could therefore have its way, particularly in lowering taxes, raising military spending, and cutting benefits for the poor. Three main factors created a favorable climate for Reagan's budget and tax cut legislation. The steeply graduated income tax rates that inflation was pushing onto working- and middle-class incomes; rising regressive Social Security taxes; and increasingly heavy state and local tax burdens.

In 1980 and 1981, then, it seemed that the combined economic, class, and social interests supporting Reagan could become the core of a new majority party. During the last few years, however, these elements have lost their cohesion, and the Republican drive to expand its base has, in fact, had the effect of dividing its supporters. The administration's 1986 tax reform proposal, for example, clearly had an implicit political purpose: by lowering all tax rates, eliminating many tax breaks, and shifting a significant share of the tax burden from individuals to corporations, the tax plan was intended by party strategists to give a populist boost to Republican hopes of realigning the parties. Instead of being perceived as the instrument of the rich and of corporate America, the GOP would appear as the defender of the common man.

The tax reform has not much changed the prevailing image of the Republican party, although it has prevented Democrats from taking over the issue. What the legislation has done, to some degree unintentionally, is to split the business community: manufacturing corporations heavily dependent on such now-eliminated tax breaks as the investment tax credit opposed the measure. Businesses involved in wholesale and retail sales, as well as in services and high technology production, supported the bill, having little use for the investment tax credit and gaining significantly from the lowering of the top corporate rate from 46 to 34 percent.

The division over taxes in many ways coincides with deep divisions among American corporations over trade policy. Many of the heavy industries that are hurt by the loss of the investment tax credit are also those most threatened by foreign imports: they consequently support varying forms of trade protectionism. In contrast, many of the retail and wholesale companies seeking lower corporate rates deal in imported goods, and are adamantly opposed to tariffs and other restrictions on trade.

Some Republican strategists are privately considering an attempt to develop a base of corporate supporters among the "winners" in the current competition among various industries—a perilous tactic because of the difficulty of predicting economic success. The independent oil industry, for example, was central to the 1980 Republican coalition. Flush with cash from oil deregulation and rising oil prices, independent oilmen from Texas, Oklahoma, and Louisiana provided much of the early financing for the campaigns of successful conservative Republicans running in states and districts throughout the country. By 1986, however, the independent oil industry had become a "loser," and many of the industry's leaders are seeking support for a protectionist oil import fee.

Another Republican alliance coming under strain is that between the country-club Republicans who have controlled the party organizations in most states, and the increasingly restless conservative Christian political community. This alliance has been of prime importance to the GOP: between 1976 and 1984, white fundamentalist Christians accounted for a shift of at least eight million votes to Republican candidates, according to the *New York Times*–CBS polls. No other single group in those years did more to create a strong Republican coalition.

Conservative Christian political leaders, including Pat Robertson, have, however, become increasingly intent on gaining direct political power. They are sponsoring campaigns to take over numerous state and local Republican party organizations, and running their own candidates in GOP primaries. For example, in Indiana in 1986, fundamentalist Christian candidates defeated candidates backed by the party for Republican nominations in two congressional districts, severely embarrassing one of the strongest state Republican parties in the country. Similarly, fights between Christian groups and party regulars occurred in Republican congressional contests in South Carolina and Tennessee. In three out of four of these districts, the Republican would normally have been favored to win. In fact, Democrats won all four districts. Republican party regulars, dismayed by such activities, are having increasing difficulty maintaining control over nominations.

The GOP is in the midst of a balancing act, trying to hold together a great many divergent groups—including well-to-do East Coast Protestants, anticommunist Asian and Hispanic refugees, southern rednecks drawn to the hard right views of Jesse Helms, the new entrepreneurs of Wall Street and Silicon Valley, urban Catholics, embattled farmers, and evangelical Baptists. For the Republicans the arms-for-hostages scandal could not have emerged at a worse time—just when they were beginning to plan for the 1988 elections. No matter what the political atmosphere may be less than two years from now, the scandal has impaired Reagan's ability to hold together the GOP coalition by his personal popularity while waiting for a successor to emerge. The controversy has also clearly damaged the ability of the Republican party to recruit strong candidates for 1988. And it threatens to weaken the ability of the three Republican party committees to continue to raise the vast amounts of money useful in smoothing over ideological and economic conflicts within the Republican hierarchy.

The rise of the Republican party has been at least temporarily brought to a halt. Democrats seem for the moment unlikely to increase their long-term share of the vote, although they may be in a good position to capture the presidency in 1988. With both parties showing roughly equal strength in the electorate, and with a substantial bloc of voters feeling little or no allegiance to either party, political competition becomes a kind of trench warfare—a prolonged engagement along an extended battlefront, with the resources of each side spread thinly along the entire line of the conflict. Each seeks to gain specific pieces of the other's territory, sometimes a House or Senate seat, sometimes a governorship, sometimes control of a state legislature, and sometimes the office of county sheriff. Each party chips away at the other's terrain, seeking to make incursions and to hold ground at every contested point.

For Democrats and Republicans attempting to build stronger parties out of fragile contemporary alliances, the coming years will be overshadowed by the two-trillion-dollar national debt. The inhibiting pressure of the debt and deficit may be more damaging to the Democrats, traditionally the party of expanded government services. They will have to struggle to balance a number of competing claims, including the claims of those hurt by Reagan's attack on the welfare state, those who demand that the party maintain support for the military, and the claims of fiscally conservative suburban voters. At the same time, however, the Republican party faces a parallel dilemma. Rural politicians from the Sunbelt to North Dakota foresee significant defections to the Democratic party among farmers demanding additional federal support. Republicans in the Northeast and Midwest are insisting that education and job training programs vital to their constituents be restored. Political life during the coming years will turn on bitter disputes over cuts in spending that the affected groups will resent, and tax hikes that many will resist. Neither prospect offers much hope for a political party seeking to expand its base of support and to obtain a decisive majority.

# Right Turn?

*Tikkun*, Vol. 2, No. 2

Over the past decade, two issues have been central to political conflict in the United States: taxes and the power of business. The rise of conservatism in the late 1970s and early 1980s coincided with the mobilization and unification of the corporate lobbying community and with the emergence of antitax movements in various states across the country. The role of business in the structures of the Democratic and Republican parties is one of the more complex and unexplored areas of political analysis. The distributional consequences of taxes are far better known than the intricate politics of taxation, despite the fact that taxes have become a key part of the debate between the two major parties.

In *Right Turn: The Decline of the Democrats and the Future of American Politics,* Thomas Ferguson and Joel Rogers of the University of Texas and the University of Miami, respectively, have produced a provocative and illuminating examination of public opinion and of the political influence of business elites.* Their exploration of extensive poll data raises serious questions about the ideological assessment of American politics in the 1980s made by columnists, consultants and politicians. Ferguson and Rogers's study of the relationship between key business leaders and officials of the Democratic Party, and of policy decisions tied to these relationships, sheds new light on the dark side of democracy, where money determines public policy.

At the same time, however, some of the arguments in *Right Turn* oversimplify recent political developments. Ferguson and Rogers are determined to make not only the legitimate argument that there remains a strong base of public support for a liberal welfare state, but also to make the far more tenuous claim

---

*Thomas Ferguson and Joel Rogers, *Right Turn: The Decline of the Democrats and the Future of American Politics* (New York: Hill and Wang, 1986).

that there was no conservative shift in the electorate during the years immediately prior to the 1980 election. Instead, according to the Ferguson and Rogers's thesis, the electorate has remained firmly wedded to the liberal welfare state, and the primary, if not exclusive, force pushing politics to the right is a powerful set of business interests controlling the policies of the Democratic party.

In effect, the authors have given primacy to two facts—that business exerts significant influence on the Democratic party, and that public support for basic government services remains strong—and dismissed the destructive consequences to the Democrats of internal party developments. Ferguson and Rogers reject or disregard arguments that the Democratic party splintered along a number of fault lines during the two decades preceding the election of Ronald Reagan in 1980; that the party was fractured by social, racial, cultural and economic class antagonisms; that the left itself was divided over Vietnam, civil rights, trade unionism, the women's movement, inflation, sexual liberation, homosexual rights, urban riots, abortion, court-ordered busing, affirmative action and hiring quotas. The list of schisms within the overall Democratic constituency—responsibility for which cannot all be laid at the feet of big business—is long.

Ferguson's and Rogers's focus on the political role of business within the Democratic party and on the interpretation of poll data produces some highly valuable information and insight. But their larger analysis produces a set of conclusions giving false comfort to advocates of the left agenda they seek to promote.

Their most dangerous assertion is that taxes are not really that important to the vast majority of people: "It is important to emphasize that among the general public (as opposed to business elites) the salience of the tax issue has never been great. . . . On balance, then, it seems reasonable to conclude that increased burdens on average Americans, and especially increased unfairness in the tax system, made the public more resistant to tax hikes and more receptive to promises to cut taxes. It did not, however, set off a groundswell of public clamor for the reduction of taxes."

Ferguson and Rogers reach this conclusion despite the fact that they include in their book extensive evidence to the contrary. At one point they cite a 1978 Harris poll showing that sixty-nine percent of the respondents felt their tax burden had "reached the breaking point." In addition, they cite data showing how the tax system had, over the past twenty years, become increasingly regressive: the corporate tax had been steadily replaced by the highly regressive Social Security payroll tax as a basic source of federal revenues, while the progressivity of the federal income tax was eroded by the addition of exemptions and deductions available largely to the affluent. As a demonstration of the strong anger over tax burdens, one need look no further than the overwhelming passage of antitax referenda on both sides of the continent, Proposition 13 in California in 1978 and Proposition 2½ in 1980 in Massachusetts; or to the presidential victory of Ronald Reagan on an antitax platform in 1980.

I believe it is far more productive to recognize the deep anger of an electorate facing not only rising tax burdens but stagnant incomes, and then to explore how business and other conservative interests successfully exploited this political mood, while liberals in general and the Democratic party in particular failed to respond. There is no question that the business community and the affluent manipulated public discontent with tax burdens in the late 1970s so that local, state and federal tax reduction legislation would bring about regressive redistributions of income.

One of the central failures of liberals and of the American left during the past twenty years, however, has been the inability to recognize the basic, legitimate economic self-interest of the voter. Strategists for the Mondale campaign made this mistake when they calculated that voters would not object to paying another one hundred dollars a year in taxes to lessen the federal deficit. Ferguson and Rogers argue that poll data which shows many voters in support of Reagan while personally in disagreement with specific conservative policies demonstrates the continuing presence of a liberal consensus, "that there is little or nothing in the public opinion data to support the claim that the American public moved to the right." An equally logical conclusion that can be drawn from the same poll data is that many voters were willing to support a conservative president because, as the poll data shows, they believed that they would "do better financially" under Reagan. If voters are willing to make that choice, it suggests that the liberal consensus is fragile, rather than strong, particularly when put to a means test.

Ferguson and Rogers, however, conclude that "public attitudes toward major policy questions have remained programmatically liberal," which then leads them to pose the question: "How does one account for America's right turn in the 1970s?" For Ferguson and Rogers, race, class, and cultural tensions within the Democratic party over the past generation are largely irrelevant. Equally unimportant is the very real difficulty facing Democratic liberalism at a time when the economy has not produced increases in family income since 1973, and when wages for the hourly worker have declined.

Instead, the authors of *Right Turn* find that the shift to the right lies in a series of disastrous decisions by a power bloc that actually controls the Democratic party: "principally capital-intensive and multinationally-oriented big business and its allies among real estate magnates, military contractors, and portions of the media. As we have sought to show, all the crucial decisions that have brought the Democrats to where they are today were made by actors who either had close ties to this bloc or were—as in all Democratic cabinets from Kennedy through Carter, or the principal economic and foreign policy advisers to Mondale in 1983–84—themselves prominent members of it."

Ferguson and Rogers contend that this "power bloc of capital intensive industries, investment banks and internationally oriented commercial banks" had its roots in the formation of the New Deal coalition. "Although this bloc represented only a small part of the business community in the 1930s, it was immensely powerful. It included many of the largest and most rapidly growing corporations in the economy—including such firms as General Electric, IBM, Pan Am, and R. J. Reynolds; many major oil concerns, including Standard Oil of New Jersey, Standard Oil of California, Cities Service, and Shell; and major commercial and investment banks, including Bank of America, Chase National Bank, Brown Brothers Harriman, Goldman Sachs, Lehman Brothers and Dillon Read." Their evidence cited for this is a forthcoming book by Ferguson. It is unfortunate that more specific information from this forthcoming book could not have been included here.

Other studies of campaign finance, however, do not provide support for the Ferguson-Rogers thesis. Alexander Heard, in his seminal 1960 study, *The Costs of Democracy*, showed that throughout the New Deal years from 1932 to 1952, Democratic support from "Bankers, brokers, manufacturers, oil, mining, utilities, transportation, real estate and insurance"—which covers a large part of the "new power bloc"—steadily declined, while Republicans remained overwhelmingly favored by these interests. In that period, oil and mining interests favored the Republican National Committee by a six-to-one margin, the same margin as bankers and brokers. Herbert Alexander, in his 1972 book, *Money in Politics*, found that members of twelve prominent families—the Fields, duPonts, Fords, Harrimans, Lehmans, Mellons, Olins, Pews, Reynolds, Rockefellers, Vanderbilts and Whitneys—many of whom are tied to the multinational interests cited by Ferguson and Rogers, gave overwhelmingly to the Republican party between 1956 and 1968. In the four elections of those years, these families gave $4,620,-000 to the GOP and just $470,000 to the Democratic party. In 1968, Alexander found that officers and directors of the American Petroleum Institute gave $431,000 to Republicans and just $30,000 to Democrats. Similarly, military contractors that year gave $664,000 to GOP committees and candidates, and just $110,000 to Democratic counterparts.

All this is not to minimize business influence in the Democratic party. Instead, the study of business strength in both parties requires far more research and documentation than Ferguson and Rogers have included in *Right Turn*, a book that touches on themes critically important to the balance of power in the United States. Whenever a political party or movement becomes ascendant—as the Democratic party did in the Great Depression, and the GOP did briefly at the start of the 1980s—a host of interests seek to gain control in order to direct the flow of benefits; and in this competition, varying segments of the business community have consistently been the most successful participants.

As the nation now enters what appears likely to be a period of sustained trench warfare between the two parties, each struggling with minority status, the exercise of special interest influence will become increasingly subtle. In this environment, proponents of both the left and right will be forced to conduct tough, exhaustive studies of the forces at work in the electorate, in campaign finance and in the management of policy, both during campaigns and while in office.

At the moment, the Iran-contra affair as well as the 1986 Democratic take-over of the Senate indicate that the Republican party has lost the momentum it had from 1978 through 1984, and the likelihood that the GOP will win majority party status has, for the moment, receded. As a result, the Democratic party has gained breathing room in the extraordinarily difficult process of reas-sembling a working coalition. Ferguson and Rogers, whose goal is a revived party of the left, have over the years often broken new intellectual ground and will most likely continue to do so. A central strength of their adversaries on the right, however, has been an assiduous commitment to exhaustive research, a commit-ment, as documented in *Right Turn*, reflected in the explosion of financial support provided in the 1970s to such conservative think tanks as the Heritage Foundation, the American Enterprise Institute and the Hoover Institution.

While no political analyst or theoretician can be expected to cover with equal thoroughness every aspect of political life, and while *Right Turn* provides a wealth of highly detailed and extremely useful poll data, a persistent weakness of the left, demonstrated once again in this book has been a kind of broad vilification of powerful interests, a process which allows the actual forces at work to escape accurate characterization and analysis. The result has been a series of defeats for the left in presidential elections. For both Democrats and Republicans seeking to formulate effective campaign as well as policy strategies, the more precise and grounded the information available, the more likely that Election Day results will not come as an unwelcome surprise.

The value of *Right Turn*, and of Rogers's and Ferguson's work in general, is the willingness to challenge accepted wisdom and to suggest that political outcomes are determined by forces not routinely reported upon in newspapers and on television. Their work has obliged others to explore new terrain and has functioned to widen the scope of political analysis. More detailed information would add strength to one of their basic, fundamentally accurate, conclusions:

The Democratic party could, after all, put forward a broad popular program of manifest appeal and benefit. They could mobilize those vast reaches of the electorate (poorer, younger, blacker than the rest) who now abstain from voting altogether. The reason they do not do this is not because they do not know how, but because they do not want to. And they do not want to because such a mobilization would require that the people mobilized actually be offered something, and elite Democrats have very little that they want to give. While they would like to defeat the Republicans, they are not about to subsidize a broad popular coalition inimical to their own economic interests.

While it is certainly true that a drive to rebuild a left coalition through full employment, higher wages, workplace protection, unemployment insurance, ex-panded health care and so on would incur the enmity of the business elite and the corporations which undergird them, the most vital task facing committed scholars like Ferguson and Rogers is to address the contemporary conflict be-tween those in the bottom third of the income distribution who feel that they need and will profit from such government programs, and those in the middle-third who feel their own standard of living eroding, who resent and fear the less privileged, who no longer trust the federal government, and who balk with all their strength at paying with their tax dollars for government expansion. It is on this humble terrain, as well as in the boardrooms and clubs of the rich and powerful, that political parties are built and shattered, and that crucial elections are won and lost.

# How the GOP Got into the Tall Cotton

*The Washington Post*, May 3, 1987

Over the past generation, the politics of the South have been a driving force in determining the balance of political power in the United States. The civil rights movement, the rise of the Goldwater-Reagan wing of the Republican party, and the steady collapse of the New Deal coalition all have roots in the political upheavals of the South. George Wallace gave meaning to the idea of conservative populism, and his campaigns for the presidency in 1964 and 1968 went to the heart of Democratic vulnerability on issues of race.

At the beginning of this decade, it was southern "boll weevil" Democrats who provided President Reagan with the critical margin of votes required to enact the budget and tax cuts of 1981, marking the first substantial and successful attack on Democratic redistributional policies. Now, it is the South which will test the ability of both major political parties to hold onto the allegiance of two key constituencies as those constituencies are represented in the 1988 presidential election by televangelist Marion G. (Pat) Robertson seeking the GOP nomination and the Rev. Jesse Jackson seeking the Democratic nomination.

The 11 states of the Confederacy have become a bedrock of presidential Republicanism, providing an increasingly firm base of 138 electoral votes for the GOP nominee, just over half the 270 votes required to win. As the region becomes more cosmopolitan and more demographically representative of the rest of the nation, the Republican party has begun to take hold at the local level, in white urban and suburban districts from Durham to Dallas. Republicans now boast that they are marching down the postwar interstate highways "like Sherman's army." Says GOP consultant John Morgan, whenever you "see a McDonald's or Pizza Hut going up, you know the Republicans are coming."

The South, in effect, has been a major source of support for the conservative movement and for the Republican party. The political consequences of the white reaction to the civil rights movement and the emergence of a two-party South have been to push the nation rightward. This development is a substantial challenge to one of the basic conclusions drawn by political scientist V.O. Key,

Jr., in his classic 1949 study, *Southern Politics*, perhaps the best book on American politics ever written. At the end of *Southern Politics*, Key wrote:

> Southern liberalism is not to be underestimated. . . . Fundamentally within southern politics there is a powerful strain of agrarian liberalism, now reinforced by the growing unions of the cities. (This liberal drive) is held in check in part by the one-party system which almost inevitably operates to weaken the political strength of those disposed by temperament and interest to follow a progressive line. Moreover, if the Negro is gradually assimilated into political life, the underlying southern liberalism will undoubtedly be mightily strengthened.

Two-party politics has emerged in the South, but it has not created a new beachhead for liberalism. Instead, politics in the South remains dominated by issues of race. Republicans calculate their chances of winning a state senate or county council district on the basis of the percentage of registered blacks, the fewer the better, and Democrats throughout the South are repeatedly thrown on the defensive as they desperately attempt to maintain a fragile alliance between blacks and a minority of the white community. The union movement in the North has fallen upon hard times; in most of the South, active government opposition, including the opposition of Democratic governors, has stymied union organization. "The modern-day version of civil rights is you can't be for labor unions," says South Carolina Democratic National Committeeman Don Fowler, noting that it is critical for many Democratic governors to favor anti-union right-to-work laws. "Power [in southern legislatures] is still Democratic," notes Democratic consultant Bill Hamilton. "If we ever lose a significant part of the economic elite, financially we are in trouble. There is no [Democratic] party structure." Republicans have used their party to institutionalize conservatism, while Democrats, instead of becoming a party of the left, struggle to maintain ties to the economic establishment.

Earl and Merle Black, twin brothers born in East Texas who now teach respectively at the universities of South and North Carolina, have produced the most significant and comprehensive study of the politics of the South since Key. Their work demonstrates with statistical and descriptive precision why Key's prediction of a strengthened southern liberalism has failed to materialize. *Politics and Society in the South* is, in many respects, an attempt to update Key's seminal work, filling in the history of nearly forty years.*

Not only was the black assimilation of the 1960s into southern political life abrupt and often violent, instead of the gradual assimilation anticipated by Key, but the potential for an agrarian liberalism has been effectively eliminated by the rise of an aggressively conservative, white middle class. The Black brothers cite a series of surveys taken between 1972 and 1984 which attempt to determine feelings of warmth or hostility toward groups and symbols. In these surveys, white southerners expressed the strongest affinity for "police," "whites", "military,"

---

*Earl Black and Merle Black, *Politics and Society in the South* (Cambridge, Mass.: Harvard University Press, 1987).

"conservatives" and "Republicans" while providing lukewarm or negative responses to "unions," "liberals," "civil rights leaders" and "women's liberation."

"From the standpoint of liberal campaigners," Earl and Merle Black write, "the political landscape of the southern white middle class is bleak and forbidding. The symbolic terrain is filled with groups and causes for which proximity probably spells political disaster, and the positions frequently championed by liberals generally do not coincide with the values prevalent among middle-class whites." At the same time, according to the authors, prospects for an alliance between blacks and working-class whites is equally bleak. "Successful campaigns against the haves [the upper-middle class] presupposes this group's isolation, an isolation not at all supported by the facts. To the contrary, the evidence of political symbols suggests numerous ties binding the white middle class and the white working class. . . . In contrast, black southerners were completely distinct, completely separated from white workers and the white middle class."

Earl and Merle Black conclude that "The Democratic party is acutely vulnerable to racial, social, and ideological cleavages that have no easy solutions," and that, regardless of which party wins a specific contest, "Statewide elections in the new southern politics will typically determine which segments of the white middle class will rule, that is, whether the self-described 'moderates' or the 'conservatives' of the educated middle class will hold the key offices, command the public institutions, make the policies, and distribute the patronage and perquisites of a rapidly growing region."

*Politics and Society in the South* is a major contribution to the understanding of the South, the most volatile region in the nation. It is the first of what are projected to be three volumes. In the next two books, as the Black brothers attempt to provide a full picture of the contemporary South, it will be of great use to their readers if they are able to go beyond the academic and statistical study of the region to use their extensive knowledge of the players in southern politics, a politics that is the equal of the ward-based struggles of Chicago and or the media-dominated battles in California. While the overall conclusions of *Politics and Society* are accurate, in further detailed study the authors might find answers for the exceptions to conservative rule, resolving how, for example, economic populism remains a vital force in Louisiana, and how the once-segregationist George Wallace ended his career as Alabama governor on the basis of an alliance between working-class whites and blacks. The power of establishment politics is nowhere stronger than in the South, but it may well be a mistake to overestimate the invulnerability of that establishment.

# The Southern GOP's
# New Button-Down Personality

*The Washington Post,* June 14, 1987

The power structure of the Republican party in the South, once a sparse network of affluent ideologues committed to the agenda of hardline conservatives like Barry Goldwater, has been transformed into the political home of an ascendant middle class, uniformed in blue blazers and button-down shirts.

This transformation has produced a party elite leaning strongly toward George Bush, the candidate rejected by the South just seven years ago as the Republican presidential candidate most clearly associated with the eastern establishment wing of the GOP.

The alteration of the southern GOP goes far beyond the political preferences for one candidate over another. A generation ago the southern party leadership was the advance guard of a conservative revolution that overthrew the Wall Street wing of the GOP.

The new southern Republican party is based on the explosive growth of an urban-based middle class that scarcely existed before the 1960s. The party also includes former Democrats who left their party as blacks gained power in the wake of the civil rights movement.

The South, as the dominant partner in an alliance with western mountain states, was the driving force behind the nomination of Goldwater in 1964. And it was the South where the flame for Ronald Reagan burned bright enough through 1976, when he suffered repeated primary defeats in the North, to propel him to victory in 1980.

This year, however, the presidential campaign of George Bush is demonstrating how soon victorious revolutionaries can be converted into a power elite, and how quickly that elite can accommodate itself to changing demographics. From Florida to Texas, men and women who as recently as eight years ago were determined to crush the GOP eastern old guard have helped to turn the network of southern party leaders and operatives into a bastion of support for Bush, the Republican presidential candidate most clearly tied to the party's old-line, patrician wing.

Bush has identified himself with the programs and initiatives of the Reagan administration, but his base of support remains heavily dependent on the center and moderate wings of the party. His strategists are convinced that a substantial challenge to his presidential bid could be mounted only from the right, the ideological wing of the party that has flourished in the South in the past.

Over the past two years, however, Bush has moved like Sherman's army through the South—backed by a war chest expected to reach $7 million this month—to capture much of the southern membership on the Republican National Committee, a host of elected officials and an impressive array of party operatives. Bush's success reflects both the change in outlook of the southern party leadership and the changing class structure of the South. As a result, within the universe of southern Republican activists, Bush has, so far, overwhelmed such challenges from the right by candidates like Rep. Jack Kemp (R-N.Y.) and former Republican senator Paul Laxalt of Nevada.

Bush's southern supporters include such early backers of the Reagan and Goldwater movements as Tommy Thomas of Florida, John Grenier of Alabama, Dan Ross of South Carolina and Lou Kitchin of Georgia. These men may not be major figures to the general public, but they were among the first lieutenants commissioned in the Reagan-conservative movement within the Republican party, some dating back to the Goldwater campaign of 1964 or the Reagan effort in 1968.

Despite the intense antigovernment credentials that these leaders once displayed, the candidates that they have helped elect to statewide office show an entirely different orientation. From Tennessee to Florida, where Republicans have been elected governor, they have initiated major expansion of government's role in education, highway beautification and industrial development. In Florida, the Republican governor, Bob Martinez, successfully won approval of a major tax increase for medicaid, road construction, new prisons and education.

In fact, the once-revolutionary Republican party of the South has, in a number of states, reached the point where it has become the target of a new counterrevolution within the GOP: the mobilization of white fundamentalist and charismatic Christians behind the candidacy of televangelist Marion G. (Pat) Robertson.

In South Carolina, Robertson's forces have severely embarrassed—and in a number of cases, defeated—a Republican power structure with numerous ties to the Bush campaign. In Richland County, site of the state's capital, the Republican establishment resorted to arcane party rules never before applied and unpublicized meetings to fend off Christian activists intent on seizing control of the county Republican party. Throughout the South, the Christian Republican right represents lower middle- and working-class workers who reject the more urbane agenda of affluent "country-club" Republicans. The Christian Republican right has a deeper commitment to the now largely forgotten "social agenda" that Republicans talked so much about in the early '80s.

The GOP's treatment of insurgent Christians delighted a beleaguered South Carolina Democratic party. Don Fowler, a South Carolina member of the Democratic National Committee, said "what is happening to the Christians now is the same thing that happened to blacks 20 years ago" when they sought entry into a white-dominated Democratic party.

The battles within the Republican presidential nomination process reflect broad political and economic changes in the South—changes that have already altered the balance of power between the national Democratic and Republican parties.

Twenty years ago, the Republican party of the South was concentrated among a small number of the elite upper-middle class. Two decades ago, despite the rupture of the "Solid South" in presidential elections, Democratic hegemony persisted at the state and local level; the urban and suburban middle class itself was a minority, outnumbered by farmers, farm workers, and a non-union working class. The GOP was, in effect, an insurgency often led by intensely conservative, hard-right ideologues among a small segment of the affluent.

The southern Republican party of the 1980s in some respects grew out of the strongest base of the Democratic party in 1950s. In the 1950s, according to UCLA political scientist John R. Petrocik, Democratic allegiance among southern whites was strongest among "upper-status whites," whose nearly 5-to-1 commitment to the Democratic party hinged on their use of the party to retain control of government.

Before the civil rights movement, this elite retained control of state and local government through a one-party system in which the critical decisions were made in low-turnout Democratic primaries with participation highly skewed in favor of the affluent by the use of literacy tests and poll taxes.

"By the 1980s," according to Petrocik, "the class cleavage had reversed itself," as well-to-do southern whites led the charge to the GOP.

This change resulted in large part from the adoption of pro-civil-rights positions by the national Democratic party, the passage of federal legislation that opened southern polling booths to blacks and the subsequent collapse of the conservative coalition in Congress in the 1960s and 1970s.

With blacks participating in Democratic primaries, the contests were no longer so subject to elite control. In addition, the deterioration of conservative Democratic muscle in Congress made the party less attractive to many southern whites, rich and poor.

The more recent shifts in the tenor of the Republican party in the South— from radical insurgency to allegiance with the establishment—reflect one of the most rapid regional economic and social alterations in this century. In a matter of just two generations, the South has abruptly transformed itself from an agrarian-based society to a largely urban and suburban society.

During its ascendency from post-Reconstruction through the mid-1960s, southern Democracy depended on a "plantation elite [that] could virtually control the political agenda of most southern states. . . . [But], by 1980, a quantum change had occurred, and the new middle class was 23 times greater than the agrarian middle class," Earl and Merle Black write in their current book, *Politics and Society in the South.*

As a result of this economic upheaval in the South, the Republican party has shifted from an insurgency to an established political movement. Its base—the urban and suburban middle class—has expanded at a geometric rate, moving from minority status in the days when Goldwater was nominated, to social dominance in the final years of the Reagan presidency.

In effect, the ideologues of the conservative revolution have been overtaken by a massive expansion of a Republican-leaning white middle class. It is in this political and social setting that Bush—a politician who claims Texas as his home state, but whose family background and style epitomize the blue blood of New England—has steadily built up a base of support and endorsements. In a certain sense, Bush—by dint of his origins and more recent political past—can be seen as a bridge between two political cultures.

Bush's backing includes key political aides to the governors, or the Republican governors themselves in Florida, Alabama, Oklahoma, Texas and South Carolina. In Texas, Bush forces claim to have three quarters of the Republican members of the legislature and a majority of the state GOP executive committee.

John Buckley, spokesman for the Kemp campaign, has sought to downplay Bush's organizing success—"we acknowledge that there isn't a country club in the South that George Bush doesn't have an endorsement in"—but privately and publicly, competitors to Bush all agree that he has a decisive organizing edge in the South at the moment.

This network may or may not pay off on March 8, Super Tuesday primary day, but it does suggest that the Republican party is a very different animal from what it was a decade ago.

In 1980, for example, Lee Atwater proudly boasted of how he organized the Reagan challenge to the South Carolina establishment in that state's GOP primary, overwhelming both Bush and John Connally, along with such local powerhouses as Sen. Strom Thurmond and former governor Jim Edwards. This year, Atwater is managing the Bush campaign, and in South Carolina he has quietly pushed most of the same GOP establishment into the Bush campaign.

Although not directly related to the upcoming presidential fight, the same changing patterns can be seen in North Carolina. In 1976, it was the Congressional Club of Sen. Jesse Helms (R-N.C.) that engineered Reagan's unexpected victory over Gerald Ford. That contest was a key demonstration of Reagan's continued political vitality and proved to be a critical step towards Reagan's successful presidential bid four years later. And it has been the Helms organization that has dominated delegations to GOP presidential conventions.

This year, however, Helms's Congressional Club—a mainstay of conservative Republicanism in the South—was crushed by the traditional, moderate wing of the North Carolina GOP-backed Gov. Jim Martin (R-N.C.), in a head-on fight for control of the party.

The expansion of the Republican base in the South is likely to be accelerated by a political tactic devised by southern Democrats: the holding of what amounts to a regional southern primary on March 8, 1988.

Designed to revive interest in the Democratic primary among white voters, the unanticipated consequence may well be to expand interest in the more conservative Republican presidential contest.

"If people choose to vote in the Republican primary," said Alvin From, executive director of the Democratic Leadership Council then "it's going to be harder to get them back [to the Democratic party] in November."

The major development that could emerge on Super Tuesday is white indifference to the Democratic primary. According to Earl Black, a political scientist at the University of South Carolina, "Whites don't give a damn who the Democrats are going to nominate."

# The GOP's Right-Wing Center

## The Establishment's Gone Conservative— But Have the Voters?

*The Washington Post,* November 22, 1987

The 1988 election marks a fundamental change in Republican politics: The party is no longer dominated by the ideological division between moderates and conservatives that over two generations pitted Eisenhower against Taft, Goldwater against Rockefeller, Reagan against Ford.

"It's establishment conservatism today," said Lance Tarrance, "The days when there were two challenging factions, those days are over." Tarrance is the pollster for Rep. Jack Kemp (R-N.Y.), who has been conducting an uphill battle to revive the antiestablishment momentum that carried Reagan from his first presidential bid in 1968 through success 12 years later.

While Vice President Bush and, to a lesser extent, Sen. Robert J. Dole (R-Kan.) have cultural and stylistic ties to moderate Republican traditions, all of the four major GOP candidates now support aid to the contras, the Strategic Defense Initiative and additional restrictions on abortions. None is, in the tradition of a John Anderson, willing, for example, to support the Equal Rights Amendment. "The differences are milliseconds, not miles, and they are all on the right," Tarrance said.

The evolving Republican electorate has produced sharply contrasting strategies among the major contenders for the 1988 Republican nomination, but one fact stands out: The two leading candidates, Bush and Dole—who together share about 65 percent of public support in opinion polls—capture little if any of the revolutionary fervor and spirit of the early Reagan campaigns.

Tarrance's recognition of a dominant "establishment conservatism" is shared by many GOP strategists, but not all. Kemp, for example, is seeking in his stump speech to evoke a resurgence of a powerful anti-status-quo conservatism: "I may not be the candidate of the Republican establishment or the status quo," he declares, "but I will be the candidate of boundless and equal opportunity for all Americans. I want to see the Republican party be the leading party of human rights, civil rights, legal rights and equal rights for all."

The Rev. Pat Robertson's campaign also seeks to keep the Republican revolutionary spirit intact through a drive to mobilize evangelical, Christian outsiders into a crusading army determined to wrest control of the GOP away from the party regulars.

At the opposite end of the GOP continuum, Bush described his notion of the correct approach to the Republican voter of 1988 when he declared in his Houston announcement speech: "We don't need radical new directions—we need strong and steady leadership. We don't need to remake society—we just need to remember who we are." "You don't get 'new vision' candidates every four years," Robert Teeter, Bush's pollster argued. "What people want to see now is someone who can reinforce, refine and build on what Reagan did."

While the Bush campaign is prepared to gamble that Republican voters— and general election voters next November—are willing to settle for a candidate who promises to consolidate Reagan's achievements, not to innovate himself, there is no such unanimity on strategy within the Dole camp. Dole himself has clearly rejected in substance and theory Reagan administration policies that have led to a national debt of $2.4 trillion.

Dole is the only GOP candidate willing to consider tax hikes as part of a deficit-reduction package. "The American people are ready for bitter medicine," he declared two weeks ago, sounding the economic themes of his own postwar Kansas Republican roots. "We will either sacrifice for our children or we will continue to make our children sacrifice for us."

That sounds like the traditional green-eyeshaded-accountant austerity that the GOP consciously sought to eliminate from its image ten years ago. And it was, in fact, Dole's newly chosen campaign manager, William Brock who led the Republican National Committee in 1978 when it endorsed the Kemp-Roth tax cut in a move calculated to reshape the GOP into a party of optimism offering lower taxes, not sacrifice.

Brock tries to reconcile this apparent contradiction by saying that he believes Dole's current involvement in the drive to reduce the deficit will permit him to shift the emphasis of his campaign from austerity toward the argument that lowering the deficit will permit future economic growth and prosperity. He's betting that Congress will enact a Dole-backed package, which then will be seen by the public as restoring stability and growth to the market place—a major set of "ifs" on which to base a political gamble.

Another Dole strategist, David Keene, contends that the electorate holds split views on the issues of the deficit and taxation: "The average Republican voter is the average conservative and they have been concerned about both of those things, the deficit and overtaxing. What you've got are candidates twanging different strings on that heart, but both of those strings are on the heart."

Teeter, Bush's pollster, disputes this assessment. "I don't see any evidence that there is a willingness to have any kind of tax increase. . . . That's a product of Reagan." Bush has staked out relatively moderate stands on arms control, chemical weapons and education, but he has adopted a firmly antitax posture: "I am not going to raise your taxes—period."

While the stock market crash and its volatile aftermath have yet to reverber-
ate into the economy in ways felt by the average voter, they have intensified
doubts about the supply-side theories that led to the explosion of red ink during
the Reagan administration. Most observers believe these doubts will reinforce the
strength of more traditional, establishment-oriented candidates competing for
the Republican nomination, i.e., Bush and Dole. "When people get nervous, they
don't look toward someone who is going to revive the revolution," a dispirited
Kemp supporter said.

The economic setbacks to New Right economic theory come at a time when
the conservative movement that flowered in the late 1970s and early 1980s has
been severely weakened. This decline is most apparent in financial terms: Fund-
raising by the network of conservative PACs organized in the late 1970s has
nose-dived. The National Conservative Political Action Committee (NCPAC)
has been torn by internal conflict since the death of its long-time leader, John
(Terry) Dolan, and a series of lawsuits and countersuits has characterized the
hostile relationship between many of the PACs, their fund-raisers and vendors.

At NCPAC, revenues for the first six months of this year have fallen to $1.1
million, compared to $3 million in 1985 and $2.6 million in 1983. The cash flow
to the Fund for a Conservative Majority has fallen from $782,000 in the first half
of 1985 and $822,000 in the first six months of 1983, to $418,000 from January
through June this year.

The decline of the New Right and the movement toward an establishment
conservatism that places relatively low priority on such social issues as abortion
may encourage the healing of some internal party wounds. But this trend also
threatens the party's ability to continue to attract the working-class and lower-
middle-class voters who provided much of the new blood to the Reagan majorities
in 1980 and 1984. These voters, who make up roughly a third of the GOP
coalition in the general election, according to pollsters, have developed only weak
ties to the Republican party itself.

The splintering of anti-establishment conservative voters between Kemp and
Robertson is likely to prevent a coalescing of these marginal Republicans behind
either of the hard-right candidates. Instead the conflict may discourage these
voters from participating in Republican primaries altogether, lessening the ability
of the GOP, and either of its two most likely centrist nominees, Bush and Dole,
to maintain the allegiance of such voters in the general election. The old conserv-
ative-moderate split in the GOP may be gone, but the ability of the party to
attract a stable majority of the electorate has still to be tested.

# EPILOGUE

**W**HILE THE OUTCOME OF elections at the end of this decade and at the start of the 1990s will, in all likelihood, be heavily influenced by the state of the economy, there are additional underlying factors playing a major role in the political process: the long-range balance of power between the two parties, as well as the balance of power between labor and management, between the rich, the poor, and the middle class, between white and black, between the religious and the secular, between rival industrial and financial sectors, between geographic regions, and between competing elites and ideologies.

Of particular importance to domestic politics is the shift in the United States from manufacturing employment to an economy dominated by service industry jobs. This shift toward service industry employment has been a prime factor in the decline of organized labor, with the unionization of workers in banks, insurance companies, and fast food chains proving much more difficult than on the automobile line or in the steel plant. A significant political victory of the Reagan administration has been to accelerate the decline of organized labor, through National Labor Relations Board decisions favoring corporations over unions, through antilabor appointments to the Department of Labor, and through the precedent President Reagan set for private industry when he fired 11,000 striking air traffic controllers in 1981. From 1980 to 1986, the percentage of the workforce represented by unions has dropped precipitously, from 23 percent to 17.5 percent, and the number of union members has dropped by 3.1 million, from 20.1 million to 17 million.

It is very likely that future trends in employment and unionization will be detrimental to the Democratic party and advantageous to the Republican party. In financial terms, the erosion of organized labor—an erosion with a multiplicity of causes, going well beyond hostile administration policies—has produced a major loss of potential revenue for the Democratic party and its candidates. More important, however, the decline of unions has resulted in the severing of the central institutional link between the Democratic party and one of its most vital constituencies. Without the cohesion of a union, and the emphasis that a union places on the adversarial relationship between employer and employee—as well as the emphasis it places on voter mobilization—much of the recognition of the tie between partisan political participation and economic well-being is lost. This loss has done irreparable damage to the Democratic party.

The second recent major development is far more complex in its impact on the balance of power within the nation. This is the regressive redistribution of income that has taken place during the past decade. The Reagan administration, in the years from 1982 through 1987, has succeeded in achieving an increase of 10.7 percent in the family median income.* When, however, this increase is analyzed in terms of *after-tax* household income, the beneficiaries of rising living standards are concentrated in the most Republican-leaning groups, the upper-middle class and the affluent.† From 1980 to 1985 (the most recent year for which figures are available), households in the bottom 40 percent of the income distribution have seen their after-tax incomes stagnate, going from $8,960 a year to $8,925, in 1985 dollars, while those in the top 40 percent have seen median incomes rise by $2,262, from $31,334 to $33,596; most of that increase has been concentrated in the top 10 percent, where median incomes rose by $5,418, from $47,122 to $52,540. In the process, the share of total income has fallen for every quintile in the income distribution, except for the top fifth.

These findings are even more sharply delineated in a November 1987 study by the Congressional Budget Office showing that from 1977 to 1988, 80 percent of the population will have experienced a net drop in *after-tax* income. In contrast, those in the 81st to 90th percentiles will have picked up some additional cash, and those in the top 10 percent will have significantly improved their standard of living. For those at the very top, the gains have been enormous. The following table shows that distribution:

*Table showing change in average* after-tax *income for each decile of the* population, and for the top five percent, and top one percent of the income *distribution, all in 1987 dollars.*

| Income group by deciles | 1977 after-tax income in 1987 dollars | 1988 after-tax income in 1987 dollars | Percentage change |
|---|---|---|---|
| First (poorest) | $3,784 | $3,168 | − 16.3 % |
| Second | $7,609 | $7,032 | − 7.6 % |
| Third | $11,563 | $10,688 | − 7.6 % |
| Fourth | $15,449 | $14,327 | − 7.3 % |
| Fifth | $19,332 | $18,090 | − 6.4 % |
| Sixth | $23,561 | $22,310 | − 5.3 % |
| Seventh | $28,032 | $27,061 | − 3.5 % |
| Eighth | $33,849 | $33,239 | − 1.8 % |
| Ninth | $41,893 | $44,216 | + 5.5 % |
| Tenth (richest) | $75,295 | $89,766 | + 19.2 % |
| Top 5% | $97,544 | $124,678 | + 27.8 % |
| Top 1% | $186,607 | $303,829 | + 62.8 % |

---

*"Median Family Income Up Significantly, Poverty Rate Drops Slightly, Census Bureau Reports," U.S. Department of Commerce press release, CB87-124, July 30, 1987.

†"Estimating After-Tax Money Income Distribution," Bureau of the Census, Series P-23, No. 126, issued August 1983; and "Household After-Tax Income: 1985," Series P-23, No. 151, issued June 1987.

Barring a major recession or an international crisis, this redistribution of income may well serve to reinforce current Republican advantages, intensifying the class-skew of voting turnout patterns. A central characteristic of voter turnout patterns in the United States over the past two decades has been the direct correlation between rising incomes and voting behavior: turnout among those in the top third of the income distribution is more than 20 percentage points higher than for those in the bottom third.* For the Republican party, which has the highest level of support among the affluent, their most loyal constituents are making more money, and are consequently more likely to vote. For the Democrats, their most loyal constituents, the working poor and the lower-middle class, have stagnant incomes and increasingly weakened ties to organized labor, an institution that has sought to persuade its members to go to the voting booth, most often to support Democratic candidates.

In looking toward political developments in at least the near future, there are, generally speaking, two other economic scenarios to be treated as possibilities: the case of a modest recession, and the case of a severe recession. In the event of a modest recession, current income and employment patterns would undoubtedly continue to sustain the Republican party as an institution, although a candidate of either party could win the White House. While it is possible that a Democratic president could use the power of office to restore cohesion to the frayed Democratic coalition, the more likely prospect is that the Democratic party will remain seriously handicapped by internal conflicts, particularly over the issues of both race and class. Race continues to be the central conflict within the Democratic party, not only in the South, where a white Republican party has emerged as a force in state and national elections, but also in such key Democratic voting centers as Chicago, Detroit, Philadelphia, Boston, Baltimore and New York. These racial divisions are compounded by splits within the bottom half of the income distribution—often following racial or ethnic lines—pitting elements of the poor against each other and against the working and lower-middle classes. In terms of class, the conflict within the Democratic party between a liberal, reformist, upper-middle class elite, and a large body of middle- and low-income voters— for whom Democratic government no longer translates into larger paychecks and better opportunities for their children—has subsided, partly because class-based cultural norms are no longer as divisive as they were in the 60s and 70s.

Class and racial divisions are, however, likely to become exacerbated in a modest recession. As the stagnation of the late 1970s demonstrated, the Democratic party is not well equipped to resolve internal conflicts over race and class at a time when the economy has failed to give the party growing resources to distribute to its constituents. One of the most interesting elements of the Republican coalition is that its fault lines—particularly those dividing party regulars from evangelical Christians—divisions involving such social controversies as abor-

---

*Thomas E. Cavanaugh, "Changes in American Voter Turnout, 1964–1976," *Political Science Quarterly*, Academy of Political Science, Spring 1981, p. 60.

tion, school prayer, and the "absolute inerrancy" of the Bible, have for the past eight years superceded conflicts of economic interest between conservative blue-collar workers and business elites on such matters as trade and tax policy.

If there were, however, a severe recession or a prolonged economic downturn (stopping short of a full-fledged depression, the consequences of which might be so destabilizing and dangerous as to produce unpredictable political outcomes), it is possible that income distribution patterns which have been working to the advantage of the Republican party could become a powerful mobilizing tool for the Democrats. The strong shift toward the Democratic party during the recession elections of 1982, when the party picked up 26 House seats, as well as hostile public reaction to 1981 tax breaks for corporations and for the affluent, demonstrated that the combination of regressive income policies and deepening unemployment could permit the Democratic party to overcome its internal divisions, those which revolve around the issue of race, and those which are more cultural, more issue-specific, or more class-oriented.

While the distribution of income in the United States over the past decade has become increasingly skewed in favor of the top of the ladder, a skewing which has become, with the sequence of tax bills enacted during the Reagan years,* de facto administration policy, these trends have not been a significant handicap for the Republican party for two reasons. First, the regressive shifts in income began during the Carter years, when Democrats held both the presidency and the two branches of Congress. Secondly, changes in the tax code effectively redistributing income upwards have most recently been associated with the longest period of peacetime economic recovery since World War II. A significant recession might well slice through the insulation protecting the GOP and its candidates from a populist revival—a revival turning the income redistribution figures for the last decade into a Republican liability, demonstrating that the Republican party is disproportionately devoted to the interests of the rich, and invests as little as possible in the fortunes of the working and middle classes.

No matter what the outcome of future elections, the Reagan years have profoundly influenced political journalism. The successes of the Republican party in winning the votes of white working and lower-middle class voters have forced a re-evaluation of assumptions concerning the strength of class-based ties to each of the political parties, and, more important, have led to a re-evaluation of the conflict between the values held by the elite press and those held by voters

---

*From 1981 to 1986, four major tax bills were passed, the Economic Recovery Tax Act of 1981, the Tax Equity and Fiscal Responsibility Act of 1982, the Social Security Amendments of 1983, and the Tax Reform Act of 1986. The distributional consequences of these measures are discussed in the General Explanation booklets issued by the Joint Committee on Taxation for each of the measures; in the Congressional Budget Office report, "The Changing Distribution of Federal Taxes: 1975–1990;" and, for the period through 1984, in *The Reagan Record,* John L. Palmer and Isabel V. Sawhill editors (Cambridge: Ballinger Publishing, 1984).

determined to restore moral order to the lives of their own families and neighbor-hoods. The longest sustained peacetime recovery since 1945—a recovery begin-ning at the end of 1982 that produced 14 million new jobs, an annual inflation rate averaging 3.3 percent, an annual growth rate of 2.5 percent, and home mortgage rates as low as 9 percent—gave at least a temporary political legitimacy to the Reagan administration's tax cutting policies and to the movement to deregulate corporate America. Reagan's accomplishments, both in the market-place and at the ballot box, have prompted a sustained and painful reappraisal within the press of long-held beliefs about the legitimacy and benefits of tradi-tional, liberal government interventions.

At this writing, however, in the volatile aftermath of the stock market crash of October 19, 1987, the national press corp is under intense pressure to vastly expand its understanding of the relationship between economics and politics, both domestically and internationally, and to consider once more a wide spectrum of Democratic—and Republican—attacks on administration economic policies.

In one of its master strokes, the Reagan administration has used the national debt—approaching $2.4 trillion in 1987—to severely restrict the initiatives avail-able to any Democrat elected to the presidency in the near future, although the long-range consequences of the deficit remain uncertain for both parties. As the nation attempts to adopt strategies appropriate to the complexities of the global marketplace, one of the basic functions of the press can and should be to evaluate in greater detail which sections of society will face the largest burdens in carrying the weight of new policy initiatives, and which will be provided the most lucrative benefits. The press has traditionally performed this role on a far smaller stage, as it has sought to disclose which politicians have profited at the expense of which taxpayers. This function can and ought to be broadened to try to include the exploration of penalties and benefits resulting from government policies for the whole range of interests, regions, races, and classes in the country.

*November 1987*
*Washington, D.C.*

# SUGGESTED READING

Adler, Ruth, ed. *The Working Press*. New York: G.P. Putnam's Sons, 1966.

American Society of Newspaper Editors. *Newspaper Credibility: Building Reader Trust*. New York: ASNE, 1985.

Bagdikian, Ben. *Media Monopoly*. Boston: Beacon Press, 1987.

Blumenthal, Sidney. *The Permanent Campaign*. New York: Simon and Schuster, 1982.

Broder, David. *Behind the Front Page: A Candid Look at How The News Is Made*. New York: Simon and Schuster, 1987.

Burgoon, Judee K., Burgoon, Michael, and Atkin, Charles K. *The World of the Working Journalist*. New York: The Newspaper Readership Project, 1982.

Cannon, Lou. *Reporting: An Inside View*. California Journal Press, 1977.

Cater, Douglass. *Power in Washington*. New York: Vintage, 1964.

————. *The Fourth Branch of Government*. Boston: Houghton Mifflin, 1959.

Chancellor, John, and Mears, Walter R. *The News Business*. New York: Harper and Row, 1983.

Downie, Leonard, Jr. *The New Muckrakers*, The New Republic Book Co., 1976

Epstein, Edward J. *News From Nowhere: Television and the News*. New York: Vintage, 1974.

————. *Between Fact and Fiction: The Problem of Journalism*. New York: Vintage, 1975.

Fry, Don, ed. *Believing The News*. St. Petersburg, Florida: The Poynter Institute, 1985.

Gans, Herbert J. *Deciding What's News*. New York: Vintage, 1980.

Gallup Press Agenda Study. "Gallup Surveys the Press." *Editor and Publisher*. December 31, 1983.

Gannett Center For Media Studies. *The Media and the People*. New York: Columbia University, 1985.

Gitlin, Todd. *The Whole World Is Watching*. University of California Press, 1980.

————, ed. *Watching Television*. New York: Pantheon, 1986.

Goldstein, Tom. *The News At Any Cost: How Journalists Compromise Their Ethics To Shape The News*. New York: Simon and Schuster, 1986.

Hiebert, Ray Elson and Reuss, Carol, eds. *Impact of Mass Media*. New York: Longman, 1985.

Hess, Stephen. *The Government/Press Connection*. Washington, D.C.: Brookings, 1984.

————. *The Ultimate Insiders: U.S. Senators and the National Media*. Washington, D.C.: Brookings, 1986.

————. *The Washington Reporters*. Washington, D.C.: Brookings, 1981.

Kent, Frank R. *The Great Game of Politics*. Buffalo, Smith, Keynes & Marshall, 1959.

Kraft, Joseph. "The Imperial Media." *Commentary*. May 1981.

Lichter, S. Robert; Rothman, Stanley; Lichter, Linda S. *The Media Elite: America's New Powerbrokers*. Bethesda, Md.: Adler and Adler, 1986.

Lippmann, Walter. *Public Opinion.* New York: Macmillan, 1965.

Manoff, Robert Karl and Schudson, Michael, eds. *Reading The News.* New York: Pantheon, 1986.

Matusow, Barbara. *The Evening Stars: The Making of the Network News Anchor.* Boston: Houghton Mifflin, 1983.

McGinniss, Joe. *The Selling of the President 1968.* New York: Trident, 1968.

MORI Research Inc. *Journalists and Readers: Bridging the Credibility Gap.* San Francisco, Ca.: The Associated Press Managing Editors Association, October 1985.

Liebling, A.J. *The Press.* New York: Ballantine, 1964.

Linsky, Martin. *Impact: How The Press Affects Federal Policymaking.* New York: Norton, 1986.

"Los Angeles Times Poll on the Media." *Los Angeles Times.* August 11, 12, 13, 14, 1985.

Newfield, Jack. *Bread and Roses Too: Reporting About America.* New York: Dutton, 1971.

Parenti, Michael. *Inventing Reality: The Politics of the Mass Media.* New York: St. Martin's Press, 1986.

Phillips, Kevin P. *Mediacracy: American Parties and Politics in the Communications Age.* New York: Doubleday, 1975.

Ranney, Austin. *Channels of Power: The Impact of Television on American Politics.* New York: Basic Books, 1983.

Research and Forecasts, Inc. *The Connecticut Mutual Life Report on American Values in the '80s.* Hartford, Conn., 1981.

Reston, James. *The Artillery of the Press.* New York: Harper and Row, 1966.

Schneider, William and Lewis, I.A. "Views on the News." *Public Opinion.* August/September, 1985.

Schram, Martin. *The Great American Video Game: Presidential Politics In The Television Age.* New York: Morrow, 1987.

Sigal, Leon V. *Reporters and Officials: The Organization and Politics of Newsmaking.* Lexington, Mass.: D.C. Heath, 1973.

Weaver, David H., and Wilhoit, G. Cleveland. *The American Journalist: A Portrait of U.S. News People and Their Work.* Indiana University Press, 1986.

Wicker, Tom. *On Press.* New York: Viking, 1978.

Verba, Sidney and Orren, Gary R. *Equality in America.* Harvard University Press, 1985.

# The Author

THOMAS BYRNE EDSALL is a native of Cambridge, Massachusetts, and a 1966 graduate of Boston University. He began his newspaper work on the *Providence Journal*, moving on to the *Baltimore Sun* before taking his present assignment, covering national politics for the *Washington Post*. Besides being the author of *The New Politics of Inequality*, he is the coeditor of *The Reagan Legacy*. In 1981, he won the first prize for national reporting and the Bill Pryor Memorial Award of the Washington-Baltimore Newspaper Guild. In 1988, the Boston *Phoenix* named Edsall one of the top ten political reporters in America. He is married, lives in Washington, and has one child.